RIDING

Through
Thick and Thin

Also by Melinda Folse

The Smart Woman's Guide to Midlife Horses

Lessons Well Learned (with Clinton Anderson)

Grandmaster: A Story of Struggle, Triumph, and Taekwondo

RIDING
Through
Thick and Thin

Make Peace With Your Body
and Banish Self-Doubt—
In and Out of the Saddle

Melinda Folse

Foreword by Jane Savoie

TRAFALGAR SQUARE
North Pomfret, Vermont

First published in 2015 by
Trafalgar Square Books
North Pomfret, Vermont 05053

Disclaimer of Liability
The author and publisher shall have neither liability nor responsibility to any person
or entity with respect to any loss or damage caused or alleged to be caused directly or
indirectly by the information contained in this book. While the book is as accurate as the
author can make it, there may be errors, omissions, and inaccuracies.

Trafalgar Square Books encourages the use of approved safety helmets in all equestrian
sports and activities.

Library of Congress Cataloging-in-Publication Data
Folse, Melinda.
  Riding through thick and thin : make peace with your body and banish self-doubt--in
and out of the saddle / Melinda Folse.
      pages cm
  ISBN 978-1-57076-657-2 (pbk.)
  1. Horsemanship. 2. Horsemen and horsewomen--Psychology. 3. Sports for women. 4.
Body image. 5. Self-perception 6. Feminine beauty (Aesthetics) I. Title.
  SF309.F65 2015
  798.2--dc23
                          2014026446

Book design by Lauryl Eddlemon
Cover design by RM Didier
Cover photographs by Caroline Pretty
Typefaces: Trade Gothic, American Typewriter
Printed in Canada
10 9 8 7 6 5 4 3 2 1

*This book is dedicated to anyone
who shares the abject dread of
dressing room mirrors, lesson videos,
and light-colored riding breeches.*

"Don't waste so much time thinking about how much you weigh. There is no more mind-numbing, boring, idiotic, self-destructive diversion from the fun of living."

Actress Meryl Streep,
addressing her 18-year-old self

Contents

BE HONEST   13

1 Your Reality   15

How healthy (and accurate) is your body image? How do you think you look when you ride? How do you think others view your size and shape? How are the opinions of others and your environment influencing your perceptions of your own body? This chapter will help you begin to move past the fear of examining your feelings about your body, giving you a better understanding of the role you play in allowing those feelings to sabotage your joy—in and out of the saddle.

2 It's Just a Number   22

What are the messages you've received about riding and weight? Where are you on the "thought scale" of rising obesity trends among riders? What does escalating weight mean for riders—and their horses? This chapter will help you understand why a number on a scale is only one factor to consider and how learning to use your body well at any weight will release you once and for all from the imprisonment of the untruths and half-truths we may have riding along with us.

3 Get Clear on What's Real   31

How does our "interior chatter" affect our exterior (posterior) reality? How can we stop fixating on how we look and focus instead on "showing up" as our own best selves? How can we learn to pay more attention to what matters most with our horses, ourselves, and others—and leave the rest on the dung heap where it belongs? In this chapter we'll explore real ways to accept our bodies first, just as they are, and open up the whole new world of understanding how our thoughts can tip the scales in our favor.

horse's movement and responses, you'll become your own best teacher for finding that "sweet spot" that makes riding the joyful dance it's meant to be.

BE MINDFUL 209

8 Mind Over Mass 211

What holds you back or makes you anxious in the saddle? How do these thoughts become things that hold you back? Do worries about your physical flaws (whether real or imagined) overshadow your joy in riding—or keep you from riding at all? This chapter takes a more holistic approach to riding and how we can engage our mind, body, and soul in our everyday experience of working with horses. By amping up our awareness of our thought and behavior patterns, we'll become less anxious, more mindful riders.

BE POSITIVE 253

9 "See" With Your Mind 255

How do you "see" yourself riding in your mind's eye? What kind of rider do you most admire—and can you visualize yourself riding like that? What did you do today to move even one inch closer to your riding goals? This chapter adds a smattering of tools for incorporating techniques such as visualization, affirmation, and realistic goal-setting into our daily lives. As we develop and strengthen these crucial "mind muscles," we'll rise above pressure and self-doubt to clear obstacles and breeze into heightened rider self-esteem and improved body image.

10 Set Your New Course 289

How do your feelings and past experiences affect your beliefs about your body and your riding? Has feeling "less than" ever kept you from your joy ride? Do you ever avoid new riding opportunities for fear of negative outcomes? This chapter will help you learn how to examine and question your emotional "scripts" and self-limiting beliefs. By tucking this information from the scientific world into your tack trunk, you'll learn how to re-write the new behaviors that will set you on a path toward greater joy and satisfaction!

BE AUTHENTIC 345

Have you always kind of known what you need to do better in order to ride better? Do you have a hard time letting go of habits and behavior that don't serve you, even though you know you "should?" Do you find it difficult to be gentle with yourself—and yet get the job done? In this chapter you'll find all the ways the tools, strategies, and insights offered up in this book can become your own, and a permanent part of who you are and how you ride. This is where this book becomes a living credo for each of us—a trail map that evolves as we do to take us to new places with our horses, our riding, and our sense of who we are.

Have you always sort of suspected that if you could do *better you could* ride *better? Are old habits and behaviors still calling the shots, even though you know what you "should" do differently? Are you struggling with the dance between being gentle with yourself—and getting the job done?* In this chapter you'll learn how to turn the key on the tools, strategies, and insights offered up in this book for permanent change to how you think, feel, and ride. This final stretch of our trail is where you can make positive changes to your life and life-with-horses credo, and begin a quest that will evolve as you discover new places with your horses, your riding and your sense of who you are. Welcome to the lightness of self and spirit we've all been yearning for!

Foreword
by Jane Savoie

W hen I was training to make the U.S. Olympic Dressage Team in the late 1980s, I had to overcome many challenges. I did not have the most talented horse or the most money, nor did I have the best riding skills and tons of experience. At the time, I also did not have what some might describe as the "ideal" rider's body. But I knew what I wanted, and I cultivated the mental training tools to reach my ultimate goal—against the odds I won the position of reserve rider on the team for the 1992 Olympics in Barcelona (I describe this journey and the techniques I used in my two sport psychology books *That Winning Feeling!* and *It's Not Just About the Ribbons*). As I trained my mind to compete at the highest levels, I also aimed to find my fittest riding self, to become an athletic rider who could not only school a Grand Prix dressage horse correctly and appropriately, but one who could carry her own body on her horse thus allowing him to perform his best while ensuring his health, comfort, and soundness over time.

To accomplish all these things, I had to learn to be honest with myself about my body: its shape, the attributes that helped me ride better, and those that needed improvement. I had to come to terms with the ways that I could, being who I was "genetically," accomplish reasonable fitness and weight-loss goals. While my desire to compete for the United States in the company of the some of the best riders in the world required I make some dietary changes and exercise regularly (in addition to riding, I'd speed-walk and hike logging trails with my dog Emma), it also meant learning to *accept* the inherent obstacles my body shape and size offered in the light of my goal, as well as recognize and appreciate its natural qualities.

This same challenge applies to my more recent pursuit (and love!) of competitive ballroom dancing. It is only in learning to look at myself with a positive sense of who I am, of my strengths and what they have allowed me to accomplish so far (and will allow me to accomplish in my future), that I can continue to grow and evolve as an active and interested human being, ever-improving in the worlds of riding and dance. It is also this ability that enables me to coach others in a way that can genuinely ensure their advancement and (hopefully) their happiness on horseback.

Of course, I was not born with the ability to appreciate this body I am in—that is only something I have acquired over time, with age, experience, and a progressively gained enthusiasm for my individuality. There were times and certainly have been days (fittings for some of the fabulous dance costumes I now get to wear come to mind) when I've wished for longer legs, a smaller bottom, or a flatter tummy—who doesn't? But as a rider, a coach, a dancer, and a woman, I have found a greater source of contentment and improved ability to attain my goals—and help others attain theirs—when I can nod briefly toward those momentary emotions and then simply *move on*. Don't we all want to look back and see that our time was not wasted sighing over superficial aspects of what we *think* defines us, and instead was spent in the joyful and passionate pursuit of our interests?

Riding Through Thick and Thin is indeed a book that aims to help every woman maximize her time with horses, in and out of the saddle, and to find that joy and passion in every other aspect of her life. I just love the humor and sincerity in Melinda's voice—reading her words is like sitting down with your friends and trading secrets over a bottle of wine. She shoulders what I think is a significant responsibility: providing a tour of all the different angles with which we can address this issue of body image as horsewomen. The material covered is impressive—from what you might expect in terms of fitness and nutrition pointers, to valuable information about riding biomechanics, to that all-essential look at what's going on inside our own heads.

This book immediately makes me think of one of my own coaching tools—"Choose Your Own Riding Adventure"—which encourages you to think about where you want to end up in a lesson, and then provides you several options to help create the path that might best get you there (I liken it to eating at a buffet and picking the items you like best from the menu). I've had wonderful success in coaching amateur riders using this technique, a riding-specific spin off the popular

Choose Your Own Adventure® children's book series. The gist of the book series is the reader is empowered to build his or her own story, choosing the next page to which to turn at the end of each chapter. The result, whether good (you found the buried treasure!) or bad (you sadly perished in a snake pit), is of your own making.

In *Riding Through Thick and Thin*, rest assured, there aren't any snake pits, but there most certainly is plenty of treasure to be had. And you can reach it in a variety of ways. Don't feel bound to the order of chapters—by all means, Melinda encourages us from the get-go to dip in and find what feels right as a place to begin our respective journeys. Your path may lead directly from A to Z, or you may take a more winding, circuitous route, delving into all manner of ideas and methods intended to engender self-assuredness in your horse life. Either way, you'll find something of value in the pages ahead, and ultimately within yourself.

I am a lucky woman to have been able to pursue so many of my dreams—and I have thoroughly relished every extended- and fox-trot step of the way. I hope that this book enables each one of you to derive the same amount of enthusiasm and joy that I have for what I get to do, every second of every day.

Jane Savoie

Reserve Rider 1992 Olympic Games;
Coach at Olympic Games in 1996, 2000, and 2004;
Author of Multiple Bestselling Books and DVDs;
Popular Motivational Speaker (www.janesavoie.com)

Acknowledgments

If I were to try to thank every single person whose reflections, insights, questions, comments, and exclamations went into the shaping of this book, it would be a long list indeed. So in blanket fashion, I want to express my sincere appreciation to everyone who took the time to talk with me, share a story, ask a question, offer an opinion, or otherwise help me through the development of *Riding Through Thick and Thin* over the past three years. From the knowledge and insights of expert sources, to thoughts, reflections, and experiences shared by the many bloggers and social media groups who post and work regularly in these areas, to countless casual barn-aisle conversations with people I know well, the immense outpouring of help, inspiration, and encouragement is what kept me going as I wrote this book.

Of course, there are also a few I need to single out for a heaping helping of extra gratitude. To Martha, Becca, and Caroline, my friends, editors, and green-chili-loving cohorts at Trafalgar Square Books: I can't thank you enough for coming up with this concept and choosing me to write it. To my extremely generous virtual panel of experts: Thank you for your support, enthusiasm, and willingness to share the depth and scope of solid information this book demanded. Your presence in this book is what will make it a true game-changer for its readers. What a special opportunity this was to meet and get to work with you! Deep appreciation also goes to Lisa, my research and editorial right hand, for helping me gather, shape, and reshape a sea of input into an evolving outline. Thanks also to Kristen, Ali, Gena, Laurie, and any others who read portions or drafts of the manuscript as it developed.

Beyond that, I must acknowledge my sweet husband, David, who has done more than his fair share of laundry, dishes, and housekeeping during the creation of this book; my parents, extended family, and friends for patience and support even when they can't imagine where I've been the last few months; and my horses...for allowing me to experiment with the theories and ideas in these pages without breaking my arms.

Introduction | **Mounting Blocks?**

L isten. I don't know who you are. I don't know where you live, what you do for a living, or what you want from your horse or your riding experience. I don't know—or care—what you look like, what you weigh, or what size jeans you wear. (And, for that matter, neither does your horse.) But there's an issue lurking out there in our increasingly plus-sized world that I think is holding a lot of women back, and I want to know why. More than that, I want to know what we can *do* about it.

The last thing I wanted to do was write another diet or exercise or "feel good about your womanly curves" book. No, I wanted answers—to my questions and yours—and to the questions that popped up most frequently in my exploration of this complicated topic of "body image." "Body image" is a tricky term, a buzzword developed to encompass all we think, feel, and know about how our bodies "shape up," if you'll pardon the pun, in relation to other people, cultural norms, physical demands, and even our own standards and expectations. All too often body image evolves as a product of layers upon layers of *perceived* expectations—from our families, our friends, our culture, and our own observations of the world around us. How we think and feel and relate to our own bodies is personal, and whether our perceptions are based in reality or a distortion of it, to us they are as present as the horses beneath us.

It's no secret that riding horses is highly physical. It demands a lot of our bodies—whether our goals are recreational, competitive, or professional, how we ride and how well we ride is a product of how we train our bodies to do the job required. We all know that, and to varying extents, we do take care of our physical conditioning one way or another. We have to because we want to be able to work with horses.

But there's more to this, sisters. As it turns out, *body image* also plays a role in how well we ride, and ultimately, how we feel *about* riding. For most of us, horse time is also "me" time—the sacred space in our lives where we find a deep connection to our own *authenticity* (our truest sense of who we really are, deep within our core). I, along with a lot of people much smarter than me, believe that horses are here on the planet to help us find ourselves, which pushes riding and "horse time" in general into mental and even spiritual arenas.

So what we're dealing with here is not just about the aesthetic ("Does this horse make my butt look big?") or about the physics ("Am I too heavy to ride a horse safely?") or even about balance issues created by extra ballast ("How can I feel more secure in the saddle?"). This book is a hard-hitting exploration of what's *really* going on in our heads about the state of our bodies (aka "body image issues"), how *does* reality weigh in, and more specifically, how can we deal with these things to get back to—and really enjoy—quality horse time? My goal is to offer concrete tools for sorting all this out. With deliberate strategies, deep thinking, and support and inspiration from others riding along with us, we'll move, step by step, into a "lighter" existence—in body, in mind, and in spirit.

Set Yourself Free

The list of what plagues women about their bodies is long—and quite enough to wear us out. Worst of all, it's a waste of our time and a drain on our energy. Chances are, if you're a woman, there has been a time (for some of us, that would be "always") in which you questioned your size, shape, body type, the length of your legs, or the thickness of your thighs. It might even be safe to say that most of us, at one time or another, have thought we're too fat, too skinny (yes, I've heard they're out there), too tall, too short, too muscular, too...oh, whatever else you can think of.

Do guys tussle with these same questions? Maybe *some* do. I hate to generalize, but men usually seem more self-accepting as they order the chicken-fried-whatever with French fries and extra gravy while we pick away at the grilled-something salad with dressing on the side. I think there's something about *being female* that sets us up for a different kind of self-scrutiny than whatever comes loaded onto the male circuit board. And when struggles with body image overtake your reality, whether well-justified or imagined, it hijacks your best intentions and steals your *joie de vivre*—the feeling of genuine delight you have for your life and all that's in it.

Life is short. Life with horses is a gift we ought not waste over worries about our size, our shape, or how we look when we ride. But honestly friends, once we have a solid assessment about who we are—and what can and can't be changed— we can acquire an assortment of tools and develop strategies for making the most of what we have, taking advantage of opportunities that come our way, and reaching the potential that is unique to each one of us. Putting *that* process into your hands is the goal and purpose of this book.

So why am *I* the one to write it? Well, for one thing I'm professionally curious. I looked under a lot of these rocks through the years as I studied and explored the mind-body-spirit connection in all kinds of things—from tennis to taekwondo, from horses to fly fishing, from yoga to religions east and west, and from domestic art forms such as cooking and creating an ideal living space to the visual and performing arts. I've discovered some of the same threads running through all of these, and connecting the dots between body image issues and working with horses was as natural as it was enlightening. For another thing, I do have the qualifying battle scars. Although I have been a more or less "normal-sized" woman (whatever that means) for most of my life, I've gained and lost the same 10, 15, 20, and now 30 pounds (thank you middle-age hormones) more times than I would care to admit in public. And, even though I've never *technically* been at either extreme of the overweight/underweight spectrum, I can assure you I've been there *mentally*. From adolescence up until last Tuesday, I've fallen prey to all kinds of thoughts, beliefs, and feelings that I was a size very different than what I now know (and old photos verify) to be true.

So instead of presenting you with another height-weight-chart-driven treatise to make you feel more or less hopeful than you already are, or a yet another idealized program for getting you into size-6 jeans, I'm here to lead an assault on the kind of thinking that is holding us back from being the best we can be—for our horses and ourselves—at *any* weight, shape, or size. It is my hope that this book serves as a giant affirmation that sets you free, once and for all, from the self-judgment that's been dogging you for decades. And, if there *are* changes you want or need to make to eliminate any mental, physical, or emotional "wobbly bits," then this book can provide insight for discovering where you *really* are "right now," where your solid and joyful "there" might be, and how to get you and your horse on the best path to enjoying tomorrow's ride for all it's worth.

The Elephant in Our Trail

In reluctant deference to one of my least favorite overused analogies, and with all size-related puns aside, the issue we're facing is something of an elephant. In a word, it's huge. We're not just talking about weight. Or fitness. Or biomechanics. Or self-concept. Or how our mind influences our body. Or how thought habits manifest as body image. Or what our spirit and sense of connection to others has to do with it. It's all of these things. And more. Clumped together, as these "body image issues" tend to be, they become the elephant in our psyche we can't rise above, see past, or work around. If we could have, we would have. Tweaking that sage elephant wisdom about how to "eat an elephant" (not that we'd want to), we're going to tackle this big wrinkly critter one crease at a time.

The other thing about *this* elephant is that, much like the one in the room, no one really wants to talk about it. Not *really*. Oh, we'll talk about diets and exercise programs, compare cleanses and fasts, and read all our junk email about the latest miracle solutions, but who *really* shares what it feels like when you catch that awkward glimpse of yourself in a dressing room mirror? Or when you can't zip your favorite riding jeans? Or worse, when you can't even get your foot up to the stirrup or pull yourself into the saddle? Who talks about hating the "muffin top" or the dreaded "back fat" we didn't realize we had until the show pictures come back? Who confesses that our jiggly arms are all we can think about when we review a lesson video? Who admits the terror of feeling out of balance in the saddle with no idea how to "shift our load" to find that safe, secure seat we had a few (or a few dozen) pounds ago?

This, I'm happy to say after listening, searching, lurking on a lot of forums and online communities, and talking to anyone who would talk to me about any of this, is a brand new day. Throughout this book you will find story after story from those who offered to share their thoughts, motivating quotes, ideas, discoveries, humor, encouraging words, fears, and triumphs. I'm calling these heartfelt contributions (which range from a few words to a few pages) "Voices of Our Sisters"—because you are not alone on this journey! There's good company here, and regardless of whether your excess ballast is in your head, your thighs, or somewhere in between, there is community of women eager to join hands and help shove that elephant on out of the trail we're all on together.

You Are *Here...*

This book is laid out like a metaphorical trail ride. You are now at the grand entrance to a complex system of interconnected trails, crisscrossing and converging on the way to our destination. Some are well-marked and well-worn; others are less defined. It's a come-as-you-are expedition, and a build-your-own journey from wherever you are *right now* (you are *here!*) to where you want to be.

Ahead lie six clearly marked sections. You can join in at whatever connecting point you choose. It really doesn't matter which "trails" in these sections you choose or how long or deeply you choose to explore them.

- **Be Honest**—Let's face it. Obesity is on the rise everywhere, and particularly in America. And, while evidence of this dramatic trend the Centers for Disease Control pinpoints as beginning around 1980 is everywhere, in the world of riding and working with horses, packing on pounds carries with it a whole new dynamic of responsibility. Does this mean we should stop riding if we gain weight? Of course not! It does mean, however, that we have to "keep it real" about our weight, the horses we choose, our needs and expectations, our riding goals—and what it's going to take to achieve them. In this section we will assess all these factors bravely, honestly, and with the full intent to make the very most of what we have to work with, inside and out.

- **Be Fair**—Part of wanting to ride comes from our love of horses, right? So to be fair to the ones we love, first we must determine that our horses (whether we own, lease, or borrow) are physically capable of carrying us into the type of riding life we choose to pursue. After that, we have an obligation to keep ourselves and our horses fit, nourished, and healthy enough to do what we want to do, within expectations that are fair to both us and to them. We also need to ensure that our tack and equipment fits well and meets ethical standards of horsemanship. When we look at how we're working with our horses in the light of fairness, horse-manship starts to take on a very different hue.

- **Be Proactive**—Working hand in hand with our obligation toward fairness and commitment to the ones we love, it's time to be *done* with passive pity parties. Empowered by a new understanding of how to equip ourselves for the job we and our horses are excited about doing, we have good reason to grab that fitness-bull by the horns. No one is saying we have to lose weight (although that just might happen). By making a conscious choice to set ourselves—and our horses—up for success, we eliminate habits, thought patterns, and behavior that doesn't serve us, grab that Golden Lasso, and claim our Wonder Woman mojo (with or without the bustier and cape).

- **Be Mindful**—What we're after in this section is learning how to create for our-selves what the Greater Good website (greatergood.berkeley.edu) describes as "maintaining a moment-by-moment awareness of our thoughts, feelings, bodily sensations, and surrounding environment." Because mindfulness is also about acceptance, learning how to pay attention to our thoughts and feelings without judging them as "right" or "wrong" enables us to break free of our habits of rehashing (and re*bashing*) our past choices and behaviors, and tune fully into what's going on *right now*. If we let them, horses are among the best teachers of mindfulness. Not only are they always fully in the moment they're in, but working well with our horses demands that we find a way to be fully present, as well.

- **Be Positive**—All Pollyanna and fake-it-till-you-make-it jokes aside, this really is the crux of the matter. While negativity about our bodies may have become as natural as breathing over no-telling how many years, it's also as toxic as inhaling exhaust fumes. Negative energy drains and distracts us; the habit of "going negative" in your thought patterns is probably something you don't even recognize as a habit. In this section we'll learn how to stop that "stinkin' thinkin'" and surround ourselves with a positive force field to be reckoned with.

- **Be Authentic ("You Do You")**—Authenticity is actually the best way out of this body image bog we've allowed ourselves to become mired in. **We are who we are**, and as long we stay true to that, we have absolutely nothing to apologize for. As women, we are conditioned to respond to certain things in certain ways. For example, I grew up in the South, where most of us learned at a young age that adding "bless her heart," excused saying something related to someone's weight, and many of us learned at an early age that other kinds of "fat talk" earns social acceptance: "Ugh! I feel so fat today!" and "Oh no, sweetie, that doesn't make your butt look big—I think it's really flattering for your body type." Here's the truth about authenticity that you already know (you just don't know you know it): Watch your horse. Horses are the most authentic creatures on the planet. They don't know how to pretend, and they will call you on it the first second you do. Ladies, we can get as good at authenticity as our horses. Whatever you look like, whatever size you are or you aren't, all that really matters is learning to be happy in your own skin, doing what you love most.

Meet Our Guides: A Virtual Panel of Experts

Who will guide us on this trail ride? What if we get lost? How do we know the map is correct? What if we lose our cell phone service?

Friends, I have assembled a tour group like no other. In the panel of experts that will lead us through this book you will find solid information, well-documented facts, specialized experience, and inspiration that comes from the hearts of those who know every step of this trail like the backs of their collective hands.

In alphabetical order, our amazing guides on the journey ahead include:

Jacob Barandes, PhD, Associate Director of Graduate Studies in the Department of Physics at Harvard University. Dr. Barandes helps us understand the physics principles behind center of gravity and center of mass—and how *learning* the difference can make a *real* difference in your balance when you ride. Who knew physics class could be so useful?

Eric Billingslea, a 30-year personal training and nutrition consultant who works closely with the yoga studio where I practice. He explains how feeding your body in a way that "builds a fire," metabolically speaking, will keep your energy level high, your muscles fed, and your mind sharp. Favorite quote: "Your body is going to eat every three hours whether you feed it or not."

Charles Gaby, MA, LPC, psychologist and counselor who has done extensive work with the Tomkins Institute and works deeply in the area of affect script psychology and recovery from shame. Gaby helps us understand the role of shame in our self-concept, and how early experiences create scripts that we act out over and over again in our lives—until we learn to recognize and rewrite them!

Joyce Harman, DVM, MRCVS, both an equine veterinarian and expert saddle fitter, as well as author of several books on the issue of equine comfort and saddle fit (www.harmanyequine.com). This unusual combination of experience and expertise offers specific, easily digestible advice to help you make sure you have the right fit for both Western and English saddles.

Susan Harris, instructor, international Centered Riding® clinician, and creator of Anatomy in Motion®, The Visible Horse, and The Visible Rider (www.anatomyin-motion.com), explains how the horse's anatomy works with ours as we ride so we get a much clearer picture of how and why "riding light" has far less to do with *what* you weigh than *how* you use your body weight in the saddle.

Emily Kutz, certified sport horse massage therapist, delves into the how and why of discovering areas of tightness in specific and key muscle groups of a horse's body, and offers up some advice for pre- and post-ride stretches and massage techniques anyone can do.

Wendy Murdoch, an internationally recognized equestrian instructor and clinician for more than 30 years is the author of several books and DVDs (www.murdoch-method.com). Murdoch is trained in the Feldenkrais Method® and here offers invaluable insights on getting "in sync" with your horse and "finding your sweet spot" of perfect balance at any gait.

Jochen Schleese, master saddler and saddle ergonomist, is world-renowned for his saddle-making and expertise in fitting both the "horse side" and the "rider side" (www.saddlefit4life.com). He explains why both sides are equally important and offers specific saddle-fit tips and measurement recommendations, as well as emphasizing the need for regularly checking and tending to even minor fit issues.

Daniel Stewart, international trainer, instructor, and Equestrian Sport Psychology expert for the Horse Radio Network and mental training coach for the United States Eventing Association, helps us understand how our "frame of mind" when we ride impacts our "framework" as riders (our bodies' shapes and capabilities). He guides us in an important discovery: Accepting and maximizing our bodies' shapes and capabilities is far better than bemoaning their challenges and shortcomings (www.stewartclinics.com).

RT³ Regulars

Throughout *Riding Through Thick and Thin* (henceforth known as RT³), you'll run into the following trail features on a regular basis (think of them as helpful signage):

#Hoofpicks

What does a hoof pick do? It helps us get the mud, muck, debris, and "poo" out of our horses' feet. This regular ritual is crucial to protecting your horse's feet and legs. If too much gunk is lodged in there, it can damage his hooves and his ability to move correctly. It can make him sore and grumpy and not want to do anything productive.

Wait.

Isn't that also true for us when it comes to body image? If there's gunk and rocks and dung in our head about how we think we look, and how we think that defines us and what we're able to do with our horses, doesn't it make it hard to move "forward and calm" on the trail to our riding goals and dreams? If it is large or sharp or jagged, or it stays there too long, doesn't it really hurt, perhaps causing permanent damage—and maybe make us not want to ride at all?

I've included a short list of "#hoof-picks" at the end of each chapter. These are the takeaways to add to your mental tack trunk to keep your progress forward, your horse time productive, and your mind clear and clean as a whistle.

Resources

You'll find recommended books and

Shea Stewart, horse trainer and riding instructor, is also a certified craniosacral therapist for horses (www.equinebalance.net). She explains how a pain response in your horse may well be the culprit in behavior problems, and how seemingly minor incidents for your horse can set up chronic issues in his body and behavior.

Jill Valle, MA, MFT, is a Marriage and Family Therapist who specializes in body image and weight issues. Valle offers a wealth of useful information and resources, as well as immediate go-to techniques for reframing, resetting, and remembering how to embrace your body, clear your mind, and move more surely toward a life of joy and self-acceptance, in and out of the saddle.

other resources from our experts, as well as other thought leaders in the areas we're about to explore.

Voices of Our Sisters

I've mentioned this one already: Watch for the thoughts, brief reflections, and wisdom of others on this trail with us. These words were mined from blogs, online forums, personal interviews, and media. Some "sisters" asked to remain anonymous and so their names have been changed; others asked to be quoted. Either way, I know you'll love to hear them speak to these issues as only true personal experience can.

Busted!

Myth busting is a large part of this book, so I decided to scatter some of the ones doing us the greatest disservice throughout the pages ahead, both to keep them topical and to keep them from bogging us down. In all likelihood I've only scratched the surface of the myths and myth understandings out there. Let these inspire you to find others and bust them if you can!

Exercises for the Body, Brain, and Soul

You're going to have plenty of ways to get hands-on in your effort to find what you are looking for in your life—in and out of the saddle! I've included exercises that have helped me in my own journey, as well as those recommended by experts. You don't have to do them all, but begin with an open mind and sample a few along the way. Lots of these trails will lead you home.

Make This Experience Your Own

As you begin each new section of "trail" that comprises this book, I invite you to pause for a moment of deep reflection to identify at least one new outcome, change, or accomplishment you'd like to experience in this area. (Remember, you can always come back for additional helpings!) Then, setting this as your intent, look for the information, stories, and resources that connect with your own unique needs and experiences, as a woman—and as a *horse*woman.

Establishing your own interactive practice with this book will empower you as you read; capturing information as it strikes a familiar chord within you will help you take ownership of whatever practices you find useful. As you work with these ideas—and shape them to fit your life and circumstances and goals—I encourage you to explore as deeply as you find necessary to make the progress you're looking for.

Not everything in this book is for everyone—and not everything that resonates today will feel as relevant to you in another space and time. You see, *Riding Through Thick and Thin* is both as simple and as complicated as you want to make it. It can spark broad-spectrum life change or a few slight tweaks. I've created this book in layers ready for digging into, time and time again. Like any beautiful trail that is both familiar and brand new every time you ride it, depending on changes in season, experience, and even your own mentality, this path will likely yield something different for you each time you revisit it.

Let's ride!

Be
Honest

1 | Your Reality

Do you flip straight to the self-test sections in all the latest get-better tomes? Do you jump at the chance to take any social media quiz that promises to reveal something important about your psyche? Well, even if you *don't*, I'm going to ask you to entertain a few ideas brought to us by Thomas Cash, a psychologist who has spent his career studying the psychology of physical appearance, in *The Body Image Workbook*. In it, Cash lays out a methodology for identifying and challenging body image issues using a series of self-tests to guide his readers. So, let's begin our own "Be Honest trail" with a quiz of our own. While the content more or less parallels Cash's concepts, this variation folds in specific prompts recommended by our horse and riding experts. The takeaway result? Focused insights on how—and to what degree—body image issues may be affecting how we ride, how we feel about our riding, and the quality of the time we spend with our horses. (Download the RT³ Test free from my website: melindafolse.com or from my publisher at horseandriderbooks.com.)

Thomas Cash's *The Body Image Workbook: An Eight-Step Program for Learning to Like Your Looks* (New Harbinger Publications, 1997, 2008).

RESOURCES

Part 1: Your RT³ Evaluation

This part of The RT³ Test explores how you feel about your appearance in general, with a particular focus on how you *think* you look when you ride. It also factors in how much you think this image is affecting your ability to ride freely and well. On the first page of a notebook, journal, or in notes on your tablet or computer, write each of the following characteristics:

- Overall Shape/Body Type
- Height
- Weight
- Weight Distribution
- Upper Body
- Lower Body
- Leg Thickness
- Leg Length

Now beside each one, write *Very Dissatisfied, Mostly Dissatisfied, Mostly Satisfied,* or *Very Satisfied* when you consider the characteristic in conjunction with your own body, and in particular with your body as that of a horsewoman. Your answers here indicate the areas or aspects of your appearance that you like or dislike when it comes to how you look, especially as you ride or work with horses.

Part 2: How Do You Think You Look When You Ride?

The second part of our test is designed to help you isolate and identify some of the thoughts that run through your head while you're horseback, and specifically how you think your body *causes* you to ride, how you think you *look* when you ride, and how you *feel* about your own body as you ride. Don't take the wording in this part of the test too literally: if a thought or sentiment hits anywhere close to home, make note. Just as you did with Part 1 of this test, write down the following prompts:

- I don't look very good when I ride.

- I am a lousy rider because of how I'm built and the way my body works.

- Judges and other riders ignore me because of how I look.

- Everyone else at the barn looks better around and on horses than I do.

- There's no way I can win any sort of show because of how I look.

- I wish I looked like the other women I ride with and compete against.

- People at the barn don't like me because of how I look.

- Everyone thinks I'm too fat to ride.

- My riding clothes look terrible on me.

- I can't participate in the clinic/parade/show because of how I look.

After each one, note how often thoughts like these cross your mind: *Never, Sometimes, or Often.* Once we get caught in our own web of body-critical thoughts, it's hard to escape them (we're going to help you find some scissors a little later on). This part of the test reveals just *how* badly you beat yourself up about how you think you look—and how you think you look when you work with your horse. If you're somewhat oblivious to your best physical features, if you don't believe there *is* anything good about your body to think about, or if you tend to brush off and dismiss any compliment, it's time to create a different reality.

Part 3: What's Distressing Your Ride?

Negative body image emotions crop up in different situations and at different times for different people. This part of the RT³ Test helps us determine to what degree this type of distress rides along with us. In other words, *how often* do these thoughts plague our time with our horses? As with Parts 1 and 2, write down:

I feel uncomfortable, embarrassed, or self-conscious about my body . . .

Now follow it with each one of the statements below.

- When I go on a trail ride or ride at a clinic or barn where I don't know many people.

- When I catch my reflection in arena or tack room mirrors.

Jane

"Horses don't judge us by our looks, and isn't that fabulous?"

- When people see me in my "barn attire."

- When I am with a group of women who are "pretty riders."

- When I am riding with a group that contains male riders.

- When I try on riding jeans/breeches.

- When I watch videos, read articles, or peruse catalogs filled with "pretty riders."

- When I'm having trouble with my horse or my riding.

- When the topic of weight comes up in conversation with my riding friends.

- When someone comments on my appearance on horseback.

- When I see myself on my horse in photos or videos.

- When I am with riders who are in great physical shape.

- When I am with riders who are overweight and out of shape.

- During challenging riding situations.

Then go down this list of statements and mark each one as *Never, Sometimes,* or *Often.* When we encounter situations such as these that trigger anxiety, disgust, despondency, anger, frustration, envy, shame, or self-consciousness directed at our bodies or how we think we look, it is essential to have tools on hand to hammer them into a more useful form.

Part 4: Keeping Up Appearances

How much is your physical appearance defining and determining your self-worth, on and off your horse, in and out of the barn? Write the following statements:

- When I am at the barn with "pretty riders," I am self-conscious about my own looks.

- When I get a compliment or see a reflection or video of myself riding that looks pretty good, I tend to dwell on it.

- If I feel good about how I look, I enjoy my time with my horse more and everything seems easier.

- When I meet or ride with people for the first time, I wonder if they think I'm too big to be a horsewoman.

- I often fantasize about what it would be like to be one of those "pretty riders."

- If I could get control of my weight I'd have more riding friends and get invited to go on more organized rides and go to more horse-related events.

- My body type affects my ability to ride or compete my horse.

- I often compare my appearance to that of other horse people.

- If another rider or someone at the barn makes a negative comment about my appearance, weight, or shape, I tend to dwell on it.

- I feel bad for my horse; I think I might be hurting him when I ride.

- I wear barn and riding clothes that cover up what I find troublesome about my body.

- I fantasize about looking different in my riding clothes and in the saddle.

- I regularly ask my barnmates and riding friends for reassurance about my appearance.

- I avoid other people at the barn and don't like to ride in the arena when others are schooling.

- My interactions with other women at the barn, in lessons or clinics, or in the show ring are friendly and supportive.

- I am confident and at ease when interacting with men at the barn, in lessons or clinics, or in the show ring.

- I am confident and at ease when meeting and riding with, or competing against, new people.

- My experiences with people outside the barn or show ring are usually pleasant.

- My relationships with my riding friends are consistently honest and supportive.

- I am in control of my day-to-day emotions related to working with my horse and riding.

- I feel accepted by the other horse people and riders at my barn.

- I am happy when I ride and spend time with my horse.

Now go back and label each one as *True* or *False.* It's no secret that how we experience our bodies in many ways dictates how we experience life. And, when we work with and ride horses, we take that truth to a whole new level. Horses are the ultimate "mirrors" of all our thoughts, feelings, emotions—as well as our physical strengths and weaknesses.

Whether you actually "took" our self-test or just skimmed the prompts and answered them in your head, you can probably now see whether or not you have body image issues and where they may be lurking. The RT[3] Test may have rung some new, key bells in your awareness. Many (if not most) of us tend to leave it at that. We may have the best of intentions, but for some reason, our follow-through never gets out of the gate. However, if *this time* you're really ready to *ride on*, let's put our self-discovery to work and begin to make lasting changes to our body image—for the better.

In this chapter we explored our perceptions of our body image—how we both consciously and unconsciously allow others and our environment to influence our perceptions. This will help you in your work with horses because how you respond to your horse and he responds to you is rooted in emotions/feelings. Incorporating this information is a new and different game-changer in the battle against negative body image because once you remove the fear of examining your feelings about your body and the role you play in allowing those feelings to sabotage your joy, you are on the right trail.

Your Chapter 1 **#Hoofpicks** include:

1 **Find perspective.** Sometimes we really don't know *where* we are on the "scale" of things—we may think we're larger than we actually are...or smaller. In order to get to our best ride, we first have to get real about how we're built, the shape we're in, and what those thoughts we have about our bodies are *really* saying.

2 **Nix old mindsets.** Objective measurements are not indictments—they are merely a starting a place as we put together a personalized plan for *Riding Through Thick and Thin*. Start right now by getting out of that mindset (there's more of this coming) and take a good solid look at what *is* true.

3 **Get ready to be surprised.** Once we start digging for "truths" it may surprise you what you think of yourself and your riding, and what you think *others* think of your riding. And above all, what all these "thinks" are doing to your self-image and the quality of your experience with horses.

4 **Work it.** It really isn't as much our size that matters as *what we do with the body we have*. Once we go to school on this, the better we'll ride, the easier we'll be on our horses, and the more fun we'll have on this glorious trail at *any weight or shape*.

2 | It's Just a Number

Right now. Get on the scale. Even if you haven't for years.

I know. We've been conditioned to avoid this "trauma" at all cost. (Some of us may actually look the other way when we go to the doctor's office.) Often, when we do finally gut it up and "face the music," that number on the scale can slap us with all kinds of shame that's really not helpful. So, what if we call "BS" on a number having that kind of hold on our emotions? What if that number isn't a painful indictment, but just like age, "just a number?" And what if we were to treat that number as what it really is—information?

So go ahead. No one is looking. And who cares if they are? This is a new day. Your new mentality regarding weight starts right now. Step on that scale. Weigh your saddle, too, while you're at it, and add these numbers together. This is the number we're going to be working with, and knowing it is the first step toward mapping your escape from the wasteland of weight anxiety. Ultimately, your route out may or may not have anything at all to do with changing that number.

A Pound Is Not Always a Pound

Going back to the title of this section (Be Honest), we're now in the "get real" stretch of this trail, aren't we? The truth is, being heavier than what is considered "ideal" for frame and height raises a whole string of questions when it comes to riding:

• How much is too much?

• When does excess weight start interfering with riding well?

• How do you know if you really *are* too heavy to ride at all?

As we'll get into later, a pound is not always a pound for, oh, so many reasons.

"If it's just extra weight, and you haven't added any pressure (such as bracing in the stirrups), you probably haven't created a pressure issue for your horse," says instructor and clinician Wendy Murdoch. (Check out measuring pressure on p. 80.) "With 'simple' physics principles in mind, that's why a heavier rider with evenly-distributed weight is easier on a horse than a light rider with uneven pressure. And, unless we're talking about weight issues that limit movement, such as when it prevents you from putting your arms by your sides or extremely large breasts, we're still talking physics, not weight."

Coach Daniel Stewart, one of the world's leading experts on equestrian sport psychology, agrees.

"Your horse doesn't care how much *weight* you carry," he says, "it's *how* you carry that weight that matters. I really believe a horse would rather carry a balanced 200 pounds than a floppy, unbalanced, all-over-the-place 120 pounds." Coach Stewart places a much higher priority on embracing and working with the body you have than criticizing or trying to change it. "If I'm going to be heavy, I need to make sure I'm a symmetrical, balanced rider," he adds.

RESOURCES

Wendy Murdoch's *50 5-Minute Fixes to Improve Your Riding, 40 5-Minute Jumping Fixes,* and the three-part DVD series *Ride Like a Natural* (all published by Trafalgar Square Books), as well as *Simplify Your Riding* (Carriage House Publishing, 2004).

Daniel Stewart's *Ride Right with Daniel Stewart: Balance Your Frame and Frame of Mind with an Unmounted Workout and Sport Psychology System* (Trafalgar Square Books, 2004) now available in ebook and Kindle formats.

The Other Side of Overweight

No matter how much we "Battle of the Bulge" veterans lament the extra pounds that plague us, the flip side of this problem is also one that has also been around for as long as anyone can remember. I know it's hard to imagine for those of us who tend to fret about excess ballast, but there is another extreme of body image woes that is just as destructive to self-concept, both in and out of the saddle.

Despite the alarming statistics on obesity brought to us by our friends at the Center for Disease Control (see p. 5), an equally legitimate concern comes from society's superficial obsession with being thin. Ironically, this extreme of body image issues—the obsession with "lightness"—is also a longtime resident in the horse world among jockeys whose livelihoods depend on a tiny profile, as well in show rings in disciplines whose traditions demand a willowy build. Eating disorders, starvation, and all the health-related illnesses that tend to arise from long-term deprivation of essential nutrients are not news to those in these worlds.

And now, even as obesity has continued its upward spiral for more than three consecutive decades, this mentality has filtered down to prey upon a growing number of girls and women feeling an ugly new pressure to be "show thin." The barn, which for most of us is a no-makeup, bad-hair-day safety zone, has become, for some, a place of socially-driven body scrutiny, negative comparisons, and body angst that is spawning self-loathing, eating disorders, and self-esteem issues that can last a lifetime. Beyond the anxieties we all share over whether our riding breeches make our buttocks look like, as my grandmother used to say, "two pigs fighting under a blanket" (just try to get *that* dressing room image out of your mind. I challenge you), this is a real problem, and it's hurting people.

So just as show ring discrimination, judgment of peers, and self-consciousness about being truly overweight is harming one subset of riders in the area of body image, it's important to remember that even the "perfect bodies" among us may well be fighting the body image battle, albeit on a different front, where the growing prevalence of peer pressure and body perfectionism is doing just as much damage as trending obesity. Enough, already! The barn should be a welcoming

Myth Understandings

BUSTED!

There are all kinds of things we believe about body types and riding horses that we dare not or don't think to question. Some of these things are "Great Truths" handed down from equestrian to equestrian through the generations. Some are "New and Improved Truths" bandied about by the experts of the day. Some are "Personal Truths"— the ones we've simply come to believe based on the prevalent experiences and perceptions in our own lives, or in what we've observed in the world around us.

In the pages ahead, we're going to examine all these tenets of our collective "Mounted Mythology" and place a stick of dynamite beneath the ones that, quite frankly, "need killin.'" Chief among these are the myths that stand between you and your *Perfect Ride*: that joy-filled experience you imagined the first time you ever climbed onto the back of a horse. These myths may include:

- A horse can only carry 20 percent of his weight. No exceptions.

- If you're overweight and riding a horse, you're not being fair or kind to the horse.

- If your (pick one) legs are too short, boobs are too big, thighs are too thick, arms are too short, upper body is too long, muscles are too dense, hips are too narrow, shape is too lopsided (and so on—I'm sure I just scratched the surface) you'll never be able to ride well.

- If you don't have a "rider's body" (you know the one), you can't compete in certain events, no matter how talented you are.

- Judges ignore overweight riders.

It's time for each of us to do a bit of cleaning and sorting to arrive at the truths we're going to buy into. Regardless of where your own collection of riding myths comes from, some of them need to flat out *go*. With the help of the panel of smart experts you met in the Introduction (see p. 8), we're going to shine a light on the places where body image and riding come together... and change your Myth Understanding for *good*.

refuge for *all* of us. While in this book we deal mostly with the overweight spectrum, it is also crucial to snuffing body image tyranny that we give equal support to our size-0 riding sisters who are convinced they have "huge thighs." As hard as it may be to imagine (for those of us who live in the double digits), they are suffering right alongside us, falling prey to many of the same feelings, emotions, and undeserved body misery.

The Last Prejudice

It is here where we should acknowledge what is sometimes referred to as the last "safe" prejudice: "Sizism," or prejudice about a person's size, refers to stereotypes developed around the belief that *all* extremely heavy (or extremely thin) people share the same characteristics.

According to the 2008 *Rider Psychology* article, "Too Fat to Ride?" Canadian writer Shelley Goodwin writes, "In social circles where one would never hear derogatory remarks about people with disabilities, gays and lesbians, or people from other minority groups, you can still hear disparaging remarks about a person's size."

Goodwin's article goes on to say that sizism tends to be more prevalent in groups where perceptions of and desires for healthy bodies create a space for verbal and nonverbal expression of these stereotypes. It is here, she writes, that "individuals with prejudicial attitudes try to justify their position and also try to sway others to it. In many cases this is done by raising concerns over horse welfare. (And while it's true that some of these concerns may be valid, it is the generalization of these as "proof," that creates a stereotype that is just plain unfair to conscientious plus-sized riders.)

Citing a blog post written by one particularly harsh critic of large riders: "Most people will agree that it is unhealthy for the average horse to carry the weight of an obese rider," Goodwin counters with the generally accepted 20 percent rule, while acknowledging that "an 18-year-old adolescent who weighs 190 pounds may be obese according to her body mass index (BMI), but will easily fall within the

Jenni

"I was born into a line of women (grandmother, specifically) who believed that my ability to have friends, get married, have a career, be 'important' (just about everything, including breathing correctly) was determined by how skinny I was. Lovely Gram, who was a very petite girl, despite her Welsh heritage, married a man of German descent....Needless to say, I have always been short, round, and according to Gram, 'over-endowed up top.' I was never tiny enough to meet her expectations, and was always left with, 'At least you're intelligent, Jennifer; you will probably be okay without a man to support you.' Lovely, right?

"I have to add that my parents moved us away from my mother's mother for these reasons, and my mom, bless her heart, always tries her best...but some things are conditioned in childhood. Such things often do not ever go away, or if they do, they go in very difficult ways. My cousins were exposed to my grandmother for their entire childhoods and suffer from eating and other disorders. My cousins are beautiful girls. *I was* a beautiful girl. I was never a size 0 or a size 2, but I was often within or just a slight bit over where I should naturally have weighed for my frame. I spent most of my childhood and teenage years believing I was this obese monster who would never achieve anything. Now I am actually obese (medical journals are finding this is actually a side effect of starvation during formative years...thank you, low-fat diet!) and I struggle every day with the fallout.

"So my best friend, Mary, in our freshman year of high school, rode horses. She was a natural size 0—it was just genetic for her. Long, lanky, tiny-waisted, and lithe. I wanted to ride so badly but feared I was too overweight (which was probably 15 pounds over what I should have been). I feared how I would look in riding breeches. I feared the horse would stumble beneath me because I was so fat. I remember Mary laughing at me when I confessed these fears, and saying something to the effect of: 'The horse weighs a ton, literally. Get over yourself. You are not fat, and the horse will never care.'

(continued)

"A novel concept for a kid who had been on a diet since she was in third grade: *The horse will not care.* And he didn't care. You wanna know who else didn't care? The instructor didn't care. *All* the girls at the barn felt funny in breeches. *Nobody* cared how 'fat' I was. So all of a sudden I had this thing that was a 'sport,' that I thought was supposed to be a 'skinny girl sport'—and nobody cared that I was 'fat.' And while I might not have been Olympic material, it turned out I was good! I was, and I am, a decent rider—despite the fact I am 'fat and will never achieve anything in life.' (Take *that*, Grams!)

"Not just in the perspective of riders, but young girls have it rough these days. With Pinterest boards dedicated to 'thigh gap,' and the constant media run of skinny being the definition of be-all…it's very scary, and annoying. I know that annoying may seem a strange word to choose, but we all hail from the women who burnt their bras—we're the boomers of the baby boomers! Today women run companies and balance households, and can choose to be moms or not-moms, and any variation in between. Why do we subject ourselves and our daughters, sisters, and friends to the crap that goes along with our only option being 'finding a man,' being desirable for society, or whatever. Where is the champion who says, 'Be desirable for yourself'? Do we really have to wait until we are old to wear red hats with purple dresses? Why doesn't our society empower our young women to be happy with themselves, and to be brave, bold, meek, or (insert wanted adjective here!) *for themselves.*

"It's hard to shelter girls from the onslaught of 'craptacularness' that seems bent on making them hate their bodies. My youngest cousin is a fantastic gymnast. Talk about muscle and body control! She's really amazing! Her older sisters pick on her because she weighs 100 pounds. I don't think there is an ounce of fat on the kid—all muscle! But the number is all they see, and at 4 feet, 3 inches they keep telling her she's fat. No matter what we tell her, it doesn't matter. Now she's on a diet, at 12 years of age. It makes me so angry, because I was that girl once (never that fit, mind you)—not fat, just normal, and made anxious over a stupid number."

acceptable weight load for a 1,100 pound healthy horse. Knowing this," she adds, "we realize that when someone says it is animal abuse for an obese person to ride a horse, the primary concern is not about the horse's welfare but rather the dislike of someone riding who does not fit the stereotypical image of a thin rider."

According to Goodwin, ridicule, discrimination, and often, public humiliation is wreaking lifelong psychological havoc on the self-esteem of overweight equestrians, especially youth and young women. Taking a stand against this growing concern, Goodwin urges global awareness that many people, in equestrian sports and beyond, may be encountering prejudice and specifically, sizism. In building our awareness—and acting on this awareness, she writes, "we can encourage and support all equestrians in their pursuit of enjoying horses and improving their mental and physical well-being."

So What Do We Need to Know . . . About Riding and Excess Weight?

Is this a book to help a heavy rider ride better? Or is this book's focus on getting mentally, physically, and emotionally fit to "ride light," regardless of the number on the scale or the tag on your jeans?

The answer is…yes. And it depends. What do you want from riding and horses? How much joy is the time you spend with your horse bringing you? Is it limited by myths and numbers?

As we ride on from here, we'll explore some tools for figuring out your best solutions, and, if you're so inclined, arrive at a plan to help you change your reality—or your *perceptions* of your reality. Or both. And, if you also end up changing your body somewhere along the way, so be it.

"Lots of times women who are overweight don't ride much," instructor Susan Harris says. "There's always a reason—or an excuse. They're embarrassed, they're afraid they'll hurt their horse, or riding is uncomfortable for them."

And following up her earlier explanations of physics and weight, Wendy Murdoch urges us to remember that, "Function makes a way bigger difference than fat. If you use your body well, you're going to decrease the pressure you put on your horse at any weight. We just have to be honest, realistic and objective to find a way to get the job done so we can ride, and ride well.

"That's the bottom line."

<table>
<tr><td>

#Hoofpicks

</td><td>

In this chapter we explored the trends of obesity, and what it means for riders in the barn, in the show ring, and on their horses. What this helps us understand

</td></tr>
</table>

in our work with horses is that numbers on scales are only one factor. Using your body well is important at any weight. This is a new and different game-changer in the battle against negative body image because it will release us once and for all from a prison of untrue messages we may be carrying with us concerning riding and our weight.

Your Chapter 2 **#Hoofpicks** include:

1 **All "truths" are suspect.** How do you know what you *think* you know on this subject? Sometimes the "great truths" handed down from other equestrians, disciplines, and generations are the farthest thing from *actual* truth.

2 **Get in your own head.** Spending some time learning to separate fact from fiction and truth from "mounted mythology" can make all the difference in our ride. Take a careful look at your own beliefs about "too much" and "not enough" and "okay" and "not okay" when it comes to size, shape, weight, and riding well.

3 **Come to grips with what may, in fact, be real.** Getting real with your size is a process of objective assessment and acceptance of what *is* true—and deciding what you want or need to do about it.

4 **Sometimes all your body needs is...*acceptance.*** How might you begin to reframe how you regard your physical being in kinder, gentler terms?

3 | Get Clear on What's Real

Now...Be Honest...did you really take the test at the beginning of the book (p. 15)? If so, you've already asked yourself a number of questions and answered a number of prompts that may have started you thinking about how you view your own body, especially when it comes to riding.

Are we right in these self-assessments? Is how we see ourselves, or how we feel in the saddle—or in our breeches or jeans—what's *real*? The answer is... maybe. And just as likely, maybe not. As we've already discovered there's a whole lot to the issue of self-image and what we can do to feel better about how we look. Let's start to peel back the layers.

You're More Beautiful Than You Think

"Real Beauty Sketches," a compelling social experiment conducted and recorded on video by Dove® soap, was a response to researchers' estimate that only 4 percent of women around the world consider themselves beautiful. That's right, 4 percent. *In the whole world*. Dove decided to speak out about the poor-self-esteem epidemic through its "Real Women" campaign. (And no, this is not a product plug.)

The intro to the video states that it intends to "prove to women something very important: you are more beautiful than you think." (Watch it at http://realbeautys-ketches.dove.us/.) Its premise is simple: A series of women sit down behind a curtain, and each one describes her own face to an FBI-trained forensic sketch artist, who then creates a portrait based only on her self-description. Then researchers bring in random strangers—behind the curtain with the women—and ask the strangers to describe each subject's face. From these external descriptions, the artist creates a second portrait.

The difference between the sketch created when each woman described herself and the sketch of her as described by a complete stranger, displayed side by side, provides a staggering and undeniable substantiation of the researchers' findings: We *are* far more beautiful than we think.

A little more investigation into the phenomena of how our thoughts define us, if even to ourselves, revealed an important side effect: Our thoughts have power to influence not only our self-esteem, but also our choices. In a post-sketch interview, one of the women, Florence, reflects on what she calls "really bad life choices" that she says were a reflection of her lack of self-esteem: "I chose the wrong job, the wrong husbands, blamed everybody else, and defined myself by what people thought of me instead of being my *authentic self* and doing what made me happy...I didn't get the emotional comfort I needed, so I thought there was something wrong with me."

After working hard on her self-esteem over and above everything else, Florence found her relationships improving, her perceptions shifting, and people commenting that she seemed like a new person.

Exercise for the Soul: Meet Your Authentic Self

Authenticity and *authentic self* are a couple of somewhat fuzzy members of that category of terms we see, hear, and toss about, but when it gets right down to it, are just a little wiggly. As far as I can tell, the quick definition of *authenticity* is keeping your thoughts, words, actions, and choices firmly aligned with the core values you were born with.

So, then, is your *authentic self* just the most honest and real version of yourself you can possibly be? And if so, *who is she*? What's important to her? How do you know when she's in charge—and when she's not? Is there a light that comes on somewhere in your consciousness when you find the "sweet spot" of authenticity,

Deandra

"I would rather someone say to my face, 'Don't you think you're too heavy to ride?' than whisper about it to everyone but me."

like the one in the drive-thru car wash that tells you to stop right where you are, because this is where you need to be?

Knowing your authentic self—and being able to define in real terms what she values—helps you understand what really drives you at the deepest level. What brings you true joy? Where do you find inspiration? What do you want more of in your life? By building your life and lifestyle around these *authentic values*, you can create an existence that is more satisfying and meaningful.

So what are *your* authentic values? (Even though they may change or shift some-what over time, they will deepen with your effort to understand them, and therefore, get to know your authentic self a little bit better.) Ask yourself: If someone were giving your eulogy today, what words do you hope he or she would use to describe you, your character, and how you lived your life? (Find a great sample list at www. lifehack.org: www.lifehack.org/articles/communication/3-easy-steps-becoming-your-authentic- self.html). Here is my personal Top 10, in no particular order:

- Kindness
- Creativity
- Excellence
- Family
- Integrity

- Intuition
- Passion
- Patience
- Spirituality
- Tenacity

1 Your turn! Make a quick list of 10 words that sum up or describe who you are at your core, in no particular order.

2 Now, allotting a single page for each word, free-journal (write as fast as you can in a notebook or on your computer or tablet) any examples you can think of from your life right now that demonstrate how you are living that value.

3 Draw a line underneath your example(s), then beneath that make a list of actions you'd *like* to take or goals to pursue to live out that value.

4 Sit back and take a look at your word list, and then your actions and goals, and ask yourself some hard questions:

What activities in your life right now do not align in some way with this list of values?

Keep in mind that your values change over time, and this list may be completely different at different times or phases of your life.

Who or what relationships in your life take you farther away from your authentic self?

I'm not suggesting you jettison anyone or anything that doesn't fit; just be aware and make choices accordingly about where you put your time and energy.

LIKE WATER RUNNING INTO A TRENCH

Here's where we make the turn toward understanding not only why we are where we are in this body image conundrum, but how our mental, physical, emotional, and lifestyle habits are keeping us stuck. How we habitually think about, talk about, and compare our bodies to others' not only sets, but perpetuates our body image. Habit, you see, is like a trench water runs into—and if you've ever been camping and dug that little trench around the outside of your tent when it looks like rain, this image will be as vivid to you as it is to me. (And truthfully, I've never been camping when it *didn't* rain.)

Regardless of how our real life body image realities are playing out for each of us, it is our myth understandings, false ideals, and negative comparisons that have helped us dig our own body-image-habit trenches. Years of related thoughts, actions, and choices in our behavior have formed the unconscious habits that keep these trenches full. While we may *talk about* change and *want* change, until we figure out how to stop filling our trenches (creating different habits of thinking, believing, and behaving), *nothing is going to* change.

Where do we begin? Body image, it turns out, is about much more than *how you think you look.* It *is* that, yes, along with a whole complex, multifaceted range of mental, physical, and emotional connections that drive how you actually experience your life in the body you have. Remember Thomas Cash and *The Body Image Workbook* from the RT[3] Test we took earlier (see p. 15)? In his book, Cash uses a series of exercises and self-evaluations to help pinpoint habitual thinking and emotional responses to this body we live in. Then, step by step, he explains how to repair the damage we may have inadvertently done to our body image, which he defines as: "More than a mental picture of what you look like, your body image consists of your personal relationship with your body—encompassing your perceptions, beliefs, thoughts, feelings, and actions that pertain to your physical appearance."

Taking Cash's book into the riding arena, it is clear to me that there's a whole lot of habitual thinking going on of which we are most likely unaware. With these thoughts, feelings, and actions (behavior) keeping our habit trenches full, even our mastery of technical riding skills is no match for what lies beneath whatever confidence we have in our proficiency. How we feel in our bodies when we ride is precisely *where* our body image connects to our riding.

Cash says that as much as one-third of your self-esteem is related to how positive or negative your body image is. "Often a poor body image lowers self-esteem," he writes. "Poor self-esteem means feeling inadequate as a person; it means you have low self-worth and don't highly value yourself." Knowing what we do about how our horses read and mirror us, it's easy to understand the unwitting cycle a negative body image sets off in how we ride, how we feel about our riding, and in our relationships with our horses. The good news Cash shares through his work is that by changing our habitual thinking we can make improvements in our body image that will not only bolster our self-esteem, but also bring comfort and contentment to our relationships (especially, I'm sure, with our horses!).

THE MESSAGE IN THE YO-YO

Many of us (myself included) relate all too well to this quote from the famous late humorist, Erma Bombeck: "In two decades I've lost a total of 789 pounds. I should be hanging from a charm bracelet." The truth is many, if not most, people who lose weight regain it again. When we're heavier than we want to be, losing weight always seems like the answer. However, losing weight is rarely the panacea we imagine it to be. What drives the yo-yo cycle of gaining and losing the same weight over and over seems to be the reality that even when we lose weight—even significant weight—*our body image may not change at all*. It's only a matter of time until the interconnected cycle of thoughts, feelings, and behaviors around that same old body image kick in—and pop goes the button on our skinny jeans.

INTERIOR REMODELING

Like a posting trot, the up and down of yo-yo dieting may have become the rhythm of our relationship with our body image. While for some this does serve to keep actual weight within a certain range, for others chronic dieting can spiral into more serious issues, such as escalating body image distress and eating disorders, wreaking havoc on metabolism that eventually makes it next to impossible to lose any weight at all. And what's worse, it's all for naught. In one of Dr. Cash's studies, for even those whose body image *did* change after losing 50 or more pounds, when they regained as little as 5 pounds their self-esteem and body image reverted right back to where it was *before* they lost the weight.

When it comes to weight loss, many experts now challenge the dieting solution completely, and move us more toward effective weight management through lifestyle change (the kinds of lifestyle changes this book is all about). And, surprise,

Anne

One of my barn friends, we'll call her "Anne" (not her real name at her request), had a medical condition that arose, in part, due to her excess weight. She already rode a very large horse and was in good enough shape to show at a very high level, and she did very well (some might say *in spite of* her weight). However, when her doctor put her on a medication with a side effect that made her dizzy to the point of vertigo, it became clear to her that if she wanted to continue riding she was going to have to lose the weight—and tend to her overall health in such a way that she could quit taking this medication.

She opted for bariatric (weight loss) surgery and a whole slew of lifestyle changes, including improved nutrition and exercise and breathing and meditation, and she dropped 80 pounds in a record (but reasonably healthy) amount of time. Of course, her main motivation was being able to ride her breathtakingly beautiful horse again, so her commitment was solid and unwavering.

Here's the funny part, though: After her first time back in the show ring following her weight loss, she reported feeling *exactly the same* minus the dizziness brought on by the medication. She had always been "all business" about her riding and nothing changed there. She knew she was wearing smaller clothes (she was, in fact, now wearing that elusive size 6), but overall, everything else felt the same.

It was only when she saw pictures from the show that she realized how different her body looked. She had been looking at herself in the mirror for months, watching her size steadily go down. She had bought new clothes in a downward progression from size 20, to 18, all the way to the 6s she was wearing on show day. When she examined the photo of her whole show class, all the horses were about the same size and color, and all the riders were dressed in traditional black-and-whites with standard, pretty much identical helmets. She looked and looked and then looked up, puzzled. "I can't find myself!" she said.

Then she looked again. "Oh, wait!" she exclaimed at last. "I had to change out my chin strap and it was flesh-colored instead of black." Tears filled her eyes.

"There I am!"

surprise, significant and permanent weight loss tends to show up as a side effect. Citing a University of Vermont study that provided clinically obese people with body image therapy similar to what Cash offers in *The Body Image Workbook*, Cash reveals the myth-busting truth: "People who need to lose weight to improve their health should separate the goals of weight loss and body acceptance," he writes. "By first learning how to have a positive relationship with your imperfect body instead of a relationship full of loathing, desperation, and abuse, your ability to shed excess weight may be strengthened."

Translating Cash's advice to us as riders brings forth the overarching concept behind this book: while "exterior remodeling" is well and good if that's something you want to do, it is far more important to work on the "interior problem." For us as horsewomen this difficult "beneath the surface" work means addressing every choice we make in how we ride and work with horses (as outlined in the chapters that follow). At the trail's end, we may or may not still want to lose weight. The point is, if we do this work well, *weight* becomes a nonissue. When we decide that we do want to make physical changes, our "interior remodeling" will set us up for success that will retire that yo-yo for good and make us much more likely to reap the emotional benefits of reaching and maintaining a healthy weight and lifestyle.

"The more invested people are in their appearance," Cash writes in *The Body Image Workbook*, "the more it preoccupies them—in their thoughts, emotions, and behaviors." He adds that while people think this preoccupation will help them raise their sense of self-worth, the opposite is actually true: It turns out that the more we fret about the size of our seat, the more our self-esteem decreases.

I don't know about you, but I'd much rather spend all that time and energy on my horses.

IT'S YOUR CHOICE

In his book Cash explains that people tend to deal with body image challenges in three basic ways:

• **Appearance Fixing** This is anything we do to try to change our looks, from fretting about the offending characteristic to trying to cover it up or otherwise make it look better. (This, I would assume, includes my stretchy jeans, oversized t-shirts, and hoodies.) This also includes always being in some stage of planning your next diet—or continuously adding to your exercise DVD collection (Argh! Got me again!).

Another appearance-fixing tactic, Cash tells us, is called *compensation:* the things we do to "make ourselves feel better" that don't address the issue we're really concerned about (I'm guessing a new haircut, different makeup, and long red acrylic nails all put me back in the "yep" column again). While these things may make us feel better momentarily, the underlying angst remains. (Even worse, those nails backfire when you're trying to tighten a cinch!)

We might also always seek reassurance about our looks ("Tell me, really, does this saddle make my butt look big?"). We, of course, hope to hear "No!" to "fix" our concern, although rarely does this appease for long. Even when others *do* tell the truth, we probably won't believe them!

• **Avoidance** Just as you may guess, this tactic means we'll go to any length to squelch any sort of body image discomfort. (In my experience, this could include drowning these worries in hot fudge.) Often sporting some version of "I'm just not going to think about it," we avoid all mirrors, photos, and video. Unfortunately, however, while refusing to think about "how big my thighs look in these breeches" or "how my belly bounces during sitting trot" may offer *some* temporary relief, it's kind of like telling yourself not to think about pink elephants. As we'll see later, our brain doesn't register the negative—so what we're trying not to think about is still in there, front and center in our subconscious, walloping our self-image. Sometimes avoidance keeps us on the sidelines and out of situations that may invite any sort of body discomfort. (This is what makes some plus-sized riders quit showing—and others even stop riding completely.)

• **Acceptance** A far better course, our assembled experts agree, is to accept those negative feelings instead of just avoiding them (we're going to learn how to do this, beginning on p. 47). Does this mean giving up on losing excess weight and resigning ourselves to being a plus-sized rider? As we'll explore in detail later on, the shifts we can make in our lifestyle and habits will likely set a new course for our thoughts and emotions around our appearance on horseback.

SEPARATE FACT FROM FICTION

"The whole issue of weight and dieting and self-image is a tangled one," says Jill Valle, a Los Angeles-based, licensed family therapist who specializes in body image and weight issues for women and adolescent girls. Because we are so influenced by what Valle terms "media mythology," it really *is* hard to separate truth from pure fiction when it comes to resolving body image issues and settling in at our fit and healthy best.

Valle agrees with what we've already pinpointed: The key to success here is looking at this process as a *lifestyle change* that reaches beyond any "diet" or "exercise program." What we're talking about here is getting in touch with the physical realities of our bodies, regardless of size, and exploring the connections between thoughts and emotions around what truly is "healthy" and "ideal" for each of us as *unique individuals*—not according to some intersection of numbers on a chart.

"What is prevalent right now is a lot of differing opinions of what's 'healthy,'" Valle says. "'Ideal' weight doesn't always correlate with ideal health, just as 'overweight' doesn't always mean 'unhealthy.' Some women may be larger," she adds, "but in touch with reality, and they may actually be healthy *and* heavy."

Valle recommends that for those who need to make lifestyle changes, as she prefers to call them, it is extremely important to make the distinction that what we are pursuing is *very different* from what the multimillion-dollar diet industry sells as being "on a diet" or "off a diet."

"The question we must ask instead," she emphasizes, "should be, 'What are we putting *into* our bodies, what are we doing *with* our bodies, and how does that align with or conflict with our goals?'" (In our case, "Is sitting here on the sofa and eating this cupcake moving me closer or farther away from being a healthy and athletic rider?").

Valle concurs that the controversy—even in our own minds—about what our own "ideal" or "perfect" weight and conditioning is makes it very difficult to sort the real and healthy from the "media mythology." (I was amazed at how her observations and thoughts as a therapist working with all kinds of women on these issues meshed with what I had discovered in my own research among coaches, trainers, and women riding at all levels and disciplines in the horse world.) Together we looked at the normal body image issues most women face through the lens of a woman who also wants to ride horses (and ride them well), and we agreed on the three key places where body image and riding intersect—and you'll recognize them! Yep: thoughts, feelings, and actions or behavior. Because these three are, in fact, a continuum (a shift in any one of them affects the other two), Valle explains that it really doesn't matter where you "jump in." (We'll delve into how to ride this magical continuum in the coming chapters, but for now just know that the realm of strong, healthy connectedness is waiting at the end of this trail for each of us.) In addition, we named three "types" that demonstrate these continuum intersections (each of us may find ourselves inhabiting one or all of these, at one time or another):

• **The Floppers** These women have no relationship with their own bodies *at all.* Deeply mired in some of the "body mythology" we've already explored, they have no idea what is or is not true about their bodies, or even where their body parts are in space and relation to one another. You've seen them or been them in the saddle: They come in *all* sizes and shapes and tend to "flop around" as they ride, with no idea how their poor balance, lack of body control, chaotic energy, and chattering minds and mouths are putting themselves and their horses in danger. What these women see, feel, and understand about their bodies has nothing to do with objective reality.

• **The Fighters** These are the women (and sadly, many teenage girls) who have been dieting for so long they don't even remember how *not* to obsess over their latest diet and exercise regimens. They may have had some successes in the past, but they've failed so many times that they've all but given up on the idea of ever getting to their goal weight and staying there. They're riding, but not as well as they think they could without what they consider "extra bulk." They worry about their horses and feel guilty (and a little bit defensive) over just about everything to do with their riding: form, style, and how they might seek to improve.

• **The Dancers** These women are few and far between, but somehow they've turned the corner. They understand, take care of, respect, and are at peace with their bodies, and have learned to make the most of their physical attributes to overcome whatever challenges happen to be "riding along with them." They know how to use a powerful combination of clean-burning nutrition, a conditioning and strengthening regimen they can live with, and a mindful connection with their energies and abilities that allows them to move with their horses like dancers across a ballroom floor. (By the way, we're going to learn how to use these, too!)

I don't know about you, but at the moment I've got one foot planted in the Fighter camp and the other tentatively tapping its way toward the Dancers. The question, I think most of us would agree, is how in the world do you get right up on stage with the Dancers? After talking to more experts than I can count and poring over all the latest sports nutrition and fitness data I could get my hands on, here's the best answer I can give you: We each have to *make the shift* in our minds (and in our lifestyles) that will connect our mind, body, and spirit in a whole new way, and on our own terms.

Beware the "Trance"

When our real or imagined shortcomings begin to define and delimit our experience of life, we can become paralyzed by a "waking dream" that author Tara Brach calls the "trance of unworthiness." In her book, *Radical Acceptance*, Brach

Myths of Description

BUSTED!

If for now we can just agree that it's really okay to be *whatever size and shape we are,* as long as we don't hurt our horses, let's talk about the mythology of body description. The self-proclaimed "Evil Queen of Comedy" Joy Nash takes deadly aim at the perceptions attached to the term "fat" in her million-plus-hit YouTube "Fat Rant" (watch it here: www.youtube.com/watch?v=yUTJQIBI1oA). In it, Nash reframes "fat" into a descriptor no more offensive than "tall," "short," or any other word you might use to physically describe a person without inferring it makes him or her good or bad.

"I personally feel like 'fat' is a descriptive word," Nash explains in her video. "So, therefore, it has no negative connotation for me. I know that there are many out there who choose to use it as an insult or derogatory term, but to me—it simply is not. 'Fat' takes less time to say than 'overweight' or 'plus-sized' and, since I am a writer by nature, and I have affixed neither a negative nor positive spin to the word myself, it is the word I use. The insult, 'Yeah, well... you're FAT and STUPID!' makes about as much sense to me as the insult, 'You're TALL and STUPID!' or 'You're DARK and STUPID!'"

The word only has as much power as we give it, Nash says, and if it is just a descriptive word in your vocabulary...well, then, it's perfectly okay to say, "I am a fat girl." Or, as I heard a young woman say just the other day, "I am not fat, I *have* fat. I also have toenails, but that doesn't mean I *am* toenails." Finding this brand of solid self-acceptance and self-compassion can be key to letting go of the negativity about your body that could be bogging you down as much, if not more, than excess pounds.

describes this feeling of futility and inertia all too familiar to those of us who have ever struggled with "yo-yo" weight.

"I know I should be able to handle the problem," she writes, "but no matter how hard I try, I can't get where I need to go. Completely alone and shadowed by the fear of failure, I am trapped in my dilemma. Nothing else in the world exists but that."

Think about it. How many otherwise wonderful moments in your life—and

BUSTED! Myths of Shape

MYTH: "My (choose one) legs are too short, boobs are too big, thighs are too thick, arms are too short, upper body is too long, muscles are too dense, hips are too narrow, shape is too lopsided for me to ever ride well."

TRUTH: According to Wendy Murdoch, "People with long torsos, short legs, and short arms are going to have a center of gravity that's higher—and maybe not quite enough leg to get around the horse, but this is a challenge of physics, not weight." Speaking in equations, she adds, "Weight is mass times gravity. Pressure is weight times force. Proportion, however, is linear: 'this' length versus 'that' length. And above all, gravity is the law."

Susan Harris agrees, adding, "You can't change short legs, a big frame, a long torso, and so on—it's the body God gave you! And while you *can't* change the fundamental shape and conformation of your body, you *can* learn how to work with your body's characteristics to maximize your effectiveness in the saddle."

"Any body shape can ride to success," concurs Coach Daniel Stewart. "You just have to find your own definition of what success is for you —within reason."

As an example, let's discuss thighs for a minute (which I usually try not to, unless I'm talking about especially in your *horse life*—have been tarnished by your self-consciousness over weight or appearance? As a young teenager, I remember watching the other girls at my boarding stable ride their horses bareback, wearing tank tops and cut-off shorts, galloping in like free spirits, turning the hoses on one another as they rinsed off their horses after a ride. I'm not sure whether it was more the fear of galloping bareback or dread of how I imagined I looked in shorts, but these otherwise halcyon days were times of misery and longing. Longing to be free. Longing to feel

chicken). Veterinarian and saddle-fit specialist Dr. Joyce Harman says the main thing to consider about our thighs is not their size but whether we are able to get our legs into the correct riding position. For example, Dr. Harman says that a problem she frequently sees that increases load and pressure on a horse—and therefore his discomfort—is improperly adjusted stirrups. This is particularly problematic for people with long thighs, because too-short stirrups can push the rider's weight too far back in the saddle—a problem for any horse with even the lightest of riders (we'll discuss this stirrup issue at greater "length" on p. 168).

Dr. Harman says it is actually the thickness of your thigh—and the location of this thickness—that is a very important factor in finding not only the right horse, but also the right saddle, the right stirrup position, and your body's place of perfect balance. To determine thigh thickness, it's important to look at how much fat and muscle (yes, muscle counts, too!) is on the inside of your thighs. She says you can "have a lot of 'backside,' and that's not as much of an issue," and she emphasizes that we need to be looking to *balance* the thickness. Again, as an example, when you have thick thighs, you're going to want a more narrow horse (more on this on p. 59); if you have thinner thighs, a wider horse will work just fine.

the pure joy they exuded, which I was certain had something to do with looking the way they looked. I realize now, looking back, that it was only my perception that was holding me hostage. This was the "trance of unworthiness," putting my joy on hold until I dieted a little harder, exercised a little more, and somehow "earned" the freedom I craved. In truth, no amount of dieting or exercise would bring me the carefree abandon I saw in the other girls' full-throttle *joy* in riding and being with their horses and one another.

This feeling of unworthiness, Brach explains, creates a vicious cycle: The more unworthy I felt, the more separate and vulnerable I felt. "Underneath our fear of being flawed is a more primal fear that something is wrong with our life," Brach explains. "Our reaction to this fear is to feel blame, even hatred, toward whatever we consider the source of the problem: ourselves, others, life itself."

SNAP OUT OF IT!

After spending a lifetime working with the sick and the poor and the hopeless, Mother Theresa observed that the biggest ailment and cause of suffering she observed was not a registered disease, per se, but rather, "the feeling of not belonging." In our own society, Brach says, this condition has now reached epidemic proportions. "We long to belong and feel as if we don't deserve to." This seems as prevalent in barn

RESOURCES

Tara Brach's *Radical Acceptance: Embracing Your Life with the Heart of a Buddha* (Bantam, 2003).

aisles, show rings, and on group trail rides as is does in any of the areas where we may compare ourselves to others. Whether or not it's justifiable, when we feel this isolation and fear of rejection, we're ripe for the sort of self-loathing that perpetuates our suffering itself in a continuous loop until something comes along to snap us out of our "trance."

"We learn early in life that any affiliation—with family and friends, at school or in the workplace [and especially, it seems, in the show barn!]—requires proving that we are worthy," says Brach. "We are under pressure to compete with each other, to get ahead, to stand out as intelligent, attractive, capable, powerful, wealthy. Someone is always keeping score."

In our riding, this scorekeeping becomes all the more compelling when our own "flaws" hit our radar screen, and it's "game on" to try and manipulate our bodies—and therefore our appearance—to fit into whatever "perfect picture" we have bought into. And then, when we think we don't "measure up" (by whatever measuring stick we pick as our poison), the "trance" sets in, and we are locked in a struggle that may well stay with us for life.

Looking back now, I'm both amused and saddened at how my perception of falling short of my own "gold standard" measuring stick of worthiness—galloping bareback in cut-off shorts (and laughing all the way)—kept me isolated from the *joy* I could have felt in riding horses with friends in the summer sunshine. What's worse, that wasn't the only time my self-consciousness over a bigger (but by no means fat) body forced my budding adolescent awkwardness into full bloom. That was when my own dance with the "trance of unworthiness" began. And yours?

THE WAY OUT

Brach says that when we allow ourselves to become entrapped by our feelings of self-judgment, anxiety, restlessness, and dissatisfaction, the "trance of unworthiness" can hold us captive for years in a cage of our own making. Usually we're not even aware we're in it; it's only in looking back (like I just did) that we see the waste of precious moments we'll never be able to get back.

The answer? Accepting everything in our moment-to-moment experience without judgment or plans for changing it. That's right. *Everything.* Thunder thighs and all.

"The way out of our cage begins with accepting absolutely everything about ourselves and our lives," Brach writes. That doesn't mean we should put up with anything harmful, she is quick to add. The way out of our "trance" begins with simply allowing ourselves to *feel what we're feeling* without resisting, judging, or feeling compelled to *fix* it. Seeing ourselves—possibly for the first time in our conscious lives—with a big, open, kind, and loving heart is your trail marker for making the turn toward what Brach coins *radical acceptance.* And this is both the beginning *and* the culmination of this journey we're now on together.

I know. You're skeptical. As we say in Texas, "This ain't your first rodeo." You've tried other solutions and come up empty-handed (and empty-hearted). All I ask is that you sit deep, stay centered, and commit to what's ahead. Don't spook when you recognize some too-familiar shadows and scary objects. As we move along this trail together, our first concern is identifying and then letting go of whatever has been stopping you. As our friend Coach Daniel Stewart (we'll hear a lot from him in coming pages) is fond of saying, "Most often what we struggle with as riders mirrors what we're going through in life. The solution is to expand our self-image beyond what is troubling us—and troubling our riding."

Does that mean we're not going to make any changes? Hardly! Am I telling you, "It is what it is...accept it and get over yourself?" Not at all! Are we going to ignore real and serious issues that could be impeding your riding or even putting you or your horse at risk? Absolutely not! You'll see how your own issues in the saddle connect with other areas of your life, and that it doesn't seem to matter which one you approach first—or which responds first—the others inevitably come along.

In this chapter we explored the concept of "interior work" and how it affects our exterior appearance. This will help us in our work with horses because in order to "show up" as our best selves, we have to stop fixating on our bodies and pay more attention to what really matters most in our relationship with our horses, ourselves, and others. This is a new and different game-changer in the battle against negative body image because when we learn to accept our bodies *first,* just as they are, a whole new world opens to us.

Your Chapter 3 **#Hoofpicks** include:

1 **Use the right measuring stick (or tape).** It may be okay to weigh more. We DO more. Charts are just guidelines for the undereducated. The real measurements are:

- How do you feel?
- Are you healthy?
- Do you have enough energy to do what you want and need to do?
- Are you strong, effective, and safe in the barn and the saddle?
- Is your horse happy and healthy?

2 **Go for quality.** We choose only the highest-quality feed for our horses, carefully matched for the level of activity they do. We measure carefully and religiously add whatever supplements they seem to need to be healthy and look their best. We feed them on time and make sure they get enough roughage and drink plenty of fresh water. We only give them healthy treats. We exercise them, stretch them, warm them up cool them down, make sure they have adequate rest, and keep their health care on schedule. Why do we have such a hard time doing the same thing for ourselves?

3 Start putting it together. As you start to tie what you *think* about your body and your riding with your actual physical realities, give yourself permission to stick with this quest. Follow each trail of new information a little way, and consider the possibility that perhaps you've been given a bum steer or two by well meaning others, the media, or your own fears.

4 Be open. To change, to acceptance, to whatever it takes to learn what is real, authentic, true, and right—and let go of all that's not. This means facing your issues squarely and figuring out your own best answers. This may mean taking others' observations to heart. It may also mean (lovingly) telling them to go jump in the nearest lake. Only when you sit with your own *authentic truth* can you begin to separate what's real from what's not.

Be
Fair

4 | **Fit Your Ride**

If you're a larger rider, the obvious horse solution is getting a bigger horse, right?

"Maybe," says Dr. Joyce Harman. But horse size is not the only thing to look at, Dr. Harman and several other experts say, pretty much in unison. "People think a bigger horse can naturally carry more," she adds, "but a draft horse might not carry as much easily as a short-coupled, more squarely-built Quarter Horse."

Dr. Harman says that studies have actually shown that "bigger doesn't necessarily mean better." There are lots of factors to consider when evaluating how well a horse is built to carry the weight of a rider-of-size. "Your horse doesn't *have* to have perfect leg conformation," she gives as an example, "but you do need to keep in mind that if a horse happens to have a conformation issue, any increase in workload puts more stress on that weakness."

We've all done it...gone horse shopping and one that is less than ideal steals our heart. Sometimes it works out (ask my horse, Trace—my husband says he hit the horsey jackpot), but when it comes to choosing a horse for his weight-bearing capacity, this is a decision that truly must be calculated with a cool, well-informed head. Especially when you are a heavier rider, the trick is to perfect your ability to spot horses that are good—or bad—choices for you, whether you're looking for a horse to buy or lease, taking lessons, or going for a recreational trail ride while on vacation.

Getting real about your weight *and* a prospective horse's conformation is key to preventing pain, heartache, and expense later on trying to keep that horse sound. This, my friends, is one time when we *do* have to put on those big-girl panties and

make decisions that will protect the horse from possible injury and yourself from boatloads of guilt.

"If you're considering a horse that is otherwise wonderful, but has terrible feet," Dr. Harman counsels, "and especially if you're heavier and you want to do more than stroll around, it's a good reason *not* to buy, lease, or take lessons on that horse."

On "Suitability"... and Asking the Right Questions

"Suitability" is an old-fashioned term in the horse world, once used to encompass a horse's mental, physical, and emotional appropriateness for a rider—and whether horse and rider are a good match in terms of size, shape, and temperament.

"This is an old idea that has somehow gotten lost," says Wendy Murdoch. "We get caught up in our fantasies and lose touch with our own realities. It's essential to have the appropriate size and build of horse. He needs to be a good *shape* for you—one that also takes into consideration the breadth of your pelvis and the length of your thighs."

Evaluating a horse's suitability to carry extra rider weight must also consider what you're planning to do with that horse. "Rider weight *does* make a difference in certain sports and disciplines," Harris says on this topic. So whether you're planning speed or endurance events, or even strenuous recreational activities such as long or hilly trail rides, suitability can be a sliding scale that depends upon the demand you'll be placing on the horse. (See Dr. Harman's explanation of "load" as being sometimes about weight and sometimes about conditions, and always about the combination of the two on p. 74.)

"You have to be realistic about whether a horse is, as they say, 'up to your weight,'" Harris says. "That is to say, can he do this job without excessive fatigue?"

According to the February 2014 issue of *Horse Illustrated* magazine, more and more public riding facilities are setting and enforcing weight limits. This is quite the sticky wicket, as you can imagine. On one hand they don't want to insult or turn away paying clients, but on the other, if you go back to those climbing obesity statistics, it's easy to see that stable and riding school owners have an obligation to protect their horses—and their long-term livelihood—by setting and enforcing these limits.

"Every horse has his limits," Harris agrees. "So don't be insulted if some stable doesn't have horses whose limits match your needs."

This doesn't mean you should give up if you don't meet these requirements, she is quick to emphasize, telling us to "just be realistic and keep looking until you find the right place." Harris says that more and more stables are dealing with this "upward" trend by buying more draft crosses. This is where the larger rider has to learn to ask the right questions.

"When you call, say: 'I'm a larger rider, doing my best to get fit, and I do need a horse that's up to my weight.' And, if they don't have one, the next question is, 'Do you know someone who does?'"

Learning to express that you are seeking a "weight-carrying horse" (Harris says this is a good way to phrase it without a whole lot of explanation) is key to being as clear as you are matter-of-fact in setting the right tone for these conversations.

While rider weight is a very sensitive subject (believe me, writing this book proved that more times than I can count), I think we all can agree that the well-being of the horses we ride has to come before everything else. Yes, "overweight" adults can ride—and some of them can ride really, really well. The factor most crucial to this kind of success, however, is being realistic...and Being Fair to the horse. It is every rider's responsibility either to choose a horse whose size and build is appropriate for the load he's being asked to carry, or to take whatever steps are necessary to ride the horse she wants or already has.

Myths of Mass

MYTH: "A horse can only carry 20 percent of his weight."

TRUTH: Perhaps one of the most mis-used percentages in the whole horse world is that a rider and tack should never exceed 20 percent of the horse's weight. No, I am not arguing the per-centage. I know there's solid science behind this particular rule of thumb—and that lots of people a heck of a lot smarter than me worked very hard to arrive at that precise percentage.

But here's the thing. It's called a "rule of thumb" for a reason: It's a basic principle with broad applica-tions, and there's a lot more to it than just "thumbs."

In the *Horse Science News* (horsesciencenews.com) article, "How much Weight Can a Horse Carry?" Liz Osborn shares the threshold of weight limit established by recent research (she references a 2008 study published in the *Journal of Equine Veterinary Science*) based on detailed measurements of eight horses ranging from 885 to 1375 pounds, packing anywhere from 15 to 30 percent of their body weight. "When carrying 15 and 20 percent of their body weight, the horses showed relatively little indication of stress. It's when they were packing weights of 25 percent that physical signs changed markedly, and these became accentuated under 30-percent loads."

Signs of stress in these horses as reported by this group of scientific researchers included faster breathing and higher heart rates whenever tack and rider weight totaled more than 25 percent of the horse's weight. And, one day after trotting and cantering with more than 25 percent of their weight on their backs, the horses' muscles showed "substantially greater soreness and tightness." The report also said that the horses least sore were those with "wider loins" (that part of the horse's back between the last rib and croup).

Osborn writes, "Based on these results, the study's authors

recommend that horses not be loaded with greater than 20 percent of their body weight. A 545-kilogram (1,200-pound) horse, then would be best off carrying no more than 109 kilograms (240 pounds) of tack and rider."

She also points out that this research from the Ohio State University Agricultural Technical Institute came to exactly the same conclusion on weight guidelines as the US Cavalry Manuals of Horse Management, which were published in 1920.

Now, I'm not one to debate with the US Cavalry—or our Ohio Tech researchers—but studies, it seems, are just that, and I do have a question or two about all this. What do we know about the fitness level of each horse in the study? What about the fit of the tack they were using? Although this study's measurements did confirm that the musculoskeletal structure and build of the horse does matter when it comes to carrying heavier weight comfortably, and while the riders in this study were experienced and instructed to "ride quietly" and "stay over the horse's center of gravity," I'm still wondering how much "wiggle room" we have on these percentages. Based on what I've learned from the sources I've queried, dozens of variables can dramatically affect the amount of weight a horse can comfortably carry.

In 2013, a UK study from Duchy College in Cornwall sounded an alarm over increasing rider weight and reflected a growing concern that heavier riders were doing harm to their horses. Reported worldwide in a number of publications including *Equinews*, the Kentucky Equine Research Institute Nutrition and Health Daily News, this study suggested that only about *5 percent* of adult riders are at the best weight to allow optimal performance from their horses.

This study is often misquoted by online panic mongers as stating the ideal riding weight to be 10 percent of the horse's mass (and you do your own math…I know I haven't weighed 10 percent of my horse's weight since the fourth grade!). The key here is to note the use of the term "ideal" by the study, which said 15 percent was

(continued)

Myths of Mass, cont.

considered acceptable, and it wasn't until rider weight reached 20 percent and above, this study said, that there was cause for concern. "The judgment of 'too heavy' is somewhat arbitrary if it is based solely on a rider's weight relative to a horse's weight," *Equinews* goes on to say in its May 1, 2013, article. "Other factors to be considered include the horse's conformation, physical condition, and age; the rider's skill, balance, and position; weight and fit of saddle and other tack; and the type of work the horse is being asked to do (slow trail riding, galloping and jumping on a cross-country course, or acting as a vaulting mount, for example). However, research using varied loads has shown horses have higher pulse and respiration rates as well as more muscle soreness after exercise as they carry incrementally greater weights."

What this says to me is that we have to pay attention to this ratio, pay careful attention to our own level of fitness and that of our horses, consider objectively our level of riding ability and how well-balanced we are in the

saddle, look at factors including how the horse is built, the fit of our tack and what we're asking him to do, and *then* arrive at the safe number for each particular horse and rider. In other words, the details are what matter most to each horse and each situation.

"There really is no hard and fast rule about maximum weight of a rider," agrees Dr. Joyce Harman. "You've got to look at a number of factors including how the horse is built, how the rider is built, rider fitness level, and level of expertise."

She cautions us, too, on misinterpreting some of the findings of these kinds of studies, as equations and ratios depend on the pool of horses the researchers has access to. "Depending on the type of horses a group of researchers works with, you're going to get a variation in data," she says. "This explains the variations you'll find in these studies and findings. And, because measurements also vary from study to study, it makes a lot more sense to consider the studies, but to be sure to consider the other, more telling variables as well."

A Match Made in ... Horses

If after you've evaluated your situation and needs, and gotten good at asking the right questions, you've decided you are ready to find your "perfect match" in a horse, all this homework will pay off as you shop around with a very clear idea of what you're looking for and why.

Harris says that while it's still important to remember the "rule of thumb" as studies suggest (which is that most horses can easily carry up to about 20 percent of their weight), it is only when you exceed that ratio when conformation, load, fitness, and ability come into play. So for a horse that's around 1,000 pounds (and as a visual, most Quarter Horses are somewhere in that neighborhood), that's a 200-pound limit, including the saddle. A Western saddle weighs around 30 pounds; English and dressage saddles are considerably less. So, if you're riding Western and you weigh more than 170, you're going to want to dig into the secondary criteria I'm providing on the pages that follow, looking for sturdier-built versions of smaller breeds or well-composed larger breed horses and draft crosses.

While lots of heavier riders tend to gravitate toward draft horses, Harris agrees with Dr. Harman's point at the beginning of this chapter that this may not actually be your best solution—it depends on what you want to do with your horse. While draft horses do tend to be very large, Harris reminds us that they are also built for *slow* work—*pulling* a load rather than *carrying* it.

"They're not normally good at athletic work," she says. "They have big feet, big bones, and big bodies, but are ironically not always the best choices for heavier riders."

Harris directs our attention instead to what she calls "large-boned riding horses" if what we need is more speed and athleticism than a draft can offer. "The old-timers call them 'heavyweight hunters,'" she explains, "built to carry a big man on an all-day hunt. They are athletic, have a big stride and are also good for dressage." Regardless of breed, Harris says, be sure to look for horses with:

- Big bones—especially cannon bones and pasterns.

- Lower legs that are wide and flat with good tendons.
- Broad chest.
- Good spread of ribs.
- Moderately short back.
- Broad over the loin.

Dr. Harman's Number One Rule for choosing a horse that is up to carrying significant weight is solid conformation: a strong, short-coupled, flat back, sturdy legs, and good feet. (In *The Horse's Pain-Free Back and Saddle-Fit Book*, she offers great help for evaluating a horse's basic conformation just by looking to assess whether a horse knows how to use his body in a way that will allow him to carry heavier weight.) Saddle ergonomist Jochen Schleese approaches this topic by considering the horse's "surface area" (the saddle-bearing space on the horse's back). Schleese, who has built countless saddles for riders of all shapes and size all over the world, emphasizes the importance of making sure a horse has a large enough "surface area" (saddle support /weight bearing area) to accommodate the saddle size the rider needs. (We'll get more into this two-sided equation of saddle fit for both rider and horse beginning on p. 77.)

Once you determine that a horse you're considering has sturdy legs and feet, and adequate "surface area" on his back, the next step is evaluating how well he *uses* his back and what Susan Harris describes as the "circle of muscles" as he moves.

"The circle of muscles," Harris explains, "is formed by muscles in the hind-quarters, back, neck, poll, jaw, lower neck, sternum, and abdomen. When these muscles work together correctly, the horse should move in a manner that feels and appears *forward* and *upward*." Dr. Harman, actually citing Harris' book *Horse Gaits, Balance and Movement* adds, "The horse's back is central to the function of its musculoskeletal system and ability to carry a rider." She advises us to train our eyes to watch a horse move in light of these questions:

- Do his abdominals and back leg muscles (the lower half of the circle of muscles) contract as he moves to allow his back muscles to work freely?

- Can you see his back rise, his head drop, his neck extend and his back muscles relax as he moves forward?

- Does his overall movement seem to go forward and up? Or down through the sternum, toward the ground?

- Listen to his footfalls (in an indoor arena if you can). A horse that is using his body correctly will have a regular beat and less noise to show he's lighter on his feet.

While this assessment is essential to making sure a horse you're considering is capable of carrying extra weight, it's also a good way to evaluate the movement of *any* horse to ensure he is traveling free of pain or problems created by previous injury, poor saddle fit, or unskilled riders.

"When a horse is in pain," Dr. Harman writes in *The Horse's Pain-Free Back and Saddle-Fit Book*, "his back muscles contract, his abdominal muscles remain soft, and his back drops and becomes hollow. In this situation, his hind legs cannot sufficiently engage. When a horse travels in this hollow-backed posture, it places a lot of strain on stifles, hocks, tendons, suspensory ligaments, and feet. This sets him up for future problems and lameness, especially if he's asked to carry heavier weight."

Dr. Harman says that the percentage of horses that do use their backs—and their circle of muscles—correctly is very small. However, as you're evaluating a horse's conformation and movement in terms of how much weight can he comfortably carry, how well he is able to use his body is a key consideration.

Harris's tips for evaluating a horse's movement for how well he'll carry weight include making sure he has good balance, meaning he turns easily right and left, with no falls or stumbles. Watch someone else ride him, watching for these things, then have an instructor evaluate how he carries himself through turns when *you're* riding him. And there are ways to tell a horse is struggling under your weight when you are in the saddle. Harris says to watch for the following "red flags" that might indicate he is having difficulty:

BUSTED!

Myths of Equations:
Calculations and Gender

MYTH: "A horse can only carry a certain calculated percentage of his own weight. No exceptions."

TRUTH: As we talk of ratios, rules, and criteria that may or may not pertain to horsewomen most of us are picturing the blatantly male exception that may make you question the truth in the numbers.

"I know of one Top-10 endurance finisher who rides a sturdy, stocky Arab, about 14.3 hands," Dr. Harman says. "He's a big guy and weighs in, with tack, at about 235 to 245 pounds. If you computed these factors with some 'recommended' calculation, you'd never put him on that horse at all!"

Susan Harris concurs that we need to acknowledge there are plenty of big, tall men who are excellent riders—and countless top-level competitors across the disciplines who are very large. "Think of the big ol' boy reiners riding 14.2-hand Quarter Horses," she says, then adds, "and there are plenty of dressage champions and top-level international show jumpers who are over 6 feet tall, and lots of top polo players who are heavy, but very effective riders."

The downfall of all the equations and calculations, it appears, is that they don't take into consideration the variations in fitness and ability—both in riders of heft *and* their horses. And, while these big-guy exceptions do exist, if you were to delve into each one you'd likely find that many of the boys have already mastered some of the ideas and strategies we'll encounter in the trail ahead.

- When you stop, he always seems to want to stretch his hind legs out behind him like he's going to urinate.

- When trotting, his hind legs "knuckle over"—almost landing on their toes—causing frequent stumbling. (This can indicate either too much weight or a bad saddle fit.)

- He travels with a hollow back (see Dr. Harman's point on this topic on p. 61) in a way that makes him lose coordination in his hind legs.

Note: Good on-the-fly remedies if you suddenly sense the horse you are riding is having trouble under your weight may include posting the trot, riding in two-point, and getting off to give him a break.

Keep Your Horse Fit—and Free of Pain and Compensation

If you're a heavier rider, maybe knocking at the door (or well over the threshold) of that weight-limit percentage, but you've determined that your horse is sound and built well enough to ride on down the trail with you, what can you do to keep him fit, give him some relief, and ensure his soundness over time? Horses carrying heavier loads need good, consistent attention to their fitness regimen (horses need core work, too!), care for their muscles before and after work, conscientious hoofcare, and a constant eye on their posture, attitude, and movement.

- **Body and Behavior Checklist** Foremost in most of our minds is keeping the horses we love happy, healthy, and *pain-free*. This means keeping regular tabs on your horse's attitude and movement, watching for any changes that could indicate your horse is struggling or experiencing pain or discomfort. This is sometimes hard to see at first, but creating a habit here of checking out how he's moving—before, during and after each ride—will attune your eyes and attention to what *is* and *is not* normal for him. Discomfort or struggle with too much weight may or may not manifest as a behavioral problem or reluctance (some horses are more stoic than others), but establishing a quick checklist that you run through on a regular basis will keep your awareness high and enable you to give prompt attention at the first sign of difficulty.

• **Focus on the Core** Just as we do for our own bodies (and yes, we'll get into that a little bit later), we need to help our horses develop core strength that will keep their backs strong and able to move freely, while carrying their riders comfortably. Also similar to our own fitness (especially mine), core work for horses is often overlooked in favor of "bigger muscle" exercise (walking the dog is much more fun than crunches). But conditioning that may show up nicely on the outside often does little to support the infrastructure that, for our horses, creates good posture and strength needed to carry weight. Just as, for example, Pilates does for us (with small movements that don't really seem like much, but specifically target tiny interior muscles), the consistent habit of doing a few simple core exercises with your horse pays off big in keeping his back and weight-carrying muscles supported and strong.

"We need to help horses get the exercise that will strengthen the back and core to carry us without strain and compensation," Dr. Harman advises. This includes things like:

- Regular free longeing with lots of transitions.

- Walking and trotting over ground poles or small logs.

- Sustained work that requires the horse to lift his core and use his body correctly for 20 to 30 minutes a day. (Perfect justification for "playing" with your horse and doing groundwork!)

This focus on core exercise for your horse also gives you an opportunity to watch how he is moving and get a feel for what's normal and easy for him so that when you're on his back you'll be better at recognizing any resistance in his body that might indicate a problem.

• **Stretch It** Dr. Harman says that making a regular point of *stretching* your horse's muscles will not only help heal back issues and weaknesses, but will help keep injury away. (Muscles are muscles, whether horse or human. Don't *your* muscles do better and stay healthier with regular stretching?) Equine stretches need not be complicated or strenuous (this isn't horse yoga, although I do admit enjoying the mental picture), and Dr. Harman emphasizes that we should never force a stretch, because if your horse resists or tightens against your attempt to help him stretch, he is just shortening and tightening the very muscles you are

Dr. Hilary Clayton and Narelle Stubbs' *Activate Your Horse's Core* (Sporthorse Publications, 2008).

Karen Blignault's *Stretch Exercises for Your Horse: The Path to Perfect Suppleness* (Trafalgar Square Books, 2013).

Linda Tellington-Jones' *The Ultimate Horse Behavior and Training Book* (Trafalgar Square Books, 2006).

trying to lengthen and loosen. (And if you have back issues, ask someone else to do these for you. No sense hurting your own back trying to heal your horse's!)

In my experience with these stretches, once my horses understood what I was trying to do they got much more cooperative and actually seem to enjoy it. Patience (and safety!) are key when introducing these stretches, Dr. Harman confirms. Details on a few good stretches are coming up, but here are few general things to keep in mind:

• Never force.

• Small, incremental improvement every day pays off big dividends down the road.

• Try each of a few different stretches, *building up to* holding them for 30 seconds each.

• Pay close attention to your horse, letting him give feedback as your duration guide.

CORE HABITS

Stretch 1: Belly Lifts to Relax, Soften, and Strengthen the Circle of Muscles

If the horse can tolerate it, practice "belly lifts" from the ground, advises Dr. Harman. A belly lift makes an excellent addition to his regular grooming ritual, as you can add a belly lift after you finish grooming each section of his body: neck, belly lift; shoulder, belly lift; back, belly lift; hip, belly lift; and so on. A normal physical

---

Eunice

"It's definitely a different mindset for women than for men," longtime horsewoman Eunice Rush says. "Though it is true there are guys who are only on their horses for a few minutes, whereas I expect mine to carry me all day, up and down hills. I take good care of my horses, but I do expect them to work hard."

Eunice says she has tried and failed many times to lose weight, and that this is a battle she has not ever been able to win. "I'm 62 years old, and I want to enjoy the food I eat. Sure, I'd like to be thin, but not at the expense of being able to enjoy my food and my life." She laughs. "So I got a bigger horse."

In *Know You, Know Your Horse* (Trafalgar Square Books, 2012), the book Eunice co-authored with Marry Morrow, we find out that pain issues—most often in feet, teeth, and back—are responsible for 80 percent of horses' behavioral problems.

"Most horses don't want to be bad," she adds. "'They are just trying to tell us something."

There are several important things she knows she must attend to keep her horse fit to ride.

"First, the saddle absolutely has to fit right," she says. "And you may have to go through several of them to find one that fits both your horse and you." Although Eunice says she always heard the weight limit (for rider and tack) for English tack

---

reaction to this is the horse will tighten his stomach muscles, his back muscles will relax and soften, his back will rise, and his neck will drop and stretch forward. Here's how:

1 Stand next to the horse's girth area, bend your knees if needed, and reach under the horse to the middle of the sternum (belly) to where there is a groove in the muscles.

---

is 25 percent of the horse's weight and for Western 35 percent, she believes a properly fitted and correct length Western saddle seems to distribute weight better.

Second, Eunice says, good chiropractic, equine massage, and energy work is a must, as is regular care of an equine dentist. "I realized that if I'm not going to be able to lose weight," she adds, "I need to take care of my horses' bodies to keep them strong and healthy and comfortable enough to carry me."

Eunice watches her horses closely for any signs of soreness after a ride. She keeps regular appointments for chiropractic work, timed especially after long rides. She never rides for three days after a chiropractic treatment, and in the week before and after a chiropractic treatment, she schedules a massage or energy work. (Who besides me wants to believe in reincarnation and come back as Eunice's next horse?)

Once a year, each horse gets a visit from the equine dentist. What does that have to do with carrying heavier weight, you may wonder?

"If the horse's teeth are not grinding right, it puts stress on the poll, which in ripple-effect fashion, can affect alignment all the way down the spine," she explains.

Eunice says she also does regular stretches with her horses, including her favorite, the carrot stretch (more on that soon—see p. 69) to entice her horse to stretch his head and neck around regularly—left, right, and downward—to keep those muscles loose, strong, and flexible.

---

2 Run your fingers down the length of this groove. Try different pressures and movements with your fingers to get the horse to raise his back, drop his head, and stretch forward. Be very careful when you first try this. A horse in pain or one that's sensitive can kick or bite. (Take it easy, increase pressure gradually, and keep an eye on his feet and teeth!)

3 Once your horse gets used to what you're asking him to do with "regular" belly lifts, you can also do what Dr. Harman calls "sideways belly lifts" by standing closer to your horse's elbow and reaching across the girth area to the other side of his sternum, then pulling up and toward the side you're standing on. What you're looking for here is the area behind the shoulder blade to "fill" with muscle and the ribs to bend toward you, just as they do when you ask for lateral bend when the horse is moving in a circle.

Stretch 2: Front Leg Stretches to Relax and Strengthen the Horse's Forehand

Pick up a front leg, and with one hand supporting your horse's leg behind the knee, lift the leg up and forward with the knee bent. (Think about stretching the horse's girth area.)

Hold it for about 30 seconds (or as long as your horse will let you at first to establish a starting point, and then try to increase your hold time from there until you get to 30 seconds).

Repeat with the other front leg.

Stretch 3: Leg Circles to Relax and Strengthen the Horse's Legs

These were first introduced to me by a friend who studied with Linda Tellington-Jones, who is, by the way, the one who first referred to them as "leg circles" in her Tellington Method books and DVDs (www.ttouch.com). This is a deceptively simple and really effective way to relax and strengthen your horse's legs.

1 Pick up your horse's hoof as if to clean it. (In fact, I do this exercise after I clean each hoof.) Imagine that there is a pencil (some call it a "laser pointer") pointing straight down from the tip of his toe.

2 Move his foot in slow, easy circles a little bigger than the circumference of his foot, as if you are drawing circles on the ground beneath his foot.

3 Repeat with all four feet; front and hind are the same technique. Do these as part of your grooming ritual or as you tack up for a ride.

Stretch 4: The "Settle" to Relax the Leg Muscles

This should be the last thing you do, and only when both you and your horse are relaxed.

1 Pick up your horse's hoof as if you were going to do the leg circle exercise, but don't. Just stand there and hold your horse's foot until you feel him relax his leg muscles and just "let the foot go," settling into your hand. (A nice deep breath from you here might help, and definitely won't hurt!) This is a bit of a patience exercise for you; don't even try it if you're in a hurry! When your horse "lets go," it is strangely calming to both of you. You'll see what I mean the first time it happens.

Stretch 5: Carrot Stretches for the Head, Neck, and Back

My horse, Trace, always votes, "Yay!" on this one, especially when it involves a handful of alfalfa after his chiropractic treatments. Dr. Harman says that carrot stretches are an excellent way to safely stretch all parts of your horse's head and neck. (It's also a lot of fun, and a good excuse to give your horse "treats.") As with all stretches—and all horses—in the beginning you're just looking for a starting point, and then you try to work deeper from there, increasing the depth little by little, being patient and never forcing. Here's how:

1 When you first do this stretch, position your horse parallel to a wall so he can't turn in circles. (Once he knows the routine, you can do this stretch anywhere, any time. Just ask Trace.)

2 Hold a carrot against your horse's side at the level of his hip and stifle on both sides, and encourage him to reach for it and take a bite. If he's stiff in his neck or back (or both!) he may not be able to reach very far at all at first. Reward him with the bite of carrot when he has stretched as far as he can.

3 Next, encourage him in the same way to stretch his head and neck forward and down to retrieve a piece of carrot you hold between his front legs.

Dr. Harman says that with regular carrot stretches, you'll notice improvement in your horse's range of motion. She cautions, however, that with horses that are mouthy or bite, this is not a good exercise, and for some clever horses (I have one of those!) it is best to save this stretch for *after* you ride or do it on non-riding days so he won't keep bending and stretching (and making you feel rotten when you don't have a carrot to reward him!).

EQUINE BODYWORK

One of the best ways to keep your horse's body strong and healthy is to make sure that in addition to good nutrition and fitness, you pay attention to his muscles. Beyond allowing adequate rest between sessions of hard work and proper warm-up and cool-down for these sessions, you can take care of your horse's muscles much the same way you take care of your own. Two of my personal favorite kinds of human and equine bodywork are massage and craniosacral therapy—the quality of both modalities depends on the skill, training, and innate ability of the practitioner. When considering *any* bodywork therapies, for you *or* your horse, do your homework first before choosing a practitioner.

Massage

While *equine massage* is a field of study and work that requires training, certification, and lots of practice, it is also something we can learn to do well enough on our own to complement the work of a professional equine massage therapist or certified practitioners of other therapies, such as chiropractic and craniosacral therapy (see more on this on pp. 72–73). Remembering that muscles are still muscles, whether horse or human, regular massage, like regular stretching, not only makes tight muscles feel better, it also teaches muscles and muscle groups to relax more completely. And, as Emily Kutz, a certified sport horse massage therapist explained to me, by keeping muscles relaxed and supple, you can prevent a lot of joint and ligament problems, because the more elasticity you have in the muscles that connect ligaments and bones, the more they are able to give without straining, pulling or (God forbid), tearing something.

Equine massage technique varies from practitioner to practitioner and according to muscle group, and I do encourage you to educate yourself on the where, why, and how-to before attempting any serious massage on your horse. However, with no training at all, it is safe and relaxing (for your horse *and* for you) to do the following:

1 Run your hands over your horse's muscles, all over his body, pressing your fingertips lightly against his skin and feeling for any areas that seem tighter or harder than others.

2 If you find tightness or a knot, just stay on that area and apply gentle pressure until you feel the muscle loosen. You can knead a bit with your thumb or the heel of your hand. (Locate that knobby little bone on the heel of your palm, straight down from your pinky finger. That, I was once told by a very skilled therapeutic massage practitioner, is the greatest tool you have for loosening tight muscles!) The more familiar you become with your horse's muscles and what tightness in his body feels like, the better job you'll do helping him relax those muscles to avoid strain and injury.

Craniosacral Therapy

So what *do* you do when you're monitoring your horse for signs of strain and compensation and you see something in his movement or gait that looks different, or when he seems sore, reluctant, less supple, spooky, clumsy, unfocused—or just not himself? If your horse gradually starts showing signs of pain, weakness, or tightness, craniosacral therapy could be a solid first step to addressing whatever is going on.

Craniosacral therapy is a form of bodywork that restores balance in the nervous system by addressing tensions and disorders of the musculoskeletal system and soft tissues. Rooted in osteopathy, craniosacral therapy is a holistic approach to healing that focuses on the *craniosacral system*—the bones of the cranium, spine, and pelvis, and the soft tissues and fluid movement that connect the cranium (head) to the sacrum (pelvis)—that is at the center of the nervous system. The craniosacral system not only affects posture, behavior, and general health and well-being, but also sensory perceptions, such as vision, sound, focus, and proprioception (awareness of the position, location, orientation, and movement of the body and its parts). Over time, craniosacral therapy peels back, layer by layer, patterns of compensation within soft tissue and bone to reset the nervous system to improve body function and postural balance.

Shea Stewart is a trainer and instructor who became interested in craniosacral therapy for horses when she saw the dramatic difference it made after only a few sessions. Today Stewart is an equine craniosacral therapist and has studied advanced horse and human techniques. She spends her time traveling throughout Texas to work on horses and teach craniosacral workshops.

Stewart says that similar to humans, horses develop patterns of movement to compensate for a pain, weakness, or tightness, which starts a domino effect of problems. Any tightness, ache, or pain may result in compensatory postural imbalances in a horse, which may then lead to other problems, such as a sore back, stifle weakness, gait abnormalities, changes in hoof growth, or joint pain.

"Recognizing and releasing dysfunctional straining patterns restores nerve function and affects the entire horse and how he feels as he goes through life," she explains. "Correct muscle usage and better performance develops with improved posture."

The uniqueness of craniosacral therapy is that it is the only therapy that addresses deep internal straining patterns from traumas within the nervous system and the relationship of the bones from the cranium all the way to the sacrum. Stewart asserts that craniosacral therapy should be part of every horse's maintenance regimen and used in conjunction with other modalities, such as massage, acupuncture, chiropractic, and traditional veterinary care.

Chiropractic Care

Okay, I admit it. I was scared to take my horse to a chiropractor. And with good reason! There are some bad ones out there, and some who can do permanent damage to your horse. By the same token, a legitimate one can do your horse a world of good. The key, I think, is to ask a lot of questions—of the chiropractor and of those who have used him. In my case, it was the answer to the riddle of my horse's hollow-backed posture and increasingly violent bucking that I had been trying for years to "train" out of him. "Have you taken him to a chiropractor?" was usually the first thing people asked—and the last thing I wanted to do. But it worked. The chiropractor went straight to a place on Trace's poll that he said had likely been out for a very long time, based on the pattern of compensation and tightness he noticed throughout his body. Two or three major adjustments later (the look of relief I saw on my horse's face just after treatment made me wish I hadn't waited for so long), we were on our way with the task of retraining his mind not to expect pain, and his body to carry itself differently.

Dr. Harman says that chiropractic is an excellent treatment for stiffness and back pain, and that with a proper regimen of chiropractic and massage, most horses can remain supple throughout their lives. She writes in *The Horse's Pain-Free Back and Saddle-Fit Book* that horses can regain lost flexibility and normal fluid spinal motion through chiropractic care, and notes that improvement in flexibility and movement is usually noticeable within four chiropractic treatments. I saw a huge difference in how my horse travels after just one visit. Maintenance therapy is usually helpful in preventing a recurring loss of motion.

What do you look for when choosing a chiropractor? Dr. Harman says that a skilled practitioner knows how to perform chiropractic adjustment to restore motion to joints using a "short-lever, high velocity, controlled thrust into the joint with his hand or an instrument called an activator" (it looks like a small metal syringe). "If the thrust is correctly aimed," she adds, "it does not take a great deal of force."

Chiropractic adjustment that uses what Dr. Harman calls "a crude type of adjustment called manipulation" is more violent and forceful, and practiced, she adds, by those who are not educated in correct techniques. As with finding anyone who you intend to help take care of your horse, talk to as many references as you can (it took six of my friends plus one trainer I trust to convince me the chiropractor who saw Trace was okay—and even then I was still a bit wary!). In addition to references, be sure to ask about training, certifications, licensure, technique, and experience.

Mind Over Muscle

When you are asking your horse to deal with a significant load—whether rider weight, extreme distance, or tough terrain—it's good to remember that when muscles get fatigued, compensation begins elsewhere in the horse's body. Often a horse will keep going past muscle fatigue and neither of you will realize how much he's compensating until injury or soreness makes it obvious.

"Try this," Dr. Harman says to illustrate this point. "Carry 10-pound bags, walking back and forth, back and forth, over and over until you really start to feel the muscle fatigue. It's okay as long as you keep moving, isn't it? Then stop and talk to a friend for a few minutes. Now try to move again." She laughs. "That's when you realize how fatigued certain muscles are, and you're going to have to use others to compensate so you can keep carrying those bags."

Myths of Build

BUSTED!

MYTH: "If you don't have a 'rider's body,' you'll never ride well, no matter what you do."

TRUTH: Regardless of how you're built, riding well takes work and dedication. Yes, it does come more easily to some than others, but the biomechanics of riding well are much more important than being "built to ride." Consider these statements: "You're built to ride. You're going to be a natural!" and "Oh, honey, you're just not built to ride. You can take some lessons and enjoy riding for fun, but you'll never be a serious rider."

Statements like these can put your mind in a dark realm of self-doubt before you ever set foot in a stirrup. The Greater Truth we need to have a firm grasp on here is a rider with a "perfect rider's build," can actually feel *heavier* to a horse than a stubby, stocky rider who knows how to distribute her weight and balance. Without exception, every single expert I spoke with while researching this book agreed that it's not so much *how you're built* or *how much you weigh* as it is *how you use the body weight you have* that determines

whether—and how well— you can ride. Or, as Susan Harris likes to put it, "It's not what you have, but how you use it that counts."

And, while it is true that some physical features *are* an advantage in riding, *not* having these features is by no means a deal-breaker when it comes to riding well.

Harris says that if you're a larger rider—either with a naturally large "frame" or someone with a smaller frame who has put on some weight—you have options. "The important thing," she emphasizes, "is to be as fit as you can be in your core." Harris is a firm believer that with solid core strength and a willingness to work on your riding skills, riding—and riding well—is a very achievable goal for *anyone*. The key, she says, is recognizing that happiness in this pursuit is part balance, part saddle fit, part educating yourself about what kind of horse will make a good choice for you, and part finding the kinds of personal adjustments (across the board) that will bring you the freedom and enjoyment you crave in your experiences with horses.

In this chapter we explored how our horse's build and our build are *both* important parts of the RT^3 equation. This will help in our work with horses by showing us where we can and need to make adjustments in riding and exercising to keep our horses safe and comfortable. This is a new and different game-changer in the battle against negative body image because when we (and our horses) feel more comfortable, riding is the joyful experience it was meant to be—and that makes us feel good in general!

Your Chapter 4 **#Hoofpicks** include:

1   **Educate yourself on what makes a horse able carry to a little more weight.** Using the rule-of-thumb (that actually has nothing to do with thumbs) as your starting point, remember to take into consideration the horse's build, his level of fitness for the job you're asking him to do, your level of fitness, and how well you are able to use your own energy to lighten his load.

2   **Learn how to find your spot.** This is not about how you look when you're trying to get in balance and connect with your horse's movement and energy. This is about how you feel. When you find it, you'll know it.

3   **Think, listen, and respond to your horse based on your own observations and feel—over the directives or expectations of others.** Proper form can be taught, but finding the feel is something you have to do on your own. Listen to your instructors, but listen to your own body and the response of your horse even more.

4   **Care for your horse's body just as you're learning to care for your own.** Taking time to educate yourself and find reliable bodywork practitioners will help you keep your horse's muscles and frame in good shape for the long haul. Learn to incorporate habits and routines such as stretches, core work, massage, chiropractic, and craniosacral therapy will keep your horse healthy and better able to perform.

5 | Balance Your Fit

One of the keys to keeping your horse comfortable—especially when carrying a heavier rider—is saddle fit. This brings us to our next stretch of trail: the saddle-fit equation.

Wait. Before you spiral into a post-traumatic algebraic funk, let me explain: Far from a lecture on angles, ratios, shapes, and coefficients, what we are going to explore is what makes saddle fit an *equation*—why we have to balance both sides in order to find the right answer. (Is it starting to come back to you now?) The two sides of the equation I'm talking about here are:

1 How the saddle fits the horse, which we'll call "the horse side."

2 How the saddle fits the rider, which we'll call "the rider side."

Here's the not-so-great surprise: you can have a really great saddle fit for your horse, but if that saddle makes *you* feel unbalanced and uncomfortable, you will be less effective as a rider, *and* your horse will become imbalanced as well. On the other hand, you can have a saddle that fits your butt like a Barcalounger (as one of my favorite saddles does), or one that puts you in such a secure spot you can ride through anything (yep, I have that one, too!), but if that saddle is too long for your horse, or if it pinches his withers (as each of my favorites do), guess what? You're going to get lots of opportunity to practice riding through reactive hops and bucks and generally grumpy behavior. (It took me four saddles to learn this. Learn from my pain.)

The right answer, then, is a saddle that fits your horse in a way that protects his back from long-term harm while allowing him to move freely without pain or discomfort and fits you, putting you in correct alignment (more on that coming soon). This takes doing some homework, paying attention to good teachers (I've brought together some great ones for you here!), and of course, constantly checking and rechecking your own work.

Go to School on Saddle Fit

We all know saddle fit is important to comfort and performance (yours and your horse's). But here's some information that may transform the way you think about saddle fit: It's much more than a performance issue; it's also *health* issue—for horse *and* human. Keeping an eye on saddle fit is actually one of the best things you can do to take care of your horse's back and increase his years of being able to pack you around, not to mention ensuring your own ability to stay in the saddle for as long as you want to.

While a thorough examination of the topic of saddle fit is beyond the scope of this book, I encourage further exploration in this area. (It's fascinating, and really *nothing* like algebra.) But we'll check in here with a few key experts to get you started with an eye toward the crucial role of saddle fit for heavier riders.

THE HORSE SIDE

Certified master saddler Jochen Schleese says that poor saddle fit can cause incredible damage to a horse, including lameness, sacroiliac subluxations, vertebral damage, pinching of nerves along the spinal column—and all the behavioral (and memorable) behaviors

RESOURCES

Jochen Schleese's *Suffering in Silence: The Saddle-Fit Link to Physical and Psychological Trauma in Horses* (Trafalgar Square Books, 2014).

Dr. Joyce Harman's *The Horse's Pain-Free Back and Saddle-Fit Book, The Western Horse's Pain-Free Back and Saddle-Fit Book,* and the *English Saddles* and *Western Saddles* DVDs (all published by Trafalgar Square Books).

that result from these painful results, such as bucking, rearing, stumbling, and refusing to work.

One of the issues at hand in our scenario is when the length of the saddle (such as the 18½- to 19-inch saddles that accommodate larger riders likely will be) reaches beyond the "saddle support area" Schleese described for us in chapter 5 (p. 86). He says that because the horse's back ends at the 18th lumbar vertebra, a too-long saddle impinges on the kidney area, or the ovaries in a mare, and the horse will most likely react reflexively and instinctively (with what is known by some of us quite vividly as the "bucking reflex"). A too-long saddle will also not allow the back to come up, making even a willing horse reluctant to move forward. "It simply hurts," Schleese says, "and horses react to pain; they're not consciously behaving badly!" A more stoic horse, he adds, will sink his back into a hollow "swayback," which effectively doubles the rider's weight (regardless of what she actually weighs) because the rider is unable to swing with the movement of the horse.

Susan Harris agrees. She adds that while saddle fit is always very important, it's absolutely *crucial* at heavier weights—and the heavier the rider, the more crucial it becomes. On the flip side, however, Harris says that with good saddle fit and a fit, balanced rider (we'll be getting to the latter a bit later), a horse can carry more weight with less stress.

Keeping in mind there are *two* sides to the saddle-fit equation, and we're beginning with the *horse* side, Dr. Harman offers up specific points of fit to consider, especially if you're on the heavier side, including:

• **Does the tree fit the horse's back?** Whether English or Western, the tree must follow the contours of the horse's back. Considerations to watch here are length (too long creates painful pressure points at withers and loins) and width (too narrow creates uncomfortable pressure on the outer edges of the tree; too wide puts pressure too close to the horse's spine).

• **Are the panels/bars the right shape?** The panels (English) and bars (Western) cannot dig into the lumbar area. It needs to curve upward at the last rib.

• **Where's the pressure?** Underneath the seat/skirt of the saddle, pressure should only be from behind the horse's shoulder blade to the last rib on each side, and evenly distributed. You can test this in a general way by running your hand between the saddle and your horse's body. Dr. Harman says there are also two scientific ways to measure pressure (and therefore get a sense of load) on a horse's back:

A *computerized pressure pad* can be a useful, very scientific way to see exactly where the pressure is located while a horse is in motion. The computer reads the pressure every second or so and uses a color system to indicate the range of pressure sensed from highest (red) to lowest (light blue). However, Dr. Harman cautions, these pads are very expensive, and they can be misused. This can create a real "garbage in, garbage out" situation, she adds, in which people trying to sell a product can use the pad in unethical ways.

"The more people can learn/educate themselves about saddle fit, the better equipped they will be to judge what they're seeing/hearing. Remember: If you 'measure' pressure when the horse is stationary, you can't see the problem. Motion is really the only way to see what's happening."

The second way to measure pressure is using a *thermographic pad*, Dr. Harman says. There are not very many of these around, she notes, and they cost about $20,000 each. And, while thermographic pads can be useful, they can also be affected by moisture and the regular saddle pad, rather than the saddle or the rider.

"It's important to do this measurement with your regular saddle pad and riding the way you regularly ride," she emphasizes.

• **How does the saddle sit on the horse?** It needs to sit straight, both side-to-side and front-to-back.

To be able to ride horses at all—to get on their backs and ask them to do things they wouldn't normally do—is something most of us take for granted. If we

Francine

"Why *shouldn't* people who are observant of their limitations be allowed to participate in such a fabulous sport?"

take a BIG step back from all this and realize what an odd (and gracious) gift it is that these large and magnificent creatures allow a human on their backs at all, the responsibility we have to care for their backs is quite humbling. "Horses were not 'meant' to be ridden," Jochen Schleese concurs, "we have forced this on them."

Saddle fit and horse movement is a complex relationship—and a good fit is not a one-shot deal. "Saddle fit should be checked regularly," Schleese advises, "regardless of whether you are a 'heavier rider' or a 'lighter' rider (But the heavier the rider, the more often saddle fit needs to be looked at, because even small problems are magnified by weight.) Because riding *is* an unnatural activity, our weight on the animal's back will change the horse's conformation over time—regardless of the weight of the rider."

Schleese says that changes in training and conditioning routines, age, and other factors all contribute to the constant metamorphosis of the horse's back. It is of utmost importance, to check and adjust the saddle to the horse as these changes occur to be sure his needs are taken into consideration. From checking to make sure the gullet gives the horse enough room all around the withers so that when he is in motion and his muscles begin to "grow" (contract and expand) the saddle doesn't pinch, to making sure the tree points stay at the same angle as the horse's shoulders to allow freedom of movement (think "sliding doors") that protects sensitive shoulder cartilage, we must educate ourselves on what to watch for and stay vigilant for any changes that require adjustment.

"Our job is to pay attention," Schleese insists, "and to make the changes that will keep a good fit."

THE RIDER SIDE

"What may surprise you is that it's actually more important to make sure the saddle fits the rider, first, and then the horse. If the saddle doesn't fit the *rider*," Jochen Schleese explains, "*then* no matter how well the saddle fits the horse, the rider's discomfort due to poor saddle fit will always translate down to the horse." (However, Schleese is quick to add, poor fit on *either* side of the equation limits both the horse and rider in attaining optimum performance.)

The effects of poor saddle fit on the "rider side" of the fit equation, especially when amplified by weight, can result in strain and damage to our own bodies, including slipped discs, constant backache, recurring bladder infections, and hip damage (sometimes to the point of requiring hip replacement).

"The best analogy here," Schleese says, "is that you will get a blood blister faster on your heel from shoes that are too tight than you will from shoes that are too big." Taking that analogy into the saddle fit arena, he adds, "If a heavier rider sits in a saddle that is too small, the rider has no chance for a pliable seat and this effectively *doubles* her natural weight because she is not able to swing through her own back or harmonize with the swinging of the horse's back."

If you're like most people, you tend to focus on seat size alone in deciding if a saddle is the right size for you. Our experts are here to tell you there's a whole lot more to it than that. "We're not trained to think about thigh length," Harris adds. "We're over-focused on seat size."

Wendy Murdoch agrees, adding that most fitters try to put people in saddles that are simply too small for them. "Thigh length is a far more important consideration than seat size," she emphasizes. "And sometimes what you need is a wider, more *open* seat—*not* necessarily a longer saddle."

Our experts agree that the most important things for us to consider when trying to fit ourselves to a saddle must include the length of our thighs, the shape of our legs, and the *shape* of the seat of the saddle. And the immediate difference when we get this fit right, Murdoch adds, is nothing short of remarkable.

"When I get a heavier rider sitting right, with relaxed, wider-open hips and good hip rotation, suddenly she finds her stability—because the saddle fits better!

"My coach said, 'Breathe out,' today, I did, and the tension left me and my horse. I started to laugh and not be so serious and my horse loved me for it because he was able to move under my weight with more freedom than previously....At that moment I couldn't give a toss how much I weighed and how bad my self perception was...."

Because we've freed the hips and thighs, she is no longer tensing the buttocks and thighs trying to hold on," Murdoch observes. "Then she can relax enough to find her true place of balance. It's amazing!"

It's Not Your Weight That Makes You Wobbly (It's Your Saddle Fit!)

When examining rider-side saddle fit, Murdoch prefers to focus on how secure the rider *feels* in the saddle. "A rider has to *feel secure* in order to ride well," she says. "Sometimes people don't realize *why* they aren't feeling secure; they just know they feel less confident in the saddle." Murdoch says that while most people think their lack of confidence and feeling of instability in the saddle comes from having gained weight, "We need to look beyond that to see instead the poor fit of the rider to the saddle. Usually a rider is still using the same tack, despite gaining or losing weight, changing shape—and maybe her horse has changed shape, too. It's hard to feel secure if you don't get this equation right."

"Often, the feeling of instability comes from the lower leg not feeling as secure," Murdoch says. "When you have a heavy rider with a short thigh in a too-big saddle seat, for example, you've most likely got stirrup bars that are in the wrong place."

She explains that as we get heavier, our feet become less able to fall naturally where the stirrup leathers or fenders want them to go. And, since stability lies in creating that even and steady "platform for your feet" the stirrups are supposed to create, taking a look at things like stirrup length and placement can be key to

BUSTED! Myths of Mounting

MYTH: "If I'm too heavy to get on my horse from the ground I'm too heavy to ride."

TRUTH: One consistent worry I've heard from people who are concerned about extra weight and riding is the "acid test" of being able to mount from the ground. So we see people struggling their way into the saddle just to prove they can; however, most equine experts will tell you that pulling and wrenching on your horse's back just to get yourself in the saddle from the ground is not in anyone's best interest—regardless of your weight or size.

And if you're among those who refuse a mounting block because, "There aren't going to be mounting blocks on the trail," rider and author Eunice Rush advises you to think again.

"'Mounting blocks' are everywhere!" she exclaims. "If you've trained your horse to stand still beside whatever you put him next to—rocks, stumps, even a rut in the trail can offer the perfect 'leg up.'"

Rush says that after riding thousands of miles of trails on her annual camp trips, a lack of "natural mounting blocks" has never been a problem. Among her favorites are downed trees ("Teach your horse to step across and stand astride one of those, and it's a perfect mounting block") and picnic tables ("My horse automatically veers toward every picnic table he sees as if it's some sort of equine 'bus stop'"). None of this happens overnight, she is quick to add. "It takes time and patience to train your horse to stand and wait for you to climb on, but it's really one of the best investments of time and energy you can make."

Rush says one of the first lessons every single one of her horses learns is to stand beside whatever she puts him next to, and stand still while she says she "drags herself on." Her next bit of advice, however, makes it clear that nothing is further from the truth than her use of the term "drag." Rush takes great care to condition herself and her horses, and she is always vigilant for any signs of soreness or strain in her own body or those of her horses.

"It's really important to make sure you are strong enough to get yourself up and centered over your horse when you mount," she advises. "Use the horse's mane—and not the saddle or horn—to steady yourself before swinging a leg over. And *never* plop down on him." Rush says that after mounting she always sits still for a moment, then pulls her knees up beside the horse's withers and then lets her legs drop down to their natural position.

Susan Harris, echoing Rush's observations, advises the use of a mounting block whenever you can, *regardless of weight*: "It's safer for the horse and kinder to his back. I say this to everyone, but it applies especially to heavier riders."

Jochen Schleese agrees: "It's not really about the rider's weight—the higher the mounting block, the less torque and strain for saddle and horse."

I'll add here that there is also one modern apparatus I've run across several times (but have never tried) is the "stirrup extender," a device that pops your left stirrup down about 3 inches with the push of a button. Once you're on, a touch of your toe puts it back into place. Those I know who have used the device marketed under the name of EZ Up Stirrup Extender (www.EZUP-Stirrup.com) say they like it because it is strong, effective, lightweight, and Made in the USA.

improving your fit. (Be sure to check out Murdoch's book *50 5-Minute Fixes to Improve Your Riding* to learn more about how a simple stirrup adjustment can create a more solid base for your feet, as well as other key position fixes. We'll circle back to this discussion when we learn to find our "sweet spot" of true balance—see p. 195).

Crucial Checkpoints

Educating yourself now, and then taking a fresh, clear look at your saddle, your horse, and your own body to make sure you've got the right fit—on both the horse side *and* the rider side—is the very best thing you can do to prepare yourself for a new level of confidence and joy in the saddle. Speaking as one who has bought five saddles in this particular pursuit of happiness, learning how to get this equation right *before* you shop will save you a lot of time, money, and heartache. Doing your homework in advance is also the best way to shore yourself up against the advice of those in the business of *selling saddles* whose advice on "fit" comes from a whole different perspective. Best of all, by making this knowledge your own, any time your body—or your horse's body—changes over time (as both no doubt will), you'll know how to revisit specific checkpoints and make the adjustments necessary to keeping your saddle fit right, from now on!

So in the land of reality (where we all can't afford custom-made saddles or regular visits from high-end saddle fitters), what are the *crucial* checkpoints that we can monitor on our own?

According to Schleese, *saddle length* is critical (see his comments regarding the effects of a too-long saddle on p. 79), as is *tree width. Rocker* (the amount or type of curve in the panels or bars from front to rear) should be considered in both English and Western saddles. "The heavier the rider, the more of an issue it will be if the saddle bridges (the panels or bars do not keep even contact with the horse from front to back)," he says. "There needs to be accommodation for some ability for the saddle to 'rock' to take care of the extra weight of the rider and avoid digging into the horse's loins or shoulders."

"The correct saddle length is sometimes hard to achieve with a heavy rider," adds Dr. Joyce Harman, "a larger seat size requires more space, and on a short-backed horse it can be hard to get enough length on the rib cage."

Schleese agrees. "When a heavier rider is on a horse that is nearing 'questionable' in load bearing capacity," he says, "the right saddle fit can help accommodate (somewhat) a bigger butt while also accommodating a relatively short saddle support area on the horse's back. This can be done by building the top of the saddle for the rider, and the bottom for the horse." *(Note: When Schleese says "bigger butt" here, he doesn't intend insult. With him it's strictly clinical—a descriptor, as Joy Nash suggests, not a judgment!)*

Two Paths, Same Destination

I've heard plenty of debating in the circles I travel, regarding which style of riding is actually harder on a horse's back, especially at heavier rider weights (saddle fit being equal). The bulk and weight of a Western saddle make it seem like the obvious "winner," especially if the rider is a little (or a lot) heavy.

A common misconception here is that if you're a heavier rider, the quickest way to lighten your horse's load is to find the lightest saddle you can. While there may be some logic to this, it's not necessarily true that an English saddle, because it's so much smaller and lighter, is "easier" on a horse's back. I paid just enough attention in physics class for this reflection from our experts to make sense: The smaller surface area of an English saddle actually *concentrates* the weight of the rider on a smaller area of the horse's back, so the heavier the rider, the greater the pressure on the horse's back than if the load were spread out a little bit more.

"It doesn't really matter what kind of saddle it is," Dr. Harman assures us, taking us straight to the bottom line. "It still has to fit. Saddle fit is always critical, and a bad fit can cripple any horse—even with the lightest of loads." And to all who are pushing that weight limit and thinking a lighter saddle will help tip the scales in your favor, Dr. Harman says, "That's 'bunk.' The truth is that adding

20 to 30 pounds of saddle isn't going to make as much difference as good fit. Even a 40-pound stock saddle, well fit, doesn't make much difference to the horse."

Along the same lines as the lighter tack argument, it may seem that a treeless saddle might be a good option for a plus-sized rider. Dr. Harman says this kind of saddle can actually make matters worse. "When it comes to treeless saddles," she explains, "the biggest issue is that there is no place to rest your crotch. What ends up happening is like a kid on a barrel: If you have thicker thighs and a treeless saddle, you're perched up there on the horse's back, trying to balance on a tilted pelvis—with your lower legs flapping in the breeze!"

BUSTED! Myths of Nostalgia

MYTH: "It's my old show saddle! I love this saddle! I've always used this saddle, so I know it still fits me!"

TRUTH: This is an important enough distinction to warrant its own myth. Just because a saddle fit you well at one time of life, doesn't mean it always will, even if you weigh exactly the same now as you did then. Trust me: Things tend to move around with age, and saddle fit is a fluid art. Dr. Joyce Harman says she sees this all the time. From former pony clubbers to junior champs, all kinds of riding disciplines have people riding around in saddles that no longer fit them. The truth is (and this is a big one) there are very few things more important to taking care of your horse's back—and supporting your own riding skills—than getting the saddle fit right on both sides of this equation.

As Dr. Harman described this scenario to me over the phone, I admit I rocked back in my desk chair and tried to balance on a tilted pelvis. As if she could see what I was doing, she then related her own personal experience in a treeless saddle.

"Even at the walk or trot I just didn't feel that secure," she said with a laugh. "And the horse could feel it, too! And at the canter, it was really ugly—I was all over the place! I just couldn't get my feet underneath me. I was always sitting back or rocking forward."

Dr. Harman says she thinks this is why lots of larger people don't feel as secure in treeless saddles, and they don't realize the saddle is the cause, rather than their weight.

"Your hips will only open so far," she says. "And if you happen to have thick thighs and/or you're on a wide-backed horse, the treeless saddle means your hips may have to open farther than they are capable, so you have to rock backward to keep your hips in the sockets!"

Now don't get me—or Dr. Harman—wrong. This is nothing against treeless saddles.

"A treeless saddle can work with other combinations of horse and rider," Dr. Harman says. In fact, this is an issue treeless saddle companies are trying to address right now, so stay tuned. And while the solution, which includes creating "seats"—what are essentially "little trees"—in them, Dr. Harman says you still have to apply the ratio of thick-thighs/wide-horse to the equation or it won't work: heavier people are likely not to feel as secure, even with planned improvements.

Bottom line? Ride in a saddle appropriate to the discipline that makes you the happiest, but make sure your saddle fits you *and* your horse well—and remember to check it often, especially if your body (or your horse's) body is changing.

And it just might be...(we're getting to that part next).

| **#Hoofpicks** | In this chapter we explored the importance of saddle fit—both for your horse and for yourself. This will help you in your work with horses by putting you in |

the driver's seat, as it were, to make sure your fit benefits your ride, your own health and safety, and that of your horse. This will be a game changer in the battle against negative body image because when you and your horse are comfortable with a saddle that fits both of you, you can begin to work on all the other layers of understanding and accomplishment that will enhance your partnership.

Your Chapter 5 **#Hoofpicks** Include:

1 **Read the signs.** If your horse seems to be struggling or uncomfortable or acting out, do some troubleshooting. Pain issues—most often in feet, teeth, and back—are responsible for 80 percent of horses' behavioral problems. And often pain and discomfort are related to saddle fit.

2 **Stay on top of your saddle fit.** Whether you ride English, Western, or something in between, take time to learn both sides of the saddle fit equation—how your saddle fits you *and* your horse. This two-sided equation must *always* be balanced, regardless of discipline! Learn your checkpoints and make a habit of monitoring both sides of your fit: If and when things change with either your body or your horse's, you may need to make adjustments to keep your saddle-fit equation balanced and working in your favor!

Be
Proactive

6 | Get Fit to Ride Light

Are you fit, fat—or maybe a little of both?

Surveying current height/weight charts provides a sense of how completely "all over the place" the "experts" are on "ideal" weight for our *frame size* (that is, whether our bodies are built on small, medium, or large support structures). For years height/weight charts gave us the "10-pound variable" for frame size (meaning, I suppose, that to allow for variations in body composition you can be over or under that "ideal" weight by 10 pounds and likely still be in the ballpark). Some also gave us an ideal wrist measurement or circumference for small, medium, or large frame size. Nowadays the Body Mass Index (BMI) measurement is most widely used to determine specific weight-related classification (and stigma) that predicts our likelihood of impending doom from weight-related diseases, such as Diabetes or heart disease.

I know plenty of very smart people have worked very hard to develop this scientific way of alarming us into better eating habits. (For me, this worked. Trust me. NOBODY wants to see the word "obese" on her medical chart.) And while it's true that BMI is probably as good a way as any to see where we are on the body-weight continuum, I'm pretty sure the BMI geniuses didn't allow for haphazard measurements that can skew results, not to mention *body type*—what physical trainers classify as *ectomorph* (long and lean), *endomorph* (soft and round), or *mesomorph* (thick and muscular)—and *lifestyle* (active versus couch potato) and *body composition* (how much muscle we're dealing with, seeing as we can weigh more even when small, depending on our ratio of muscle tissue to fat). This (and possibly a few too many green chile cheeseburgers) is how I got classified as "obese."

I'll be the first to admit that I do weigh a lot. I always have. I have always been a solidly built "good-sized girl." I've never really been *that* big (staying in the size 10 to 12 range most of my adult life—and struggling against the same 20 to 30 pounds since adolescence), and I carry it fairly well, thanks to the muscle living beneath my pudge. Thankfully—due to heredity, good early nutrition, and a lifelong habit of exercise and competitive sports—I also have very dense bones. Am I also overweight? Yes. And, since I *am* gaining weight around the middle for the first time in my life, it's a health risk I know I need to do something about. But am I really *obese*? Well, my BMI says so. (One of my friends told me I should stop telling everyone, but it struck me as funny—or maybe ironic—that this happened during the writing of this book in which I decry the toxic effect of labels on our self-image!) After considerable whining and fuming, I decided I might as well laugh about it and use the ridiculous label to spur myself into action.

So, as I deal with my own freshly diagnosed obesity, my mind turns to others in the horse world who may relate. What we do for fun is more strenuous than the average modern lifestyle. It creates strong muscles and dense bones. Even the wiry dynamos out there probably weigh quite a bit more than their sedentary, non-horsey sisters. You can't toss 50-pound bales of hay, carry buckets of water, muck stalls, guide a fully loaded wheelbarrow with any degree of accuracy toward a dung pile, or complete all manner of other horse-world realities without some serious strength. And strength weighs something.

So how much is *too* much when it comes to riding our horses? How do we know if we are a strong and solid partner to our horse, or just an uncomfortable load he must bear?

Horse-Breed Body Types

We understand without question how and why a horse's breed and body type sets him up for success (or not so much) in certain disciplines and activities. Why can't we do the same for our own bodies? Coach Daniel Stewart helps us move away from judgment and toward practical solutions that help us make the most of what we *do* have going for us and mitigate those things that are, well, less than ideal. He makes a clever comparison between horse breed and human body types—see if you can identify which horse body type most closely resembles your own in the chart on p. 96. (You may find that you have the characteristics of more than one category.)

Knowing that our genetically determined shape can be altered somewhat by changes in our behavioral patterns and choices (I would almost swear that yoga makes me taller), by following some specific "framework" fitness strategies in between rides we can embrace our body type and learn to work *with* our natural shape instead of against it.

"Once you have a better understanding of how your shape and size influences your riding," Coach Stewart says, "you can develop an unmounted program to solve your mounted imperfections."

Pound for Pound Defiance

Our weight, as Eunice Rush reminds us, is not always an indicator of health.

"I'm actually much healthier now than I was when I was younger and weighed less," she admits. "And I feel better. I eat the right foods (and lots of them) and feel better and stronger than I ever have."

She points out the images of women we see in the media are not at all realistic for most of us. "Sure I'd like to be a size 5," she laughs, "but I don't want to live that way."

Horse Breed	Body Characteristics	Framework
Shetland	Small, lightweight with short limbs. You tend to gain weight evenly and regardless of weight have a low center of gravity and good natural balance.	Increase strength and stamina with lightweight strength exercises and lots of stretching to build strong, supple muscles.
Connemara	Short to medium height, broad around the middle. Short limbs, tend to gain weight easily, especially in girth and legs. Low center of gravity helps offset loss of equilibrium in the saddle.	While you can be overweight and still ride well, you'll do better to concentrate on stamina exercises and healthy eating habits to get fit, supple, and strong.
Quarter Horse	Medium height and muscular, with broad shoulders, flat torso, and muscular limbs. High center of gravity challenges your balance.	Work on overall flexibility and balance; use lightweight strength and stamina exercises followed by stretching to stay strong, flexible and supple.
Thoroughbred	Medium to tall height with long slender limbs and small, well-defined muscles. Extra weight tends to go to your midsection. Balance and stability issues created by high center of gravity and narrow base of support are offset by long legs.	Improve balance and symmetry; coordination enhancing exercises will help you use your long body and limbs most effectively.
Warmblood	Tall and shapely, "hourglass" figure; muscles strong and well sculpted without being overly thick. High center of gravity makes balance a challenge.	Improve balance and symmetry to make the most of your long legs and athletic ability and overcome issues with equilibrium.
Anglo-Arabian	Thin, lightweight "pear-shaped" upper body, wide hips, and robust thighs. Low center of gravity and wide base of support provide balance advantage; tend toward weight gain in hip and thigh area, which challenges mobility of lower torso, as well as contact between legs and horse.	Employ a good stretching program that targets hips and a stamina program that focuses on thighs; good nutrition keeps excess weight off hips and thighs.
Draft Horse	Tall with big bones, broad chest and shoulders, thick midsection, flat behind and solid limbs. With weight carried high in your body, you have a very high center of gravity. High body mass index interferes with flexibility and grace. Even a small loss of balance is aggravated by size.	Work with a balanced program of stamina, flexibility, symmetry and balance, while working to keep your body mass as low as possible through healthy eating.

Courtesy of Coach Daniel Stewart

Myths of Gait

MYTH: "It's okay. I'm just going to ride at the walk."

TRUTH: If we are on the heavier side and tell ourselves that our weight is not going to hurt our horses because we're not asking them to go fast (we don't feel balanced and secure in the saddle at anything faster than a walk, anyway), then it's time to face reality. The truth is that a rider puts a lot more pressure on the horse's back at a walk or even at a standstill—at whatever size and weight—than she does at faster speeds.

As we've already touched upon, those of us who spend a lot of time owning, riding, and working with horses are going to weigh more than many of our more sedentary sisters. It takes a lot of muscle to toss a bale of hay over a fence, drive a fence post into the ground, shoulder a sack of feed and carry it to the barn (for as may reps as there are sacks of feed to unload). Hoisting a saddle, yanking on a lead rope or longe line with enough authority to get the attention of a wayward thousand-pounder—this is the stuff our muscle mass is made of, and it defies insurance height/weight charts.

In the next section we'll explore the point our experts have already made: why a fit, skilled, balanced rider—even at what the charts deem "significantly overweight"—feels lighter to a horse than a floppy, unbalanced supermodel. (I have to admit, I'd like to see one of those runway waifs ride through a serious spook.) Despite this great truth, I must acknowledge that sometimes excess weight creeps up on us (on top of our muscle) and *does* become an impediment to our riding. This may be a few extra pounds, or much more than that. Each of our bodies handles weight differently, and if we can step back from the emotional side of "being overweight" and take an objective look (much like the conditioning scale we use to make sure our horses are where they need to be in terms of *their* weight and girth) it becomes much easier to make whatever adjustments are right for each of us.

In terms of being fit to ride, there are two important things to look at, and it is very hard (if not impossible!) to separate one from the other: *Body composition* is our fat-to-muscle ratio; the other is our actual *level of fitness*—how strong, flexible, and conditioned we are for riding well.

In Coach Daniel Stewart's first book, *Ride Right with Daniel Stewart* (available in ebook and Kindle formats), Coach Stewart discusses at some length the amount of muscle required to ride.

"Riding uses almost every muscle in your body," he writes, "and it's not unusual for you to use as many as 10 or 15 different ones to achieve a simple movement." These are all kinds of muscles, he explains, from the ones that help you maintain your posture and the ones used to guide and direct the horse, to those that open and close your hips. We'll talk about how to condition the most important of these "riding muscles" later on, but for now we just need to recognize that these muscles, once developed enough to work well, add significantly to the number on the scale. The perk here is that since muscle is metabolically active tissue, having more of it on board will likely improve overall body composition. The key is tweaking nutrition a bit to help that along.

Finding Your Why

When I visited with Wendy Murdoch about the idea of "riding light," she told me that the one single common characteristic of all her students who have lost significant weight—either for the purpose of riding better or so that they could ride at all—was the *single moment of commitment*, a time when they knew for certain that they were going to "do this thing" and nothing was going to stand in their way. Pamela Peeke, MD, MPH, FACP, author of *Fit to Live*, calls this moment of commitment the "power why." Dr. Peeke says that by discerning that precise moment—the mother of all your motivations for getting fit—you keep yourself strong in the face of cheesecake,

Rhonda

"Even though I have a good, sturdy horse, a picture that a friend sent me from us riding the previous summer made me sick. I looked at myself (all 252 pounds), sitting on my horse and thought, *OMG! What on earth am I doing?*

"I knew right then it was time for a change! I haven't ridden my horse since November, which is when I joined Team Beachbody® (www.teambeachbody.com) as a coach. When I started I was at 247 pounds; to date I made a vow to my best four-legged friend to get to a proper riding weight and for us to both be fit and healthy (he is a little on the chunky side, too). I am also helping other horsey acquaintances get into shape for their buddies, and I would love to help more. I guess I look at it as I am not just helping the riders, I am helping their horses, too."

as well as defiant when tempted to let your workout schedule slip away.

Dr. Peeke says that to fully understand our "power why," we have to approach it from the fear side. Think back to the RT[3]

Dr. Pamela Peeke's *Fit to Live* (Rodale, 2007).

Test at the beginning of this book: *What's your deepest fear around the issue of weight or body image or fitness when it comes to riding and your love of horses?*

- Is it that you'll never win your division, and judges will ignore you because of your size?

- Is it that you won't be able to give your horse effective aids?

- Is it that you'll one day struggle to get on your horse in front of other riders?

- Is it that you worry about whether your weight may be hurting your horse?

- Is it that your own health may deteriorate to the point that you can't ride at all?

Dr. Peeke says once we isolate and name our deepest, darkest fear about our weight, we then must stop, take a deep breath, and imagine what the *opposite* of that fear would be. The opposite image propelled by our deepest fear, Dr. Peeke says, is our "power why." *That's* what we *really* want.

Exercise for the Mind: Train Your Brain

Set up a simple grid like below and jot down your top three greatest fears regarding your weight and your horse, and then imagine what the opposite of each fear would be and write it in the column to the right. The "opposite thought"—your ideal outcome—may not necessarily involve losing weight or becoming an Animo Italia riding breeches model. It could be that your greatest fear is continuing to try to ride while obsessing over weight issues, and your "power why" is simply to be at peace with your body, in *and* out of the saddle.

Deepest Fear	Imagined Opposite	Power Why
Example: Everyone at the barn laughs because I'm too fat for my horse.	Everyone at the barn admires the way my horse and I work together in partnership.	I am a horsewoman to admire and have a wonderful partnership with my horse.

Curmudgeon Wisdom

Back in the 1990s I worked out religiously with a cranky old Fort Worth, Texas, fitness trainer named Chuck Weisbeck. While his methods and machinery were somewhat antiquated, even at that time (5-gallon paint cans filled with concrete and attached to a metal bar with hardware store chain, as well as assorted sizes of canned goods that served as dumbbells—and probably occasionally his dinner) what he said to me as he waggled his knotty old finger at my "too fat" upper body was (and still is) spot on. Chuck's book *Body Sculpting the Weisbeck Way* is long out of print but worth finding, and his legacy as trainer to countless pageant and bodybuilding contestants, local celebrities, and everyone in between, was earned one rep at a time. I laugh out loud now every time I hear something that was one of his "things" from way back then, now being touted as the latest and greatest in today's diet-and-fitness mêlée. So, with a nod to the late, great Chuck Weisbeck, here is a snapshot of his macro, time-tested advice, in a grumpy-but-effective nutshell:

> Chuck Weisbeck's *Body Sculpting the Weisbeck Way* (Eakin Press, 1993).
>
> **RESOURCES**

• **"Keep it simple."** Chuck's first pearl to the new initiate was always, "No white stuff, no bubbles," meaning nix the refined sugar, white flour, saturated fat, and carbonated beverages. I've read a lot of research and perused a lot of programs, and this seems to hold true as a common thread for quality control for the feed that goes into our own buckets. I don't know about you, but as a veteran dieter I've done all the tracking, counting, weighing, measuring, and pinching I want to. I have to have something easy, accessible, and above all, *so automatic I don't have to think about it.* Chuck's mantra was just the ticket.

• **"Do it."** I think Chuck said this *before* St. Nike added the softening "Just." It seems that when people cross this demarcation line of commitment to make "it" a priority, "it" happens (see Murdoch's "moment of commitment" and Dr. Peeke's "power why" on p. 98). That doesn't mean the trail is an easy one, but when we put our mind in a different place, success—reaching that end destination—becomes our only option.

• **"Stop whining."** I remember Chuck standing over me as I hoisted that rusty barbell plate overhead from a prone position. Between gritted teeth I was interviewing him about what I was doing and why even then, although neither of us realized it. "Stop whining," he grumped. (For the record, I don't think I was whining. Just *questioning*.) "It's not hard to eat right and work out when you stay focused on the result."

That made little sense to me then, but it does now. Keeping your eye on the result—the bigger prize than the cheeseburger calling your name—makes good-sense nutrition and regular exercise just *what you do*: on the road, under stress, overworked, underappreciated, worried, sad, happy, mad, glad—regardless of whatever emotion or circumstance is trying to lure you toward the fast-food drive-thru.

• **"You'll thank me someday."** Chuck used to say we'd thank him when could open a jar of pickles when we were old without asking for help. These prophetic words, brought into our riding arenas, mean that conditioning work we do *now* will pay off in our riding our horses better and with greater ease, effectiveness, and enjoyment far into our future. And, coming back to the pickles, it's important to note that the conditioning work we do to help us *ride* better will also help us *live* better, now and into the days ahead. Let's get to it!

Muck Out Your Nutrition

You knew we would get here. Nutrition (notice I did *not* say "diet") is a crucial part of rider fitness. Or, as experts like to say in one way or another, "You can't exercise your way out of poor nutrition." In fact, according to studies by the American Journal of Clinical Nutrition, *what we eat* and *how much we eat* is much more important to maintaining a healthy weight than *what we do*. Therefore, taking a close look at the fuel we're providing our bodies is an inescapable part of keeping ourselves fit to ride—regardless of our size or shape. This should not be news to those of us who carefully measure and supplement our horse's feed, and sniff and paw at hay before we buy it to make sure it's of the quality that will fuel our horse with the energy he needs to perform well and maintain a healthy weight. Above all, even if you (like me) rarely ask your horse to do much at all, good nutrition keeps him looking good!

Wait. Don't go. I didn't say you have to change anything just now. Let's just sit with this idea for a bit and consider whether we can adapt what we already know about keeping our horse's body fit and strong.

After combing tomes of current literature by some of today's leading authorities on nutrition and fitness, here are a few basic ideas for cleaning up and simplifying your nutrition. By making (and keeping) a few basic rules for how you fuel *your* body (in much the same way you analyze that tag on your horse feed) you're taking your first tentative steps toward the lifestyle changes that will help you learn to love (or at least appreciate) the skin you're in.

• **First thing every morning, build a fire.** I did not make this up. And, although I've heard this particular piece of advice phrased a bazillion different ways, this metaphor, presented in an afternoon nutrition seminar by Eric Billingslea, a 30-year personal training and nutrition consultant who works closely with my favorite local yoga studio, has stuck with me better than the much more elaborate and scientific explanations I've run across.

The gist of Eric's summation of all the great "clean eating" truths comes down to three basic elements of nutrition that we need to pay attention to: lean protein, complex carbs, and quality fats. When we combine these elements correctly, we stoke the fire of our metabolism to burn fat as its fuel. (If you've ever been camping or stayed home on a snow day, you know that if you build a fire right from the get-go, it doesn't take much effort to keep it burning all day long. You just have to keep adding the right fuel—and in the right amounts.)

Marry

"My shape is very square, and I'm larger boned, so losing 40 pounds didn't really change me a ton," says horse trainer and co-author of *Know You, Know Your Horse* Marry Morrow. "I went down two sizes in pants but only one size in tops (I have very broad shoulders). I still try to wear clothes that 'hide the belly.' I still don't see what I would like to see. (Although to be honest, much of it is the older look on my face that bothers me! I'm getting close to 60, and it's not graceful.) One thing I did really find interesting when I lost weight was how much more I tend to sit with my legs crossed—I didn't realize I had stopped doing that with the extra 40 pounds because it wasn't comfortable.

"On a horse, I feel better. It's a feeling of freedom to know that I'm not hurting my horse or his back. When I was heavier and would finish riding, I would slide down off the horse and feel a bit sore, my legs would be tired, and now I can ride quite a bit longer and don't feel pain when I get off. (I'm still not wild about the pictures of me on a horse, though—I still look right at my belly!) I can visualize myself being another 40 pounds thinner. I was there once! I would like to see the belly fat go and maybe some face fat, too.

"Losing weight for me is not about certain diets. It's calories in, versus calories out, and what I use for those calories. I have an app on my phone called 'My Fitness Pal' (www.myfitnesspal.com). I love it, as it has tons of food recommendations, and it's easy to add up your calories; it tells you how much fat, protein, and so on. And it has a place to put in your *own* recipes so you can find new ways to cut calories on what you fix at home. It also has a place to put in your exercise, and it takes *those* calories off your total. So, if you have a 'bad eating day' you just exercise more so you don't go over your goal of calories. Horseback riding for 30 minutes burns 117 calories. Grooming a horse for 20 minutes burns 99 calories! If you break down and eat a cookie, plan to take that second ride and burn it off!

"One week at a time is my motto, and I try to follow a Mediterranean 'diet' with mostly organic veggies and fruit. Of course, I had to figure out how to cook and eat many new things, as I had *no clue*! I try to make something new once a week, and I try to keep something that I *shouldn't* eat out of my life for one week. For instance, my first goal was that I could not drink a pop for seven days. On the seventh day, I could. It was interesting, as I did this for a month and found out on the day I *could* have a pop, it didn't taste very good. After a few months, pop was not even something I would *think* of having.

"Humor is a must for losing weight. I tend to laugh at myself when I'm struggling. I go to the barn and look around my feed room. I have my horses on the best feed that I can find (no fillers for my boys!). I have big tubs chock full of the vitamins and minerals they need to be healthy. Waiting until second cutting for the hay means it is not full of junk but just good healthy grasses. They get fed all-natural supplements to help keep the bugs away. They are detoxed organically twice a year. Then I go out into the barn and I'm so proud of their healthy look: just the right weight, hair shiny, feet wonderful. I do energy work at least once a week and give them a massage after riding before turnout. On rainy days, I do extra grooming. I work so hard to keep *them* happy and healthy, so seriously, what's wrong with working as hard on myself? (If I could just get them to look after me the way I look after them!)

"When I have a bad day I keep telling myself I am *not* going to be a Kirstie Alley: Up and down and trying to be 'proud' of the fat—no way!

"A real milestone moment was when I had to buy new clothes because my pants kept falling off. I usually hate shopping, but that one day I did celebrate! And getting on a smaller horse and not feeling bad about it made my day. My ultimate goal is I would like to own one more horse in this lifetime: a young one, start to finish. I don't want to go horse shopping and have to think about the horse's bone structure to carry 'my weight.' I want to look for and find my dream horse, no matter what size he/she ends up being."

• **Complex carbohydrates.** These are the "logs" for your metabolic fire; they come bundled in starchy root vegetables and whole, unrefined grains (Chuck said, "No white stuff," remember?) and should be consumed two times a day, at breakfast and at lunch. This fuel is necessary to getting and keeping your metabolic fires burning. To keep these "logs" from burning up too fast, Eric reminds us that regardless of whether it is a meal or a snack, it's important to always add protein and healthy fat to your complex carbs. Simple carbohydrates, such as fruit, can be consumed at other times of the day, he says, as long as you include a fat and a protein. Note that baked potatoes (in limited quantities) are okay; French fries, sadly, are not. Sweet potatoes are better than white potatoes; in fact, with any vegetable the deeper the (natural) color—and the more colors you can pack into a meal—the better. Always.

• **Lean, animal protein.** As the "kindling" of your metabolic fire, protein keeps your metabolic fires burning steadily all day — as long as you "tend" it every two to three hours by tossing on a little more complex carb "kindling" to "turn up the fire." Protein, experts agree, should come from a variety of sources every day. (This also keeps you from getting grilled-chicken burnout.) There is also some solid science behind choosing lean, clean, animal protein (chicken, turkey, beef, fish) over dairy and vegetable proteins, because the latter metabolize differently and are not as available to our bodies. We also have to eat a lot more vegetable protein to get the same benefit as a quality piece of lean meat. (Sorry, vegetarians!) "Every cell of your body needs protein," Eric says. "You don't want to burn your protein!"

• **High-quality fats.** "Don't run from fat!" Eric emphasizes this point again and again. He and lots of others believe that by providing your body with plenty of healthy fats (and many put fish oil and flax seed oil supplements in this group), you refresh your fat cells with cleaner burning, better quality fat that is then more usable to your body as energy. Among these are avocado, nuts, seeds, and high-quality extra virgin olive oil (EVOO). He's such a fan of this stuff he has his clients take a tablespoon of EVOO after every meal. (It's kind of gross at first, but I have to admit it grows on you.) I did ask Eric if we could take the olive oil "with popcorn" instead of "straight up." He was not amused.

When my subsequent exploration of top fitness literature echoed Eric's advice again and again (trust me, I hiked the proverbial Everest that is our current diet and fitness industry), I came to the same stunning conclusion you're probably about to reach:

I knew that.

A great book called *The Power of Habit* by Charles Duhigg delves into what makes the critical difference between something we know—like "always eat a good breakfast"—and the true integration of this information into our decisions and choices every single day until they become habits. Duhigg decodes the "habit loops" that drive both the things we repetitively do (sometimes without realizing it) and the reasons we do these things in the first place. We'll dig into this ahead (see p. 290), but for now just remember that, as Aristotle once said, "We are what we repeatedly do. Excellence, then, is not an act, but a habit." By incorporating a few small habit changes in the way we fuel our bodies, we begin the ripple effect that will lead to excellence in our physical strength, stamina, and health that will empower our riding in a whole new way.

Will we lose weight? Probably. But that's not really the point. Even if we stay right where we are (weight-wise), we'll *ride* stronger and lighter—and feel better doing it. If you change *nothing else* in the way you eat, a few simple tweaks to your daily habits will create some game-changing neuropathways in your brain that can add up to big rewards in no time. These include, in no particular order:

Charles Duhigg's *The Power of Habit* (Random House, 2011).

RESOURCES

• **Eat breakfast every single day, and make it a good one.** Going back to "building the fire" (see p. 103), this is the daily wake-up call you give your metabolism. With lean protein, complex carbs, and fat on board to start your day, you'll fire up your metabolism in a way that you can keep it burning all day by simply adding small quantities of quality fuel at regular intervals. Good old eggs, it turns out, are not the cholesterol villains they were once thought to be; in fact, they make a pretty awesome breakfast protein. (Our grandparents knew this!) Most experts now recommend eating the whole egg (whites and yolk), but if you're still worried about it, egg whites only also make a fine choice. Combine with a complex carb (Eric recommends steel-cut oats with some dried fruit to sweeten), and you're good to go. It's easy to eat the same thing for breakfast and lunch every day. (No decisions required! Keep it simple, remember?) But if you're the type to get bored (and you are not concerned with sodium or preservatives), turkey bacon and turkey sausage also make good lean protein choices.

• **Eat every two to three hours.** Not a lot, mind you, but something—and always in that lean-protein-complex-carb-quality-fat combination that will keep the metabolic fire burning. If you're someone who tends to skip meals, Eric made a point I can't seem to shake: "Your body is like a newborn baby," he said. "It feeds every two to three hours, whether you choose to eat or not."

What Eric means is our body's demand for more fuel on the fire is a constant. If we eat the right proportions of *quality* food, our bodies use that first and then release and burn off our excess fat stores. However, if we don't take *in* quality fuel on a regular basis, our bodies go straight to the next easiest thing to break down—the animal protein already on board, our hard-earned muscles. As a survival mechanism, our body will consume our own muscle protein first, leaving our stored fat as emergency rations in case the "starvation" continues. This protective mechanism is what seals our chubby fate when we don't take in protein and complex carbs often enough to keep our inner metabolic cannibals at bay.

• **Drink plain water and lots of it.** This one is so deep in the "not new" category I had to dig deeper. Forget the percentages and ounces and appetite-suppressing part we all know. Going back to that fire analogy, imagine that the water you drink is rinsing your "fat ash" away (yes, I did that on purpose. You won't ever forget it, will you?). Water helps move what your metabolism just burned right on out of your body as waste, either through your pores as sweat, or through your urine and bowel movements. This bit of mental imagery was a good one for me, and it's amazing how tweaking this one habit makes a constant intake of water grow on you.

The trick, our buddy Eric explains, is spreading out our water consumption throughout the day. How much is enough? Eric recommends a gallon; most experts say to drink enough to keep your urine clear. If you wait till you're thirsty, you're already dehydrated. (Apparently we all walk around in varying degrees of dehydration and don't even realize it.)

I discovered that putting a filled, 24-ounce, insulated water bottle on my bedside table when I go to bed at night and making sure to finish it when I first get up in the morning starts the ball rolling for me. I make sure to have a big glass of water with breakfast, one mid-morning, one at lunch, one mid-afternoon, and one with dinner. Every time I drink something that *isn't* water, I try to refill my cup or glass with the same amount of water and drink it right then. After about two weeks of doing this, I was surprised by two things: First how much I started to crave the stuff, and second (possibly more important), how many restrooms I have located in my daily travels around town.

With a little priming of intent, you'll establish your own routine and tricks; by connecting a full bottle or glass of water to specific parts of your day (every time I get in the car I now fill up my water bottle), you'll be surprised how easy it is to get the whole gallon consumed by dinner. My doctor told me he fills a gallon jug each morning and makes sure it is empty before he leaves his office at the end of the day. (This, he said, minimizes "night-time interruptions.") My favorite water bottle is 24 ounces; I know I need to have six of them a day. You can use a smartphone app such as iHydrate (Mobile Sports, Inc), LoseIt, or MyFitnessPal, or a simple old-school tally to keep up with your daily intake. Regardless of whatever else you do in terms of nutrition, this is a habit worth forming.

• **Go for high-quality feed.** Consider the importance we place on the quality feed and forage we choose for our horses. If we do the same for ourselves, one food choice at a time, our overall nutrition will likely improve considerably. Simply put, just decide to do the best you can every time you need to choose a meal or snack. If you can afford organic, pesticide-and-hormone-free meats, fruits, and

BUSTED! Myths of "Healthy" Foods

According to www.trim-downclub.com, it is not only *what we eat* but also a few key things *we need to eliminate* that make all the difference when "mucking out" our diet. Staffed by certified nutritionists and registered dietitians, this online support community lives by a common commitment to eliminating five "healthy" foods with sneaky hidden agendas, including:

1 **Juice concentrates.** With all the fiber processed out, our bodies read it as pure sugar.

2 **Margarine.** Trans fat is far more harmful and infinitely less tasty than real butter.

3 **Wheat bread.** Even whole wheat triggers the cortisol release that sends glucose into our blood streams that is only helpful if we're actually running from a bear or fighting off a mountain lion; otherwise, it just causes our bodies to store all this extra energy as fat.

4 **Processed soy.** *What?* Apparently, that seemingly virtuous tofu, soy milk, and soy protein has a dark side; all the good stuff has been processed right out of it.

5 **Corn products.** Much if not most of the corn we get these days has been genetically modified, and this GMO corn triggers fat storage in our bodies. The corn we find on the cob and in cans is not the only culprit: Read labels carefully, because corn starch, corn syrup, corn syrup solids, and some things that don't even have corn in their name are chemical corn derivatives that make processed food taste better and stay fresh longer. And since our bodies don't know what to do with it, they just store it. As fat.

vegetables, great. If you can't, or if those things aren't available to you, just do the very best you can, keeping all your food fresh, lean, and as close to "whole" as you can get. As a general rule, the more processed it is, the more likely it is to pack on unwanted pounds. Try to "shop the edges" of the grocery store (packaged and processed foods generally live in the center aisles—see Dr. Pamela Peeke's advice on p. 115), order the freshest and simplest foods on restaurant menus (and always add veggies if it makes sense!), and limit sugary, salty snack foods.

HORSE SENSE FOR HUMANS

I'll admit I was skeptical when I first opened Haylie Pomroy's book *The Fast Metabolism Diet*. It seemed a little bit hypocritical to even look at it, considering my longstanding anti-diet rant. I never would have touched a book with such a title if it had not been for two things: First, it was recommended to me as a possible source during my interview with licensed therapist and mental health counselor Jill Valle, who shares my aversion to the "D-Word." And second, prior to earning considerable stripes in the human nutrition arena, Haylie Pomroy started out as an *equine* nutritionist. After serious study (with noteworthy results) in animal science, Pomroy says she gained pivotal understanding of the huge impact metabolism has on body composition and performance.

Haylie Pomroy's *The Fast Metabolism Diet* (Harmony, 2013).

"That's where I first learned that food can be used, systematically and purposefully," she writes, "to shape the body the way a sculptor shapes a lump of clay." As Pomroy amassed an amazing perspective on nutrition, she began to make some important connections. "The more I learned about animal nutrition," she says, "the more I thought about how some of the concepts could be applied to people—that *our* diet could also be managed to speed up metabolism and increase the metabolic rate of burn."

The book's title, it turns out, is ironic—Pomroy turns the word "diet" into an acronym that those of us who feed things on schedule every day readily understand: D-I-E-T (**D**id **I** **E**at **T**oday?). We need to understand the importance of feeding *ourselves* as regularly and well as we do our horses, Pomroy says. It's also time to shift our thinking about how we use food. Rather than a source of comfort, pleasure, or reward, food needs to become for us merely how we set our bodies up to do what we're asking them to do. When we begin to think about food in the light of how we feed our horses, we gain new ground mentally and emotionally around what food does—and what it's for.

We know how adjusting feed and supplements and exercise produces visible results in how our horses look, feel, and perform. When we extend that thinking into our own physiological arena, we find very much the same principles at work. "I love horses," Pomroy writes. "I ride them and study them and admire them." (See? I told you she's okay!) "I also think they can teach us important things about metabolism." She then references something I know will be familiar to you. Some horses are "easy keepers" and do just fine—even get fat—on very small amounts of food. Others we can feed and feed and feed and they still have ribs showing. The difference? Metabolism!

Pomroy explains that in animal science, something called "feed-to-gain conversion" is how you calculate feeding a steer for the best marbling (fat distribution), and how you calculate feeding a horse for optimal fast- or slow-twitch muscle fibers, depending on whether you're looking for speed out of the gate or stamina for a long haul. Puzzled that no one had ever applied these solid, well-tested scientific principles to the care and feeding of humans, Pomroy decided to do just that, with staggering results, according to her case studies and testimonials.

By putting her understanding of how food triggers biochemical change to either speed up or slow down metabolism, Pomroy called on this science to get results in her human clients with lasting results. Her discovery produced weight loss, yes, but even more important, it improved cholesterol counts, blood sugar levels, and much more. By, teaching people how to "let food work for them," Pomroy helped countless people create the physical results they were looking for—and lifestyle tweaks that keep them strong, healthy, and free from the cycles of dieting and self-criticism that goes along with weight that just won't seem to come off.

What's the magic of applying animal science to human dieters? Pomroy's focus on how we feed and strengthen the systems *within* our bodies empowers them to do a better job of keeping that metabolic fire going and is what makes everything we do work better, from now on.

"I am the metabolism whisperer," she writes.

Referring to herself as a "personal trainer for your metabolism," Pomroy kicks wayward metabolisms into gear by calling into the play the work of systems we all know we have, but (if you're like me) may not be sure what they do. By feeding and supporting what she calls "the five major players" (liver, adrenals, thyroid, pituitary, and body substance—white fat, brown fat, and muscle), Pomroy's program prescribes specific foods and exercises in a three-phase rotation you do each week. Each phase only lasts a day or two and not only does it confuse your metabolism into action, it lays the tracks for a lifestyle shift that will help you keep your metabolism stoked. While the variety does keep it interesting, it *is* strict and precise—just like that carefully measured scoop of supplement you add to your show pony's food to make his coat shiny or his feet healthier.

Calling upon whole, "real" food (like so many of the clean-eating programs I ran across), Pomroy's program sends chemicals, preservatives, dyes, and artificial anything packing. Quoting the American Medical Association, which has coined a word for these non-foods—*obesogens*—Pomroy teaches us that not only do our bodies not know what to do with these substances in terms of breaking them down, but they disrupt the balance of our hormones and how our bodies metabolize fat. Ironically, she adds, most of the packaged "diet" foods you find on your supermarket shelves are loaded with these chemicals. She asks her readers, "How would you rather your liver spend its day: Breaking down chemicals you eat under the pretense it is food, or working on burning the fat off your butt, belly, chin, and thighs?"

"Some people can't lose weight even though they don't eat very much," Pomroy writes. "Their metabolic flame has died out and they can't get it lit again. The logs are wet, the garbage has piled up, and the whole process has become dysfunctional. They need a jumpstart. They need to be reignited." Our metabolism, she explains, reflects what we do by creating a body that can survive the conditions it is subjected to.

The truth is, transforming how we deal with our weight issues goes far beyond physical and dietary changes. "Re-ignition" involves a mental and emotional paradigm shift in which our past successes or failures will have nothing to do with our new reality. It requires that *moment of commitment* that Wendy Murdoch referred to back on p. 98—the "power why" Dr. Peeke explained on p. 99.

Enter at "A," Tosca Reno, author of *The Eat Clean Diet* and several successful spin-offs. Like Pomroy, the use of the "D-Word" almost got Reno thrown off our elite virtual panel of nutritionists, but her story makes her a role model worthy of study. Reno made a name for herself in the bodybuilding world and even became a *swimsuit model*, for crying out loud, by taking a big step back from the diet industry and coming up with a much more logical (and livable) solution. I first ran across Reno's book several years ago and put it aside, thinking, "Well, that's a great story, but it's just too hard." And now, after my tour of research for RT³, I'm looking at Reno with a completely new understanding. She had this figured out all along.

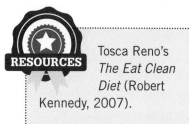

Tosca Reno's *The Eat Clean Diet* (Robert Kennedy, 2007).

Lisa Hark, PhD, RD, describes Reno's story as "one of inspiration, motivation, and hope for anyone trying to improve his or her lifestyle." Like so many, when Reno weighed in at over 200 pounds, she never imagined her life could be any different. Her "power why" was wanting to "do better" for her kids, not horses, but the important parallel here is that at some point she *made the decision* to reclaim her life, and that's when she discovered potential she never imagined.

Hark says that what makes Reno's story different (and for our purposes, darned near perfect) is that in a diet-driven culture, she made a conscious decision *not* to "diet" at all. Instead, she decided to reshape her nutrition by eliminating any foods that were processed and nutritionally devoid. Starting simply by replacing junk food with lean proteins, complex carbohydrates, and small amounts of healthy fats (we've talked about all of these—see p. 106), Tosca Reno's personal transformation from an obese 20-something to a swimsuit-model 40-something is the least of it.

Reno was the first person I ever heard use the term "eat clean" to describe this lifestyle of dietary logic that relies on whole, real foods from every food group and stays as close to what nature provides as possible. The big payoff is freedom from endless dieting, feeling better, having more strength and energy to do what's important, and developing resistance to chronic "lifestyle" diseases. And, oh yeah, probably losing some weight. And while we'll probably enjoy the way that looks, it's not even the point of these programs.

GO THE DISTANCE

We can't always eat perfectly (unlike our horses!), but we *can* promise to always look for the best choice available. And remember, *nothing* is a permanent deal-breaker. Slip-ups happen; enjoy them. And then get back on track *with your very*

Myths of Nutrition

BUSTED!

MYTH: "I eat mostly packaged dinners from low-calorie and diet brands, and that's all I need to control my nutrient intake."

TRUTH: Studies show that processed food.packs on the pounds. In *Fit to Live,* Dr. Pamela Peeke provides eating and lifestyle guidelines that by now will be sounding quite familiar: 20 to 30 percent lean protein, 40 to 60 percent complex carbohydrates, 20 to 30 percent "good" fats. Dr. Peeke also gives us great food-shopping advice, including:

• **The Rule of Five**—Always make sure there are at least five different colors of fruits and vegetables in your cart. (This is harder than it sounds!)

• **Shop the Perimeters**—The outer aisles are where, for the most part, you'll find fresh, unprocessed foods. (The center aisles are where the packaged, sugary, starchy, additive-laden foods live.)

---

next food choice. This is not about any particular "diet" or "program"; it's about creating a nutrition-conscious *lifestyle.* Through the small, common sense choices we can make every single day, we can improve the quality of our nutrition by staying true to just a few simple promises to ourselves. It's about living your life, doing your best, and *trying not to worry so much about it all.*

Some days will be easier than others. Some days you will do all the things I've mentioned so far; others you may only do a few. And other days you may get bucked off completely. Olympic superstar Dara Torres says that when everyone goes out for burgers, even when she's in training, she'll order the burger (with extra veggies), lose the bun, and have the fries. We, too, can stay true to our goals—and also enjoy the exceptions—as long as we keep our focus steady on the long-term prize.

In later chapters we'll explore the formation of habits, the role mindfulness can play in making these lifestyle shifts, and how changing our thought patterns can impact our behavior. But for now, just remember that if you stay this course, the results will show up in *how much better you feel* and *how much stronger you get.* One day you'll stop thinking of these things as choices at all; they'll just be "what you do" to stay as strong and healthy as your horse. You may even have trouble remembering what the big deal was about making these lifestyle changes in the first place.

Beyond the Feedbag

There's another factor to consider as we set ourselves up for riding success regardless of weight. It is another much-maligned word that produces the, "Yeah, yeah, yeah," response in me (and just about everyone I know). It's the "E-Word": Exercise.

We've established that horsewomen are athletes; that's part of why our BMI doesn't tell the whole story. We know that riding is hard work and uses most of the muscles in our bodies. And it's no secret that horse and barn chores are a non-negotiable workout. So, even if we're heavier than we'd like to be, we're not a bunch of flabby couch potatoes. We've got muscles aplenty, and they *do* work hard.

But what if we could refine, define, and develop the musculature of our bodies in a way that could help us—and our horses—even *more* when we ride? What if this physical "framework" (the "outside") would complement how we're feeding our bodies (the "inside") for results that would exponentially increase our enjoyment when we ride? What if this, like our nutritional muck-out, is just a matter of understanding and creating a few minor lifestyle shifts that will produce major results?

The trick is to streamline and simplify a body tune-up so that the "E-Word" becomes as much a part of our day-to-day routine as eating clean. There will be days when it all falls apart, of course, just like occasionally pizza-and-beer night is *going* to happen. (I insist on it!)

SO, WHAT IF WE DON'T?

Okay, you may be thinking (assuming you made it this far): *I'm in good enough shape. I've been riding for a long time. And yes, I have put on some weight, but I'm still as strong as I need to be to ride well. I'm not that heavy, either, so I know I'm not in any danger of hurting my horse. So…is all this "framework" really necessary?*

In a word, *YES.* As Coach Daniel Stewart explains, regardless of how much you weigh or what kind of shape you're in, whenever your riding muscles start feeling fatigue (aka, they aren't in optimal shape), several things begin to happen—and none of them are very good for your horse:

• **Poor posture.** When fatigued, the muscles of your torso collapse and your shoulders and lower back begin to round. Slouching forward, even slightly, may offer a little relief, but it also shifts your balance in a way that makes you less stable and causes your horse to have to work harder to maintain *his* balance. What's more, the subsequent gripping and clenching we do to hold on leads nowhere good.

• **Decreased mental capacity.** Fatigued muscles, starved for oxygen, search for more fuel. Guess where they most often find it? Your brain. As your brain oxygen gets hijacked to keep your muscles working, things like coordination, concentration, focus, reflexes, and decision-making all take the backseat. When you're on the back of a horse, is that *really* where you want them?

• **Poor biomechanics.** Even if you are naturally symmetrical, have good balance, and are breathing properly, a lack of solid conditioning that results in fatigue in the saddle will take that edge from you. When you find yourself wondering why you've suddenly developed postural flaws you've never struggled with before—it's muscle fatigue that's the culprit. (We'll visit the subject of biomechanics soon—see p. 157.)

• **Increased risk of injury.** Obviously, the effects of muscle fatigue put your balance and stability in the saddle at risk. While this may not mean you'll be coming off your horse (though that's a distinct possibility), it does open the door to other riding-related injuries, such as lower back and knee trouble, and pulled or strained muscles.

• **Weakened natural aids.** As your muscles are busying themselves trying to find fuel and relief, they really can't be bothered with delivering the clear, precise aids your horse needs and deserves to help him understand what you're asking him to do. As your communication with him deteriorates, so does the quality of your ride—and ultimately, your relationship with your horse.

"The next time you feel tired in the saddle," Coach Stewart advises, "remind yourself that you're an athlete. Sit up straight, take in a deep breath, and push yourself a little bit harder so that your horse doesn't have to work extra hard to carry your tired body around."

So ladies, shall we embrace our inner athletes—for our horses' sakes?

THE HOLY TRINITY OF FITNESS

For riders, a balanced program of strength, stamina, and flexibility make up the "Holy Trinity of Fitness." This is probably not news to you. But how can we add a healthy side dish of off-horse conditioning work without capsizing a plate that's already too full? The good news is that adding as little as 30 minutes a day of focused conditioning exercises (especially if you're doing *zero* minutes right now) will probably yield results that will make you want to keep doing that much—and maybe even more.

"If you knew the only thing that separated you from better riding and less risk of injury or strain was about 15 to 30 additional minutes a day of training you could do from your home or barn without expensive equipment, what would stop you from starting today?" asks one of my favorite rider fitness resources, certified

Myths of Denial

BUSTED!

MYTH: "I'll ride as a way to lose weight."

TRUTH: Riding a horse well at heavier weights actually requires greater strength and balance than riding at lower weights. Or, as one anonymous interviewee put it, "It's a whole lot more to balance, and a whole lot harder to get *back* in balance."

Because of her own concern for the well-being of horses, this rider was quick to add, "God created such a wonderful animal to put up with so much from us. We don't sit right, we can't feel right, we don't use our reins or legs correctly—and when we get on a horse and we're not in shape to ride him correctly, it's just not fair." (There it is again, the call to Be Fair....)

My interviewee paused here and measured her words carefully, fully aware of their potential sting, but wanting desperately to get her point across.

"I don't want to encourage anyone who is overweight to ride who isn't willing to make the changes and improvements in themselves that they need to in order to ride well—especially at heavier weights. So I'd say unless you're willing to spend the time, energy, and discipline to do the right things for yourself and your horse, I'm against it."

personal trainer Heather Sansom of EquiFITT.com. She concurs that the muscles we use when we ride *are* different—or rather, we use them differently—than in any other sport. And particularly when we're trying to create a "framework" so we can ride lighter regardless of weight, we need to be *intentional* about the conditioning activities we incorporate into our lifestyle. How is being *intentional about conditioning* different than just plain *conditioning*, you ask? Well, I'll tell you: Conditioning just for the sake of conditioning can be (and is for me) kind of a sporadic approach to doing things I know I should do, whenever, however, and if I can. Being more *intentional* about it means I have a bigger plan at work, and I am making a deliberate choice to follow this plan in order to achieve a desired result. For me, "be intentional" belies more of an end-game focus than "just do it." While to some this may seem like a word game, I tell you it works wonders in helping me stick to my program.

While we all know that riding is good exercise (we often remember this quite clearly the morning *after* a long ride), and it does condition our *riding muscles*, it is not, in and of itself, nearly enough to make the kinds of changes in our bodies we're seeking. It's also important to remember that riding also tends to create or aggravate asymmetry and strength imbalances in our bodies—and tightness where we should be supple—that takes specific work to overcome. To address these issues, we must also work "off the horse" with a consistent training routine that is as much a part of our day-to-day routine as brushing our teeth. If we're faithful to these off-horse routines, we can mitigate strength imbalances before they start to set up muscle strain, repetitive-use injury, or even the tightness and muscle knots that interfere with our ability to connect with the motion of our horses. According to Heather Sansom, "Creating balance and flexibility, muscle memory, proprioception (body awareness), core strength, and cardiovascular endurance (stamina for long show days/ long rides) is more effective when you can work on these areas *out* of the saddle *between* your rides....Working 'off horse' allows us to take our muscles through their full range of motion, taking the time we need to reset our body's muscle memory patterns and sense of 'straight' so that we can begin to use our bodies to assist our horse's movement effectively."

FORGET SKINNY—GET STRONG!

Strength training for most athletes is remarkably similar: We all have pretty much the same muscle groups, and they get stronger in pretty much the same ways. Thinking back to Chuck Weisbeck's cement-filled paint cans and array of canned goods (p. 101) and forward to the high-tech gyms, swanky health clubs, and country-club-fitness centers I've experienced since, it seems that it's not so much *how* or *where* you strength-train, just that you *do* it with enough consistency to make a difference.

While it's true as Coach Stewart mentioned on p. 98 that riding uses almost every single muscle in your body, the muscles most important to riding are in your back, hips, legs, butt, shoulders, and abdominals. "It's important to strengthen each and every one of your riding muscles," he writes in *Ride Right with Daniel Stewart*, "because weakness in one muscle will compromise the integrity of the muscles surrounding it."

Coach Stewart, who has developed a lot of rider-specific exercises targeting these muscles, says the key to striking the ideal balance between stamina, strength, and suppleness in your riding muscles is to use very light weights, do lots of reps, and be sure to include all these muscle groups on a regular basis.

The result? Sinewy and "moderately strong" muscle that will give you the strength you need for effective cues and aids and good posture—with the flexibility to move easily with your horse. The difference in conditioning a rider's muscles over a tennis player's or a football player's, Coach Stewart explains, is that the *strength* a rider needs is the ability to use muscles as *economically as possible* in order to continue riding strong *without resting* these muscles. This is very different from the strength required to make a single hit with as much force as possible, and then rest until the next one.

Coach Stewart describes this pairing of efficiency and effectiveness as the "dynamic duo" (remember Batman and Robin?) of muscle control. "Muscles contract two ways," he explains. "Dynamic and static. Regardless of which way they contract, they are always subject to fatigue."

Remember this: *In riding, dynamic and static muscle contractions work together to create the continuous effectiveness and efficiency you need to work them without rest.* This is one of those factoids you may be tempted to skim. Don't. It offers clues to finding success when building your own routine.

According to Coach Stewart, *Dynamic muscle contractions* (isotonic) involve *visible movement*, such as opening your hips while posting to the trot. *Static muscle contractions* (isometric) are *invisible*, such as the core strength expended to control your posture. Even though you can't see these muscles working, they work very hard *all the time*; when they fail or fatigue you'll see (and feel) it in slumped or sagging shoulders or rounding in the back.

Conditioning for this special kind of strength takes focused work, along with a solid understanding that will stand you in good stead as you work toward the next feat of "riding light," whatever your size—the biomechanics that help create what our dressage friends call "self-carriage." (Only now we're not talking about the horse.)

Specific exercises are really up to you! This training need not be complicated or expensive; however, Coach Stewart says that regardless of the strength training exercises you choose, there are seven important rules to follow:

1 **Always warm up and stretch.** Five minutes of rider stretches before each ride will save *you* from injuries that create setbacks and keep you out of the saddle.

2 **Lift the proper amount.** Light weights only! While individual strengths vary, this means lifting the weight you can lift repeatedly for a long period of time without sacrificing form.

3 **Exercise in your "normal riding position."** This feels weird at first (and I'm sure it looks weird, too), but it makes total sense. You want the conditioning work you're doing to translate directly to your time in the saddle.

4 **Do each repetition slowly and smoothly.** Make the *contraction* phase last three seconds and the *elongation* phase last four to ensure the maximum benefit

you'll never see if you rush through your reps. "Just because it's lightweight doesn't mean your reps should be faster," Coach Stewart reminds us.

5 **No bouncing.** This means putting a full, one-second pause *between* the contraction and elongation of each rep. Failing to do this will not only rob you of the full benefit of this exercise, but "bouncing" without putting these essential pauses in your reps can lead to injury.

6 **Perform isotonic and isometric contractions.** When we ride, we're asking our muscles to perform both *dynamic* (*isotonic*, or movement you can see) and *static* (*isometric*, or tightening, squeezing, or "zipping up" your muscles) work. While most exercise programs focus solely on the dynamic side of this coin, a rider needs to follow every dynamic movement with a five-second static hold, which means we pause, check and straighten our posture, and "zip up" our core.

For the uninitiated, this odd term describes visually how we pull in and tighten the full length of our abdominal wall progressively (as if we're zipping up a jacket), starting at our pelvis, traveling up our abdominal wall to the top of our ribcage. Cassandra Stephens of ABSolute Pilates (cassandrasabsolut-epilates.com) gave me another great visual for holding this without getting too stiff: imagine your core as three boxes: one is your pelvis, one is your midsection, and one is your shoulders. Now imagine that these boxes are stacked and aligned evenly, with rubber bands attaching them. You can move any of these boxes as you need to, but when you tighten those rubber bands, the stack realigns into a straight, even tower.

7 **Don't overdo it.** More is not better, and results show best when muscles get enough time to recover fully (48 hours) between sessions.

Echoing this last rule, in her book *Age Is Just a Number*, Olympic swimmer Dara Torres tells of how she had to learn *not* to compare herself to other swimmers, other training regimens, and other people's ideals. I think we can all relate to this scenario. Who among us has not looked at another rider and thought, *if I worked*

RESOURCES

Dara Torres' *Age Is Just a Number* (Three Rivers Press, 2010).

harder I could look, ride, or show like that? We need to take Torres' lessons from the pool into our riding arenas: We have to do what is right for our own bodies to retrain our frames to be better, stronger, and more supple riders—*this*, for once, isn't a competition.

Exercise for the Body: Conditioning Simplified

As you can imagine, designing your own program carries its own risks and rewards. I recommend you keep it all extremely simple. (If you're like me at all, you will be tempted to complicate it to the point you won't even want to do it. Ask me how I know this.) While making specific improvements and correcting muscle imbalances may require more specialized work, to maintain the level of conditioning you have requires a quick daily overall routine you can do in a matter of minutes, followed by a good stretch to the muscles worked to keep those muscles long *and* strong.

Here's the simple version a trainer taught me years ago that has stood the test of time for her clients trying to maintain an overall level of conditioning: You can work all of your major muscle groups with three things: squats, a four-part crunch series, and pushups.

• **Squats.** Sit in an invisible chair, then stand up. That's it. The only rules are: Don't let your butt go below your knees or your knees extend forward past your ankles. Do these in sets of 10 with a quick rest in between. Start with three sets and work up to 10.

• **4-Way Crunch.** 1) Lie on your back with your fingers interlaced behind your head, knees bent, feet flat on the ground. Lift your chest and shoulders straight up toward the ceiling; repeat till you feel a burn. That's your starting number. 2) Now straighten your legs and lift your heels toward the ceiling for as many reps as it takes to feel that burn in your lower abs. Write that number down. 3) Now take your left elbow to right knee, and repeat till your feel it in your left side. That'll do. 4) Now repeat with your right elbow to your left knee till you feel the pinch. Don't overdo this one: start where your body allows and work up to a max of 25 of each with good form. Remember to breathe out upon exertion (when you "crunch"), and keep your abs "zipped" and your belly button pulling toward your spine as you perform each move.

• **Pushups.** Can't do pushups? Try to do just one with good form. (If you can do more, great.) A Pure Barre instructor told me (to my great relief) that just holding your pushup in the "up" position with a straight body, square shoulders, and straight arms (core zipped!) for as long as possible will work the same muscle groups as actual pushups and start to build the kind of strength that will eventually allow you to lower yourself with good form into a single perfect pushup. Once you can do that, you're ready to build toward adding one pushup a day until you get to 10, and then start working on adding additional sets of 10, with three sets as a good goal, while 10 sets of 10 puts you in line for a golden lasso. (This is a Wonder Woman reference, for the unenlightened.)

Build Core Strength for Stability
"Regardless of the shape and size you have to work with, the fitter you are, the better you'll ride," says Susan Harris. "This applies especially to core muscles (those deep inner abdominal, back, and pelvic floor muscles) you strengthen with Pilates-type work. These are what help a rider maintain balance, even during jolts and sudden movements. People who do Pilates or other core work regularly usually find that their riding improves by leaps and bounds as their core gets stronger."

Sometimes we think of our "core muscles" as pretty much the same as what everyone uses to refer to as "abs." However, in addition to your abdominal and back muscles, your "core" is actually a complex, interconnected group of muscles that lives *beneath* what we tend to generalize as the "abs." (I can tell you *exactly* where they are and how they make themselves known in a most excruciating way when first you expose them to specific work.) Your core muscles actually extend in all directions *beyond* your "abs," and pretty much connect to everything besides your head, arms, and legs! In fact, you use your core for just about every move you make.

It's no secret that I love hot yoga because it is pretty much a complete workout that builds flexible strength, core stability, flexibility, and stamina beyond my wildest dreams in just three to four 90-minute sessions a week. (A word of caution here: not all hot yogas are created equal; be sure to do your homework, listen to your body, and be smart about how hard you push in the heat. Hydration, nutrition, and common sense are keys to safety and success when working hard in high temperatures.) And after spending my required 30 classes in Pilates (that's what founder Joseph Pilates says it takes to "rebuild" your core), I saw a huge difference in my riding and my posture, as well as finding muscles I didn't know existed. Pilates, like yoga, is something you can do safely every day—but two to three days a week is enough to maintain your progress and slowly build to new levels.

Another exercise craze gaining popularity that also translates well to equestrian fitness is barre—the serious core- and body-sculpting work previously reserved for

BUSTED! Myths of Location

MYTH: "If I just find the right gym, I'll have a place where I can go to really get in shape."

TRUTH: According to "Why Home Workouts Rock," an article on healthyroads.com, people who exercise at home stick to workout routines much better than those who visit gyms, and adults who work out at home are 32 percent more likely to follow an exercise program than those who used a fitness center. So not only can a home workout be much easier to fit into your day, it gets the job done. (Thank you, HealthyRoads! Goodbye, gym guilt!)

dancers. Pure Barre (purebarre.com) is the one I've tried; there are others, as well. This is extremely targeted work comprised of small movements that make huge differences in your body in short periods of time, including visible results in the first 10 classes, and results you can feel (once the searing soreness subsides) in the first couple of weeks. This is a pretty good place to tell you that when you start something new in the way of core exercise—especially something intense—it is in your best interest to go back several days in a row. (My instructor said to "gut it up" and do four classes in a row at first. She was right.) This is very hard to make yourself do, but it spreads the soreness out and prevents the dreaded (and down-right incapacitating) "second day soreness."

All three of these fitness "disciplines" are game-changers; in a perfect world we'd do them all. But if you have a real life (including a job, a family, and of course, horses!), finding the kind of time needed to get to any exercise class regularly can be difficult, if not impossible. And, if you're an all-or-nothing thinker (as I sometimes tend to be), a few missed classes can put any of these disciplines in the rearview mirror. I've come to the conclusion that just like with nutrition, the trick here is to establish your own "core practice" in whatever discipline seems to work best for you, do your utmost to get there as often as you can, and find simple ways and means to maintain your progress even during times when you *just can't.*

Exercise for the Body: Amp Up Your Stability in 10 Minutes a Day

When it comes to working on balance and stability, one of the most interesting pieces of exercise equipment I've run across is a BOSU ("Both Sides Utilized"), which is essentially an exercise ball, cut in half and mounted on a flat base (hence the term, "both sides"—you can stand on the "bubble side" or the "flat side," I'm really not sure which is worse). Just standing on the BOSU forces your body to call into action your core and stabilizing muscles; performing any number of simple exercises on it helps you develop them, and your balance, like nothing else (www.bosu.com).

According to Aussie author and healthy life mentor, Sally Symonds (www.an-eventful-life.com.au), the BOSU first came into vogue around 2000 and has gained great popularity for its bonus effect of strengthening the muscles of your core and improving coordination throughout your entire body. Just about any exercise that can be done on the ground can be maximized on a BOSU.

What is especially exciting to me about the BOSU is I can *always* find 10 minutes a day to do my basic workout (squats, crunches, and pushups—see p. 124), and by doing this work on that happy, half-bubble I love to hate, I can sneak in some core work, as well! No matter what else is going on in my life, that 10 minutes a day helps me make sure I stay fit to ride even during the busiest or most complicated seasons of my life. (So when the opportunity to ride does eventually arise, I'm ready to enjoy it!)

You can find all sorts of resources for good BOSU exercises and adaptations—from simple to scarily complex—online. Once you have mastered basic BOSU survival skills, however, I also want to direct you to Coach Daniel Stewart's 2-DVD rider fitness set (see sidebar, next page). Designed by Coach Stewart to teach anyone who rides horses how to treat and train herself like an equestrian athlete, his program uses the BOSU, along with a variety of other equipment and cross-training exercises geared toward improving your balance, suppleness, posture, stamina, and core-strength.

There are a lot of do's and don'ts for using a BOSU (they buck!), and while most of these rules are pretty much common sense, it pays to go slowly, be patient, and spend some time just learning to balance on the thing before you try actual exercises. It's also good to note that success in BOSU-related exercises lies in a *gradual* increase in your degree of difficulty. Be sure to do a 5- to 10-minute cardio warm-up and stretch to help prevent injury. It's best to perform each exercise first on the ground to make sure you understand it, then progress to the BOSU when you're sure you're ready for the ride.

BUILD STAMINA THAT WON'T QUIT

"You perform a triathlon every time you ride," says Coach Daniel Stewart. "Instead of swimming, biking, and running, you walk, trot, and canter!"

What I think Coach Stewart means by this sage bit o' wisdom is that when we ride, our effectiveness depends on our body's ability to tolerate and resist the different types of fatigue. When fatigue sets in, our posture changes, our muscles tighten as if to brace against it, our breathing changes, and at some point, our mental focus starts to fade, compromising our decision-making and cognitive functions including timing, judgment, and body awareness.

> Coach Daniel Stewart's *E3 Extreme Equestrian Exercises* 2-DVD set (www.stewartclinics.com).

RESOURCES

Coach Stewart identifies for us three types of stamina: muscular, cardiovascular, and psychological. "The good news is that an increase in one type of stamina nearly always causes an increase in the others," he says. "The not-so-good news is that to increase your stamina, you're going to have to do a little hard work."

• **Muscular stamina** refers to how long you can use your muscles and hold good posture and form before fatigue and muscle burn make this impossible. Improve muscular stamina with things like progressively longer/more intense rides, circuit training with light weights, and perhaps a barre class like I described on p. 126 (in which shaking muscles indicate complete fatigue and are the goal of each class—and this, the instructors always exclaim, means your muscles are getting longer and stronger).

• **Cardiovascular stamina** refers to how long your heart and lungs will supply fresh oxygen and blood to your brain and muscles without rest, and how quickly you can recover after a rest period. Build cardiovascular stamina by consistently pushing your body (gently!) past the point when you would normally stop. This is something Coach Stewart calls "progressive overload," which he says is well worth the hard physical work it entails. To avoid too much impact on my legs and joints, I like to mix up different sources of aerobic exercise each week, such as walking, rowing, jogging, and swimming.

• **Psychological stamina** describes how well you can keep your mind focused, even when your body starts feeling fatigued. To improve your psychological stamina, your task is to ensure that oxygen-rich blood gets to your brain in steady supply; do this by keeping your oxygen delivery system in tip-top shape. The cardio work helps with this, as does building muscular stamina. Another strange and delightful side effect of hot yoga, I've found, is that developing the ability to resist the urge to wipe sweat (or lie down on the mat and moan) and instead remain focused on correct form for each posture builds psychological strength that translates especially well to pushing through fatigue in the saddle. (You know...we're talking about ignoring sun, wind, and biting insects so you can finish a lesson with focus you never imagined possible.)

Exercise for the Body: Behold the Lowly Jump Rope

Traversing several sports and more trainers than I can count easily is a single piece of exercise equipment that is inexpensive, highly portable, and easy to use. *The jump rope.* It was while watching my 75-year-old Taekwondo Grandmaster do a jump-rope demo before a self-defense clinic audience of children and adults (and remembering how he starts every class and workout of his own with the ragged old jump rope that hangs on the wall beside his desk) that I realized the power and longevity of this simple practice he had kept all his life. If his stamina is any indicator I'd say we'd all best go get ourselves a jump rope and hop to it. Making a 3- to 5-minute jump-rope routine a part of our daily fitness regimen is one of those things we can definitely find time to do to warm up our muscles and build and maintain our base-level stamina without even thinking of it as "exercise."

What's more, the stamina, agility, and focus it takes to complete a good jump-rope conditioning routine takes this apparatus from child's play to serious contender.

Coach Daniel Stewart offers a great equestrian-specific jump-rope exercise called "Skip to the Trot," which he claims enhances our sense of rhythm, balance, breathing, body awareness, symmetry and mental focus: "While other aerobic activities—jogging, for example—help develop your stamina, they do very little to improve other areas a rider needs to work on," he writes.

If you haven't used one of these little dynamos since gym class, spend some time just playing around with a jump rope and getting your rhythm sorted out before attempting anything more complicated than simple "skipping" (and believe me, if you haven't done this for a while, simple skipping for 2 to 3 minutes is plenty complicated!). If you feel sassy, try hopping on one foot, then the other, then switching back and forth between them. Once you're pretty confident you have your "jump rope legs on," here's Coach Stewart's twist on this timeless classic:

1 Stand with your knees bent, kneecaps facing forward and down, putting your body in exactly the same position it's in when riding. Now, with your eyes focused forward, keeping your knees bent, skip rope normally. Once you can do that, instead of keeping your hips fixed in place, start opening and closing your hips in time with your footfalls, imitating exactly the motion of a posting trot. (I never said this would be easy.)

2 While "skipping to the trot" as described above, now concentrate on your breathing as you "post" rhythmically, keeping a rhythm similar to your horse's stride, eyes up, hips relaxed, absorbing shock with your calves. (Visualization really does help here. Once you get your rope swinging more or less automatically you can settle into your trot as if you really were riding around the arena!)

3 It is highly likely that in doing the above two steps you will drift around a bit. (I think I crossed several county lines.) We all have a dominant side, a stiffer side. (Hey! So do our horses!) And if you tend to ride too much forward or backward, you'll see evidence in the direction you move during this exercise. Using this as a bit of a diagnostic tool, Coach Stewart advises us to draw or mark a square on the ground and try to "skip to the trot" within its borders. (Again, easy to say, *hard* to do!) If and when you can keep your "pony" in the center of this square, work up to two minutes of skipping to the trot while holding your symmetry and balance without losing form.

4 Rest for one minute, and then try the same exercise (still posting and staying in the square) *on one foot for 45 seconds*. Now rest 30 seconds and try it on the other foot. Most likely, Coach Stewart says, you will have more trouble with one foot than the other. (It was very hard for me to tell which was worse; let's just say I could *almost* do it with my left foot. Looks like I'll be working on this for a while.) "If you can skip more easily on one side than the other, it may indicate a muscular or coordination imbalance between your right and left side." Coach Stewart advises us to "skip to the trot" three times a week to build stamina and correct our asymmetry problems.

INCREASE YOUR FLEXIBILITY TO FIND RHYTHM AND RELAXATION

Flexibility has earned its place in the rider fitness "Holy Trinity" for several reasons. First, a flexible body (and when I use the word "flexible" here, upon the recommendation of Coach Stewart, I mean it bends and moves easily and is supple) has elasticity that helps protect you against injury. Second, flexibility permits your body to move freely with your horse's in an uninhibited way. Finally, by achieving flexibility in your own body, you help your horse—he will mirror your suppleness, rather than your stiffness! In the short term, flexibility on horseback improves rhythm and relaxation. In the long run, you're going to be riding more relaxed, for longer periods of time, and for many years longer than you will without this crucial addition to your fitness regimen.

A good flexibility routine should include some basic daily stretching for all major muscle groups, plus specific stretches before and after every ride:

• **Before you ride,** a few targeted stretches help undo muscle tightness in your neck and back created by sitting at your desk, and tightness in your hamstrings and hip flexors caused by sitting for prolonged periods or driving. They also help decrease muscle stiffness and lengthen muscle tissue, protecting it from trauma and tearing.

• **After we ride,** stretching encourages hard working muscles to relax, improves blood circulation, and helps remove lactic acid to reduce soreness.

Emily J. Harrington, CPT, equestrienne fitness trainer, and multiple AQHA world champion and top-10 World Show finisher, writing for America's Horse Daily, offers stretching advice for equestrians. When we ride, she says, the body is out of its neutral alignment: The inner thigh muscles (adductors) are stretched. Hips and outer thighs are abducted and shortened. Pointing to the archetypical bow-legged old cowboy who has likely spent more time on the back of a horse than his own two feet, she adds, "Stretching the whole body after every ride will help the body recover to neutral position."

Warm Up FIRST

In my early years as a martial artist, we started stretching as soon as we arrived for class. Now as one of the older members of this same community, I realize the importance of doing some gentle warm-up before even starting to stretch. Breaking a sweat before I stretch is my key to good, deep, effective stretching, and ultimately, a good class.

Transferring that knowledge and experience to the riding arena, we have a dual responsibility there. Just as we are careful to warm up our horses' bodies before asking for serious work, we need to extend that same consideration to *our own* bodies! Remembering to treat ourselves as athletes, just as we do our horses, is key to making small modifications to our barn and riding routines that will protect and build our flexibility.

So, keeping in mind that warm muscles stretch more easily, a conscious effort to warm up our muscles will soon become habit if we tie it to things we are already doing. This needn't be anything elaborate: you can get the job done by walking to the barn or arena or pen at a faster pace, or by jogging in place for a few minutes when you first get out of the car, or making a point to groom your horse with a little more vigor. A Pilates instructor who also rides told me she ties certain warm-ups and stretches to her grooming, tacking up, and pre-riding routine: she "zips up" her abs (see p. 123) as she brushes her horse and picks out his feet; stretches her shoulders, chest, and back when she goes to get her tack from its locker; and stretches her hamstrings, quads, hips, and lower back after she returns her grooming box to its place and before leading her horse to the arena. She repeats this process, in reverse order, after her ride to hit the same muscle groups again, then follows with a few specific other stretches at bedtime (and, by the way, before she gets out of bed the next morning).

If we use her level of body awareness and care as our gold standard, any steps we can make in that direction will help us build routines that care for our flexibility. And even better, by making a point of paying attention to our muscles as we go about our regular pre- and post-ride chores, we can keep our bodies flexible and our muscles supple, without any extra "routine" at all!

Double Down Whenever You Can
Assuming you've achieved a level of fitness that allows it, several people I talked to extol the virtues of planning their rides as post-workout rewards. (If you're not there yet, it could be something to work toward!) Not only does this amplify the effects of both activities, but because warm muscles stretch easily, riding after a light workout can produce some surprising immediate results. And, when done consistently, this habit builds stamina (see p. 129 and Coach Stewart's explanation of "progressive overload" to use this strategy to gradually increase your stamina by tagging up workouts and riding). "There's nothing like riding your horse right after you've gone to the gym," says equestrian Monica Brant. "If you've never tried it, you might be surprised how much your horsemanship improves after a workout."

Michelle

"As a typical female, I have never really loved my body...Being on a horse is the one place I feel comfortable, confident, and capable—always have!"

"It's not the actual stretching that helps your horseback riding, but rather the long-term flexibility created by including stretching in your daily routine," says Katie Mital, BS, ACE, CPT/CES, a certified personal trainer from Bend, Oregon, in an article in *The Trail Rider* magazine. She adds that riders who don't stretch develop stiffness in their hips, hamstrings, chest, and shoulders due to maintaining a constant position in the saddle. The "heels down" position may stretch our calves, but the "closed" sitting position held for long periods of time by our knees and hips allows the muscles around these joints to become tight.

Remember These Stretchy How-Tos
When a 2004 Centers for Disease Control study concluded that athletes might benefit by participating in a warm-up that mimics the intended sport, we can only assume that Coach Daniel Stewart was nodding and grinning. He's been instructing his riders to always work their muscles with their body in the same position it's in when they ride for decades. It truly does make a difference that moves it to the top of the "work smarter, not harder" class of equestrian fitness advice. Here are a few more tips for getting the most from your stretching and flexibility routines:

Stretching Do's
• **Go with the flow.** We already know that breathing is important in our strength work, but it is equally important to learn how to breathe with your stretches for maximum effectiveness. Try to "flow" in and out of every stretch with focus on your breathing. Start the stretch with an in-breath and hold the stretch for a 10-to-15-second

out-breath. Repeat for a total of 30 to 60 seconds for each stretch. Never hold your breath. (If you find yourself holding your breath while stretching, you're probably also forcing the stretch. Stop both!)

• **Flirt with your edge.** I heard this in a yoga class once and it has stuck with me since. Of course we know not to stretch *past* the point of pain—or to hold a painful stretch. But there's a point in there somewhere that is just *at the edge* of where it hurts a little. When you find that edge, back off a tiny bit to the spot where it's not quite uncomfortable, but still fairly intense—that's where you want to hold the duration of your stretch. And remember, only *you* know where *your* edge is—and it can change from day to day. Listen to your body!

• **Respect the differences.** We can't all be ballerinas or gymnasts. Every body is different in its level of natural—or earned—flexibility, and every day is different in every body, as well! Things like fatigue, hydration, soreness, tension, stress, you name it, can affect how deeply we are able to stretch. The point is to find your edge with every stretch, every day, and work within that to get the best stretch you can for **that** muscle on *that* day. Just because you could put your palms on the floor yesterday and today you can barely touch your toes doesn't mean you need to push harder. As they tell us in yoga, "100 percent effort, done with correct form, gets 100 percent result," *regardless* of how deeply your body will go into a stretch or posture on any given day.

• **Take your time.** Once we get to the barn, we're all eager to ride. On busy days, it may be tempting to do a few quick stretches and call it good, or skip stretching altogether when you're really pressed for time. Don't. Taking this time for yourself and to prepare your muscles for your ride not only makes your ride go better, helps protect you from injury, and maintains an overall level of flexibility, but following your routine of deliberate stretching and breathing also puts an important pause in your routine to help clear your mind, amp up your awareness, and calm your emotions. So start slowly, hold those stretches and breathing for 10 to 15 seconds, relax, and repeat each stretch at least three times.

• **Think balance.** Not only should a good flexibility routine contain, over the course of each day, simple basic stretches targeting all the major muscle groups, as well as special stretches for "riding muscles," but we also must be sure to stretch (and work) opposing muscles in balanced pairs: chest and shoulders; back and abs; biceps and triceps; quads and hamstrings, calves and shins. This keeps one group from overpowering (and therefore shortening or weakening) the other. As we do this, we need to pay attention to our balance left to right: strive for equal flexibility on both sides of our bodies. If one hamstring is tighter than the other, for example, it may be at greater risk for injury; spend a little more time stretching and breathing into that tightness each day to build balanced flexibility over time.

• **Focus on what you're stretching.** This may sound funny, but when you visualize the muscle as you're stretching it (and you can find anatomy charts online if you're curious and want to be specific) and you "see it" in your mind's eye getting longer as you breathe and hold that stretch, it helps you create a deeper stretch. And, if you feel tightness approaching pain in a muscle as you stretch it (especially when you're hovering near that "edge" I talked about on p. 136), breathing into that tightness often encourages it to release. Slow, static stretches of low intensity and long duration are best for muscle lengthening; so if you have specific muscles you want to address, this kind of extra focus really pays off!

Stretching Don'ts

• **Don't bounce.** Bouncing can cause micro-trauma in the muscle, which must heal itself with scar tissue. The scar tissue tightens the muscle, making you less flexible and more prone to pain. Always stretch muscles slowly and with consistent tension.

• **Don't push.** Stretching is a gentle conditioning activity. Pushing too hard, doing too much too soon, rushing through your sequence, or trying to force a stretch (that is how I tore a hamstring not once, but twice!) defeats your purpose and invites (begs for!) injury.

- **Don't stretch a cold muscle.** Stretch during your warm-up, between activities or strength-training sets, and during your cool-down for maximum results.

- **Don't overstretch injured muscles.** It's tempting when you experience a slight pull to try to "stretch it out." I'm not sure if that's even possible, but I do know if you stretch a painful muscle too much you're going to make matters worse and do damage that will keep you out of action far longer than if you just call it a day, ice it, and come back and try again once it's better.

- **Don't push harder if you feel pain.** Really, this should go without saying, but if you do hurt yourself while stretching, stop right then and there and get some ice on it. Trainers generally agree that ice is the best thing for the first 48 hours (15 minutes at a time, every 2 to 3 hours, using ice bags, cold gel packs, or bags of frozen peas), then alternate ice and heat to restore blood flow and healing to the muscle.

- **Don't be afraid to ask questions.** While the Internet is fine and dandy for getting ideas and finding basic information about stretches and exercises, sometimes there is no substitute for a good, old-fashioned human being to answer your questions (and any questions your questions generate). Consult a sports medicine specialist, athletic trainer, physical therapist, or health-club advisor to improve your stretching technique and double-check your form to make sure you're getting that 100-percent reward for your efforts!

Exercise for the Body: Stretches for Equestrians

With contributing knowledge from Coach Daniel Stewart; Won Chik Park, 9th Degree Taekwondo Grandmaster; Robin J. Levine's article "Flexibility Training for the Rider" (ratemyhorsepro.com); and Monica Brant's "Stretching for Better Horsemanship, Part 2" (*America's Horse,* January 2015), here is a general stretch routine for all us horse gals.

• **Chest stretch.** For upper-body work, always stand with your feet shoulder-width apart and your knees slightly bent. Standing up straight, place your hands gently on your head, elbows bent and out to the sides, upper arms parallel with the ground (as if you're going to do a sit-up or crunch), and press forward with your chest as you pull both elbows back.

• **Shoulder stretch.** Bring one arm across your chest and use your other arm to gently push that elbow toward your body. Breathe. Repeat for the other side.

• **Chest and shoulder combined stretch.** Standing in a doorway, raise one arm straight up over your head and place the back of it against the the top of the doorway. Press your body forward to feel the stretch in your arm, chest, and shoulder. Switch sides and repeat. Alternatively, stand with your back to a fence or rail, grab the top of the rail behind you with both hands, and lean forward, bringing your shoulder blades together on your back to open up your chest. Hold and breathe.

• **Back stretch.** Lying on your back on the floor, bend both knees and bring them up to your chest, wrapping your arms gently around them as far as they will go. Pull gently until you feel a stretch through your back. Hold and breathe.

• **Bicep stretch.** Reach both arms behind you, thumbs turned out, until you feel a slight stretch in the front of your upper arms; intensify this stretch by trying to clasp your hands behind your back.

• **Triceps stretch.** Bend one arm and grab the elbow with your opposite hand, gently pulling the elbow up beside your ear (on the same side). Allow the palm of the hand on the arm you're stretching to rest on the back of your shoulder as you stretch.

• **Forearm stretch.** With one arm outstretched in front of you, use your other hand to gently pull back on your fingertips as you push outwardly with the heel of your palm. Then flex the hand of the arm you're stretching down so your fingertips point to the ground, and use your opposite hand to put gentle pressure on the back of that hand, pushing it toward your body.

• **Quadriceps stretch.** Standing on one leg (hold onto something if you need to!), bend the other leg at the knee, and with your same-side hand, grab that foot and pull it toward your buttocks. When your foot reaches your buttocks, hold it there and push the bent knee backward until you feel a good stretch up and down the front of your thigh.

• **Hamstring stretch.** Stand up straight, "zip up your core," then bend forward, reaching toward your toes with your legs straight. Just let your fingers dangle wherever they stop, and keep breathing and gently reaching for your toes as your hamstrings release. Now "roll" back up, using your core muscles, until you're standing straight again (this protects your back and sneaks in a little extra core work). Next, cross one foot in front of the other, "zip up," and bend forward again, reaching for your toes. Switch feet and repeat.

• **Calf stretch.** Stand with your hands on a wall or fence post for support, extending one leg behind you. Stretch the heel of the extended leg to the ground as you push forward on the wall or post. Breathe into the stretch. Switch legs and repeat.

• **Shin stretch.** Sit with your legs parallel and straight out in front of you. Reach for the tops of your toes and grab them if you can, gently pulling your feet back toward your body. To intensify this stretch, see if you can lift your heels off the ground. Breathe and repeat.

• **Gluteal stretch.** Lie on your back on the floor and bend one leg at the knee, with your other leg extended straight in front of you, its foot flexed and its heel on the ground. Use your hands to gently pull your bent knee toward your chest as far as it will go. Hold it there and breathe. Intensify the stretch by trying to bring your knee to your same-side shoulder. Switch legs and repeat.

• **Abductor (outer hip muscle) stretch.** Lie on your side on the floor, with your legs bent, one stacked on top of the other. Lift your top leg in an "opening" motion, moving the top knee away from the bottom knee while keeping your feet together. Hold the top leg as far "open" as you comfortably can and breathe. Lower and repeat two more times, then switch sides.

• **Adductor (inside of thigh) stretch.** Sitting on the floor, bend your knees and bring the soles of your feet together (martial artists call this the "butterfly stretch"). Press your thighs down toward the floor (use your hands to intensify the stretch). Hold, breathe, and repeat.

• **Abdominal (core) stretch.** Lie on your back with your arms extended down by your sides. Arch your back gently to lift your chest up off floor until you feel a nice stretch all along your abdominal wall. Be careful not to over-arch or tilt your head too far back—you don't want to put pressure on your neck.

• **Hip stretches.** Opening up your hips is one of the most important things you can do pre-ride. Sit in a chair (or on the ground with your legs stretched out in front of you), and rest one ankle on the opposite knee. Use your same-side palm to press your bent knee toward the ground. Stop when you feel a good stretch in your hips and breathe. Repeat three times and switch sides.

• **Leg swings.** This is a perfect pre-ride stretch because it is wonderful for loosening and getting good movement and circulation in your glutes, core, abductors, adductors, hips, hip flexors, and the often tight ilotibial (IT) bands that run down the outsides of your legs. Stand beside the arena or paddock fence with your feet parallel, holding onto the rail with the hand closest to it. Plant the heel of your outside foot (the one furthest away from the fence), and swing the leg closest to the fence forward and backward in a straight line, as high as is comfortable, 20 to 30 times. Then face the other way and switch legs. Next turn and face the fence, holding on to it with both hands as you swing one leg side to side in front of you, as high as is comfortable, 20 to 30 times, and then switch legs.

OR TRY A COMBO PLATTER

So…what if you don't have time to do the "ideal" number of separate workouts for the Holy Trinity of strength, stamina, and flexibility? What if your weeks are, like mine, a running challenge to get people and animals fed, make clean clothes happen, and maintain a reasonably dirt- and disease-free home—not to mention meeting work deadlines, tending to barn and horse chores, spending some riding time, and paying at least a minimum of attention to personal needs (dentist, anyone?). Oh yes, and then there are the urgencies of life that won't wait, like birthdays, car trouble, paying bills (not that those things are at all similar, I was just thinking about last week). When in the *real* world do we have time to do what it takes to rebuild our frames? If you, like me, look for places to double up (and double down on results), this could be as good a solution for you as it is for me.

The answer Dara Torres discovered and relates in her latest book *Gold Medal Fitness* is a form of resistance stretching called Ki-Hara, which she credits with maximizing her workouts and making a huge difference in her overall physique. Ki-Hara is a form of combined flexibility, strength training, and core work refined by Steven Sierra and Anne Tierney of Innovative Body Solutions (www.ki-hara.com). The gist of it is moving your arms and legs in specific rotational and diagonal patterns to continually engage your core muscles and gain strength and flexibility in all ranges of motion.

Torres explains that Ki-Hara teaches the body how to contract its muscles *while* they're being stretched and strengthened ("eccentrically") and while engaging and energizing the core ("concentrically") in ways that are most effective for strengthening and preventing injury. "Ki-Hara trains muscles in the way they are used most frequently," she adds. "This strengthens the body dynamically."

The object of this kind of stretching is "taking a muscle from its shortest position to its longest position, while continually resisting (contracting) the muscle." Also known as the *e-centric pause* of strength training. (Remember how Coach Daniel Stewart told about the *contraction phase* and the *elongation phase* of strength training? If not, see p. 122.) Resistance stretching asks you to oppose elongation throughout the entire range of motion to build muscles that are longer, stronger, and more flexible.

Dara Torres' *Gold Medal Fitness* (Crown Archetype, 2010).

Building on what she learned from her Ki-Hara work, Torres created one of the simplest tools I've run across for dealing with painful muscle tension and working on overall muscle flexibility and strength. The *Resistance Stretching with Dara Torres* DVD (look for it on the Ki-Hara website) requires no equipment and allows you to start wherever you are and progress at your own rate. While this DVD is not specific to riding and riding muscles, it does target common back and hip tightness and inflexibility. Its aim is to build strength and balance, while protecting from injury by locating and releasing areas of muscle tension while realigning the body.

EASY DOES IT

With a nod to our Holy Trinity of Fitness (strength, stamina, and flexibility), Coach Daniel Stewart advises us to consider what kind of work we each need to do *in each area* to fit our body type, activity level, and personal riding goals. Instead of the "great guns" approach (which has shot me out of the "new exercise program" saddle more than once), Coach Stewart advises moderate progress forward, beginning wherever you are *right now* and building, *one step at a time,* on whatever you've already got going for you.

"Try to find a few sneaky ways to increase your activity (in all three areas of the "Trinity") until you get to the next level," he advises. Adding simple things like an extra ride each week or a couple of targeted, rider-specific exercises each day will likely do the trick.

Coach Stewart also advises us to go at this with lighthearted focus, intent on adding (and ultimately maybe subtracting) "just a little here and a little there" until you find your body conditioning (and body image) improving, almost as if on its own. By making small, deliberate, and consistent choices across all three areas—varying your activities to keep it interesting and giving your body whatever rest and recovery time it needs—you will not only make the fitness gains you're looking for, but you'll create the lifestyle tweaks that will naturally maintain these changes.

And of course, before starting any new workout routine, be sure to check with your doctor to discuss the best exercises for your specific needs. It also goes without saying (but I'm going to say it anyway) that if you buy exercise equipment, read the instructions and learn to use it safely and correctly. A barrel racer I know required stitches after an unplanned dismount from a foul-tempered exercise ball. (It wasn't pretty, let me assure you.)

Make a Plan You'll Really Follow

"I believe that you, too, can achieve optimal fitness if you make getting and staying in shape a priority," Dara Torres says in *Gold Medal Fitness*. "Adapt your workout routine to your body's ever-changing needs; approach working out as an integral part of taking care of yourself; and then go for it."

Torres would probably be the first to tell us that juggling work, home, and training priorities (and we can plug "horse" somewhere in there) is always going to be a strain on our time and imagination. It is all relative. Busy is busy. No matter who you are, or at what level you work or play, there are only 24 hours in each and every day. "Gold Medal Fitness," Torres says, "is within reach for all of us, regardless of our age, shape, weight, or long list of responsibilities. But," she adds, echoing what instructor Wendy Murdoch observed about that moment of commitment (the "power why"—see p. 98), "you've got to *want* it."

Okay, enough talk. It's time to lace up those sneakers for some off-horse work. (Does anyone else hear the theme song from *Rocky* starting?) For a quick snapshot of workout planning that really works, I bow to Torres' advice. In *Gold Medal Fitness* she says to think not in *days*, but in *weeks*. By setting up your plan at the beginning of each week, and tailoring it to whatever time you'll have available *that particular* week, you can get your already full hands on long-term training success. When you try to "find time" or rearrange your life on a day-to-day basis—or when you set up unrealistic "routines" that look too far ahead, you're asking for trouble.

TAKE IT A WEEK AT A TIME

At the start of each workout week, set aside a little time with your calendar and ask yourself:

• What's on my calendar at work this week?

• What's on my family/social calendar?

• What are my riding/horse-chore commitments? (Time promised to our horses counts too!)

• What time do I want to be in bed each night?

• How early can I get up each morning?

• Are there any "holes" in the middles of my days when I could fit in a quick workout?

Depending on what kind of calendaring solution you live by, block off the time that's already spoken for and highlight the spaces available for exercise. Now you're ready to plan your workout week. Treat these as *serious appointments* and don't reschedule or cancel for anything short of *true* emergency. (This will probably

BUSTED! Myths of Our Own Making

MYTH: "No matter how much weight I lose, when I look in the mirror, all I see are 'thunder thighs.'"

TRUTH: In addition to the myths that we hear from others, there are still other, more "personal" kinds of myths we either made up for ourselves at some point in our lives or they came to us from critical others (see Jenni's story on p. 27). These may be things that are true about our bodies, but we find them unacceptable. Or, they may be completely *untrue*, except in our own perceptions. But let's face it, true or not, our body perceptions are our realities, no matter what others—or sometimes even the mirror—may tell us otherwise.

In its extreme, this kind of personal mythology is part of the body image battle that involves eating disorders—think of the nearly skeletal young girl who looks in the mirror and still sees "fat" thighs. In its mildest form, our personal mythology about our bodies just haunts us and steals our peace with who we are. I know a little something

about both ends of the spectrum and have seen and heard it plenty about it in those I have spoken to in the process of researching this book.

I reached my adult height and weight during the sixth or seventh grade. With my body image's formative years spent towering over the other girls (and most of the boys), I always felt much larger than I actually was. I've always been solidly built—born with a sturdy mesomorph frame that naturally carries more muscle; my prepubescent weight never played nice with the nurse's office height/weight chart. My worse dread was being weighed at school and realizing how much heavier I was than most of my friends, many of whom happened to be of much slighter build. I also hated it in the doctor's office, where my height and weight was more often than not off the charts.

When I compared myself to the other kids my age, I felt gigantic. I wasn't, but that feeling made me self-conscious about my body, sometimes to the point of keeping me from doing things I wanted to do (like wearing shorts and going to swimming parties). I played competitive tennis from the time I was about 11, and my love and passion for the game compelled me to be fit and strong. Fortunately for me, in addition to Chrissie Evert and Evonne Goolagong, the female tennis heroes of that day were also Billie Jean King and Martina Navratilova. While I still wished for the lightness and the long, lean physique of the first two, I accepted that my "thunder thighs" and "Amazon shoulders" equipped me for a strong, serve-and-volley game, which was a new thing for female tennis players in the seventies. It was a begrudging appreciation, but at least while on the courts, my body was just fine.

Fast-forward a few decades when an illness at last allowed me to drop the extra weight that plagued me. I was *at last* happy with my body. My family told me I looked awful, but seeing my ribcage and hipbones so clearly was my own private joy. Here's the weird part, though. While objectively, I realized the size-4 clothes I wore verified my body nirvana, I didn't *feel* any different.

And weirder still, when I looked in the mirror—or caught sight of myself in a reflection—I still saw the "chunky" athlete!

It was then I realized the power of the mind over self-perception. It was a glimpse of what that skeletal anorexic girl experiences with her own mirror, and I am thankful, both that I didn't slip down that slope *and* that I experienced that body image distortion firsthand. Now, bringing all my own experiences with body image desperation and distortion, along with my lingering body angst, into the horse world, I can truly see how damaging this negative personal body mythology can be.

One of the most troubling things about buying into our own personal body mythology, in my opinion, is the cycle it sets off in our heads that can actually make these misperceptions into self-fulfilling prophesies. Looking back at pictures of myself during the time of my life when my own mind was telling me I was Amazonian, it's easy to see the truth. I wasn't big *or* fat. I was very, very average, especially as an adult. Nevertheless, because *(continued)*

Myths of Our Own Making, cont.

my mind attached itself early-on to my misperceived enormity (played against a societal obsession with thinness that blossomed at about the same time as my body anxieties), it was "game on" for the succession of self-loathing, yo-yo dieting, and actual weight gain that perpetuated the problem.

Coach Daniel Stewart refers to this mental phenomenon as "confirmation bias," which he defines as when you "purposely try to confirm your negative biased opinion by recalling negative things that can prove it." The real problem with confirmation bias, he adds, is that if you convince yourself you're unworthy, you might unintentionally give less than 100 percent because you feel it won't make a difference. "In the end, your bias might just get confirmed," Coach Stewart says, "not because it's true, but because you made it happen by not giving your all."

The sad thing about this is it doesn't have to happen. It's not based on truth, but rather, on something we, for some reason, decide to tell ourselves "is how it is."

take some mental retraining, which we'll get to later, but for now let's get your planning process in place.)

Get a good idea of which exercises you're going to start with in each category, remembering the Holy Trinity of Strength, Stamina, and Flexibility. Time each "appointment" so you know for sure how long each kind of training in your workout schedule takes going forward. While you may not have enough time every single week for everything you want to do, just do the best you can to keep your Holy Trinity balanced.

And another thing: Torres emphasizes the importance of giving yourself at least one day, and preferably two, each week for *complete rest*. Not only is this time to let your muscles recover and repair, but rest days are perfect opportunities to recharge your mental batteries, spend time with family and friends, and hang out with your horse.

Exercise for the Brain: Power Up Your Weekly Conditioning Calendar

I've played around with lots of workout tracking and scheduling methods (including all the mental ones that NEVER materialize) and here's my hands-down favorite. I do all my workout planning on Sunday evenings, and while I'm scheduling my conditioning time, I am sure to block off my horse or barn time (and all the other major commitments in my life, as well). In later sections of this book, we'll get into some other routines and practices you may want to add to this calendaring mix, particularly in the area of mindfulness. As you make a bigger commitment to taking care of yourself, this strategy will be your lifeline to a new, more balanced reality.

1 **Enable Google or Sunrise calendar.** Install the app on your smartphone and bookmark it on your desktop. (I love the Google calendar best, but both work across devices.)

2 **Work first from your desktop.** On whatever day you set for your planning each week (as mentioned, I do mine on Sunday nights), click on Google calendar on your computer. Customize your view, depending on how your mind works best. Once your calendar is formatted, you can access it from any device.

3 **Set your workouts as "appointments."** Look at the week ahead. Which days and times offer your best opportunity for conditioning work? Mark these as appointments and plan to keep them. Your goal is to have at least three sessions (and, for you overachievers, no more than five without rest).

4 **Schedule your rest days.** At least one day after three or four consecutive days and at least two days' rest after any stretch of five consecutive workout days.

5 Color code your workout "appointments." This will give you an overall visual of your balance of the "Holy Trinity." I used yellow for stamina, red for strength, purple for flexibility, and turquoise for rest. See more ideas about this below.

6 Add attachments. This button on Google calendar gives you a place to save (and find quickly when needed) lists of exercises, an exercise log, pictures of stretches, ideas for sequences, or other materials you find to help you learn or refine a workout.

7 Find time. This might be my favorite button on the Google calendar. Just like having a personal assistant, when you're looking down the barrel of a horrendous week, you can ask it to "find time" in your schedule for a workout. Amazingly, it usually can!

8 Add notes. Keep track of how things are going, journal about progress, and highlight things you want to remember or explore more deeply.

9 Drag and drop. Things change and sometimes we have to adjust our lives. The drag-and-drop feature makes this easy, too. Just move the pieces of your life around as needed to fit and fill the frame of every week. The key to making it all happen is getting the pieces in there in the first place!

A quick note for the technology-impaired or -resistant: If you'd rather saw off a body part than boot up a computer, this concept works just as well with a regular calendar or a plain sheet of paper with the days of the week listed in columns as shown below. Get yourself a colorful set of highlighters and color code your weeks in exactly the same way for exactly the same visual report card of how well you've balanced your conditioning—and your life!

In her 2014 Huffington Post article, "Color Coding Your Life," Lori Stevic-Rust, Ph.D. ABPP, puts profound wisdom behind the idea of color coding as a serious tool we can use to create and maintain the coveted work/life balance. If you (like me) have worn out reams of not-quite-useful strategies on an epic search for this kind of overall balance, take hope. Stevic-Rust's explanation of how she uses electronic calendaring technology to capture, sort, and nail down what's truly important (using color codes for *everything*), just may set us all free.

"True balance doesn't really exist but establishing priorities and maintaining a commitment to them does," Stevic-Rust says. Clarifying that this kind of balance also does not demand "equal to" or "the same," but instead refers more to a feeling of contentment and satisfaction, she compares a color-balanced calendar to the healthy balance of colorful foods we are encouraged to load onto our plates and into our shopping carts to ensure optimum health. "Perhaps our mental health requires a colorful calendar as well," she quips. "Color coding my life has been a guide to keeping me balanced and mindful. Envision what you want, see your balance and push forward with better focus."

To color code items you've already entered in your Google calendar, just click edit and your color choices will appear! (Or, if you're going old school, assign a colored pen, pencil, or highlighter for each activity. I've used shades of gray below.)

Sunday	Monday	Tuesday	Wednesday	Thursday	Friday	Saturday
FLEXIBILITY: Yoga	STRENGTH: Weights	STAMINA: Elliptical	REST: Guided Meditation	FLEXIBILITY: Yoga	STRENGTH: PureBarre	STAMINA: Walk
FLEXIBILITY: Yoga	REST: Guided Meditation	STRENGTH: Weights	STAMINA: Cardio Mix	FLEXIBILITY: Yoga	STRENGTH: PureBarre	REST: Guided Meditation
FLEXIBILITY: Yoga	STRENGTH: Weights	STAMINA: Elliptical	FLEXIBILITY: yoga	STRENGTH: PureBarre	REST: Guided Meditation	REST: Guided Meditation
FLEXIBILITY: Yoga	STRENGTH: Weights	STAMINA: Elliptical	REST: Guided Meditation	FLEXIBILITY: Yoga	STRENGTH: PureBarre	STAMINA: Walk

• Use the **category** button to assign a name to a color, and then color code: strength, stamina, flexibility, and rest activities entered on your calendar.

• Next, assign a name and color for the *other* parts of your life with which your conditioning routines will have to peacefully coexist: work, home/family, horse time, friends/social life, volunteer work, personal business, health and mainte-nance appointments, and so on.

• Designate a bright color for contemplative work (you'll learn more about what this means in pages to come), reserving time for things like journaling, meditation or prayer, mindful walking, and working with affirmations. These will show up as colorful little slivers, regularly and evenly scattered throughout your week.

Your color code planning tool will help you work both forward and backward—forward as you look at your weeks in advance to make proactive decisions about how you will be spending your time, and then back over past weeks and months in regular and deliberate reviews to gain and maintain a clear and colorful snapshot of how well you've been able to set limits and stick to your true priorities. (Your friends and family will soon learn the meaning of, "Sorry, I already have too much green this week," and "I really have to honor my orange this week because it's been missing for the past few." You may initially get some ribbing on this, but once people start seeing your life transform, they'll be getting their color on, too!)

Whether you're using a smartphone, a desk- or laptop, or a pencil and paper, the only hard-and-fast rule here, my experts agree, is to *find the recording method that works for you, write down your workouts a week at a time, and then* **do** *what you've planned.* According to the *Journal of American Medicine*, people who write down their workouts (and track what they eat—see our discussion of nutrition on p. 102) have a 50 percent higher success rate in terms of sticking to their program and getting the results they are after.

THINKING IN BLOCKS

I've always heard six weeks is the ideal stretch for following a single workout, but in her book Torres says five—and seeing as she's the Olympic Champion, let's humor her.

There is a progression most bodies go through when getting used to working out regularly. When I first started hot yoga, one of the instructors there had it nailed *to the day* what each of the first 10 days would feel like, and that there would be a slight "bump" in my weight (not cool!) after about two weeks of work. Then after that, he assured me, with regular class attendance, plenty of water, and a clean diet, the weight would start coming off very quickly. He was right (including the, "Why in the world am I *doing* this to myself?" whine on Day Seven). And sure enough, every time I've been away from hot yoga for a while, the first 10 days back pretty much follow that progression whether it's been a few weeks, a few months, or a few years. (Sadly, I've not yet learned the obvious lesson here.) Similarly, Torres says the "break-in period" for her program (and I'm willing to bet this goes for most any integrated "framework" program) follows a fairly predictable pattern:

• **Week One** is always the toughest. It's all about getting used to the movements themselves and the new level of activity. *Key Strategy:* Be good to yourself and your sore muscles, stay hydrated, get plenty of rest, and soak in a tub with Epsom salts post-workout. It really does help. Oh, and remember that this part won't last forever. Week One is also the time when you're most prone to injury, so pay special attention to warming up, listening to your body, and making sure you've got your form and alignment right on every exercise or stretch you include. (I maintain that everything in the world is on YouTube, so if you really need to check your form, Google it!)

• **Weeks Two and Three** are about building strength and refining your techniques, schedule, and routines. This is also a time for getting inside your head and telling yourself to feel really good about what you're doing for yourself—and your riding. (More about this mental game in coming chapters.) *Key Strategy:* One of my yoga instructors likes to describe this "break-in" period as "opening your body's checking account" into which each workout is a deposit, and everything else you do (including riding!) is a withdrawal. This thinking really helps me keep the pressure on to stay "in the black"!

• **Weeks Four and Five** are similar to Week One in terms of difficulty, but for a different reason. By now you're really, really tired. A good tired. A you-earned-it tired. But exhausted, nevertheless. The perk here is that you begin to see and feel results: You feel stronger and straighter and more agile, and you'll find you have more staying power and shorter recovery times. *Key strategy:* Go a little easier, work a little bit under your maximums and be kind to yourself. This may also be a time of thinking you can maybe miss a workout here and there. *Don't.* It is a slippery slope where one missed workout turns into three. And one skipped workout week turns into a few. Before you know it, you're back on the sofa eating Cheetos and wondering why you feel so sluggish, why your horse isn't going for you as well as he was, and why riding is suddenly less fun. Be on guard for this overwhelming urge to slack off, and squash it with your unflappable, newfound, color-coded determinations.

Move to a New State—of Being

As you move through this process of transitioning to a new lifestyle of clean eating and deliberate "framework" that will keep you riding well at any weight, it's important to record whatever milestones are important to your journey. By *recognizing* and *affirming* your milestones, turning points, and big moments along the way, you'll continue to build on your successes. Acknowledge each accomplishment as a reward you've earned fair and square. As the weeks progress, you'll begin to notice that you feel better—and ride better. You'll stand up straighter on the ground and sit up straighter in the saddle. You'll move more deliberately, feel more assurance, and exude the confidence that signals clear connection to an inner power source. This is the mind-body bond we can all benefit from, whatever our weight, and as it becomes our new *state of being*, we'll find ourselves well beyond any borders where scales, mirrors, and supermodels rule.

#Hoofpicks

In this chapter we explored the concept that diet is not about deprivation. It is about giving your body healthy fuel to burn. This will help you in your work with horses by providing the energy to pursue the "Holy Trinity of Fitness," while adding enjoyment and endurance to your riding time, with less risk of injury. This approach is a new and different game-changer in the battle against negative body image because it emphasizes *fitness* over size.

Your Chapter 6 **#Hoofpicks** include:

1 **Try something new to improve your conditioning every week.** Maybe it's an extra ride to soak up a beautiful day. Maybe it's one of those targeted, rider-specific exercises you usually just read or watch the video about. Just one new thing to try each week (if you like it, you can add it more often!) can get you to the next level.

2 **Take a new picture.** By looking at your body differently—and appreciating your body type for its potential advantages—you can shape your nutrition and fitness routines to bring out that potential. Learning and accepting what is and is not possible, doable, or even good for your body will make a big difference in how you measure success.

3 **Make plans you can really follow.** Most people have really good intentions when it comes to eating healthier, exercising better, and doing both more regularly. What separates the warrior women from the whiny girls is the ability to calm down about all this, focus on a few things you *can* and *will* do, and put them on the calendar like a dentist appointment, each and every week.

4 It's a moving target. In today's world—and especially if you're trying to squeeze horse time into an already over-packed schedule—finding time to exercise is tricky at best. The key to success here is realizing that each week may require a completely new plan. Sit down and schedule your calendar at the same time every week (only you know when that is), picking from your menu of favorite (doable) activities within the "Holy Trinity," and stick to that plan like glue. The next week can be different, but by going one week at a time, one workout at a time, you'll climb out of the procrastinators' pit and into the winner's circle.

7 | Unpack Your Biomechanics

Close your eyes right now and imagine your perfect ride. Whether it's the ultimate reining pattern, the flawless dressage test, the clean course, or the winning time, I can bet on one thing: It's *effortless*, right?

It may also be in slow motion, brimming with joy and eliciting a rush of euphoria unlike anything else. What would it take to *really* ride like that? How can we move beyond any concerns we have about how we look or what we weigh or whether or not our breeches are too tight and just *get that feeling*?

That vision is attainable for all of us, and this is where we start unpacking the rest of how we "get there" from wherever we happen to be right now. So far on this journey together, we've trudged through the technicalities: We're on the right horses, we have the right saddles, we've cleaned up our nutrition, and we're renovating our "framework." (Or not. You may still be just thinking about all that.) What we do from here on out is going to be key to *unlocking the joy* we've been yearning for: that "perfect ride" feeling that, right now, seems just beyond our grasp.

"Rider biomechanics," explains Coach Daniel Stewart in his book, *Ride Right with Daniel Stewart*, "is a term used to describe the way in which *your body* functions and interacts with the *body of your horse*." Put simply, it's learning to move with your horse.

And on the converse, Coach Stewart says that any "biomechanical imperfection" we as riders may have will likely be mirrored in how our horses move. "It's impossible for a horse to be balanced and symmetrical if you're not," he explains. "And one imperfection always leads to another."

Now, these "imperfections" may not be as big as we imagine our thighs to be.

In fact, they may be so small that we've already dismissed them as trivial. But little things like how well and when (and whether!) we breathe makes a big difference in how the horse moves. In fact, each detail of our body's position and function (whether we realize it or not) is connected to many others. With the help of our experts, we'll explore the ins and outs of how you hold your head; the position and shape of your lower back; and even how your toes can affect the "big picture" of flexibility, alignment, and fluidity of motion.

Sit deep and settle in—this is a dense, winding part of the trail, and it offers to take you to a new place in your experience with horses.

A Shared Balance

"Horseback riding is the only sport I know of where one species sits on another," says Susan Harris. She helped clarify for me what "balance" in the saddle really means.

"When we ride," she explains, "we're actually trying to *share* balance with our horse. That means we have to get *our* balance centered with the *horse's* balance." (And all this time I thought it was all about me.) Harris says that finding this place of *mutual balance* calls into play the four basic requirements of any seat—English, Western, and all points in between:

1 **The rider has to feel safe and secure.** This is "thing one" for a reason, Harris says. "We have to be in balance or we *won't* feel safe *or* secure. And if you're not in a position that feels safe and secure," she adds, pausing for effect, "you can't think of *anything* else." (Isn't that the truth? Raise your hand if you've been there! My hand's *way* up.)

To feel safe and secure in the saddle at any gait (and any weight), Harris says there are three very important things to remember:

• Let your legs "hang," rather than "hang on with your legs."

- Breathe properly.

- Make sure your body feels balanced and centered (see p. 158) *before* going faster.

2 The rider must be able to communicate with her horse. This involves your seat, legs, hands, and reins. "Sometimes we think of this as 'control,'" Harris says, "but it's really more about being clear; more of saying, 'Will you please do this for me? You're trained for this!' than 'Don't you dare!'"

3 There must be cooperation between horse and rider. Harris classifies as accidental "those things we unintentionally do to our horses that hurt, confuse, or upset them." (Sheepishly raise your hand if you think you might have ever been guilty of this...yeah, me too.) Harris likens this "accidental abuse" to a toddler riding on a parent's shoulders in which the happy tyke is thrashing around, kicking, squealing, and having a grand time, completely unaware that she's pounding Mom in the face. "She loves you and has no idea she's hurting you," Harris explains, "she's just oblivious. We want to make sure we ride in a way that is *not* oblivious. We want to be kind and considerate of the horse. The better we ride, the less 'accidental abuse' will happen."

4 There must be unity. This, Harris says, is what brings it all together. "Whether you're walking, posting a trot, or cantering through a field of daisies, you and the horse are moving as one when *your balance* and *your horse's balance* are connected. It's the ultimate," she says, the excitement in her voice rising as she describes the feeling. "It's the thing that keeps us working at it—and the thing that makes me want to keep riding until I'm 95."

Here's the catch. "You can't have Number 4 until you have Numbers 1 through 3," Harris says. "It's progressive *and* cumulative." But what about that question you're begging me to answer? Is this euphoria reserved only for those who have reached their ideal shape and size?

Nada and nope.

"Mutual balance has nothing to do with your size or shape," Harris says. "It's all about how well you get together with your horse. There are a lot of riders with a lot of different shapes, and instructors need to always look at their *ability* rather than their *disability.*"

For example, she says, if a larger rider has a "pear shape," that means she has a low center of gravity and will be able to sit nice and deep in the saddle. (Remember Coach Daniel Stewart's Anglo-Arabian body type? See p. 96.) For

BUSTED!

Myths of Maximum Impact

MYTH: "My boobs are too big for me to ride well."

TRUTH: The upper-body ballast issue, for women, is one of those sensitive subjects that garners instant recognition among anyone chest-endowed who has ever sat a trot.

In the November 2011 edition of *USDF Connection,* the official magazine of the United States Dressage Federation, Susan Hoffman Peacock explored this top-heavy issue in her article, "Less Bounce to the Ounce," which offered up some useful insights we can all take shopping. Not only does finding the right sports bra, as Peacock puts it, "quell the bounce" (as well as

doing away with other common sources of discomfort including chafing, digging, pinching, and other atrocities) but what most female riders don't realize is how much excessive bounce can affect not only their own balance, but also their horse's.

I know it's hard to imagine how bouncing boobs can throw a 1,000-pound animal off balance, but hear this out: Quoting a University of California at Berkeley newsletter, Peacock points out that when riding, our bosoms do a whole lot more than move up and down. They move front to back, side to side, and in one study involving a DD cup size, researchers measured more than 8 inches of vertical movement every rider of every shape, size, and body type, Harris urges us, and our instructors, to *always* ask, "What *can* we do?" rather than focusing on what's difficult or (currently) out of reach.

"IT'S A FUNCTION THING"

When it comes to finding unflappable balance on the back of a horse, Wendy Murdoch agrees "there's a 'spot' you're looking for—you're either there or you're

while the subject was running (I *don't* want to know how they measured that!). Now think about your horse and how he's affected by the slightest shift of your weight in the saddle, and you can begin to see how a big bosom has a say when it comes to the issue of balance.

Not only does all that motion cause a lot of wear and tear on our bodies; the *weight* of large breasts also plays havoc with our posture and creates strain and unconscious bracing throughout our upper torso. This constant source of muscle fatigue makes any sort of fluid movement in our upper body next to impossible.

So what's the answer?

First, find a sports bra that fits, bra-fitting experts agree, and find a retailer accustomed to fitting larger bra sizes for high impact sports. Regardless of whether you think this is a concern, it's still a good idea to make a well-fitted sports bra a priority, and to keep this unsung and vital piece of riding equipment in good repair. (Or, as the sign on the dressing room wall at one sporting goods retailer reminds us, "No sports bra should ever celebrate a birthday." This might be a bit extreme, but you get the idea.) Check out: Titlenine.com, Roadrunnersports.com, Seejanerun.com, and Herroom.com.

"It's not an attractive sight when a rider's chest bounce grabs more attention than her horse's movement," Peacock observes. "When it comes to riding, support might not be beautiful, but being *supported* is."

not there—and it doesn't matter if you're heavy or if you're light, the spot is pretty much the same."

Murdoch, who makes her living acquainting riders with their balance, says that as long as your horse is suitable and you ride in this spot where you're most secure and balanced, then, "Ride, baby, ride!"

"This is not a weight thing," she adds. "It's a function thing. When it comes to balance, it doesn't really matter what *weight* you are. And while a rider who was thin when she first learned to ride and later got heavy may have to relocate where that 'spot' of balance actually is, it really isn't the added weight that's the issue as much as balance. And, if you've always been heavy you just don't have that other awareness."

Exercise for the Brain: The Pencil on Your Finger

To illustrate this complicated point of physics in its simplest form, Murdoch tells us: "Imagine that you are balancing a pencil at its balancing point on your finger. Do you know where that is? If the pencil gets bigger around (thicker), does that point change? No! As long as the weight is distributed evenly, the center of balance stays the same with increased weight. Weight gain and riding balance works much the same way; however, the difference in finding our 'spot' of balance becomes more challenging when you consider how that weight is distributed, and other changes in anatomy that go along with things like childbearing and menopause and the natural thickening in the midsection that often accompanies aging."

Murdoch says that the balance differences and challenges she sees most are among women who rode earlier in life and have come back to horses. Their bodies are just different, in weight or in shape—and sometimes, in both.

"After childbearing the shape of your pelvis may have changed," she explains. "These women are seeking balance in their old place, and it's as if someone moved the kettle from the kitchen to the living room. It's still there, it's just in another place, and you simply have to look for it a bit to find it!"

Hope

"If you say anyone over a 36DD can't ride, does that mean that a 32F could, even though the volume of breast tissue she has is the same as the 36DD, roughly? HOW WOULD YOU MAKE THESE RULES? (Personally, I'd rather someone just spent more time making better sports bras.)"

The good news is that while the natural course of life for many women can, as Murdoch puts it, "Pull the rug out from under your balance," she has discovered in working with female riders that once she shows them where it is (and how to find it), "They're like, 'Thanks!'...and that's it—we're done!" Murdoch shrugs. "You just have to find that balance point in the body you have *now*."

Murdoch, who is no stranger to weight issues herself (we bonded over that boomeranging 10-15-20-and-now-30 pounds we've both gained and lost too many times to count), says there was a time in her own life when she had gained weight and didn't feel very good about herself. Through it all, however, she says she never really felt that the additional weight affected her ability to find her balance on horseback.

And (spoiler alert!) finding your balance is *not* just about the physical, although that's the most obvious piece of the puzzle. Finding mental and emotional balancing points also requires some trial-and-error hunting, and in much the same way. It's important to note that when learning to find *any* type of balance, once you learn to look for it—and know what it feels like when you find it—it's easier to find again and again, at any speed.

There is one important difference, however, between finding your physical balance point and that of mental and emotional balance, Murdoch acknowledges. "Unlike the physical, these other two kinds of balance are moving targets," she says. "You can't just find it once, grab it, and hang on to it. Finding our mental and emotional balance when we ride is something we learn—and remember—and find on a daily basis. Kind of like, well…life!" (We'll refine this more complicated search for the "other" types of balance soon.)

BALLAST AND BALANCE

"It's easy for people to make unfounded statements about the issue of balance, especially in discussion groups, without adequate science behind what they're saying," Murdoch cautions. "I encourage you to check out the science behind anything you hear or read before putting much stock in it. Go back to trusting yourself and your own feel and instincts, and not relying too much on others to tell you what to do."

To help provide a tool for this kind of information sifting, as well as clues for developing your own sense of feel for your place of perfect balance on the back of your horse, Dr. Jacob Barandes, Associate Director of Graduate Studies in the Department of Physics at Harvard University, weighs in (if you'll pardon the expression) on what our *center of mass* has to do with our riding, especially after a significant weight gain.

"What is center of mass?" you may ask (along with, "Will I need a textbook for this?"), and Dr. Barandes is here with the short answer:

"An object's *center of mass* is the 'average location' of all its mass," he explains. "If you have a barbell with 100 kilograms on each end, then its center of mass is right in the middle. (Think about the pencil Murdoch described—see p. 162.) If the barbell is really lopsided, with 100 kilograms on one end and 1 kilogram on the other end, then the center of mass is going to be very close to the 100-kilogram end."

Why is this important? To help make it clearer why an understanding of "center of mass" is so important to finding our natural place of balance for riding a horse, Dr. Barandes explains, "The center of mass is the special point with the following property: Whichever way we have oriented the object, it will only balance on a golf tee if the center of mass is directly above the point of contact with the tee."

So, taking this understanding off the tee and into our own arena, it means that a person will balance on the top of a horse if the person's center of mass is directly above the horse's. Depending on your shape and proportions, holding this place of perfect balance is a sliding scale of challenge.

"A person with a very low center of mass, a 'bottom-heavy person,' will probably find the experience much easier," Dr. Barandes says, "because if the person wobbles a little bit, her center of mass will stay pretty much in the same spot—right near the point of contact with the horse. But a 'top-heavy' person, having a center of mass that is much higher up, might have a tougher time staying balanced on the horse, because if the person wobbles a little, her center of mass could easily move pretty far from directly above the horse."

Dr. Barandes says that developing our own intuitive "feel" for the natural place of balance in our own bodies when we ride is really all about finding the location of our center of mass, and then realizing that a change in our shape (or posture!) will change the location of our center of mass. "After all, if I huddle up into a ball on the floor ('What a week I had!')," he quips, "my center of mass is going to be way lower than it would be if I were standing on my tiptoes with my arms up in the air." Taking this analogy into the saddle, it's easy to see how alignment that keeps our center of mass in a straight vertical line directly above our point of contact (our seat) on the horse will maintain balance that keeps us in our "spot."

Exercise for the Body: Playing for Balance

1 When you're sitting on your horse, quietly make small changes in the curve and position of your lower back and pelvis. Move a little more forward; lean a little more back. Play with posture and leg position. What feels better to you, more stable and solid, at the halt?

2 Now ride around a bit and make the same kind of small adjustments in posture and position and see how it feels to you as your horse moves.

3 Observe how your horse reacts to each variation in your posture or position. Does he stretch his neck down, lower his head, and take a deep breath? If so, *you're there*! You're in balance over *his* center of balance.

I have to admit that discovering physics' serious worth to us as riders was a little bit like that sobering moment when I realized I had just used algebra in cooking. But when we wonder whether our weight gain is affecting our balance in the saddle, this physics lesson underscores the importance of examining the *distribution* of the weight. And, going back to Coach Daniel Stewart's body type comparisons (see p. 96), consider the way your body is fundamentally put together, where

Eunice

We first met fellow horsewoman Eunice Rush in chapter 4 (see p. 66). Here she shares another story to help us all "lighten up" a bit with a little laughter:

"I have never been one of those willowy thin cowgirls who can wear tight jeans and big belt buckles. I have never ridden elegant, fine-boned horses. I, in fact, have plenty of backside ballast, and ride big-boned horses that always weigh in over 1,100 pounds.

"However, it was that big ballast that paid off one day when I and some riding friends got caught out in a storm. Three of us ladies decided since it was a beautiful sunny day, we would ride the local abandoned railroad bed from one small town to another. We trailered over to the trailhead and took off. It was a nice 10-mile ride between fields, and we were the only ones on the trail.

"One friend (we will call her Karen) was that willowy thin rider on a nice little Quarter Horse. The other (we will call her Sharon) was midsized but on a smaller, fine-boned horse, and then there we were—Bo and I.

"We rode our 5 miles into town and stopped to have a Coke and a rest at the park, and had just started back when we noticed a dark cloud coming in from the west. By the time we reached the outskirts of town, the wind had picked up. Karen decided she was going to try to make it back to my house because it was actually closer than the trailer but down a highway. She left us at the edge of town. Sharon your extra poundage has accumulated, and whether the weight you've gained really *is* a negative factor. What you may discover is that by lowering your center of mass and widening your base of support, a little extra weight may be working to your advantage!

Coach Stewart says that the wider our "base of support" (hips), and the lower our center of gravity, the more balanced we'll be at any weight. So what does that

---

and I thought we would try to make it back to the trailer. Then, about a mile out of town, the wind *really* hit.

"I knew if we could make it back about half a mile there was a road with a farm and a barn, so we turned around and took off as fast as we could. Now I know you might not believe it, but by now the wind was so strong that I had to hold on to both the saddle horn and the cantle to stay on board—every time my bottom left the saddle seat ever so slightly, the wind blew me up and out. When I got to the road where we would turn, I found that Sharon was not behind me. The farm belonged to a woman from my church, and I knew she was an EMT; I figured my best bet was to get to her in case Sharon had been hurt.

"Bo and I skidded to a stop in her barn just as the rain and lightening hit, and it had passed by the time we started back out in search of Sharon. The wind had died down, and we soon saw her heading our way. She explained that the wind had actually blown her and her (elegant, light) horse right off the path toward a deep ditch that ran along the track bed. Realizing the danger, she had gotten off and sought shelter behind a big tree until the wind passed. So as you can clearly see—big ballast is better!

"We found Karen camped out in a garage on the outskirts of town, safe and dry. The weather channel later reported the storm had brought 100-mile-per-hour, straight-line winds, and even a tractor trailer truck had been blown over near where we had been riding.

"Way to go, Bo!"

mean to the equally distributed or the top-heavy rider? Do we all just need to eat more cookies?

Not so fast, our experts agree. Once you know and understand *where* you are on the balance spectrum, you'll know better what to work on (conditioning, not cookies, they advise) to level the balance playing field and shift the odds more in your favor. First building core strength as an equalizer, you can then build your "Holy Trinity" conditioning program to address your body's specific needs.

BRACING IS *NOT* BALANCING

Ever tried to stable your "wobbliness" by bracing a bit more in the stirrups than you know you should? Yeah, me too. It only seems logical that if we have those things hanging right there beneath our waggling feet, we might as well use them to stop the flopping, right?

Ironically, this is the *last* thing that will help us get balanced.

"One thing that can make us really uncomfortable in the saddle — and also the first thing we naturally do when we feel unstable in the saddle," Wendy Murdoch says, "is bracing in the stirrups. Studies actually show that for every one pound of body weight you add to the weight in your stirrups, you put *four* pounds of pressure on your knees, whether you're overweight or not! That's the reason why, if you don't have good balance, and you use your stirrups to brace, your knees are *not* going to be happy."

In her book *50 5-Minute Fixes to Improve Your Riding* (see p. 23), Murdoch offers a way to help you use the balancing point of your foot (the area just behind the ball of your foot that *rests* on the stirrup) to find *stability* instead of bracing: "By simply resting that part of your foot in the stirrup (with just enough pressure to keep it in there—and no more!), you will have more flexibility in your hip, knee, and ankle joints," she writes, "and your foot will be more secure in the stirrup." With this fix, Murdoch assures us, in addition to finding the stirrup length and position that feels most secure, we can find stability *without* bracing.

Two extremes Murdoch says she sees all the time in riders with stability problems include having their feet too far forward (with pinky toes jammed against the outside branch of the stirrup), and too far back (with the toes barely in the stirrup, and then gripping with the toes inside their boots — as if that will help you hang on!). "I find that most riders have very 'opinionated' feet," Murdoch writes. I'll have to admit, pondering what my toes were doing when I was more worried about my "big, floppy body" (perception is reality, you know) sounded pretty silly to me at first, but upon trying Murdoch's foot fixes, I realized what a big difference even small habit changes could make in my riding.

When your feet are solidly in the stirrups, you're neither flopping *nor* bracing; you've created for yourself a stable platform for your feet, just as if you were resting your feet on solid ground. Plant this image in your head, play with the positioning of your feet, and develop your own "solid ground sensation" for *your* opinionated feet.

Lift from Your Core

One of the things common to martial artists, dancers, figure skaters—and any others who seem to float effortlessly above the reach of gravity—is the ability to *lift* from their core. We learned about how a strong core keeps us stable in the saddle and explored all kinds of ways to build core strength back on p. 64. But what else can our core do for our riding?

In addition to acting as dynamic stabilizers for your whole body, your core muscles are also responsible for transferring force between your extremities—harnessing, pulling together, and transferring power and efficiency between your upper and lower body in a way that can create amazing vertical lift with a feeling of lightness, or floating, that indeed seems to defy gravity. I discovered this initiation ability of core muscles quite by accident.

I had been going to Pilates for six or seven months, and due to time constraints, had not darkened the door of my Taekwondo *dojang*. Nor had I worked out or practiced Taekwondo forms at all. One day I decided to go to a noon class where some of my oldest and dearest Taekwondo friends met each week to work out. There is one black belt form, called Kumgang, which requires jumping and twirling in a 360-degree circle several times in a row. I'm not going to belabor this, but I have never been much of a jumper. And to jump and twirl...well, I passed the test, but I can promise you it wasn't nearly as pretty as I would have liked it to be.

On this day I lined up with the others and began the form. When we came to the jumpy-twirly part (yes, it has a name, but that's not really important to this story), I doggedly began my jump and spin, expecting the same old sluggish circle that barely got my feet into position for the next technique. To my complete surprise, I found myself way up in the air (for me, anyway!), and making that full 360-degree turn before I was fully ready for the next part. I wasn't the only one who noticed; my expression of shocked delight made everyone in the room laugh.

"What in the world have you been doing?" They all wanted to know. "Just a little bit of Pilates, two or three times a week," was my bewildered answer.

As equestrians on the trail to riding lighter, it only makes sense that training, engaging, and tapping into our core as we go about all the other things we know to do as riders, regardless of discipline, will enable us to start making this powerful connection that every successful dancer, jumper, gymnast, martial artist, and basketball player most likely figured out in one way or another long before I did.

"Think of a time when you saw a pair of dancers who were so light on their feet they appeared to be floating above the dance floor," prompts Dr. Joyce Harman. "The goal for every rider ought to be about 'dancing with your partner' in an enjoyable way. It should look and feel light and easy. Struggles should be occasional; it's not a constant physical battle. We see a lot of people 'driving' horses. The really *good* riders, of any weight, *float with* their horses."

What she refers to here—moving "up" with the horse—is key. To see what she's talking about, Dr. Harman encourages us to watch videos of riders in the Olympics and World Equestrian Games and look for this quality. Once you know what you're looking for, she adds you'll also see what it means to "ride downhill," and you'll see how the horse responds to this by becoming hollow-backed and moving incorrectly.

"It's easy to get distracted by flashy leg movements, transitions, and everything but correct movement," she says. "But if you start to look at a lot of good and bad, you'll see the difference and what that difference creates."

This ability to "float" with your horse involves learning how to not only locate, but to *lift* your center of balance, which is a skill that was articulated and taught by the late Sally Swift in her Centered Riding® method. Although Swift is gone now, her Centered Riding legacy remains and is still available to all of us through her broad network of certified instructors (including Susan Harris and Wendy Murdoch) and her bestselling books and DVDs. "Centered Riding is based on a knowledge of human and horse anatomy, balance, movement, and on understanding how the mind affects the body and how both affect the horse," CenteredRiding. org states. Centered Riding helps riders of all ages and abilities to develop "a more balanced, free, and coordinated use of self [so that] both horse and rider can move more freely and comfortably, and develop their best performance."

> **RESOURCES**
>
> Sally Swift's *Centered Riding; Centered Riding 2: Further Exploration;* and *Centered Riding 1* and *2* DVDs, all from Trafalgar Square Books (www.horseandriderbooks.com).

PIVOTAL CONNECTIONS

This is a place where the trail widens a bit to include some fundamental concepts you're going to need for the terrain ahead. It's a place to relax, take in our surroundings, and get our bearings before heading into ideas that will start to layer our understanding of this new trail—and what makes it unlike those we've ridden before.

Centered Riding teaches that a centered, balanced rider with good awareness of her body can help her horse move with balance and freedom of motion, which leads to efficiency of movement and beauty in the horse's gaits. A dedicated long-term student of the Alexander Technique, which teaches students how to bring about better "use of self" in all activities through a set of principles of movement and habits, Sally Swift made a pivotal connection between Alexander principles and riding horses, and then incorporated this understanding into her Centered

Riding method. Although this infusion didn't change any of Swift's basic principles of horsemanship, her deep study of key Alexander ideologies led to incorporating ideas such as self-awareness and mindfulness, which Swift termed "the use of the self," into her teachings.

So how does a rider develop better "use of self"? In Swift's second book *Centered Riding 2: Further Exploration* she uses the terms *ground* and *center* to answer that question for us.

Grounding

Grounding is a sensation of feeling connected to the earth *through* the horse. By building this sensory awareness, the rider can better find her balance. Wendy Murdoch explains that grounding provides stability by serving as the shock absorber that allows our bodies to yield into the movement of our horses' bodies. It has to do with staying supple, especially in the hips, knees, ankles, and toes, while keeping the torso in alignment with gravity. To accomplish this, Murdoch advises, "let your legs hang down like wet dish towels around your horse. You also want your shoulders grounded as if your elbows had heavy weights attached to them. You want this 'grounded feeling' through your arms and legs while the torso remains erect. This posture is a source of incredible strength."

Exercise for the Body, Brain, and Soul: Simple Grounding

I borrowed this idea from a favorite guided meditation of mine, one that has really helped me feel the sensation of grounding, both on and off my horse. Try this first sitting or standing on the ground and then from atop your horse—first at a standstill, then walking, and then faster gaits.

Take deep breath and imagine a golden light (sunbeams make for nice imagery here) is entering the top of your head, traveling straight down your spine, through your seat (if you're sitting) or legs (if you're standing) and into the ground beneath you.

As you visualize this light moving down and through your body, allow your body to follow it, sinking downward toward the earth. Make a deep connection with the earth, and allow that light to glow inside you until your whole body is glowing and sinking down, down, down, solid, relaxed, connected. (When you try this on your horse, visualize the light encompassing his whole body, too, moving from your seat into his body, filling the length of his body, then moving down through his legs and into the earth.)

What Ungrounds Us?

Have you ever been riding along, really feeling your horse's movement, floating along completely connected — and then . . . not so much? According to Murdoch, things that cause us to "lose our grounding" when we ride include:

• Stiffening our bodies.

• Bracing against the stirrups.

• Curling or gripping with our toes inside our boots (look for more about this in coming pages).

"We have to teach ourselves to override that natural reflex by letting ourselves absorb the motion in our joints while stabilizing with our postural muscles," she says. "When mounted, the body needs to have the potential to lower toward the earth (the joints are not inhibited internally). Your body will sink into the saddle, increasing the depth of your seat, even though you won't see any visible change in position. All the joints in your legs need to be loose enough to function, and you shoulder girdle needs to rest on the ribcage to provide quiet, following hands."

Centering

There are all kinds of connotations for the term "getting centered," but let's begin with the physical—where "getting centered" means, according to Susan Harris, that "our center of gravity is below and behind our belly button."

It is a subtle thing, and it takes more than a little quiet practice on your own to find it, but once you learn how to find and settle into that center of gravity whenever you need to, Harris assures us, it's nothing short of magical—the gateway to that riding euphoria we're stalking. She also considers centering to be key to feeling safe and confident in the saddle at any gait or speed, for any size rider. When your center is *out* of balance, your body instinctively does whatever it needs to do to survive. This may include such unattractive, ineffective, and downright dangerous things as hunching forward and gripping with your knees in what Harris calls the "fatal fetal crouch."

"Even a gentle horse doesn't respond well to that," she says. "This posture throws your weight forward and makes the horse feel insecure, too."

If you're lucky, this response to a lack of balance on your part will just stop your horse dead in his tracks, since a clutching, out-of-balance rider "shuts the front door" on the horse by pressing on some of the muscles that control free movement in his front end. If you're *not* lucky (some horses really don't handle the "fatal fetal crouch" well at all...ask me how I know this), you're either in the dirt or touring the next county by now, hanging on for dear life.

"Helping a rider find her *internal* balance and learn to move with the flow of energy is more important than all the 'heels down, shoulders back, chin up, chest out' advice we instructors can give," Harris says. The real trick, she adds, is learning to find that centered balance *in motion.* Harris says this key Centered Riding technique is what she likes to teach to her students first, and she does so by starting them out bareback or on a bareback pad with a vaulting surcingle (which has handholds). "You can really feel the horse's muscles under you," she explains. "You feel like you're *part* of the horse. If you can find this feeling early on and feel safe and comfortable with it, it will be easier to find it when riding with a saddle."

Harris advises doing this "center finding" exercise at a walk only to start with, and with your instructor on hand. "It is very important to go very slowly and only speed up when you are completely comfortable," she adds. From there, your instructor can help you feel this same place of balance while riding with a saddle in the "two-point" or "jumping position."

Marry

"I am a larger lady, but being honest, I do struggle with some other people who are very large and want to ride," says Marry (we first met her back on p. 104). "I think you have to be sure your size matches the horse: such things come into play as the length of the horse's back and leg structure to handle a larger rider—it's not just about getting a 'taller' horse.

"And, in my opinion, and as a human who *is* large, you need to have good balance to be fair to the horse. There are plenty of really large people who ride very well, have good balance, and there are others who honestly make me wince when I see the horse dipping and going off pattern because of the rider's lack of balance in conjunction with her size.

"I think if we love our horses we are also *honest* with them and with ourselves. Wanting to be *fair* to them, we should care about how our size affects their structure and lifespan, and that can be a reason for the goal of losing weight. It's not easy and I'll never be a skinny girl, but I do enjoy riding more since I have recently lost 40 pounds. (Now for the next 40!)"

"When you can find your balance in this position and take bounces in your knees," Harris says, "you are preparing yourself for trotting and posting at the trot."

Centering also takes you to your center of control and energy; when riding, this "center" is deep in the lower body as we've discussed, allowing your seat to be stable and secure. Taking what we've just learned about our center a step further, it is a way to manage the flow of energy into, out of, and around our bodies—a practice commonly found in the martial arts (Aikido, specifically, which is a defensive martial art of "spiritual harmony"). Centering redirects the *energy* of outside concerns (stress, tension, and negative thoughts) to the center of your body, creating a sense of inner calm.

Exercise for the Body, Brain, and Soul:
Center Yourself

1 **Focus on your breathing.** Breathe deeply, drawing in air as far as you can, holding it for a beat, then releasing it slowly. Repeat: in through your nose, out through your mouth. As you release each breath, imagine that you are also breathing out any tension or tightness you feel in your body, starting with your toes and working your way up to the top of your head. With each breath in, imagine that you are "breathing into" (or forcing your breath into) each area of tension so you can release even more of it on your next out breath. Clench and release any muscles you find that are still tight, and keep breathing "into" and "out through" them until the tension is gone.

2 **Locate your center.** Aikido teaches us to visualize our "physical center of gravity" as being about two inches below our navel. Whether or not our center of gravity has any true connection to center of mass (opinions vary on this, but do remember Dr. Barandes's explanation of center of mass on p. 164), focusing your mind on this place in your body creates a greater sense of balance and control. When doing this on your horse, relax your hips and visualize your center of balance shifting downward until it "finds" the right spot, "changing your balance on the inside," as Susan Harris explains. Once you've made a connection to this place of power in your own body, breathe in and out deeply at least five times, and allow yourself to really feel a sensation of deep stability and calm.

3 **Redirect negative energy.** Learning to redirect negative energy is how we can transform thoughts and feelings that aren't serving us well into action that does. I don't think I have to tell you why, as we ride our horses, understanding how to make this continuum work for us can not only improve the quality of our rides, but also help keep us safe, helping our horses draw from this centered stability so they, too, can relax and enjoy the ride.

Still breathing deeply, from your center, allow yourself to notice any negative thoughts and feel any negative energy related to the situation you're in. (Are you annoyed by the sound of a neighbor's lawnmower? Are you afraid your horse is going to spook or take off?) Imagine that with every out breath you're blowing all the scary "what ifs" and negative energy right into that space in your center, where its calm, white light will transform the negative into powerful positive energy. With your next inhale, focus your mind on what you *do* want, and state it in present-tense positive: "I'm calm and strong. All is well." By focusing on what you *do* want, letting your tensions go, and settling more deeply into your own center, you can use the negative energy from the outside to fuel a positive effective response within.

Learning to use centering is a matter of practice, and the more you practice the easier and more automatic it becomes. Make a conscious effort to learn this technique, trying it often in all kinds of situations—from the quiet moments to the epic stressors. Creating opportunities to practice centering will give you confidence that when you're really feeling negative about yourself, your situation, or how you look or think you can ride, you'll know what you can do to control your energy and keep both you and your horse balanced, safe, and riding on.

Get a Lift from the Martial Arts
While it's true that studying martial arts teaches you to lift from your *core*, I'll be the first to tell you (and as I've already admitted) this comes more naturally for some than for others. As a second-degree black belt and longtime student of Taekwondo, it continues to mystify me how some people, regardless of shape and size, can manage to catch so much more "hang time" in the air when executing a flying kick than others of us who have to work extremely hard to get off the ground at all. It turns out that this is not so much about conditioning (believe me!) as it is natural predisposition and core strength; however, there's also an *energetic element* to it that cannot be ignored.

Myths of Riding Instruction

MYTH: "My instructor is a good rider, and that's all that really matters."

TRUTH: Regardless of who you are and what you're trying to accomplish, our experts agree that good riding lessons are invaluable. "Lots of people want to do the right thing," observes Dr. Joyce Harman, "but they're not getting anywhere because the instructor they have doesn't understand the concept of 'up' and 'lightness' and what these riders really need to get there."

So how do we go about finding that "floaty" lightness that looks and feels effortless? And for instructors, how do you teach that to a rider with body issues, real or imagined? Susan Harris says that while most instructors know quite a bit about how the *horse's* body works, they must also understand how the *human* body works, and

how to work within each rider's range of motion—the comfort zone that works for her. Balance and alignment (see pp. 158 and 182) are key to keeping the rider's joints free to move as they need to and release any tension in her body that interferes with her abilities in the saddle. And, while some soreness is inherent in any athletic endeavor, instructors should never ignore serious joint and back pain.

"Riding instructors have a responsibility to help students use their bodies correctly," Harris adds. "A good instructor observes and listens to the students, and adapts instruction to the individual, instead of forcing everyone into the same mold. People of all shapes and sizes can become excellent riders, but each must do it in her own way."

Finding the right instructor to work with you and your specific body challenges is key to discovering your own riding excellence, and Susan Harris offers the following tips for vetting a riding school or stable to make sure you're set up for success.

1 **Make sure you're at a stable with instructors that will help, not criticize your body.** Also, make sure the stable has horses that are "up to your weight" (see our discussion of this on p. 56) and gentle and steady enough to ride safely.

2 **Be realistic.** This pertains to where you are (your geographical surroundings) and what riding instruction options are available to you right now.

3 **Be willing to take it slowly.** "There are a lot of very important 'learn to ride' exercises meant to be done at slow gaits—or even sitting still," Harris says. "Don't discount these and don't be in a hurry to go faster. You can learn a heck of a lot at a walk."

Dr. Joyce Harman and Harris agree that good riding lessons with an instructor who understands this concept of "lift" are invaluable. The goal for instructors, she says, ought to be to help their students find the feeling of dancing with their (equine) partners in an enjoyable way.

"Riding should look and feel light and easy," she explains. "Struggles should be occasional; it shouldn't be a constant physical battle. It's not a matter of a bigger bit, bigger spurs, and pulling harder."

Until this book, I never really made the connection between my martial arts and my riding (although lots of people have—see Resources, below). Dr. Joyce Harman was the first to flat-out mention the parallels to me, and it was a conversation with her that compelled me to play around with these principles I already knew very well. Digging a little deeper, I discovered that James Shaw, a student of martial arts for over 30 years and author of *Ride from Within* illustrates how Tai Chi concepts can aid equestrians as they seek balance and rhythm, and Mary Wanless (creator of Ride With Your Mind®) also observes the connection between riding and martial arts, particularly in stances. (Duh! The Korean word for Taekwondo's most solid and balanced stance is *juchoom sohgi*, also known as "horse riding stance.")

Another riding resource is Mark Rashid, a renowned horseman *and* black belt in Aikido who understands the energetic components common to martial arts and riding horses especially well. His book *Nature in Horsemanship: Discovering Harmony Through Principles of Aikido* delves into this connection—consider this passage where he talks about a particularly difficult stretch in his Aikido training, which caused him to examine his most fundamental beliefs: "I could either continue holding on to them as I had been," he writes, "or I could take a long hard look at them and see if there was something more for me within them, perhaps something that I had been missing. What I found would not only change the way I look at Aikido, but it would also have a profound change in the way I looked at and approached my horsemanship as well."

RESOURCES

Mark Rashid's *Nature in Horsemanship: Discovering Harmony Through Principles of Aikido* (Skyhorse Publishing, 2011).

Mary Wanless' *Ride With Your Mind®; Ride with Your Mind Essentials;* and *For the Good of the Rider* from Trafalgar Square Books (www.horseandriderbooks.com).

James Shaw's *Ride from Within* (Trafalgar Square Books, 2005).

Karen Muson's *The Art of Riding* (www.theartofriding.com)

Richard Strozzi-Heckler's *Aikido and the New Warrior* (North Atlantic Books, 1993).

THE "UPS" AND "DOWNS"

Dr. Harman and Harris note that while some people who are naturally athletic, flexible, and fluid seem to just "float around" without much effort (the "up" type), others, regardless of actual weight, are more lumbering—they walk, ride, and *move* in a heavy way (the "down" type).

"At Centered Riding, we say that's moving 'down in our weight,'" Harris explains, "and if you're one of those, you may have to really work to bring your weight, energy *and* core up."

And, Dr. Harman adds, just like there are "up" people and "down" people, there are "up" or "down" horses. If you've ever witnessed a horse's movement both before and after being taught to lift his core (through lateral and gymnastic work), you've seen the difference it makes in how he moves and carries himself. Sometimes, it looks like a different horse.

When a savvy old horse trainer named Karl Black began trying to help me with my horse, Trace (check out the ongoing chronicle of our struggles in my book *The Smart Woman's Guide to Midlife Horses* and read the story of Trace and Karl in my "Life With Horses" blog at Equisearch.com), the first thing he did was teach him how to lift his back and core to get past some physical habits formed around an old, unresolved chiropractic issue. Once a single chiropractic adjustment restored alignment and removed the source of Trace's actual pain, the challenge was to retrain his movement after what was likely 15 years of compensation. This slow and steady work over the course of an entire year changed how my horse moved and looked so much that several people at my barn who have known Trace for years thought I had finally given up and gotten a new horse. Trace's lifelong habit of moving "down in his weight" was aggravating his physical problems; my riding the same way was only making matters worse. (We've got *him* fixed...now we're working on me!)

Susan Harris relates a personal story that demonstrates how the principle of riding "up" plays out, once you are able to find and refine the ability to align your center of balance and use your energy to "float" with your horse:

"I went to a clinic where they had a computerized saddle scanner that showed (using color indicators) the pressure pattern and the amount of pressure being put on a horse's back as you ride," she relates. "On the computer screen, ideal pressure shows up as light blue. From there, the colors reflecting increasing pressure go from dark blue to purple to dark purple to red to dark red, which is the most harmful and potentially damaging to the horse.

"Now, I'm *not* a lightweight rider, and I took a horse that had just had some major chiropractic work, and I had him in a saddle that only almost fit. Even as he was just standing there saddled, not moving, the computer showed two red pressure points at the back of the saddle. I got on and the red spots got darker. Then I asked him to bring his back up and the spots turned blue. We moved out, and throughout our ride, as long as I stayed in balance and kept him round, it stayed light blue.

"Next we had a physically lighter (but inexperienced) rider get on him. She couldn't get those spots out of red no matter *what* she did! This showed me that, as long as the horse is capable of handling the rider's weight, a larger rider who rides in balance and 'up' may actually stress a horse less than a lighter rider who's stiff, out of balance, or 'down' in her weight."

Get It Straight

Has an instructor or a well-meaning friend ever said, "Sit up straight?" as you rode blithely by? Has anyone ever said, "Sit back!" and when you *do* sit back (until you feel like you're in a recliner waiting for your beer) did they say, "There, that's better"? Do you think you're putting exactly even weight in your stirrups...only to get home to find a large pressure sore on the inside of *one* leg, and not even a rub on the other? As you discovered these things about yourself, did you notice that your horse seemed stiffer or had "trouble" on one side or the other? There are a lot of issues that come into play around how we sit in the saddle, and Coach Daniel Stewart and instructor Wendy Murdoch are going to help us "get it straight."

WHAT DOES "SITTING UP STRAIGHT" FEEL LIKE?

"We all have a somewhat skewed image of what our riding position looks like," says Murdoch. "We look in the mirror and just see the front of us. If we were to look from behind and from the side, we'd get a very different picture!"

We're now entering Murdoch's official turf. She is internationally known for her expertise in rider biomechanics and has spent a career teaching all kinds of riders how to do what great riders do naturally. But Rome wasn't built in a day, and neither is this kind of riding.

First, Murdoch tells us firmly, it's really not about how you look—or what you weigh—but rather the positioning of your skeleton that determines how you hold your frame when you ride. She brings this point to life in her DVD *Ride Like a Natural: Sitting Right on Your Horse* with one of those classroom skeletons (this one's named Elmer), demonstrating what "sit straight" in the saddle means. (Here we go, back to high school again, but this time we're just down the hall from algebra and geometry, in the spit-wad zone of biology class.)

"We don't even know what 'the position of our skeleton' means until we're challenged in a way that breaks our illusion that what we're doing (with our bodies) is keeping us safe," Murdoch says. What she's referring to is all those things we habitually do when we ride *in an attempt* to feel balanced and straight, but which may actually be putting us in greater danger. And, she adds, "'Straight' does not mean 'rigid' or 'braced,' but rather *allowing* your skeleton to settle into that magical place of balance that aligns with your horse's center of balance." (Remember what we learned about all this earlier? See p. 158 for a refresher.)

Murdoch says that this is what she teaches her students on a daily basis, and even though it starts with visual demonstrations to show us what we're looking for, personal experimentation (preferably on a safe and tolerant horse) is key to learning what "straight" feels like in our own bodies.

"Here's the place where you're solid," she tells her students by guiding them through a series of carefully choreographed variations on their positioning in the saddle. "And here's the place where you're *not*. Now *you* find it!"

"People often then ask me," she goes on, "'How do I look now?' I tell them, 'I don't care how you *look*! How do you *feel*?' We're so concerned with our appearance we forget to *feel for function*. And people are also unwilling to experiment—to see what might *feel* better to them than what someone has told them *looks* better."

Because we are the ones who actually live in our bodies, Murdoch encourages us to become our own best teachers in this matter. She says that by increasing your own awareness and connection with your body, you are much better able to judge what "sitting up straight" feels like inside your own skin where your own skeleton actually resides.

"We're trained to try to please someone else and not to listen to ourselves," she explains. "We're *not* trained to feel—or to observe and experiment with how small changes affect ourselves and our horses. We have to learn to listen to ourselves and to our horses, and then to do the best we can to find our own way."

That's both empowering and scary, especially if you're struggling with these issues and have, like me, bounced from instructor to instructor trying to figure out where the hole is in your riding that is keeping you from the "ease and joy" of riding horses that always seems just beyond reach. And especially when you're riding at a heavier weight than you'd like to be, the concern that brought you to this book in the first place escalates with balance and posture issues.

"We're often so concerned with not hurting our horses that we trust it all—time, money, *and* safety—to people who may or may not know what they're talking about," says Murdoch. "And regardless of who they are and what they know, they are most certainly not in our bodies, feeling what we feel."

So why do we throw our own ability to feel away without question? Why are we so reluctant to trust ourselves?

"When I see riders going to that place," Murdoch says, "I always ask them: 'Tell me again about what you do? How many people rely on your judgment? How many decisions do you make in a single day?'" And then, after listening to their sometimes sheepish answers, and watching the understanding begin to dawn on them, she follows with: "And why can't you trust yourself on something so simple as whether your position feels good or bad to you?"

Murdoch says we should all just go out and play with straightness and balance on our horses (assuming your horse is willing to engage in such play): Make a series of small adjustments to how you're positioned and ask, after each tiny change, "What happens when I do this...or that? How does my horse respond? How does my body feel?"

Murdoch states that it is true that heavier riders seem to question their abilities more. Is this an excuse? A fallback? A reason not to ride because we're afraid we may not be doing it right? Murdoch says that in her experience, the answer is often "all of the above." So this all begs a new question: Are people who are heavier more vulnerable to self-doubt because of their *overt weight issues* or *covert body image issues*? "A heavier person wears it all on the outside," Murdoch observes, "and some people seem to take advantage of this obvious insecurity—and prey upon it."

GOOD SIDE, BAD SIDE: YOUR DUELING SYMMETRY

It's no secret that every rider—and every horse—has a dominant side. And lots of times, even when we think we're sitting and riding perfectly straight, that dominant side is overpowering the other. Coach Daniel Stewart points to a few clues of this side infringement, including:

• **Riding better or more comfortably in one direction or the other.** We say our horse has a "good side" and a "bad side." Consider that the "good" and "bad" you're experiencing may be your own asymmetry adding to—or conflicting with—your horse's!

• **Feeling more comfortable on one canter/lope lead over the other.**

• **Looking the same direction first.** Some people also cock their heads a bit to one side, even when doing groundwork!

Letting our dominant side, well, dominate, is a very common riding problem, Coach Stewart says, because it can be caused by so many different factors. Because we—and our horses, too—are *born* with this dominant side (this is what makes us right-handed or left-handed), we naturally tend to do more things with that side because, well, it's just easier! And, as we live our lives favoring that dominant side in the name of comfort and efficiency, it just keeps getting stronger, more coordinated, and *more dominant* over time.

Other contributors to our asymmetry include habits, behavioral patterns, old injuries, and even occupational requirements. Again, your dominant side gets stronger because it's easier to use it: it's more coordinated, and more efficient. Can you imagine going to work tomorrow and doing everything with your "opposite" hand? It would be a long day, I can assure you. But taking a cue from my yoga class, where we do each posture twice, always reminded to "switch your hand holds" for the second rep to "build symmetry," I now see the value for making a conscious effort to use your non-dominant side whenever you can to offset that natural lopsidedness.

Over time (and left unattended), the stronger your dominant side gets, the less flexible it becomes. This, in turn affects how your joints on that side work, and eventually leads to compensation by the other side. While this may not be obvious to you in your day-to-day life, Coach Stewart says, riding puts a super-magnifying glass (or maybe a microscope) on your natural asymmetry—it always shows up in the saddle in ways we don't even realize. Coach Stewart says that a simple test (see the exercise that follows) and the determination to stay on the lookout for sneaky asymmetry can make all the difference in your riding. He also notes that correcting your asymmetry is best approached as an off-horse project.

"Remember, this is not a horse-and-rider problem, but simply a problem born out of being right- or left-handed, magnified by behavioral patterns," he says. And, while the effects of asymmetry are likely accentuated by extra rider weight, doing the work you need to do to correct it will lighten your horse's load, even if your weight stays the same. (Plus, you'll be helping your horse overcome *his own* symmetry problems at the same time.)

Exercise for the Body: Scales of Symmetry

I know you're probably thought-screaming, *What?!?!?! Not scales!* Even though we're trying to reframe weight as just a number, stepping on scales is still somewhat traumatic for most of us. But stay with me here. I promise this is about *balancing* your weight, rather than lowering it. (Or discussing it. Or criticizing it.) This exercise from Coach Daniel Stewart is about realizing that even when we *think* we have our weight evenly balanced in the stirrups, due to the natural dominance of one side over the other, it just may not be so.

1 Place two identical scales side by side on a hard, even surface. (They have to be identical so you are sure to compare equal measures!)

2 Stand with one foot on each scale.

3 Now get in "riding position" (bend your knees, shift your weight into your heels, and hold your hands out in front of you as if you were holding the reins).

4 Wait a few seconds to allow the scales to settle and have a friend record their weights. (It's important that *you* do not look down to see the numbers on the scales because this shifts your weight forward and skews the reading.) If your measurements are not equal, there's a very good chance you've got some asymmetry going on.

ALIGNMENT RULES

One of the more interesting things I ran across when delving into biomechanics of alignment beneath the classic "ears, shoulders, hips, and heels" credo we've all heard (but not fully understood) is that as we tweak the alignment of our skeleton by balancing our head and flattening our back, we are beginning the process of teaching our nervous system that *this* is the alignment we want to find when we're in the saddle.

What that means, of course, is you have to be very deliberate about all this at first. You have to ride with consistent focus on this new alignment that may be very far, or just a slight adjustment, from where you are now. If you (like so many if not most of us) have been riding around with less-than-ideal alignment, this new position may feel a little strange, especially to the muscles now being asked to work differently (or as may be the case of many of them, to *stop* working and just relax). But take heart. As you log hours in the saddle practicing this alignment, it's going to take you to a new place. (See also James Shaw's meditation exercise on p. 225 for further help finding balance and alignment.)

Regardless of which riding discipline you call your own, Murdoch says, good alignment is good alignment. "Whether you ride Western, English, dressage, or jumping, there's one thing none of us can escape," she says. "It's called gravity. Gravity is acting on us all the time—there's no escaping it—and we need to learn to work *with* gravity rather than *against* it."

What's important to understand about gravity and your skeleton is that when you ride with your head, spine, and pelvis aligned, your "riding muscles" can stay loose enough to allow your body to move freely with your horse.

Exercise for the Body: Stiffness versus Gravity (*Hint: Gravity always wins*)

To demonstrate how this works, Murdoch prompts, shake one hand. Now shake that same hand with one finger held tense and stiff. See a difference? All it takes is one tense, stiff finger to make your hand, arm, shoulder, even the whole side of your body stiff.

That's what happens when any one part of your body gets stiff and tense (as some of us do when we're *trying* to balance). Poor alignment when we ride sets up this stiffness and tension in our unwitting fight against gravity, and in my experience any fight against gravity is a losing proposition.

So how do we find the proper skeletal alignment we already touched upon that works *with* gravity rather than *against* it? Wendy Murdoch says we can likely improve our overall skeletal alignment (that leads to straightness in the saddle) by checking and correcting three main areas: head, lower back (and pelvis), and feet.

It's All in Your Head: Bowling for Balance

Did you know your head weighs about 15 pounds? Murdoch explains (using a 15-pound bowling ball as a visual aid in her DVD) that if you think about riding around with a bowling ball on top of your spine—and consider that your nervous system is constantly dwelling on the fact that if that bowling ball hits the ground, you might die (it is a *nervous* system, after all!)—you understand the neurological imperative to keep that thing balanced. (Did you just quietly straighten your spine as you read this? I know *I* did.)

"When your head is in its balanced position on top of a straight spine," Murdoch explains in *50 5-Minute Fixes to Improve Your Riding*, "you reduce the amount of work your muscles have to do to keep it upright and allow your skeleton to do most of the work. This liberates other parts of your body to move freely and counters the downward force of gravity."

What this means is that when your head gets too far forward (usually because you are jutting out your jaw in attempt to put your shoulders back, which I know sounds silly, but it *is* what we do) or too far back (a common over-correction of real or imagined alignment issues), it begets muscle tension as your body tries to counterbalance your bowling-ball noggin. But that's not the worst part. Poor alignment of the head (which Murdoch compares to high or overly tucked, chin-to-chest head carriage in horses) also creates a heavy, downward pressure through your body that makes the horse feel every ounce of weight on his back. Rather than a favorite dance partner, you become the proverbial sack of potatoes.

Maintaining good head alignment will keep your skeleton doing the work and your muscle involvement to a minimum. Best of all, as Murdoch writes, "When your skeleton supports a well-aligned head, you can then lengthen through your

Jenni

One of the challenges we all face, regardless of our size or shape, is being able to find (or rediscover) our ideal place of balance at any gait—and get back to it if we happen to find ourselves flopping around. (It happens.) The secret, it appears, is learning to readjust our position. Jenni, one of Wendy Murdoch's students who experienced finding that place of perfect balance and alignment we're going to call finding our "sweet spot," gave us a peek inside the riding lesson that changed everything for her:

"I told Wendy at the beginning of the lesson that I felt like my weight was contributing to my being off balance," Jenni relates. "Being overweight is awkward, and my body often feels off balance in a lot of situations, so it's not hard to make the jump to feeling that it's contributing to my feeling off balance in riding, too. (And I know the gym bunnies and diet busters are like, 'Just lose it, and you will be fine.' If losing it was so stinkin' easy, don't you think I would have done it already?) Being able to find that 'core seat' again, and then working consistently to stay in that core seat, is the only way to beat my balance issues. It may be harder, as the horse has more of me to sling around when she gets to slinging...but that would be more the reason to be more conscious of keeping the core seat solid."

So what kind of adjustments did Murdoch help Jenni make to find her "sweet spot" of balance?

"She had me move forward in the saddle, then adjusted my stirrups. I suffer from that hunter position of exaggerated heels—which most riders do. Heels down are important, but heels crammed toward the Earth with the stirrup shifted too far back on the ball of your foot, well, that's disaster!"

Murdoch helped Jenni find that soft spot where the stirrup should go *without* having to shove her heel down. "Your heel is still 'down,'" she emphasizes, "but the foot is more level." The difference these minor adjustments made in how she felt when riding, Jenni says, was "like coming home! I know where my body should be, and I know what it *should* feel like; I just couldn't find my way back there."

And here's the important part, according to Murdoch: Once Jenni found that "sweet spot" of balance, she had her move from the "bad place" to the "good place" several times just to be sure she was clear on where it was—and where it wasn't. Jenni needed to not only know the difference, she also needed to be able to find it on her own whenever it slipped away. Murdoch says that one of the things that frequently happens in this search for our "sweet spot" is that we may find it—and feel very sure and solid at a walk, but when we move into a jog or trot, or still more challenging, a canter, and downward transitions back down to a walk, this "sweet spot" becomes a moving target.

"The canter was the hardest," Jenni agrees, "because when you sit wrong you are tensed up, so of course you cannot follow the horse's rhythm correctly."

Agreeing that everyone needs to have a secure seat in order to find and stay in that perfect spot of balance, Jenni says she believes it boils down to getting your pelvic "bowl" level (visualize your pelvis as a basin, with the two large bones as the sides of the basin attached in front by the pubis and in back by the sacrum), your butt underneath you, and your legs in that place where they wrap around the horse. "When you find that, or have that," she adds, "it doesn't matter what kind of riding you do, you will ride it best."

Jenni says the "trick" to Murdoch's lesson was shortening her stirrups. She recommends that those of us "seeking our sweet spot" try it, too. "Ride in an old (but good and well-balanced) hunt saddle and force your legs short," she advises. "We do this for kids when we start teaching them how to ride, because it rocks them back on their butts and kind of forces them to find the balanced position."

Following this exercise, being able to lengthen your stirrups again becomes a triumph and a privilege. "Wendy probably took me up three to four holes on my leathers," she laughs. "Just because we ride dressage or Western, and have longer stirrups, does not mean we should forget that this is the privilege of the balanced, and we need to shorten it back up when we start to feel wonky."

See more about working with your stirrup length to improve your sense of balance and security in the saddle on p. 168.

spine (Sally Swift called this the rider's need to "grow up" in *Centered Riding 2*), all the way through the top of your head, creating that lift and lightness that helps and encourages the horse underneath us to lift his back as well.".

This, my friends, is the closest we'll ever come to defying gravity.

Get Flat on Your (Lower) Back

Another aspect of the body alignment key to "riding light" regardless of actual weight is the lower back and pelvis. Just like head alignment, this principal of biomechanics has nothing to do with riding discipline, level, or goals—and every-thing to do with physiology and how gravity acts upon every human body that sits on a horse. According to Murdoch, to find the stability and mobility we're looking for in our hips, we must pay attention to the position of our lower back and pelvis. "When a rider's back is stiff or hollowed, or her hip joints are restricted, it directly affects the horse's ability to perform," she says. The same, she adds, is true for the horse: "A horse with a hollow back and inability to engage his pelvis will be unable to lift his back beneath you to carry your weight with comfort and ease." (More on this on p. 61.)

Acknowledging that most of us were taught to ride with a hollowed back, Mur-doch says we are pretty much destined to grip with our legs, tense up, and pull on the reins to find stability. (I can't decide if knowing this makes me feel better or worse.) In *50 5-Minute Fixes to Improve Your Riding* Murdoch offers specific exercises for addressing our hollow-backed habits. Take this work easy, though, she cautions. These are deep, physiological changes that are best done slowly, especially if you have lower back pain or tightness. The good news is that small bits of work focused on this "fix," done consistently over time (days or weeks, depending on where your starting point is), will change your lower back position for good, building your sense of security as you create "muscle memory" that makes this new position a habit. (This is where the work we did in the fitness sections on strength and core stability, beginning on p. 125, starts to dovetail with changing the way we ride. We have to build that strength and stability before we learn how to use it!)

A hollow back pitches our weight forward and skews our balance; some of us tend to overcorrect a hollow back by rounding it *too* much (picture the "cutter's slump"). This is just as bad for our balance as a hollow back, if not worse, because it places our weight too far *back* in the saddle and is very uncomfortable and restricting to our horses. Both extremes cause us to brace in the stirrups, which is also uncomfortable for us, and our horses (see p. 168). A flat lower back, however, keeps us sitting solid in the saddle with no need to use reins, legs, or anything else for security.

So where *is* this "sweet spot"? Murdoch says we all have to find it for ourselves; every body is different, and while we may be talking about millimeters in any direction, that "sweet spot" moves from person to person, and moves when a person experiences changes in weight or shape. Start this search off the horse, altering the amount of curve in your lower back by deliberately *hollowing* and then *rounding* it (while sitting and standing in front of a mirror) until you find that "flat" place in between.

One common piece of bad advice (and I admit I certainly fell prey to it) is that you flatten your back by using your abs to "pull your belly button toward your spine." This, Murdoch tells us, is both impractical and inefficient. Rather than worrying about which muscles to contract and when, she coaches, focus on your overall alignment and function, and let your brain decide when to call which muscles into action for the desired result.

"As you refine your function, you will increase efficiency, minimize muscular effort, and you will not have to think about what muscles are working," she says.

Exercise for the Body: Seat Bones South

1 Check that you are sitting in the middle of your saddle. Then, alternately hollow and round your back in very small, slow, movements so that you can sense and feel what is happening.

2 Notice:
- Your seat bones change position in the saddle as you move your lower back.
- Your back muscles change shape, texture, and tone as you move.
- The place where your seat bones are pointing down and your back is flat.

3 Consciously change your seat bone position (point them forward and back; weight them to the left or right side) and feel:
- The effect on your lower back.
- Any tension in your abdominal area with each small change.
- How you can alter the position of your pelvis *without* contracting your abs.
- How your seat bone position affects the freedom of your hips: Do they feel more or less open? Do your legs feel longer?

BUSTED!

Myths of Skill

MYTH: "I'm not going to show, so technique doesn't matter."

TRUTH: Well, actually, it does. The truth is, as we've already mentioned (and I daresay we'll mention again), study after study shows that to protect a horse's back, a heavier rider must learn how to use her weight and energy correctly. Regardless of your riding goals, your horse depends on you to be strong, stable, and flexible, and to possess a solid set of riding skills.

Lower Body Logic

Now that we've got a solid, flat back, an upper body balanced over our pelvis, and the weight of our head balanced over all of that, it's time to look at what's going on in our lower body—and what we can do to create the flexible strength there that will connect us on a deeper level with the movement of our horses. But how can we teach all those hip, leg, ankle, and foot muscles that have been gripping for dear life to discover their own "sweet spot" and then to just *let go*?

Exercise for the Body: Lower Body Checkpoints

The secret to finding your "sweet spot" is more about knowing which parts to relax than anything else. Here are a few places to persuade to "let go, already!" as we move our focus to our lower bodies:

Open Your Hips

1 Sitting on your horse in your (possibly newfound) solid upper body alignment, just relax the muscles in your hips, allowing them to sink into the saddle.

2 Now see if you can rotate your legs a little more outward in the hip socket to allow your legs to lengthen down a little bit. Don't push; just *allow*. (Sometimes just thinking about it helps your legs reach down in a new and outwardly imperceptible way.)

Mobilize Your Ankles

1 First check the side-to-side movement in your ankles to make sure they are relaxed and moving freely.

2 Next, rotate your heels in and out.

3 Then, "roll" your ankles inward and outward.

4 Finally, move your heels up and down.

Relax Your Toes!

It's hard to imagine anywhere in the matter of riding, weight, and biomechanics, that our tiny little toes are calling the shots. But relaxation, comfort, and effectiveness in our feet and ankles play a much bigger part in our stability than most of us realize, and our toes have a whole lot to do with that! Have you ever made sure your toes have ample room to spread out in your boots? Are you aware of what your toes are doing inside your boots as you ride? (Gripping? Curling? Dancing the Rumba?) Here are some toe-related questions Wendy Murdoch invites us to consider:

• Are your toes lying flat on your boot's foot bed?

• Are they pressed up against the top of the boot?

• Do you curl or grip with your toes when you ride?

• Do you stiffen your toes when you attempt a difficult movement? (A spin? A jump?)

"While it is not possible to see what is happening inside a rider's boot," Murdoch says, "it is surprising to hear how many people do funny things with their toes when they ride." Relaxed and comfy toes can make a huge difference in our stability in the saddle, while toe tension, apparently, can contribute mightily to our instability. Toes rule. Who knew?

The first order of business is making sure your riding boots fit right. This may seem obvious, but do a quick check to make sure your toes have ample room, nothing pinches, squeezes, or rubs, and that you have the right sock to wick moisture and create the amount of cushion or padding that is comfortable to you and works well with your boot. Once basic comfort is assured, try this exercise from Murdoch:

Exercise for the Body: Ride Like a Duck

1 Standing barefoot on a hard surface, pay special attention to what your feet feel like. How much surface do they cover? Can you spread your toes to cover as much ground surface as possible so your feet feel bigger and wider? Imagine that they are wide and webbed like a duck's feet.

2 Walk around for a few more minutes with "duck feet" to implant this feeling and image in your mind. Put on your boots and see how wide you can spread your toes inside your boot.

When you get on your horse, take a moment to remember that spread-out-toe feeling, and then spread your toes inside your boot. Notice, as you do this, how much more of your stirrups you can now feel. The more your can keep that feeling and imagery going as you ride, the more supple your ankles, knees, and hips will become. It's not magic—it's biomechanics!

Great Timing

When Everett Mrakava, the Canadian Horse trainer you may have met in *Smart Woman's Guide to Midlife Horses*, was working with my horse Trace to see if he could solve the riddle of his escalating bucking, he invited me to his facility for my first ride after 30 days of training. I had no idea what to expect—or what he would expect me to do. While I had been cautioned against getting back on this horse at all after his last blow up, I still wasn't ready to give up. Still sporting a healthy degree of self-preservation instinct, however, I wasn't at all sure I was ready to put my foot in the stirrup. I did trust Everett, who apprenticed for Peter Campbell, a direct descendant of Tom Dorrance/Ray Hunt training lineage. He told me that Trace was doing well, but really needed, more than most horses, a well-balanced rider who knew how to stay connected with him.

Yikes.

"He's sensitive," Everett said, "which is good—and makes him light as a feather—but it also means if you get even a little bit out of balance it's going to piss him off."

Great.

The key, he said, was developing my own feel for what Trace's body was doing.

Jenni

"So I had my own horse, but I also rode for different trainers through the years," says our friend Jenni, whom we first met on p. 27. "One of the women I rode with was Shelley Rosenberg, back when she owned the Dressage Center in Oro Valley, Arizona. Shelley was not a size 0, and she was never ashamed of it. She was a very talented rider, and she knew she was good. She was also an amazing instructor who didn't let silly crap like 'bad self-image' or 'not owning a gazillion-dollar Warmblood' stand in her way of helping you become the best rider you can be. I have had two great instructors/trainers through my riding travels, and I count Shelley as one.

"So what happened? College happened. Work happened. Moving across the country and across states happened. Lo and behold...marriage happened. Polysystic ovary syndrome (PCOS) happened. Over the last decade, I went from working with Olympic long-listers to working with no one. And I gained weight. And I gained more weight. Somewhere along the way I lost that feeling of perfect seat and perfect balance. I lost that feeling of perfect control over my movements that we, as riders, become accustomed to. By the time I worked with Wendy Murdoch, I had been feeling out of balance for over two years. The horse never unseated me, but something was just 'off.' You know it's wrong. You are still able to ride, the horse still moves, you still post. *But it's all wrong.* And when the horse takes the odd off step, or falls out of balance under you, the whole world goes jiggly. It's like...JELLO! Very jiggly. Not fun.

"I was searching for that elusive place that I used to know so well, that used to be second nature to me. (When you 'catch ride' or ride for trainers and sit on 10

Okay, I thought, *I can do that. How hard can it be?*

As I rode Trace at a walk, Everett leading him, the first thing he asked me to do was to tell him when each of Trace's feet hit the ground—and which foot I was feeling. I was stumped at first. Feeling each footfall itself was easy enough, but how in the world was I supposed to be able to feel which foot was which? (It wasn't

---

different horses a day, that 'core seat' becomes your life. It's the difference between staying on and eating dirt.)

"Wendy realized that I had lost the placement of my pelvis and was sitting back farther. A few little changes and all of a sudden, I was solid again. The horse could round under me better, and moved out when I thought *forward*. Wendy insisted that it was most likely an older Western saddle I had been riding in that had caused my problems. She didn't think it was my weight (but I am not so sure...perhaps that's my own insecurities creeping up on me again). But the important thing was my horse was happier—I was no longer interfering with her!

"I just wanted to cry!" Jenni says about her breakthrough (not that she did, she's quick to point out, "because we are horse girls and we don't cry!") "What I learned meant I've been 'blocking' my horse for what...a decade?"

For Jenni, after years of struggling to find her "sweet spot," it finally clicked when she found the place, "a little more forward" where she felt her horse open up and move out with a new ease she immediately recognized. After pondering why she had been sitting back so far, Jenni figured it out while watching a video her husband had taken of her riding.

"I was sitting back so far to not overbalance my horse, to get off her shoulders," she says, "because I am fat, and that's the thing to do right? To sit back to get out of the way, right? Well...no! Because when you do that, your back hollows out and your seat bones dig into the horse's back.

"The horse can't move through that."

See more about working with your stirrup length to improve your sense of balance and security in the saddle on p. 168.

long before I couldn't remember what it was like *not* to be able to feel it, so the good news is this awareness, once generated, sticks.)

But I got quiet. (Everett told me closing my eyes might help. It did.) And we took it one foot at a time. First he called out each step of Trace's left front foot: "Now. . . Now . . . Now . . ." It felt a little silly, but eyes closed, I felt for it. We walked around and around the arena, calling each foot, one at a time, until I really could feel when it hit the ground. This was one of the silliest and strangest—and possibly best—riding lessons I've ever had in terms of getting connected with this very simple motion of my horse. I wasn't sure exactly what to do with this information, but for me, it was riding enlightenment.

A similar experience came at the trot one day when I was riding with a friend who is very accomplished in the show ring. I was trying to learn how to post, but I had no idea what I was doing. (All I knew to do was rise up and sit down and trust that I'd eventually get in rhythm with my horse. Let's just say it wasn't happening.) Now remember, I learned to ride by sheer survival instinct, and I'll be the first to tell you my form and expertise as a rider is, shall we say, limited (and rooted in the sincere desire to stay on the top side of my horse and avoid hitting the ground at all costs). But on that day, in the name of making my horse Rio a little happier to move out for me, I was trying to post. My friend Carol watched me for a while, and then (I'm sure with all the tact she could muster) said, "Um, which diagonal are you trying to post to?"

I heard the diplomacy in her tone; I just had no idea what the right answer was. *Which diagonal? What the heck is a diagonal?* Seeing my uncool confusion, she rescued me. "Watch his outside shoulder," she said. "When it goes forward, you go up."

Ahhh. When I tried it, I actually felt an instant change in Rio's body. It was if he heaved a great sigh of relief and said, "*Thank you, Carol!*" (I suspect that if he'd had a credit card and a dialing finger, he'd have sent her flowers.) It made all the difference in our ride that day—and every day since then. And, although I didn't make the connection with this "feel" immediately, just like with my ponied walk with Everett, pretty soon I didn't have to watch for that outside shoulder to come forward; I could just feel it.

To get connected and in sync with the movement of our horses, we have to train our awareness to feel, in the overall motion of the horse, the progression of each gait. Once we can do that, we can begin to help our horses move more freely beneath us, timing our aids to their movement in a way that sets their bodies up right and allows them to lift their backs correctly to bear our weight.

"When a horse is able to lift his back, he is better able to bear a rider's weight," Wendy Murdoch explains. "If he drops his back, his hindquarters go out behind him and all the rider weight comes down on his back. This is very uncomfortable, and it causes the horse to put his head in the air."

According to Murdoch (and lots of others), this is a matter of timing: being able to ask your horse to do what he needs to do, when he is most able to do it. By understanding and being able to feel the details of your horse's body movement at each gait (now…now…now…), and being able to keep yourself aligned with gravity, even (and especially!) during transitions, you'll find a new "place" to ride that's easier on your horse *and* more comfortable for you.

Exercise for the Body: Just Feel It

I invite you to experience your own lesson of enlightenment. (If you have a quiet horse and someone to lead him at the walk the first few times, it's much easier to feel the footfalls with your eyes closed.) I try to practice this exercise for a few strides as I begin each ride, just to remind myself to pay attention to what *my horse's body* is doing.

1 Make sure your back is flat and solid (see p. 192). If a shove to your lower back pushes you forward, causing your seat bones to point out behind you, your back is too hollow. If a shove to your lower back causes you to slump forward, losing connection with your seat, your back is too round. "A good, solid alignment in

your back is what will allow you to feel the motion of your horse's feet," emphasizes Murdoch.

2 At the walk (just as I did with Everett and Trace), concentrate on one of your horse's footfalls at a time (right hind...right hind...right hind...) until you can feel it without question.

3 Then try to feel all four feet as each foot makes a step (now...now...now...). It's harder than you'd think, but once you feel it, it gets easier and easier to find again. Note: While it's natural to start this exercise trying to feel a front leg move, Wendy Murdoch says it is actually much easier to start with the back. Once you've got the feel of back feet moving, Murdoch recommends finding those elusive front feet by watching your horse's shoulder, and then your thigh. "If you place your hand on your thigh," she says, "you'll actually see that your thigh mirrors the movement of your horse's shoulder on that side."

A couple more tips when finding your "feel" with this exercise:

• **Catch the swing.** While your thigh mirrors the movement of your horse's shoulder, your lower leg follows the left-right swing of your horse's rib cage as he walks forward. Murdoch advises us to simply notice and allow this gentle swing as your seat maintains its forward-back motion. We don't want to force or exaggerate the left-right swing because too much side-to-side in the horse's barrel causes our weight to shift side to side; this decreases the forward motion of the horse and makes it more difficult for him to lift through his back.

• **Have a nice flight.** It's important to understand the four distinct phases of a horse's step at the walk in order to time your aids correctly. "You can't ask a horse to do something different when his foot is already on the ground," Murdoch explains. "You want to time your aids to the flight phase—when his foot is traveling through the air." The four phases to every step the horse takes, regardless of gait, are:

Laurie

Laurie, a lifelong rider who shows her horse Zip in Western Pleasure, is well acquainted with the need and challenge of staying connected with your horse at all gaits for optimum performance. Still, sometimes, and for no discernible reason, she was feeling out of balance and "in Zip's way." Hoping to feel more solidly and consistently connected in the saddle, she began looking and listening for new insights related to finding this suddenly elusive connection.

"When I read somewhere that the secret to riding well is staying out of your horse's way, I started thinking about what that meant," Laurie says. "I've ridden for a long time and I know that some days it is all completely fluid—and others it's more of a struggle, for me *and* for my horse. I've always wondered what causes that 'click' where we are just floating along together—and how can I help that happen on every ride?

"So I started playing with where and how my weight was distributed in the saddle, feeling what it felt like to be 'in the way,' and then looking for that point of balance where I felt myself and my horse just relax and move together.

"It took a little while, but I found that place," she says, with a laugh, "and it was actually not where I thought it would be—a little further forward in the saddle than I realized. But ever since that day, any time I start to struggle or feel my horse struggling, I just think, 'Get out of his way!' And then I find that place again and things improve dramatically."

Phase 1: Landing—The horse's hoof contacts the ground.

Phase 2: Support—The just-landed foot first bears weight.

Phase 3: Breakover—The foot "hinges" to begin a new step.

Phase 4: Flight—The horse's foot is actually off the ground.

BUSTED! Myths of Invisibility

MYTH: "Overweight riders don't have a chance in the show ring."

TRUTH: In the show ring, one myth in particular pervades—and most people don't talk about it. As one top-level dressage rider (who only told me this on the condition of anonymity) explains, "When you're showing, you know that judges have an expectation of what to look for. Judges do tend to ignore larger riders — completely."

Why is this?

"Many of them have an attitude and think, 'Just because they can afford a good horse doesn't mean plus-sized riders should be riding at this level,'" she says with a shrug. "I know that part of it is they just don't want to see good horses hurt, so they try to discourage larger riders by marking them low or ignoring them."

Shortly after this conversation, this rider got a nice surprise at a large regional show. (Synchronicity, anyone?) Afterward, she had opportunity to talk to one of the judges. The judge, who freely admitted this unspoken bias, said that when she first saw this rider enter the ring, she immediately dismissed her because of her size. Then the judge spoke the words that became the siren call for this book:

"Because you rode so beautifully and moved so well with your horse, it became impossible to ignore you."

Because of this rider's dedication and skill, despite the bias she knew existed, a "plus-sized rider" won that class, proving that it *can* be done.

Wendy Murdoch says she recalls once watching a very large

woman ride in a reined cowhorse competition. This woman, who was *quite* large, Murdoch emphasizes, "was *really* good. She was aggressive and focused and rode *extremely* well. She *won* that competition, and to look at her, many would have assumed she couldn't ride at all!"

In a 2014 episode of FX's popular television show *Louie*, "So Did the Fat Lady," we see how this "cloak of invisibility" spreads across the lives of all who struggle with weight and the perceptions of others—and how these negative discernments can get tangled (and play havoc) with self-worth. In one of this show's pivotal moments, Vanessa, a plus-sized waitress who asks the main character Louie out on a date, gives a shrill voice ("Why do you hate us so much?") to the silent shaming and pitying of larger women that goes on all around us.

"And why *are* we afraid to talk about such things?" asks Sarah Baker (the actress who plays Vanessa in the show) in a May 12, 2014, follow-up interview with Cara Buckley of *The New York Times*. "Really, is being a fat girl such a terrible thing?"

Whether this episode of Louie was a mere coincidence of entertainment, or a zeitgeist of talented, unapologetic, and unthin women laying claim to their fair share of the center stage, for those who struggle with body image issues and riding, this mainstream message of authentic empowerment exposes an ugly social construct for exactly what it is, in our horse world and beyond. I think our horses, as *originators* of this kind of open-heart authenticity, must be proud.

Circling back to Wendy Murdoch's earlier advice, let's connect the dots here between learning how to find your own "sweet spot" of balance and connection and now extending that willingness to discover and learn to your efforts to *really feel* what your horse's body is doing at every gait. "Don't overwork this," she cautions. "Just take a few moments during each ride to play around with feeling something new, and then go on and ride—and just enjoy your horse."

In small ways, through small adjustments, and with conscious practice over time, we can heighten our own awareness and learn to respond to our horses based on our own observations and feelings—not the directives or expectations of others. As we touched upon on p. 178, many of us, especially if we're struggling with body image and weight issues, are so accustomed to relinquishing responsibility for what we feel and what we need to do, we allow even well-meaning instructors to plant seeds of doubt in our own abilities to figure things out for ourselves. Part of repairing our own self-concept is doing this work and learning to trust what we feel and what we learn from our own practice on our horses. "It's not easy to be self-responsible," Murdoch acknowledges. "Or to learn to trust yourself. For some reason, it's so much easier to give all that over to someone else."

Murdoch challenges each of us to patiently persist in building (and trusting) our own awareness and to learn to be objective about our riding without getting caught up in the "I can't do this!" emotional rollercoaster. (And who among us hasn't fallen prey to *that* wail after a particularly horrid experience in the saddle?) "It's so difficult to be objective," she admits. "That's why we're so quick to find another person to tell us what to do."

It's important to note here that what Murdoch suggests (and neuroscience proves out) is effective because learning to ride is a primarily *kinesthetic learning experience* (that's a 10-pound phrase that means "learning by feel"). When you learn to find your place of balance and connection with the movement of your horse by experimenting with small changes on your own, rather than just following the directives of an instructor, you create neural pathways that help teach your nervous system the difference between being in your "good" position of solid balance and being anywhere else.

And that's a solid truth that remains on the inside—no matter what we look like on the outside.

In this chapter we explored how all the ways we use our bodies when we ride, from the distribution of our weight to our comfort in moving, our muscle mass is integral to riding. This will help in our work with horses by improving how our horses respond to our new awareness of our balance and movement. This will be a game-changer in the battle against negative body image because now every move we make will express newfound confidence in our bodies.

Your Chapter 7 **#Hoofpicks** include:

1 **Follow your thrill.** Contrary to some opinions floating around out there, one riding discipline isn't better than any other when it comes to heavier riders. Ride in the style that makes you happiest and feel your strong and balanced best. Rider skill is always the determining factor — and as long as your saddle fits well, the style of riding you choose is really of no consequence to your horse.

2 **Dabble in subtlety.** How you use your energy to center, ground, straighten and lift when you ride requires subtle shifts "inside" that pay off big in balance and connection and relaxation when you ride. Feeling this connection takes practice, an ability to "get quiet," and a willingness to open to a whole new way of riding.

3 **Delight in self-diagnostics.** Since much of this work is so deeply interior, only *you* can really pinpoint what you need to do to make progress. As you continue to work on your fitness program and try to incorporate some of these "softer" strategies into your riding, you'll begin to see where these

roads intersect (and where you need to concentrate your conditioning work).

4 Work small. Mental shifts, heightened observations, and tiny adjustments "inside" translate here to very big, long-term results. This is, quite literally, deep work in our riding that we may never have even considered before—or allowed ourselves time and freedom to play around with. Enjoy this part! The good news is, it will get easier and easier to find this awareness, and ultimately, for it to become a permanent part of how you work with horses.

Be
Mindful

8 | Mind Over Mass

Even as he considers "mental coaching" for young riders as "preventive medicine" to stop negative thought patterns *before* they start, Coach Daniel Stewart prescribes for adults something he calls "corrective medicine" to help them break down bad habits and replace them with more positive and productive ones. "The well-known catch phrase, 'Just do it!' may work well for young riders," he jokes, "but sometimes, for adults, it needs to be 'Just *un*do it!'"

When it comes to being overweight, the mental work required to undo old patterns of thinking and behavior may feel like a lost cause, or at the very least, not something we really understand. However, as we are about to discover, there is now some serious science behind the idea that brains *can* rewire, your mind *can* change, and things *can* be different—from the inside out. *But how do we get there from here?* First, you have to be willing to do some thoughtful (and possibly intense) work within this idea of "corrective medicine," and quite possibly, change the way your mind processes the concepts of "health" and "lifestyle" that you've more than likely been wrestling with for some time now. And even though *mindfulness*, *breathing*, *visualization*, and *affirmation* may sound like fluffy, ethereal words, if you're willing to entertain a few new ideas, these terms could pack a wallop when it comes to changing your life—and your riding.

The trouble with buzzwords is that at some point, after you've heard and read them several dozen times, you start to glaze over. Don't do it here! Before we go further, let's get the "official definition" of mindfulness out of the way: According to *Psychology Today*, mindfulness is "a state of active, open attention on the present. When you're mindful, you observe your thoughts and feelings from a distance, without judging them good or bad. Instead of letting your life pass you by, mindfulness means living in the moment and awakening to experience."

Applied to our riding, mindfulness can be the single greatest thing you can do for yourself, your horse, and every single ride. As you'll see in the coming sections, awakening your senses, heightening your focus, learning to conquer and reframe negative thought patterns, rediscovering your joy, and retooling habits to set your feet firmly on the pathways to your dearest riding goals are only a few of the side effects of embracing mindfulness as a way of life.

How and where do we begin? In this section, we'll be exploring a full spectrum of ideas and information, sensations and stories, exercise and expert advice along the *thought-feeling-behavior continuum* Marriage and Family Therapist Jill Valle described for us earlier (see p. 40). We'll gather a few new (and maybe a little bit unusual) seeds of change, and plant them in the research I've tilled to cultivate some new and empowering answers with our unique needs and circumstances in mind.

This is the point of departure from the usual trails you might expect to ride in a book about horses and riding and horsemanship; we're going to explore a few paths you may have glimpsed but have never ridden before—and discover together where they lead. While each of the areas in the coming chapters can be its own journey (and its own library of books), we're going to venture just far enough down each trail to show you some special connections for equestrians, along with resources, expert advice, and information about using these ideas to transform how you are in the barn, how you are around horses, and how you ride.

The Mindfulness Connection

Jill Valle says that things like mindfulness and yoga are great ways to tune in to your body, especially when you are trying to make significant lifestyle changes you want to fully commit to.

"Mindfulness is a communion of mind, body, and spirit that is crucial to positive attitude—especially about positive changes," she explains.

Valle, whose extensive training at The Mind Body Medical Institute at Harvard Medical School, along with a 15-year private practice, focusing on women and adolescents and body image issues, is well-equipped as a self-professed proponent of mindfulness in any endeavor. She feels that this could be the missing piece for a lot of riders who have struggled unsuccessfully with weight and body image issues. Mindfulness is the antidote for a lot of ills, she says. "We spend so much of our lives doing things *mindlessly*. Eating—especially overeating—is often emotional, and fat is emotional protection."

Valle incorporates mindfulness work into whatever overall strategies she helps her clients craft to cultivate a more positive body image, including specific focuses on:

• Accepting our bodies as they are, *right now.*

• Learning the basis of and how to disregard the unhealthy messages we receive from the media.

• Taking a holistic approach to health and fitness (think back, friends, to what we've covered so far!).

• Making the healthy lifestyle changes we need to.

This is where we get down to the real work of discovering what's been stopping us from reaching our personal and riding goals, and where we start to put together our own strategy for making changes for the better. This may include changes in our weight/fitness (we're empowered with some practical ways to do that now), and changes in our perception—how we think about our bodies, ourselves, and our potential as horsewomen. In Valle's words, now shaped into the question we've been waiting to ask, "How can we get 'unstuck' from the beliefs that do not serve us?"

EVERYDAY MINDFULNESS

"Mindfulness brings presence to the moment so you can notice what's been going on behind the scenes," Valle says.

Huh?

What's hard to realize, she explains, is how much is going through the back of our minds at any given time, sometimes even when we think we're paying attention to the moment at hand. A simple commitment to mindfulness, she asserts, is the antidote to the "autopilot" condition most of us spend more time in than we realize. "It doesn't require a big commitment to daily meditation to develop a mindfulness practice," Valle explains. "There are many easy ways to be mindful, every day."

Exercise for the Soul: 5-3-1

Valle recommends this small but powerful "everyday mindfulness" exercise she created for her patients, which she calls "5-3-1." She recommends using it any time you catch yourself feeling anxious, upset, or overwhelmed.

Stop, take a deep breath, and then ask yourself:

• What are **5** things I see in the room (or barn or arena) around me?

• What are **3** things I hear?

• What is **1** thing I feel?

(Try this right now and feel your blood pressure drop a few points.)

Valle says that using this exercise when we feel overwhelmed takes us out of our 'loop,' and returns us to the moment by making us an "observer." Noting that while very few people *really* meditate, this little 5-3-1 exercise is something her patients find they can actually use. "The result," she adds, "is more often than not a desire to explore deeper practices."

After speaking with Valle, I decided to give her 5-3-1 exercise a field test the very next time I felt overwhelmed by my life's magical roller coaster ride. It didn't take but about 20 minutes before I got a pop-up reminder that the farrier was coming later that afternoon, so I left my office early, picked up my daughter from school, and headed to the barn. On the way I got a business call deemed "extremely urgent" that necessitated an evening ahead full of damage control. As I pondered this mess, my daughter informed me she had nothing to wear to an important event the next day (oops), and I looked down to discover my inspection sticker was expired on my car. Did I mention we were out of hay?

Taking a deep breath, I pulled into the parking area near our barn.

- **5 things I saw around me?** 1) Horses grazing in a turnout pen; 2) the barn manager welding something on his trailer; 3) a friend giving her horse a bath in the washrack; 4) another friend hand-grazing her horse; 5) kittens playing on the clubhouse lawn.

- **3 things I heard?** 1) The buzz and popping of the welding equipment; 2) horses in the pen behind me running down the fence line; 3) a tractor coming back from raking the arena.

- **1 thing I felt?** Warm sun beating through the windshield of my car.

Did this exercise change any of my circumstances? Not at all. But somehow, everything suddenly felt more doable. I'd wait for the farrier, make some notes as they occurred to me for my later emails, set a reminder to call and order hay the next morning (they were closed for the day) before I left the house early enough to get my car inspected on the way to work. After the farrier was finished, my daughter and I could go to the mall, grab a salad in the food court, and find something vaguely wearable for the next day's event. (As a parent I do believe in natural consequences—this one being, "You get what you get when you shop the night before for an outfit." In Texas that all rhymes perfectly.)

Yes, it turned out to be a late night, but yes, it all worked out. And I'll have to say the turning point toward calm control was Valle's 5-3-1.

RAISIN THE BAR

There is a well-known mindfulness exercise involving a raisin that originated with Jon Kabat-Zinn, Ph.D., Professor of Medicine Emeritus and creator of the Stress Reduction Clinic and the Center for Mindfulness in Medicine, Health Care, and Society at the University of Massachusetts Medical School (he's also author of nine books on the subject of mindfulness—he *is* his own library!).

Exercise for the Soul: The Raisin Exercise

At Kabat-Zinn's MBSR clinics, the mothership of the "Raisin Exercise," it is practiced as follows:

1 First examine the raisin, noticing its wrinkly texture, color, size, and shape.

2 Smell it. (Did you even realize a raisin has a smell?)

3 Put it in your mouth, but *don't chew*. Notice how the raisin feels on your tongue, roll it around a bit and feel it soften.

4 After an excruciating period of this activity, you're invited to bite down and taste the inside of the raisin, then to chew and chew and chew until it is nothing but raisiny goo.

5 Finally, swallow, feeling the goo slide down your throat, noticing the aftertaste once it's gone.

I don't know about you, but this is not how I usually eat raisins. Or anything else for that matter. For the record, I did try this exercise with a McDonald's french fry, and I'll have to say that while goo stage was admittedly gross, I still enjoyed that french fry more than any other I can remember.

The point of this exercise, writes Kabat-Zinn in his book *Full Catastrophe Living* is to illustrate to ourselves how difficult it is to pay attention and be truly present with what we're doing—and to think about just one thing at a time. Mindfulness techniques such as the Raisin Exercise are designed to quiet a busy mind, helping you become aware (and stay aware) of the present moment *only*—so you get less caught up in what happened in the past and what you think might happen in the future.

By creating what Kabat-Zinn calls "an island of *being* in the sea of constant *doing* in which our lives are usually immersed, a time in which we allow all the 'doing' to stop," we open ourselves to the richness of learning how to slow down, make time for ourselves, and nurture a greater sense of calm and self-acceptance in our lives. With the idea of learning to make thoughtful changes in our lifestyle, creating moment-to-moment awareness of what's going on in our heads will help us dismiss patterns of self-talk that are not serving us and cultivate new ways of seeing old problems.

"Mindfulness is much more than *just* meditation practice," writes Kabat-Zinn,

RESOURCES

Jon Kabat-Zinn's:
Full Catastrophe Living (Delta Trade Paperbacks, 1991)

Wherever You Go, There You Are (Hyperion Books, 1994)

The Power of Meditation and Prayer with Sogyal Rinpoche, Larry Dossey, and Michael Toms (Hay House, 1997)

Everyday Blessings with Myla Kabat-Zinn. (Hyperion, 1997)

Mindfulness Meditation for Everyday Life (Piatkus, 2001)

Coming to Our Senses (Hyperion, 2006)

Letting Everything Become Your Teacher: 100 Lessons in Mindfulness (Dell Publishing Company, 2009)

"It is also a way of life that reveals the gentle and loving wholeness that lies at the heart of our being, even in times of great pain and suffering."

But enough about pain and suffering—and raisins, for that matter. Here's an exercise that you'll probably like better. (I'm pretty sure your horse will, too!)

Exercise for the Soul: Mindful Grooming

In the spirit of the moment-to-moment awareness created by Kabat-Zinn's raisin exercise, I give you the raisin exercise's horsier cousin, what I'm going to call "mindful grooming":

1 Go to the barn. Greet your horse and then tie him somewhere free of distractions.

2 Get your grooming tools and lay them out near your horse in the order you will use them.

3 Examine your horse. Notice his expression, the tone of his muscles, the texture of his coat, how he's standing.

4 Take a deep breath and smell your horse, the hay, the barn around you. (Only horse people appreciate this particular brand of aromatherapy.)

5 Place your hands on your horse and feel his coat. Take another deep breath as you notice the warmth of the horse's body and the subtle motions of the surface of his body. Wait, without doing anything other than stand there with your hands on his neck or shoulder, until both you and your horse relax. (Wait for the big, deep sigh from one, or likely both, of you.)

6 Get a brush or currycomb and begin working slowly over your horse's body. Feel each stroke of the brush or each circle of the currycomb. Time your breathing with the use of your tools. If something irritating enters your mind, take another deep breath and concentrate only on the path of your brush. Feel the smoothness of your horse's coat with one hand, while the other follows the brush.

7 Brush in smooth, continuous strokes. Gently massage any areas of tightness you feel in your horse.

Invoking all your senses as you share this time and space with your horse may bring more enjoyment of this everyday grooming experience than you have ever experienced before. And while you may even feel a little sheepish when you think of all the times you've run into the barn, given a few hasty swipes of the brush (...just on the part where the saddle goes...) and "groomed" your horse without being really, truly *present*, take heart. In the words of the late, great Maya Angelou, "When we know better, we can do better." Grooming our horses is just one way we can practice being more present in each moment of our lives. Mindfulness simply means giving your mind fully to *whatever* you're doing. As you go about your day and especially your more routine and mundane activities such as barn chores, remember Kabat-Zinn's Raisin Exercise and make up your mind to, be *present.*

Focusing for a few moments on a single raisin (or horse) isn't a silly activity if it builds the skills we need to make life-changing adjustments to our everyday experiences. With everything that splits our attention, moment by moment and day after day, at an all-time high (and climbing), mindfulness is becoming an indispensable tool for not only coping with escalating stress levels, but also for discovering and nurturing a still place within ourselves from which ideas, solutions, and new habits can begin to form.

The Meditation Prescription

Meditation is one of those things that gets tossed about and tossed aside, almost as many times as the "D- Word" and "E-Word" (see pp. 111 and 116). At the time of writing, a Google search of the word "meditation" yields 33,900,000 results. So no, I'm not going to tell you how to meditate. I will say that, like lots of other powerful things, meditation itself is deceptively simple. And, depending on how

busy your "chattering monkey mind" is, it can be really, really difficult to
    just
        sit
            still
                and breathe.

Breathing is key to most of the meditative techniques I've used or read about, from the most elaborate visualizations—or guided meditations—to the simplest techniques. We'll dig into all of that in a bit, but first let's explore what meditation does for you. After centuries of practice in Eastern religions and philosophies, meditation has finally, blessedly, hit the mainstream in such a way that it is attracting big research dollars from the National Institutes of Health to the United States Marine Corps. In the February 2014 issue of *Time Magazine*, mindfulness (of all things!) was the cover feature. In her article within, writer Kate Pickert delved into the work of the mindfulness guru and MIT-educated scientist we've already met: Jon Kabat-Zinn. In Kabat-Zinn's 1979 book, *Full Catastrophe Living,* he revealed the results of eight-week, stress-reduction clinics that required, as their primary underpinning, a daily practice of 45 minutes of meditation. That's right. 45 minutes of sitting still and just focusing on the sensation of your breath coming into and exiting your body. And *not* thinking about anything (everything!) else. Sounds simple, doesn't it? Try it. You won't believe all the places your mind can wander in just 45 minutes when left to its own devices.

As Kabat-Zinn explains in his book, the idea is not to *prevent* your mind's meanderings. Rather, when you find yourself off on a tangent, the object is just that: *find yourself there,* and then gently lead your awareness back to your breathing.

I've sat in meditation classes where we were encouraged to close our eyes and imagine our minds as blank canvases. As thoughts appeared on the canvas, we were told to imagine they were leaves fluttering gently down to a stream where the water carried them away (elaborate and involved a lot of concentration, but it *was* pretty). Another instructor said to visualize the mind as a vast open blue sky and thoughts as clouds that drift across the sky until they are out of view.

As for the 45-minute commitment, seven days a week, eight weeks running, well, that may sound hardcore, but Kabat-Zinn's results speak for themselves. To write her article, Pickert attended an MBSR class, both in hopes of gaining better insight (we writers do that sometimes; I'll tell you about mine shortly), as well as seeking to find a better way to deal with the stressors of her own hyper-connected life. She reports being frustrated, at first, by the constant bombardment of thoughts and distractions.

This is not unusual, experts agree; in fact, in today's world it would be unusual *not* to feel completely weird and useless just sitting still and doing nothing for 45 straight minutes. We're multitaskers, and we're proud of it. We make mental grocery lists in the dental chair, we talk on the phone while giving the dog a bath, and we pay bills while we're watching TV. We've gone so far down this technological rabbit hole that there's even a commercial featuring a girl in the middle of a *yoga* class, reaching down and transferring money on her smartphone right in the middle of standing bow. As if that were a good thing.

How many people have *you* seen talking on their cellphones while riding or longeing their horses? I often attend NCHA cutting events near my home in Fort Worth, Texas. Because I live near Will Rogers Coliseum, one of my favorite escapes is going over there periodically throughout these two-week stretches to watch the horses work, but also just to watch the warm-up end of the pen where trainers are loping horses. To me (and this may be just plain weird, but it's an example of finding your own way in the mindfulness arena) there is a meditative quality to watching a horse lope in long, slow circles—and these horses can go for days. What bothered me most the last time I visited is that not just one or two, but almost *all* of the folks out there loping horses were *on their cell phones*! The truth is, we've rewired our brains to the point where it feels odd, even when loping a six-figure SuperStakes contender, *not* to be multitasking.

However, study after study shows that multitasking, while completely *possible*, is not quite the solution we think it is. In fact, it *lowers* our overall productivity—and worse (for our purposes here), robs us of the opportunity to be *present* in our bodies and in our lives. In other words, multitasking creates mind*less*ness.

Because modern neuroscience has now determined the neuroplasticity of the human brain—which, in plain terms, means you can, in fact, change your mind, and even better, "rewire" your brain—it also confirms our ability to rewire our *attention*. (So even for those of us whose smartphones have become an appendage, there's hope.) What's more, because these studies show that attention—and mindfulness—is like a muscle: It strengthens with exercise. Here's what Kabat-Zinn tells the enrollees at his MBSR clinics when they begin his eight-week course: "The most important thing to remember is to practice every day. Even if you can make only five minutes to practice during your day, five minutes of mindfulness can be very restorative and healing."

What people often fail to understand, he explains, is that meditation is really just about paying attention. And, since paying attention is something we all know how to do (at least occasionally), meditation is really not as foreign or irrelevant to our life experience as we may think.

RT³: JUST SIT STILL AND BREATHE

Following Jill Valle's tracks on the 5-3-1 exercise (p. 214) and shortening Kabat-Zinn's original formula of 45-7-8 to something more doable—and armed with the understanding that increasing our mindfulness will aid us in our quest for the joyful, productive lifestyle we long for—let's all commit to building our mindfulness by sitting *still and breathing* (nothing fancy yet, just breathe) for at least **20** minutes a day, **5** days a week, for **4** weeks. If you really do this—commit to spending at least 20 minutes, five out of the next seven days, sitting quietly and dragging your focus back to your breathing as many times as it takes—chances are you will discover a new oasis of calm in your life that is well worth whatever you have to do every day to make it happen. And even better, this small commitment now will begin your mindfulness practice, setting the stage perfectly for new habits and practices to come.

I know. It's hard at first. It feels really silly. And a little bit selfish. Do it anyway. And, knowing full well that your mind is going to be hopping around like a bunny on candy-coated carrots for the first few sessions, vow only to notice when

the thoughts come, and drag your awareness back to your breathing. You may have
to do this over and over again for the whole 20 minutes, but the only object is to
sit there and keep trying. (Some people subdue their "chattering monkey mind"
by actually saying, "in," as they breathe in, and, "out," as they breathe out.) Over
time your spaces of mental "nothingness" will expand and your mental bunnies
will slow, fade, and appear less frequently. People I know who have committed to
a regular meditation practice report that once you get this habit established, 20
minutes will seem like nothing. And everything.

THERE'S AN APP FOR THAT

Actually, there are many—473,000 results on a Google search for meditation
apps, and at the time of writing, 497 different apps on iTunes alone—out there
just waiting to help you start your meditation practice. While simple breathing
works just fine, if you want to move deeper into this practice there is a huge variety
of different kinds and styles of meditation aids out there. (Ironically, the smartphone can now be our best mindfulness support, reminding us when it's time to
meditate, and then connecting us with the app that makes the experience as rich
or as simple as we'd like it to be.) One needle in this huge haystack recommended
to me by my daughter, of all people, is called Stop, Breathe & Think (stopbreathe-
think.org). It starts by asking, "How are you?" And invites you to check in with
yourself through a series of categories/questions:

1 **Stop, Breathe, Think**—The app invites you to dim the screen for 10 seconds while you close your eyes, take a deep breath and think about how your mind and body feel. A "ding" brings you back just in the nick of time before you fall asleep. (Or maybe that's just the way it works for me after a long day.)

2 **Check In**—The app then asks you to rate yourself:
  • Mentally, and then physically, choosing between "Great," "Good," "Meh," "Poor," and "Rough."

  • Emotionally, you get to pick up to five facial emoticons from "smiley" to "frowny."

3 **Results**—Using your answers, the app then offers you a customized meditation for your day: A 6-Minute Equanimity Meditation can help me be more balanced, open, and nonjudgmental (maybe). A 5-Minute Gratitude Meditation promises feelings of happiness, joy, and enthusiasm (it's a *meditation*, not a magic wand), and a 6-Minute Relax, Ground, and Clear Meditation offers moments of feeling physically and mentally settled and calm (look for baby steps in the right direction at first; bigger results come with regular practice). I'll have to say this app helps me quite a bit (I usually go with all three…), especially when trying to settle in for a blissful evening of writing (you're holding the result), or coveted time with my family, or a few hours with my horses, Trace and Rio, following a crazy day of directing the communications of a large downtown Methodist church and about a dozen active ministries. (Anything that can settle my mind following a day of mental ping-pong-slash-whack-a-mole is the best endorsement I can think of!)

MOMENTS OF MINDFULNESS

If the idea of meditating still makes you fidget just thinking about it, there are a number of different ways to incorporate moments of mindfulness in your life (sans cushion). As the creator of Tai Chi for the Equestrian James Shaw demonstrates, you can even "get your meditation on" in the saddle.

Exercise for the Body and Soul:
Standing and Sitting Meditation

The goal of this exercise from Shaw's book *Ride from Within* is to develop a new awareness and understanding of balance on the ground first and then on the horse, with the goal of achieving a state of quiet, centered stillness in the saddle.

"This exercise teaches you the different roles the bones, muscles, and mind play in your balance," says Shaw. "It will help develop the roadmap to a place of quiet connection with your horse. You will embark upon a path, which is a pattern of initiating movement by using your mind, breath, and body."

1 Stand with your feet parallel (neither pigeon-toed nor splayed), shoulder-width apart. Your legs are straight, neither locked nor bent, knees relaxed, arms hanging naturally at your sides, hands relaxed.

2 Look forward toward the horizon. Smile and breathe.

3 Imagine the crown of your head floating upward, as if pulled from above. (This idea and visualization puts your head and neck in proper alignment without creating tension in the muscles of your neck.)

4 Now imagine that you are just a skeleton, no muscles are holding up your bones. How would you have to "stack up" your bones to remain standing?

5 Turn your attention to where your weight is in your feet. How is your weight distributed? Is it equal between your two feet, or is there more in one foot or the other? Is it evenly spread across your "footprint," or is there more weight on the insides or outsides of your feet? Is there more weight in your heels or on the balls of your feet? Make a mental note of what you find (and how it may differ or support what the scales told you in Coach Daniel Stewart's balance exercise—p. 187). As we began to discuss previously, and now start to put into active practice, your natural distribution of weight has an important connection

to your riding: where your weight is in your *feet on the ground* tells you where your weight is in your *seat in the saddle*. (We'll return to this in the mounted portion of this exercise.)

6 Focus your mind on the balls of your feet. Note that most people stand with their weight back in the heels of their feet. In that position, you lack structural alignment and you have less strength. Standing with your weight in your heels puts you at the "end of your rope" as far as balance is concerned—the slightest push on your chest will send you backward and out of balance with very little chance to recover.

7 Now move your attention to your breathing. Take two or three deep, slow breaths, and with every breath relax a little more. Similar to our earlier grounding exercise (see p. 172), use every out-breath to allow your body to sink deeper toward the earth.

8 Return your awareness to your entire body, and then recheck the distribution of your weight. Has it shifted into the balls of your feet? If your weight is still in your heels, allow it to move into the balls of your feet. Keep this feeling in mind as you prepare to begin sitting meditation on your horse.

9 Mount your horse and remain at the halt.

10 Look forward to the horizon. Smile and breathe.

11 Expand your crown upward. Visualize your head lifting, as if being pulled from above, so you feel like you're floating upward. Feel the lift through all your vertebrae, starting with the top of your spine, not by stretching your neck up, but by imagining that you're expanding the space between each vertebra in your spine, all the way down to your pelvis.

12 Holding this relaxed "floating upward" sensation, turn your full focus to your seat bones as they sit in the saddle. Try to feel the "bone-to-leather connection," and see how your weight is distributed, much as you did previously in Steps 6 and 8 with your feet on the ground.

13 Recall the adage that "where your weight is in your *feet* is where your weight is in your *seat*." Just as most people stand with their weight back in their heels, most riders place their weight back in their seat bones. Is this true for you? And, just as when most people shift their weight forward to the balls of their feet they say they feel like they're leaning forward, most riders, upon moving their weight to the center of their seat bones, say they feel like they're leaning forward. While this feeling is entirely normal, it's also inaccurate; with your weight in the center of your seat bones, you've actually found your center. With time, this position will feel "normal"—not to mention stronger, more supple, and better connected with your horse.

14 Return your focus to your seat bones and their "bone-to-leather" connection. How big are they? Can you visualize them as big as golf balls? Tennis balls? See them and feel them with your weight balanced in the sphere you are envisioning.

15 Turn your attention back to your breathing. Take two or three deep, slow breaths, and with every out-breath, relax your body downward and a little more deeply into this new seat position.

16 Now just smile and sit quietly on your horse, continuing to breathe, feel, and appreciate the relaxed, deep, balanced seat you have right now. Your goal is to have this seat and this state of mind whenever you ride.

Another good way to make this powerful tool yours without subscribing to what you might conjure up as the stereotypical meditative scenario is *moving* meditation. Any type of repetitive task will work well for this (mowing, raking an arena, painting fence, and shedding out your horse's winter coat come to mind), as well as some types of yoga. I am a fan of walking meditation, often referred to as "mindful walking."

There's a catch to turning repetitive tasks into moving meditations—it gets dangerously close to multitasking; it's not as simple as you may think. (But I'll let you slide here if you really can't make yourself sit still for 20 minutes.) Take walking meditation, for example. As Jon Kabat-Zinn explains in *Full Catastrophe Living*, "We carry our mind with us when we walk, so we are usually absorbed in our own thoughts to one extent or another. We are hardly ever *just walking*, even when we are 'just going for a walk.'" Focusing your awareness *only* on your walking (feeling the ground beneath you, feeling your weight moving heel to toe, taking in the sensory input from the natural world around you without mental commentary) is much harder than it seems. This practice is not just about watching your feet—it's about being *aware* of walking without being *consumed* by it.

Usually, we walk for a specific reason, such as getting from Point A to Point B. As we're walking, we're generally thinking about Point B: *How much farther? What time will I get there? What am I going to do after that?* And especially if we're walking to build stamina (as part of our commitment to our Strength-Stamina-Flexibility Holy Trinity—see p. 118), our mind is busy: *How's my heart rate? Gosh it's hot/cold/windy/about to rain! How much longer could this hill possibly be? How much farther do I need to walk today to offset that piece of pie I ate yesterday?* And then there are the real-life concerns we tend to take on our walks with us: *What am I going to do about that confrontation at work yesterday? Am I ever going to get this book finished? The car needs new tires. What will we have for dinner? Yikes! We have no food—I really need to go to the grocery store.* As we're walking (and composing a mental grocery list), another thought intrudes: *Oh no! I forgot to put out the trash cans! Will I make it back in time?* (This may add a speed component to intensify our walk.) Speed-walking now, the self-chastising begins: *Why can't I ever manage to get in bed at a reasonable hour? The house is a disaster and I offered to host a family dinner this weekend! Aaaaack! Grocery store! But first, I'd better pay bills. And the horses need to have their feet trimmed—and it's also time to have their teeth floated.*

Before we know it, we're standing in front of Point B, wondering how we got there. Sound familiar?

A New Way to Walk

Walking meditation, on the other hand, is a completely different experience. It's all about feeling the many physical sensations of walking itself. And, when you drill down to this level of awareness, you can't help but be amazed by the complex balancing act continuously taking place on the relatively small surface area of our own two feet.

The awareness we need to return to the "simple" act of walking involves focusing on the movement and sensations in our feet, legs, torso, and arms, all working together to propel our body forward on the path we choose. Once we are able to focus on feeling all these sensations, we can start to integrate our breathing, and then time it to our steps (in, 2, 3; out, 2, 3). As we walk, our gaze should be fixed softly about 4 feet in front of us—*not* on our feet. The object is to cultivate an *internal observation* of the sensation of walking, and just like our breathing and meditation exercises, when we catch our attention wandering, we gently bring it back to the physical sensation of just walking and breathing.

Remember how you learned to feel the four phases of the horse's stride (see p. 202)? Now it's time to become fully aware of each phase of *your own* stride:

Phase 1: Landing—When one foot contacts the ground.

Phase 2: Support—When your weight shifts and the just-landed foot first bears weight.

Phase 3: Breakover—When your other foot "hinges" to begin a new step.

Phase 4: Flight—When your other foot is actually off the ground.

Citing cases of actors "learning to walk" onstage as if for the first time, and people who, due to illness or injury, must re-learn to walk, Kabat-Zinn emphasizes that with walking meditation, the object is *not* to get to a Point B at all. In fact, he prefers walking in a prescribed circle or back and forth in lanes so there *is* no Point B. This ensures we are alone with our mission to keep the mind at rest with no place to go, nothing to do, and nothing more interesting than being present with each individual step, as if it were a completely new experience.

"This doesn't mean that your mind will go along with your intention to *just be* with each step for very long without a concerted effort to keep it focused," Kabat-Zinn cautions. "You might soon find it condemning the whole exercise, calling it stupid, useless, idiotic. Or it might start to play games with the pace or with balancing, or have you looking around or thinking of other things. But if your mindfulness is strong, you will quickly become aware of this activity and just return your attention to the feet, legs, and body."

Exercise for the Soul: Set Your Day for a Quieter Path

In the class I attended led by Eric Billingslea (we met him earlier in the book in our discussion of nutrition—see p. 103) he made a revolutionary suggestion. He challenged us to do a 45-minute, morning "slow" walk that he promised to be the metabolic equivalent to three hours of aerobic exercise at any other time of day. While I'm not sure of the science behind his claim (and I really don't think it counts as the stamina-building component of our fitness regimen), there were enough svelte disciples of his nodding their heads knowingly in that packed room that I decided it was worth a try. I invite *you* to give it a try, too, because not only does it help fulfill our "framework" component, it makes for excellent mindfulness practice.

Here's how it works:

1 **When you first awaken in the morning, get out of bed and begin walking.** Billingslea says we can use the potty, but not to turn on lights, let the dogs out, start the coffee, or anything else that might now be part of your normal wake up routine. (This confuses the dogs.)

2 **Walk as slowly as you possibly can (think slow mo).** Walk heel to toe, bringing total awareness to your breathing and the physical sensation of walking, returning your awareness to just walking and breathing every time you catch your

mind wandering. Tread your prescribed path through your house, without stopping, for 45 minutes. (This is *way* harder than you think it will be. It also takes some pre-planning and path-clearing. Did I mention that it confuses the dogs?)

3 Illuminate your path. Since it was still dark when I got up early enough to do this, I put a few candles and nightlights along the path, and I *did* slow enough to light them all on the first pass. This was actually kind of cool and ceremonial. I began calling my daily slow-walk my "freeform labyrinth." (After making fun of it for a few days, both my husband and my daughter joined me. They suggested we add music. I ignored them and just kept walking.)

What amazed me about the 45-minute walking meditation (coinciding, I later realized, with Kabat-Zinn's Stress Clinic prescription of 45 minutes a day in sitting meditation, so there's obviously something to this recommended timeframe) is its predictable progression. When I began, my mind was fully cluttered with thoughts of all I had to do that day, problems that didn't get solved the day before, and a few problems that couldn't be solved at all. The first five-to-six minutes were a struggle, and I was continuously dragging my awareness *back* to that heel-to-toe motion of each foot, one after the other. Somewhere during minutes seven or eight, however, something strange happened. No longer was I struggling—my mind really *was* a blank canvas. Occasionally a stray thought would dart out of the underbrush and make a run for it, but it was quickly and quietly escorted to the curb by my desire to keep my canvas clear. At some point after that, probably around the 15-minute mark, I settled into "The Zone," and from there, the rest of the time flew by. More mornings than not now, I am sad to hear the timer buzz, calling an end to my peaceful walk to start my day.

I have found that since I began these morning meditative walks—and I now try to bookend my days with regular sitting-and-breathing meditations in the evenings (made much easier, by the way, by my moving meditation experiences)—I am much more likely to find that same quiet, contemplative "blank canvas" mental place when I ride. It's a different dynamic, of course, but I do feel quieter on the inside, and it seems like my horse can feel that, too.

Exercise for the Soul: Walking Meditation on Horseback

In her *Yoga & Riding: Techniques for Equestrians* DVDs, instructor and bestselling author Linda Benedik explains how in the saddle, the walk can become a moving meditation, both in the arena and on the trail. Here's how:

1 Find a walk tempo that is comfortable for you and your horse.

2 Clear your mind, and coordinate your breath and movement with the movement of your horse.

3 Find a sense of stillness within yourself and focus on it, becoming fully present in the sensation of each moment, feeling the rhythmic integration of your breathing with the breathing and movement of your horse.

4 With each step, honor your horse with the gratitude and appreciation you feel for his company and his willingness to carry you upon his back.

This one takes some practice, but is well worth it, and makes a delightful way to end each ride, leaving both you and your horse with an incredible sense of union as, through breath and movement, you've become one.

SYSTEMS CHECK

Being aware of what's going on in your body at all times is part of becoming comfortable with it—through all its shape and weight fluctuations. To help you add this vital tool to your RT³ toolbox, I'm offering a couple of variations on classic, body-scan meditations. The systematic, full-body "check-in" has been around for a very long time. Jon Kabat-Zinn says that by training yourself to put specific and intentional focus on each part of your body in a deliberate, consistent progression is effective not only for understanding and relating to your body, but also for developing attention that is at once both concentrated *and* flexible. Isn't that *exactly* what we need when we ride?

RESOURCES

Linda Benedik's *Yoga & Riding* DVDs, and her book with Veronica Wirth *Yoga for Equestrians,* all from Trafalgar Square Books (www. horseandriderbooks.com).

Exercise for the Soul: Body-Scan Meditation

1 Starting with the toes of your left foot, move your focus slowly up your left leg, acknowledging any sensations you find as you go.

2 Direct your breathing in and out of each place your attention settles, from your toes all the way up your left leg. (Imagine that each part of your body now has the ability to breathe on its own.)

3 At the top of your left leg, go across your pelvis, straight down to your right toes, and then slowly back up your right leg to your pelvis, stopping wherever you feel any tightness to let that place "breathe" away the tension.

4 Move upward through your lower back and abdomen, and then up your torso, through your chest to the base of your shoulders. Stop and breathe in each region, determining as you go how large each area of attention should be. This will vary with your level of tension. Allow your awareness to be your guide.

5 At your shoulders, first go right, letting your attention travel down to your right fingers, and then back up; move across your chest to your left shoulder, down to your left fingers, and then back up to your left shoulder and across to the center of your chest. Breathe each time you move your focus.

6 Move up through your neck and throat to your face, around the circumference of your head, and then up to the top of your head.

7 End your scan by breathing through an imaginary opening in the top of your head.

8 Imagine that your breath, now flowing freely from each part of your body, from your toes all the way up through the top of your head, and then back down to your toes again.

"By the time we have completed the body scan," Kabat-Zinn writes, "it can feel as if the entire body has dropped away or has become transparent, as if its substance were in some way erased. It can feel as if there is nothing but breath flowing freely across all the boundaries of the body."

This, my friends, is exactly where we want to be as we struggle to dismiss the limitations imposed by our bodies—or by any pre-existing *ideas* about our bodies. And this is where meditation can take us.

Exercise for the Soul: Body Scan on Horseback

Once you've tried the basic body scan a few times and have marveled at the complete and utter limp-noodle relaxation you can achieve, try it on horseback. (You be the judge of whether your horse is an appropriate mount for this exercise. And, if you have a friend willing to lead your horse in the early stages of this exercise, so much the better!)

1 Starting at your left stirrup, check in with your toes. Are they spread and relaxed (see p. 196)? Breathe through your toes. (Anatomically tricky, I know, but by now you know you can do it!) Any tightness in the ball/arch of your foot? Breathe through it, and then move up your calf to your knee, thigh, and left hip, breathing through each part as you go—stopping for an extra breath wherever you feel tightness.

2 Go "across the saddle" and drop down to your right toes. Breathing as you go, move back up through your feet, ankles, calves, knees, thighs, and hips. Each breath and release is your indicator of whether to stay or to move on to the next part.

3 Check in with your pelvis and lower back—your *center*—and then move on up through your abdomen and into your chest, breathing through each part as you go.

4 From the top of your chest, move toward your left shoulder and straight down to your left fingers. Open and close them (gently!) on the reins to breathe and release any tension. Let your attention then travel back up to your left shoulder, across to your right shoulder, and then down to your right fingers, where you again gently open and close your fingers to identify any tension, and then breathe to release it. Return back up your right arm to the center of your chest, continuing to breathe "through" each part as you go.

5 Move up through your neck, jaw and face, breathing into and through any tension you find, traveling around your head and up to the imaginary "blowhole" in the top of your helmet.

6 Take a few deep breaths here, and imagine this breath moving into and through each region of your body, in and out through the top of your head, as you remain settled deeply in your secure position on the back of your horse.

Try this first at a standstill, then at a walk, and then at a trot. Ultimately, you will be able to do a version of the horseback body scan at any gait—and anytime you feel out of sync with your horse. With this powerful tool at your fingertips, you'll be able to quickly locate and remove any tightness in your body that is impeding your ride.

Take a Breather

As you've no doubt noticed by now (in your life and in this book), one of the things we're always asked to focus on as part of everything—from physical performances of all kinds (from sports to music to dance), to spiritual practices (from contemplative prayer to various mindfulness and meditation techniques such as those I mentioned earlier in this chapter), to health-related activities (from childbirth to panic disorders to pain management to stroke and cardiac rehab)—is your *breath*. And, as silly as it may sound, the very first thing we forget to do whenever we're concentrating or upset or stressed is *breathe*. (Not for long, of course, because our life literally depends on it.) Especially when we're riding horses, in everything from our first riding lesson to a Grand Prix dressage test, the advice we always get (and often forget) is to *breathe*.

"It is in your best interests, as a rider and as a human being, living on this planet," Coach Daniel Stewart says, "to learn—and remember—to breathe properly."

WHAT *IS* "PROPER" BREATHING?

The best way to define "proper" breathing is first to tell you what it's *not* and how improper breathing can sneak up on you when you least expect it. While of course when we stop breathing *completely* (as in holding our breath) we do notice it pretty quickly, what we may *not* notice very quickly, or sometimes at all, is the shallow, thoracic (chest) breathing we fall prey to. While we *are* technically breathing, this type of breathing is not doing us or our riding any good. According to

Coach Stewart, when your chest inflates, but your belly stays flat, it interferes with the vital exchange between your respiratory and circulatory systems (blood and oxygen) that takes place mostly in your lower lungs. "If the fresh air isn't getting there," he reminds us, "it can't be sent 'upstairs'" (to your brain).

"Chest breathing" is not only highly ineffective for getting vital oxygen into our bloodstream (which then fuels your brain *and* muscles); when we hold air in our upper torso we expand and lengthen our torso in a way that creates tension in our chest and shoulders *and* raises our center of gravity (remember our physics lesson on p. 176?) to make balance more difficult (which in turn raises our stress level and makes us breathe even more shallowly). This is how the common habit of breathing too shallowly (or holding your breath) adversely affects our balance, mental focus, *and* muscle strength.

In her book *Ride With Your Mind Essentials*, renowned instructor and clinician Mary Wanless also addresses the power of breathing on horseback. She says that if you find that you're running short on breath as you ride, it may not be so much a fitness problem (especially now that we've done all that great "framework") so much as a *breathing* problem. To diagnose this, Wanless invites us to "follow" our breath in and notice where it tends to stop, both when we're riding and when we're just sitting still. We may be holding or limiting our breath more than we realize.

Wanless says that holding our breath when we ride is not unusual (whew!), nor is the habit of taking short in-breaths that almost qualify as a gasps. To complicate matters, with that quick in-breath that inflates only our upper chest and pushes the chest and shoulders up, sometimes we then forget to breathe out. So common is this in the dressage arena, she notes as an example, that dressage judges often remark on how riders have their very best moments when they ride down the centerline at the *end* of their test—when they finally allow themselves to breathe all the way out because the test is over!

At any level of riding, breathing properly in the saddle makes a big difference. Breathing deeply and learning to use your diaphragm to force air all the way into your lower lungs to create a "belly breathing" habit will relax your muscles, improve your balance, and clear your mind to allow you to stay present and mindful. In *Ride*

With the Mind Essentials, Wanless compares the diaphragmatic breathing we need to employ when we ride to the breathing used by opera singers and those who play wind instruments. (Ever watch Kenny G hold a note on his saxophone for what seems like days? This is the image I associate with this piece of advice from Wanless, and what I think we need to keep in our heads about breathing properly when we ride and work with our horses.) "Good riders bear down and breathe continually, without a sense of effort," she writes, "The muscle use of bearing down can only be maintained indefinitely if it is accompanied by diaphragmatic breathing."

To help you understand what Wanless means by "bear down and breathe" (it's really not as intense or difficult as it sounds) consider this exercise for teaching your body to breathe this way (compliments of 9th Degree Taekwondo Grandmaster Won Chik Park):

Exercise for the Body and Soul: Breathing Lesson

Quite by happy accident, I learned this technique years ago from a world-renowned martial artist, Taekwondo Grandmaster Won Chik Park, who in response to my questions about "proper breathing" (and to address my habit of holding my breath) took a few minutes to demonstrate the "ancient recipe" for training your body to breathe deeply and well. It is amazing how much of a workout breathing can be! His impromptu demonstration has stuck with me for more than 25 years…maybe it will work for you, too.

1 **Sit quietly.** Wherever you are and however you're most comfortable, close your eyes and breathe in through your nose, visualizing as you do the air coming into your chest, abdomen, and finally, all the way down to your belly, until your belly has expanded all it possibly can.

2 **Breathe in more.** And more. And still more, until you start to wonder if you might pop like the balloon you're probably starting to look like.

3 Pause. Hold it for as long as you can; try to hold the "full" stage a little bit longer with each successive breath.

4 Exhale. Through slightly pursed lips, let the air out slowly, little by little, taking twice as long to exhale as you did to inhale.

5 Exhale more. Keep this up until you feel "empty" of air.

6 Now exhale more. And more. Still more—until you feel your balloon's "sides" starting to touch.

7 Pause. Hold it as long as you can; try to hold the "empty" stage a little bit longer with each successive breath.

8 Begin again. Slowly start to take in air until your lungs are full again. Repeat this entire process continuously for your entire breathing practice session.

This kind of breathing leaves your mind with very little else to do, Grandmaster Park explained. And by putting that pause at the "top" and "bottom" of each breath, you develop the self-discipline to regulate your flow of air under anxiety. While daily practice of this breathing exercise does a lot of good things for your physical self, it also trains your mind to use your breath to relax and focus (key to using the mindfulness techniques we touched on earlier in this chapter). And, best of all, when we breathe easy and are relaxed and focused, our horse follows suit.

Let's follow up with two exercises, featuring some of my favorite breathing imagery, one from Coach Daniel Stewart and one from Mary Wanless. Their ideas for building the "belly-breathing habit" will keep oxygen in your blood, improve your mental focus, stabilize your balance, and prime your muscles for the relaxed staying power key to a deep and secure seat.

Exercise for the Body: The Belly Balloon

Concentrating on the inside of your lower abdomen, imagine that you're filling a balloon that flattens your lower back as it expands and fills the entire space inside your belly. As it pushes your diaphragm down, it allows you to get that good deep breath "down into your belly." (I know, the anatomy on this is a little shaky, but the imagery is clear!)

1 Sitting in the saddle at a standstill, do a quick check of your alignment (see p. 187).

2 Now turn your awareness to your breathing, making sure to inflate that "belly balloon" against your spine in your lower back until you feel your lower back flatten and your seat bones point straight down. Hold that place, and continue breathing, as if the sole mission of your in-breath is to keep your lower back flat.

3 Sit with your back flat and your breath rhythm going for as long as your horse will tolerate it.

4 Now move out at a walk, keeping the rhythm of your breath and the sensation in your lower back as a constant as you turn your attention to how your horse is moving under you. Notice when your breath shortens, pinpoint where your breath is stopping, and then—as you did in the meditation exercise on p. 225—"ask" that tightness to "let go." Then breathe back into your belly. Note: If necessary, stop your horse to "breathe through" the tight spots if you need to. Eventually this process of finding a breathing rhythm and keeping it deep and relaxed throughout your body will be automatic—something you can do on the fly!

Exercise: Bear Down and Breathe

This cure for the quick, shallow breath is a great Mary Wanless visual (she's the queen of these—I'm still breathing through the imaginary gills she inserted at the bottom of my ribcage in *For the Good of the Rider*, another of her books).

1 As you're breathing in, visualize pulling your breath *downward,* all the way down to your bikini line.

2 If you feel any "clogs" along the way where the in-breath seems to stop, add some "block dissolver" (picture Drano® for your airways), and with your breath, ask the block nicely to let go. "Be quietly persistent," she coaches us, "taking the time it takes to find a way through it."

On your out-breath, imagine a tap (or valve) on your midline at bikini-line level. Picture the air you have breathed in leaving your body through that tap. (Wanless invites us to make the sound, "Phsst!" as we "breathe out" through this new valve. I, however, choose to refrain from the audible air release, as it might make my horse think it a signal to cross the county line immediately. I encourage you also to use caution if your horse is similarly sensitive.) The purpose of this "tap" in your bikini line, as Wanless explains it, is to "keep your guts pressing out against your skin" (that's the "bearing down" down part she mentioned earlier) on the out-breath.

TAKE A (BREATH) BREAK

I have a stressful "day job." We'll just leave it at that. Len, a colleague, happens to be a devoted student of all sorts of ancient prayer and contemplative spiritual practices. He's a very chill guy, highly accomplished at remaining oblivious to the craziness around him. While this may get him into a little trouble with the "Type As" from time to time, I'll have to say I admire his peaceful, unruffled demeanor. This is someone who takes "staying present" *very* seriously.

One day Len walked into my office and asked, "How often do you look out your window?"

I followed his gaze just past my computer screen to the view outside and the fountain that babbled just about a foot beyond the panes.

"Um, I don't know," I said.

"Once *every hour* I want you to look out there at that fountain, take a deep breath, and just follow the path of the water," he instructed as if being a "Doctor" (albeit D.Min.) meant he was allowed to deliver spontaneous spiritual prescriptions. "Observe how it bubbles up and cascades over the round, smooth stones, and then ebbs back into the basin."

I looked again. Sure enough, the water was just as he described it. I realized that as many times as I had likely glanced out that window, I had never noticed *any* of that before.

So I took a deep breath. As the air traveled well past the point in my chest where I suddenly realized it usually stopped, I realized how good—and rejuvenating—that deliberate and deep breath felt, so I did it again. This time I forced the air all the way down "into my belly," just the way Grandmaster Park taught me all those years ago (see p. 238). The difference in how I felt was staggering. It was as if someone turned on a light in my brain.

That simple exchange in my office taught me three things about breathing that have stuck with me since:

1 We are usually unaware when our breathing gets shallow.

2 A few slow, deep breaths and simple observation of the natural world for a few moments *each hour* can make a huge difference in our overall state of well-being.

3 No matter how much about all this we *know,* it is very easy to forget to *do* it. This is true in our time at work, at home with our family, and when spending time with our horses.

"Each time you sit in an alert and dignified posture and turn your attention to your breathing, for however long," Jon Kabat-Zinn writes in *Full Catastrophe Living*, "you are returning to your own wholeness, affirming your intrinsic balance of mind and body, independent of the passing state of either your mind or your body in any moment."

So once every hour, whether you think you need to or not, *just breathe,* do it deeply, and take in the world around you. It is a beautiful and interesting place when we take the time to notice it. And, going back for a moment to any body image anxieties we may be harboring, breathing deeply and well helps us eliminate stress, recharge our brain and muscles, and if we're feeling lethargic and sluggish, just might make us more inclined to do something good for ourselves than to reach for a snack that will only make us feel worse.

It's important to take these exercises out and practice them often until they become so "second nature" that you don't even notice the blowhole in the top of your head, the balloon in your belly, your negotiations with your "breath clogs," or the tap spewing air out your bikini line. And of course, the more you practice your breathing in your normal, day-to-day activities—or as part of your standing, sitting, or walking meditations—the easier it will be to incorporate it into your horsemanship where your horse can enjoy the benefits of your relaxed, flexible control, mental clarity, and helpful aids.

Incorporating good breathing into your riding and into your life is yet another giant step toward the joy and confidence you'll soon feel and radiate far beyond the size of your jeans. We're traveling now where our riding, mindfulness, and body image issues are starting to share the same stretch of trail. Keep on reading, friends...and now I'm also going to suggest that *you* write, too.

Journaling Answers

Anyone who knows me very well or has read my book, *The Smart Woman's Guide to Midlife Horses*, or attended one of my "Dust Off Your Dreams" or "YourLife, Up!" retreats, knows I'm pretty sold on journaling as a way to find your own answers. In fact, you've already read my recommendation to write things down "in your journal or notebook" a few times in this book. Here's why I hold journaling up above all the other strategies I know of for figuring out some of our life's conundrums: Journaling taps into your subconscious in a way no amount of ruminating or talking or rehashing can. It's a private, personal avenue for exploring what's going on in your deepest self that opens your own unique path to discerning direction, helps you discover your own answers, and reveals connections between experiences that may well have eluded you in the busyness of your day-to-day life.

I have also noticed through the years of studying this phenomenon that there is almost nothing in the self-help world that *doesn't* ask you to journal. Journaling, it appears, is the universal, one-size-fits-all prescription for problems and struggles, large and small. *But what makes it work?* Isn't this just more time spent indulging in self-absorbed whining instead of working toward "real" solutions?

To my surprise and delighted, I discovered the best answer to these questions yet in the writings of the late Dr. Ira Progoff. In an article in the *Atlantic Monthly* in 1961 (you can access the full article on his website, www.intensivejournal.org, but I'll boil it down for you here), shortly after Dr. Progoff began serious work with his Intensive Journal Program for Self-Development, he totally nails down why journaling is the key to finding our own answers, and the ultimate tool for creating the profound and authentic change we desire.

Comparing a life with an issue to be resolved (such as a negative body image or actual excess weight) to a "weak stream with a boulder in it," Dr. Progoff said to remember that the stream is our flow of life energy; the boulder is whatever is blocking it. While traditional psychoanalysis tries to get rid of the boulder by "breaking it up and analyzing it out," the weak stream remains weak. A far better solution, Dr. Progoff theorized, is to "gain access to the source of the stream and find a means of enlarging it." By enlarging the stream's source, the stream deepens and expands until it becomes "a river deep enough to *rise over* the boulder." According to Dr. Progoff, opening this "depth" within ourselves helps us increase and expand our stream of life energy to overcome whatever "boulders" have rolled into our path.

For those of us brought up in a world of tangibles and matter-of-fact common sense, this whole metaphor about the stream and the boulder may seem a little flaky. But stick with me here. It's this simple, really: To facilitate this process of finding what you're looking for on this trail (whatever made you pick up this book in the first place), and to keep up with the answers you uncover (and the subsequent questions they may raise), it is extremely helpful to keep a journal. This journal will serve not only as a record of your inner experiences and growth on this journey, but it will also plant important clues for you to discover later on—you won't even realize they *are* clues as you write them, but trust me, when you look back on these pages from the perspective of a few months, a few years, or a few decades down the road, you will be amazed at what you see that you *don't* see right now. As Dr. Progoff discovered through years of work with journaling and teaching others to journal their process, recording our progress (and, perhaps, lack thereof) is key to making use of information and insights we don't even realize have been inside us all along. (Ruby riding boots, anyone?)

THREE PAGES A DAY TO CHANGE YOUR GAME

Back in the 1990s I dove headfirst into *The Artist's Way*, in which author Julia Cameron teaches us how to tap into the power of our subconscious through a simple journaling technique she dubs "Morning Pages." This amounts to writing three full-sized pages longhand, first thing every

Dr. Ira Progoff's *At a Journal Workshop* (Tarcher, 1992).

RESOURCES

Julia Cameron's *The Artist's Way* (JP Tarcher, 1992).

David Allen's *Getting Things Done* Revised Edition (Penguin, 2015).

morning. Before your feet hit the floor. Before your coffee. Before you talk to anyone about breakfast or clean socks or lunch money or unpaid bills.

This daily practice of "catching" your subconscious *before* your "chattering monkey mind" wakes up (hence the need for quiet) and *before* your "real day" starts is as amazing as it is appealing. Just wait until you see what kinds of things pop out of your mind each morning, unencumbered by the need to make any sense of it. Calling Morning Pages "the bedrock tool of a creative recovery," Julia says there is no wrong way to do this exercise. "They are not high art," she adds. "They are not even 'writing.' They are about anything and everything that crosses your mind—and they are for your eyes only. Morning Pages provoke, clarify, comfort, cajole, prioritize, and synchronize the day at hand. Do not overthink Morning Pages," she cautions, "just put three pages of anything on the page...and then do three more pages tomorrow."

Morning Pages is a practice that will benefit you with your horses, with your struggles over body image, and with just about any other "boulders" blocking your stream. As comforting as it is vague, the simple, repeated act of "dumping" what's on your mind after each night's sleep-processing gives clarity to even the murkiest of situations. Once Morning Pages become your habit, you'll find the time you spend writing your three pages to be a place of peace and centering in the face of life's daily storms, from the quick and ferocious "squall lines" to the steadiest of monsoons.

As much as I loved filling spiral after spiral notebook with my rambling mélange of interesting (to me) thoughts and exciting ideas—interspersed with garden-variety whining—I realized, after re-reading some of my pages from nearly a decade prior, that the same things have been my "boulders" for most, if not all, of my life. Since I was still whining about the same exact things decades later, did that mean all that journaling was just riding in circles and never finding the way out?

Whether you're talking body image issues, boundary issues, or confidence issues at the canter, it's entirely possible that what you're struggling with now is rooted in something you've dealt with before in one form or another. Morning Pages tend to shine a light on these patterns and "spirals" in your life. Although Cameron seemed to feel that the value of Morning Pages lay in getting these thoughts out ("Keeping or tossing Morning Pages notebooks is a highly personal choice," she counsels. "I have had people shred, toss and burn their Morning Pages. I have had other people hold onto them for years. I myself save my Morning Pages, although I seldom reread them."), for me the value of this exercise did not end there. You see, I didn't *intend* to reread them, and I *thought* I had disposed of them, but when I ran across that notebook 10 years later and read it, just for kicks, smug in my certainty that I had "moved past" what turned out to be a lot of whining, I got a surprise. I was still mired in the same emotional bogs. Issues, places and faces had changed, but the patterns were alarmingly consistent.

So if you're patient with this journaling exercise (and willing to dig around a little in your own messiness), you will likely find new insights and connections hidden among your seemingly impossible to-do lists, unfinished household and barn tasks, dietary self-loathing, and unmet goals. Within the pages of this jumbled-up tangle of first-thing-in-the-morning thinking (thoughts that otherwise would have slipped away unnoticed), there are important clues for finding the way forward on our trail. But how do we find them? What actions should we take? Or, as I am always fond of saying in response to any sort of psychobabble, "Okay...so what?"

THE BIG "SO WHAT?"

After a few years of asking this question, the answer came—as these kinds of answers almost always come—in a time and place I least expected it. Tucked inside the privilege of participating in one of Dr. Ira Progoff's Intensive Journal™ Workshops, I found a prescribed process for not only what to do with these random morning spewings of my subconscious, but how to put these thoughts and reflections into the larger context of my life's experiences so far, and where I might be going next.

Myths of Privacy

MYTH: "If I write down what I'm feeling inside, someone might see it and judge the dark side of me."

TRUTH: If you worry, like I do, about your morning ramblings being read (and likely misinterpreted) by others (my mother taught me as a youngster never to write down anything I didn't want the whole world to read), I've come up with a way to capture and process the "useful stuff" that comes up in Morning Pages and jettison the rest.

I journal most mornings, and then, at some point later in the day—or week—I read these pages back. If there is something worth exploring further, I create a dated prompt in an electronic file (which I cleverly call "Journaling Prompts"). If there is an idea or insight I'm particularly proud of and don't mind sharing, I recopy it in an "official" journal; if it's something I need to take action on, I add it to my "GTD" master to-do list. (Thank you, David Allen, for your Getting Things Done® system, without which I wouldn't get anything done… *ever.*) If I need to explore a matter in more depth (using Progoff's method), I add an appointment on my calendar (using the title of the prompt I recorded electronically), and I keep it like the therapist's appointment it is. Then, I feed my original pages to the shredder. There. Information gathered, managed, processed, explored…and all evidence of insanity deleted—no blood, no foul. No disappointed heirs. (As in, *"Wow, I never had any idea Great Grandma was such a basket case!"*) I offer this unofficial privacy measure with the hope that it brings a measure of comfort to those who, otherwise, might be too terrified of exposure to journal at all.

Like Morning Pages, the Intensive Journal™ method has nothing to do with writing; it's a hardcore self-examination tool for those of us intent on getting to the "core" of our emotional lives. (In other words, we're training another kind of "core strength" here.) Dr. Progoff's "Daily Log" reminded me of Cameron's "Morning Pages" in that it was a tool for a quick, stream-of-consciousness, longhand mind-dump. It was not, however, first thing in the morning and it wasn't limited in length. Still, the process felt similar. The defining difference I love about Dr. Progoff's Intensive Journaling is that the exercises included after the Daily Log (find them in his book *At A Journal Workshop*—see Resources) include opportunities to create understanding and healing through:

- **"Dialog"** (albeit imaginary) with people, events, the world around you, and in our case, *especially* with our own bodies. This exercise yields amazing insights about your own thoughts and attitudes and often creates healing within.

- **"Stepping stones"** that trace the unfolding of a situation, issue, attitude, or event. This is an empathy-builder that can shed light on relationships and dynamics.

- **"Intersections"** ("roads taken and not taken in your life") where you see how and where past decisions and actions changed your course. This can be both a nice side trail to self-forgiveness and a wake up call for missed opportunities.

While journaling for journaling's sake *is* cathartic, I've found that, for me, anyway, it's in the revisiting and processing that we discover the insights worth doing something about. Progoff's Intensive Journal™ offers one such solid, time-tested *process* we can return to again and again as our lives, experiences, challenges, and opportunities emerge. I'm sure there are others. When we can choose a journaling method that offers a pathway to inner wisdom, and a process for using what we find to move forward from whatever has been holding us back, we find ourselves on the fast track to progress we may never have imagined possible, with answers that come from within us as and when we're ready for them.

It's easy to see the effect of this kind of internal "groundwork" in your riding and your connection to your horse. "I believe the pages render us *present* in our life," Cameron writes. And, because our horses require our presence above all else, journaling seems to have a direct effect on how calm and clear we are with *them*. Horses, as the ultimate mirrors of our emotions, also make marvelous listeners and journaling partners (if you've never sat with your horse and journaled, you're missing a wonderful and sometimes quite surprising experience). It never ceases to amaze me what comes out in a journal and how the self-awareness journaling creates builds clarity, confidence, and authenticity (there's that word again!) that makes our time and our work with horses everything it was meant to be.

Chicken or Egg?

It may not have escaped your notice that two of the mindfulness exercises in this section are to be done "first thing" and "before you do anything else." I noticed that, too, and after a little exploring and asking questions of the experts, including visiting Julia Cameron's blog where this issue was addressed quite well, here's the verdict: Morning Pages are best done first. Cameron actually refers to them as "Meditation for Westerners." However, if you also want to add another kind of mindfulness exercise to the beginning of your day, my recommendation (backed by Cameron and others) is to start with Morning Pages and then add a moving or sitting meditation, depending on your attention span or personal preference. Several who commented on Cameron's forum agreed that emptying your mind onto your Morning Pages actually helps clear and quiet it, making actual meditation easier!

| #Hoofpicks | In this chapter we explored how we can engage mind, body, and spirit into the experience of riding and working with horses. This will help us in our work with horses |

by creating greater awareness of our thought and behavior patterns to become less anxious, more mindful riders. Incorporating this practice is a new and different game-changer in the battle against negative body image because when we focus on our authentic selves rather than our (often-imagined) flaws in our appearance, we free ourselves of what's been holding us back from the experience with our horses we've been looking for.

Your Chapter 8 **#Hoofpicks** include:

1 **Cut a new trail.** This section was a virtual smorgasbord of mind/body/spirit exercises to help you connect with your higher self, deepest wisdom, inner goddess (pick your phrase!). What this means and why it's important to at least give some of these things a try even if they feel and sound weird at first is that these are the vehicles for slowing down the chatter in our "monkey mind" that aggravates and perpetuates our body image issues and any number of other inner struggles we face. By learning to make these practices our own, we'll be able to connect with the parts of ourselves that are beautiful, perfect, and 100-percent-right in every single moment we're alive on this planet (and with or on the backs of our horses).

2 **Think of mindfulness as a "pick two" menu.** Start and end your day, every day, with one of the paths to mindfulness you learned in this chapter. Try them all on for size—and give each one at least a month of regular use before deciding whether to keep it in your permanent tack trunk. (The truth is different strategies will work better for you at some times and in some situations than others; getting comfortable with all or many of these exercises will greatly increase your self-help arsenal.)

3 **Finding "quiet places for your soul" is your "groundwork."** You will begin to experience other times or occasions—especially while riding—that can bring this sense of calm collection right back to the forefront. You'll be equipped to discover the difference mindfulness techniques can make as you check in with yourself, your emotions, your life's circumstances, and set yourself up for a smoother ride through your day.

Be
Positive

9 | "See" With Your Mind

Visualization is another one of those wiggly, overused words (we've had a few already in this book) that can provoke eye-rolling in anyone who hasn't directly experienced the powerful difference a well-crafted "picture in your mind" can make. *Well-crafted* is the operative word here. From weight loss (we *can* get where we need to be) to specific accomplishments (lead changes…great spins…) to flawless performance (a clean round…a dressage test littered with 10s…), visualizations are the tool that most success coaches (and *lots* of riding coaches) keep at the tippy top of their bag of tricks.

Here's an example of how visualization can work: When working with a client who had tried and failed to pass an important exam five times, even though she was well-prepared, licensed therapist Jill Valle grabbed the visualization tool and went to work.

"I took her through a whole session of feelings," Valle relates. "'What would it feel like to pass the exam?' We did a very detailed visualization of her sitting in the chair, taking the exam, knowing all the answers, completing the exam, turning it in, getting in her car, and going home. Then going to the mailbox, opening it and finding the letter from the exam board. We went through the minute specifics of every moment—right down to opening the envelope and reading the letter that said she passed. We went through all the sensory responses in each moment, including sights, sounds, smells, tactile feelings—such as the papers in her hand, the warmth of the steering wheel from her car sitting in the sun—every tiny detail we could come up with to make the visualization feel as real as possible. And, it *felt so real* that her ecstatic laughter and tears of joy *were* real, because she really *felt what it would be like* when this big milestone was accomplished at last."

And the next time Valle's client took the test? She passed.

"Visualization helps us find the *feeling place*," Valle explains, "and research has shown time and time again that when we engage our *feeling place* in our visualizations, our brains don't know the difference between the visualization and a real event."

Valle cites one such study involving stress and the fight or flight response that measured physiological response to *real* danger (almost hit by a car) and *imagined* danger (a scary movie). The measurement of physiological response to these two events was *exactly the same*, proving our minds' amazing power to trick our bodies into believing whatever we want to think *is real*.

What Gives Our Visualization Power?

As mentioned, the benefits of visualization have been well-documented, in relation to every sport you can imagine (and some you can't); to any sort of performance; to fine arts; to workouts, to fighting cancer or other illness; to physical rehab after injury. Visualization, like journaling (see p. 244), is the power tool that fits most everyone, and the better you are at wielding, the bigger result.

According to experts, keys to visualization that produces real results include:

• **Involve as many of your senses as possible.** For example, don't just *see* the mental picture of your perfect ride, engage your imagination to *hear* the footfalls of your horse and the squeak of your saddle. *Feel* your horse moving underneath you at several different gaits, the straightness in your posture, and the fluid, relaxed strength of your solid connection. *Smell* the mixture of sweat, fly spray, and fresh green grass. (I really can't imagine what you might *taste*, unless it's a big wad of gum, but you get the idea.)

• **Practice by playing this visualization over and over again.** In his 2002 *Horse & Rider* article, "Mapping Your Reining Win," veteran reiner Dell Hendricks advises us to play our visualization in our heads 100 times. "And I mean 100," he says. He explains that by visualizing our perfect runs in explicit detail so often it becomes second nature, we will subconsciously boost our performance. And, instead of merely visualizing what we're doing, Hendricks advises us to look around us at the landmarks (or those we imagine) to place us in the context of what we're doing and where we are. In other words, don't just watch it passively like a movie. "Avoid just picturing the maneuvers," Hendricks says. "Instead, visualize yourself riding each one…Focus on what you'll be feeling and the landmark you'll be looking for and riding toward next."

• **Slam the door on anxieties.** "If any negative thoughts creep in, shut them out immediately, and focus on the ideal," Hendricks says. If you're having trouble keeping doubts and worries at bay, use "thought-stopping"—Coach Daniel Stewart says you can literally just tell yourself, "Whoa!" as soon as you think of something negative to disrupt the river of doubt—then return to participating in your visualization. By mentally "changing the channel" in your mind when you feel negative, anxious, self-conscious thoughts creeping in, you return to the more important matter at hand. Find a mental image model—someone you see as strong, beautiful, fit, aware, and in tune with her body (Wonder Woman works especially well for me!)—and indulge in a Walter Mitty moment where you *are* that person.

• **Shift perspectives.** In his book *Pressure Proof Your Riding,* Coach Daniel Stewart explores riding visualizations in depth. One Coach Stewart suggestion that stuck with me is to create your visualizations from a variety of perspectives: so, "see" the ride as it would feel through your own senses, then "see" the ride as it might be viewed by a spectator (where you can sub in an ultra-fit and über-talented body double if you'd like), and another perspective that perhaps few of us think about: "see" the ride through the eyes (and experiences) of your horse. *("Gee I could have sworn she got on back there at the mounting block, but I can hardly feel a thing on my back right now… Oh. Wait. There she is. I can feel a little leg pressure…guess I'd better change leads!")* Coach Stewart advises us to shift our perspectives to and from each of these vantage points as we "play" our visualization in our mind, as if we had a camera crew operating in several different areas of the arena.

In fact (and please don't think I'm advocating for any extra time in the gym!), in a 2009 *Flourish!* article entitled "Seeing is Believing: The Power of Visualization," Angie LeVan, resilience coach, speaker, trainer, and writer, explores the power of visualization in our everyday life that actually translates quite well to our issues with body image and riding horses. She cites a study that found the same patterns activated in the brain of a weightlifter who *imagined* lifting hundreds of pounds as in the ones who *actually* lifted the weight. And in *Pressure Proof Your Riding* Coach Stewart talks about a study of three groups of riders in which the first group actually practiced a specific dressage maneuver, the second group visualized exactly the same practice, and the third group ate donuts. (I know which group I would have chosen!) While those who practiced showed the most improvement, those who only visualized the same practice actually showed significant improvement, and the donut-eaters just gained several pounds.

Perhaps my favorite of the studies cited by LeVan in her article speaks directly to our workout and conditioning goals, and offers a great mental alternative on days when you can't ride. Guang Yue, an exercise psychologist from the Cleveland Clinic Foundation in Ohio, compared people who *actually* worked out in a gym with people who did the same workouts in their heads—while lounging on a couch. While the 30 percent increase in muscle mass of the gym rats is to be expected, the 13.5 percent increase in muscle mass in the couch potatoes is a shocker! And ready for more? The muscle increase in the non-exercisers remained for *three months* following their mental training. What this proves is that we have no excuses; if we get in a bind and can't ride or condition or work out as planned, creating an elaborate visualization that we can "feel"—even if we can't lift a finger—could be the next best thing!

The crux of this whole visualization thing is that mental imagery is *far* more than just "picturing success." It directly impacts the cognitive processes of the brain, including motor control, attention, perception, planning, and memory. In fact, when we get serious with our visualizations, we're training our brain in much the same way we do our bodies during our actual rides. In addition, consistent practice of our visualizations (even if you just set aside a few minutes every day) can enhance our motivation, increase our confidence, and prime us for achieving the happiness with horses we deserve.

Exercise for Your Brain: Visualize Your Perfect Ride

If you're still not sure how much all this visualization mumbo-jumbo will really help on the quest to accept your body as it is, I invite you to try one on for size with Jill Valle's help. Remember, in each step it's crucial to engage *all five* senses: sight, sound, smell, taste, and touch. (A quick note of practicality here: sometimes, when you're dealing with horses and barn chores, taste is a sense best left unengaged!)

1 Visualize your body, strong and fit. Look in an imaginary tack room mirror. What do you see? Long, well-defined muscles? Cheekbones? Six-pack? What do you feel? A soft breeze on your skin, coming in through an open window? Is it warm or cool? What are the smells around you? Is there a faint scent of leather cleaner and oil coming from the saddles and bridles on their racks? Are you chewing mint-flavored, sugar-free gum?

2 Slip on your riding pants. What color are they? How does the fabric feel against your skin as it fits just perfectly? Can you smell the laundry soap? (Since this *is* the optimal visualization, we might as well have clean clothes!) Hear the zipper sliding easily closed and the snap clicking together with minimal pressure. Is the mint flavor gone from your gum yet?

3 Pull on your boots. Notice how soft they feel, and listen to the sound they make as they slip easily over your calves and fit, just so. See how nice they look with your riding pants. Can you smell the leather?

4 Saddle your horse. (Note: You can get as detailed as you like here with the grooming and preparation for a ride, but for these purposes, we'll just skip right to the saddle.) Lift the saddle into place and tighten your girth or cinch. Notice how nicely your tack fits your horse as you check the feel and visual measurements you've memorized from earlier in this book (see p. 79). Breathe in the scent of your horse (for most of us this is true aromatherapy!) and give him a spritz of fly spray if you're so inclined. (This may fulfill the taste if you forgot to visualize closing your mouth.) Listen to the barn sounds around you.

5 Get on your horse. Feel him take a deep, relaxed breath underneath you as you ground and center yourself (p. 172), check your alignment (p. 182), and flatten your lower back to make sure it's stable and secure (p. 192). Listen to your horse playing with the bit. Look around you at the fence line, the trees. Smell the freshly cut grass from a mower running in a nearby field as you walk your horse toward the arena or trailhead.

6 Move into to your "perfect ride." Okay, you're going to have to take it from here—your perfect ride is your business, and only you know what that looks like! Involve all five senses if you can (get a new piece of gum if you need to), and stay in your visualization for as long as possible. Feel, experience, and absorb the sensation of riding in complete harmony with your horse. The more you practice this visualization the closer your *real* ride will get to your fabulous vision. But don't take my word for it. Give it a try! (This makes a nice mental break within the confines of a busy workday. Just try not to get caught. It's really hard to explain to co-workers!)

Mind Your Self-Talk

If you're like me, the idea of doing daily *affirmations* (very specific written statements that generally follow what I like to call "3Ps" and "3Rs": positive, personal, and present; read and repeated religiously) has never really clicked. While affirmations always *sound* like a good idea—and there is solid neuroscience and psychology behind them, along with plenty of convincing anecdotes about how they "change lives"—this is another one of those "self-help" steps that has always seemed, well, just plain silly. (I blame *Saturday Night Live* for this. When you think of affirmations, does anyone over the age of 25 *not* think of "Stuart Smalley" in front of his mirror? "Because I'm good enough. I'm smart enough. And doggone it, people like me.")

I pushed all these feelings of foolishness aside, however, when I began reading the research, including a 2014 study from Stanford University that confirmed many positive results from the affirmation process, including improvements in learning, and achieving health, fitness, and performance goals, as well as improving relationship outcomes. (Doesn't that just about sum up everything we're working with in the arena of body image and riding horses?) "Like other interventions and experiences, self-affirmations can have lasting benefits when they touch off a cycle of adaptive potential, a positive feedback loop between the self-system and the social system that propagates adaptive outcomes over time," the study states. Simply put, affirmations are proven to set off a cycle of positive thoughts, emotions, and behaviors that shore up our self-esteem and gain momentum each time they're proved valid. (Remember the *thought-feeling-behavior continuum* Jill Valle talked about on p. 40?)

Regardless of your riding goals, Coach Daniel Stewart explains, developing your own unique set of affirmations around what you *do* have going for you helps lay the thought groundwork for your future success, however you choose to define it. "We have to train a rider to find whatever is in her that's positive," Coach Stewart says, "and then we can build from there."

To find a powerful parallel to this teaching for those of us dealing with body image issues, I had only to look to my own experience (and the experiences of those who share my favorite yoga discipline with me) the first time in that mirrored, miserably hot room when the instructor said, "Look yourself in the eyes and acknowledge your beauty, power, and strength."

I was shocked and sad at how hard this was for me to do. Years of body image insecurities made me want to *avoid* looking at myself in that mirror at all costs. I had done a lot of bargaining with myself over wearing that somewhat skimpy hot yoga outfit that put each and every of my body's "imperfections" on undeniable display. ("Skimpy" in my case was according to my own sensibilities—there were several far-more-perfect young bodies in there sporting bathing suits.) The instructor and literature assured me that not only was it important to the process to be able to see all your body parts well in this class, but that everyone in there was focused only on themselves and getting through the class, so there wasn't going to be any judgment from others. (I don't suppose he, being a 20-something man, ever considered that the worst judgment of my body was going to come from me!) So standing there in my little shorts and fitted tank top, there it all was, right out there for everyone to see. I took a tentative look into my own eyes in the mirror, trying not to feel silly, snicker, or make fun.

And I saw something there. Something deeply sincere and almost apologetic. A vulnerability I always responded to in others, but had never actually seen in myself. Above all, here was someone doing her best, and trying really hard to do something new and strange and good for her body. After that class I made a point of making contact with that person behind those eyes in the mirror as often as I could, and with repeated effort, it *did* get easier to look her in the eyes and acknowledge how hard she was working. As my strength and ability to do these postures gradually improved, and I began to see changes and "improvements" in my body ("Wait! Is that a new muscle? Yay!"), I *did* begin to see it as beautiful. And strong. And capable of doing difficult things with beauty and grace. Even if my standing bow wasn't anywhere near perfect, and even on those days when I lost my balance and fell out of it seven times in 60 seconds, I got back into it *eight* times. I learned to "finish strong," no matter how ugly the in-between parts got. And before too long, that almost apologetic look transformed to a confidence and self-assurance I almost didn't recognize. I was able to carry that feeling into other areas of my life: A horse I was halfway afraid of—and spent a lot of time apologizing to—became a partner in working through both of our issues. With this relationship transformed, we'd take as much time as it took, without apologies or explanations, because doggone it, we were both worth it.

Living inside a body I appreciated, even though its size didn't change that much, nor did its weight, put my whole self-concept on a different plane. And it all started with looking myself in the eyes in the mirror and thinking affirming thoughts.

Taking a turn now into some deeper woods along this trail we're on together, let's all take a deep breath as we collectively dismiss any queasiness we may feel at the thought of looking ourselves in our mirrored eyes, saying things that, down deep, we may not yet quite believe. Like urging a water-skittish colt across his first stream, let's encourage our psyches to stick a tentative hoof into the land of affirmations.

For this we're looking to "affirmation guru" Louise Hay, whose fundamental premise about affirmations is that whether or not you believe in them, you're already doing them. This is true, she says, because affirmations include *everything* you say or think. Period. (Remember the old horse training adage that every minute you're with your horse you're either training him or un-training him?)

"Every thought you think and every word you speak is an affirmation," Hay writes in *21 Days to Master Affirmations.* "All of your self-talk, your internal dialogue, is a stream of affirmations. You're using affirmations every moment whether you know it or not."

Yikes.

But here's the good news. When we become aware of this Great Truth about affirmations, and therefore more *deliberate* about creating them, we've at last found the path to making profound changes to our self-concept *and* our riding (and by now we know that these two things are inextricably connected). Whether this means a complete physical metamorphosis or just a healthy dose of self-acceptance, we're declaring to our subconscious: "Okay, I get it now. And I'm paying attention. I understand that the words I choose have the power to eliminate or create, and I'm going to be choosing them much more carefully from now on."

Wait. Let me just interrupt any negativity you're feeling about this exercise right now. This is all going to be much easier than you think. Much of what we say to ourselves, particularly around things like body image and weight, and often in regard to our riding ability, are habitual thought patterns we've developed over many years. And, just because we've *believed* something negative about ourselves or about our riding, it does not mean there is any actual truth to it. According to Hay, it's now up to us to reexamine the things we've always believed about ourselves and "make a decision to either continue to believe them because they support us and make our life joyful and fulfilled," she writes, "or make the decision to release them."

Louise Hay's *21 Days to Master Affirmations* (Hay House, 2011).

OUT WITH THE STINKIN' THINKIN'

So how do we know which thoughts to listen to, believe, and take positive action on—and which to "release?" As riders facing body-image challenges, if you haven't noticed by now, we are dealing with a very unique and particular set of circumstances. As we discussed in the "Be Honest" section of this book (p. 15), we have to be both realistic about our individual circumstances and precise in our plan to make the most of our individual opportunities. In other words, the more personal and specific our affirmations are, the more powerful they will be.

It's also important to understand how completely overrun our minds are with thoughts and the self-talk that crystalizes our most recurrent thoughts into actual words. In fact, Coach Daniel Stewart says that research shows that we think between 20,000 to 60,000 thoughts a day, and (despite our best meditative efforts—see p. 225), we actually can't go for longer than 11 seconds without "talking" to ourselves. And here's the kicker: about 90 percent of these thoughts and statements are the *same ones* you had yesterday. And the day before that.

Now we're starting to see what we're up against.

Going far beyond typical "positive thinking" and "positive self-talk," Coach Stewart offers a few great pointers for custom-building affirmations that will take root and grow good things in your riding and in your life:

• **Use emotion to influence motion.** This is about *thought spirals.* Negative thoughts spiral into self-doubt, positive thoughts spiral into confidence. Learning to see these spirals in your own thinking is the first step to creating *positive thought spirals* when you feel your confidence slipping. When I first entered that yoga room, I was looking around, comparing my body negatively to everyone in there. Assessing the seasoned practitioners laying down their mats all around me, I was not at all sure I could stay in that room with the heat and was almost certain I wasn't going to be able to do the postures. My self-talk, had I netted it and put it through a thought-to-speech app (if only there were such a thing) was likely something along the lines of: *"I'm not sure I belong in here. I'm fatter and older than everyone—except for that wiry old woman over there who has probably been doing this for years. Look at all these mirrors. Why must all the walls be mirrored, floor to ceiling? Oh! Geez! If I look at that mirrored column I see myself not once but three times! Not cool! I'll just hide back here in the middle of the back row (not the corner! Two mirrors there!) and hope no one looks at me. I'm stiff as a board, clumsy as an ox, and with all this middle-aged weight around my midsection, I can't even see my toes, much less touch them. There is no way I'm going to be able to do this. I have no balance. I'm going to embarrass myself. I'm going to fall on my face. I'll probably throw up. I might even hurt myself. I wonder if I can still leave."*

(They lock the doors when class starts.)

Now fast-forward a few weeks (after my affirmation-awakening eye contact), as I was just starting to notice small changes in my body and in my practice. I walked into the same classroom. It was still hot. The mirrors were still everywhere. The ballerinas were still in the front row. Wiry old woman still in her corner. I put my mat down in the center of the room, knelt and sat back on my feet "Japanese style" (a "sitting Zen" meditation posture called *zazen*, which is a Japanese word that literally means "sitting concentration") and caught sight of myself in the mirrored column. My thoughts were now along the lines of: *"Hmmm, my shoulders and upper arms don't look too bad at all from this angle. Boy, am I glad to be out from in front of my computer. I really need this class today. Wow. The breathing exercises are going to feel awesome today...Is that an ab muscle I see?"* I know I'm not supposed to compare myself to others, but it didn't escape my notice that I was the last one down in a posture calling for slowly lowering to a sitting position in an imaginary chair. *"Will you look at that!"* and when the instructor dialogue reminded us that all our muscles should be engaged, with "nothing loose, nothing hanging" I peered closely at my body and indeed saw nothing loose *or* hanging *"How about that?"* Looking myself in the eyes during triangle posture, arms outstretched, *"I look pretty strong and powerful in this position. Too bad I can't walk around this way all the time."*

Here are a few interesting notes about my *positive thought spiral*: At that point, I had not actually lost an ounce of weight. Had my body really changed that much? Or was I just starting to see it differently because of the consistent affirmation? (Spoiler: it was likely a little bit of both.) Did you notice that in my positive thought spiral, each thought was positive, personal, and present ("P3")? These were affirmations built from my own awareness and reality. To formalize the process, I could have written them down to read and repeat religiously ("R3"), but since this particular yoga practice uses the same postures in the same order, these thoughts did occur again and again, accomplishing pretty much the effect I needed. (Who knew I could sneak up on myself with affirmations?)

And how did this affect my riding? Having those mental images planted in the yoga room made it much easier to sit straighter, call on my flexible strength and know it was there, breathe to the bottom of my lungs, and feel that same "beauty, power, and strength" I affirmed in the yoga room right there with me in the saddle.

• **Get in the habit of thinking in positive words.** Use each negative thought or word you notice as an opportunity to practice reframing into positive. Make a game of it! This, too, gets easier with time, awareness, and consistent practice. At first, especially when you're coming off years of continuous negative self-talk, it's hard to nab these slippery little negative "thinks." But train your mind's eye to watch for them, and when you catch one, use "thought-stopping" or "thought interruption" techniques (see Coach Stewart's "Whoa!" on p. 257 and more about this on p. 305) and literally think of the positive counter. Sometimes, this takes some imagination, especially when the negative happens to have a small (or whole) grain of truth to it.

This is where we can start to lash the sections of this book together: Since we've decided to Be Honest (p. 13), this isn't a time for denial, candy-coating, or any other sort of positive "spin." What we're talking about here is an honest reframe of what you're thinking, laced with self-compassion (more on this coming up next) and realistic expectation, along with sincere commitment to a solid Be Proactive plan (see p. 91). Examples of this kind of reframe include:

Stinkin' Thinkin': "I feel like a cow in these riding breeches."
Reframe: "I may not look the way I want to in my riding breeches just yet, but

they fit me well, and are comfortable and of good quality to help me ride better. I'm working on getting in better shape, and I'm already seeing a difference in my fitness level and how that translates to my riding."

Stinkin' Thinkin': "It's no use. I've tried all this stuff before. If I had the (pick one . . . or several!) willpower, genes, time, money, energy, chef, and personal trainer, maybe I'd have a chance to have a better body and a better body image. But I'm heavy, I've always been heavy, my family is heavy, and nothing I do is going to change that."

Reframe: "While I accept my body and build (and genetics) for what they are, now that I understand how all this works, I know I can do a little better. I may never be a size 6, but I will find ways to get fit, keep my mind and emotions in a better place, and make the adjustments I need to in order to enjoy my time with my horses."

Stinkin' Thinkin': "I don't even have time for my horses—there's *no way* I have time to do all this extra stuff to get in shape and change my body image."

Reframe: "I'm curious about finding ways to incorporate some of these new habits into my life in tiny, doable steps to see if I can make improvements in my fitness, focus, peace, and joyful connection with my horse—without taking too much time away from my other priorities. (Also, I'm going to read the next section of this book to see what clues and ideas may be just the low-hanging fruit to get me started on a whole new path!)"

• **Change past negatives to present positives.** Substitute "love to" for "can't" or "hate"; "when" for "if" or "think" or "try"; and add "now" to the beginning or end of every positive.

Past Negative: "I can't get up early enough to write in my journal, meditate, and still get to work on time."

Present Positive: "I love to get up early enough to write in my journal, meditate, and get to work on time (or early!) with a clear-headed start to my day."

Past Negative: "I can't feel all these things I'm supposed to feel when I ride my horse; if I would lose weight and get in shape, it might be different, but I can't, so it won't ever get better."

Present Positive: "Now that I'm taking baby steps toward getting my body fit and my mind quiet, I love learning how to *really feel* and move with the motion of my horse."

• **Remember that no thoughts are "neutral."** Words like *think, hope, pray, wish, want, believe* are actually negative because they don't convey 100 percent confidence. Train yourself to ditch them: I *pray* my riding will improve and be more fun becomes, "As my riding improves it will be more fun!" I *wish* I would take better care of my body so I'll feel better becomes, "Because I'm taking better care of my body, I feel amazing!" And so on.

• **Capture the positive cause-and-effect relationship between thoughts and actions.** This goes back to the thought-feeling-behavior continuum we learned about back on p. 40 (and which we're about to explore further...) As we make these connections, we amp up our mindfulness and start to harness the power of our thoughts, transforming them into actions that follow suit. Even if, for now, this is still more or less theoretical, or if we start by just noticing where these connections are already occurring in our life and in our riding, it is a solid first step toward engineering bigger and bigger results. For example:

"I **meditate** daily now because I **thought** it might help me quiet my nerves before shows."

"I **regained** my focus on the dressage test because I **caught my mind chattering.**"

"I **finished the reining pattern perfectly** after a missed lead change because I **stopped the negative thought spiral** with a deep breath and an affirmation."

• **Adopt motivational mottos.** These are words or phrases (song lyrics are great) that are short, catchy, and speak to a goal or desire in some area of your life. I don't know about you, but sometimes words and phrases just jump out at me: from a lyric of the music that happens to be playing on the radio, to a line from a sitcom rerun that's on in the next room, to the title of a magazine article that pops into my awareness as I stand in line to check out at the grocery store. Sometimes affirming wisdom arrives in a fortune cookie, a talk with a friend, or in a conversation overheard. (Yes, I do eavesdrop. I also write fiction and you just never know when something you say might end up in a book.) The point is, sources for creating your affirmations are everywhere. Just listen, write down things that feel good to you—things that express who you are and the qualities of your soul that you want to nurture. Here are a few affirmations I've crafted from random sources of inspiration:

Inspiration: "Life does not have to be perfect to be wonderful." (Refrigerator magnet. Yes, I bought it.)
Affirmation: "I embrace every moment of my life as wonderful, even in its imperfection."

Inspiration: "Self-care is never a selfish act—it is simply good stewardship of the only gift I have, the gift I was put on earth to offer to others." (Educator and activist Parker Palmer.)
Affirmation: "I take care of myself so that I can offer my best self to others."

Inspiration: "We need to remember what's important in life: friends, waffles, and work. Or waffles, friends, and work. Either way, work is third." (Leslie Knope, *Parks and Recreation.*)
Affirmation: "I organize my time each day according to my deepest priorities."

Exercise for the Brain and Soul:
Build Your Own Affirmations

Using any or all of the methods I just described, develop and refine your own affirmations, grabbing onto whatever speaks to you *right now*—in your riding or in your life (because we know by now that these things often mirror one another). Add them to your journal or note them on your tablet or phone. What you're looking for here is a good, solid list of every single strength you have (or would like to have) in every area of your life. We're going to take these and infuse your daily 90 percent of recurring thoughts (endless loop style) with your own carefully crafted, positive game-changers.

PERFECT PRACTICE

A friend, Grandmaster Roy Kurban, who runs a martial arts *dojang* keeps this famous Vince Lombardi quote over the door:

> **Practice doesn't make perfect.**
> ***Perfect practice* makes perfect.**

When it comes to affirmations, this—also a favorite saying of dressage rider, Olympic coach, and author Jane Savoie—couldn't be more true. We've talked about how *powerful* our thoughts are. *More powerful still* are the words we choose to carry the vibrational frequency of our intent. *Turbocharged* are thoughts paired with emotions carried by carefully chosen words we say while looking into our own eyes in the mirror! This may feel uncomfortable at first (perhaps further into the woods than simply meeting our own gaze during yoga class), but think about it: many if not most of the messages we receive and have taken to heart over the course of our lives, especially those concerning our value and abilities, are delivered by someone looking directly into our eyes. See the importance of this eye contact now?

As we all know, anything worth getting good at takes a certain amount of practice. Practicing affirmations in the mirror is no different (just ask Stuart Smalley). As with learning to meditate, there will be missteps, false starts, and lapses—and many times when you'll have to drag your thoughts *and* your actions back to your affirmation practice. But every time you come back to the affirmations you've created, you'll find it gets a little bit easier and more comfortable as you settle into this life-changing habit. Here are some tips to getting your new affirmation ball rolling:

• **Start small.** Pick the first two affirmations from your list that you've made that speak to where you are with your body and your riding *right now.* You'll come back to the others, but for the next month or so, work only with these first two until they become a natural, easy part of who you tell yourself you are.

• **Keep 'em handy.** I'll let you figure out whether you write the affirmations you're working with in lipstick on your bathroom mirror, set them up as reminders in your phone, or make notecards you carry in your purse or wallet—just find some way that works for you that will keep them popping into your awareness throughout every day.

• **Own it.** Say your two affirmations like you mean them, as if they're *already true.* As suggested already, look yourself in the eye when you say them in the mirror. Set aside some time each day to create visualizations (we used to call these day-dreams) around your affirmations, in which you engage all your senses to touch, see, hear, smell, and taste how this new reality feels as you settle into it (revisit p. 259 for more on visualizing).

• **Learn more.** Expand your knowledge around the affirmations you create (whether the affirmation has to do with horses, riding, fitness, or nurturing inner stillness), taking note of any questions that occur to you in these areas and then seeking answers. These questions may be natural prompts for the next steps you will want to take on your journey.

"This is a life work," Louise Hay writes, "The more you learn, the more you know, the more you practice and apply, the better you get to feel, and the more wonderful your life will be. Doing this work makes you feel good!"

(Isn't that the same reason we want to spend time with horses?)

WHEN PERCEPTION ≠ REALITY

Beginning on p. 289, we'll begin to see how all this mental work can help reshape our lives into what we've always wanted, in *and* out of the saddle. Before we leave the land of affirmations, however, there are still a few more small thought-streams to cross.

First, it is important to note that any time spent whining about what we *think* is wrong with our lives is time utterly wasted—we might as well have spent it watching reality TV. When it comes to making changes, the more energy we give to *what's wrong* in our lives, and the more we *feed* that perception, the more we beckon that reality.

So how does this negative bias affect our riding and the time we spend with our horses? I'll give a personal example that is, while slightly embarrassing, somewhat illustrative (I gave up pride a long time ago). Once when I visited a friend's barn for a clinic, I arrived feeling very self-conscious; I was certain everyone there was going to be a better rider than me. My friend rides all the time; with my schedule, I am lucky to ride once or twice a week. She goes on trail rides, shows, and attends regular clinics and lessons. Me…not so much. While I was intimidated, my deep desire to ride better inspired me to "woman up," load my horse, and just go do my best.

I arrived the night before to settle in, and my friend and I went over to the arena, where we met several others who were also there to familiarize their horses with the surroundings and work them a little bit to get the travel kinks out. When everyone started loping, I just followed suit. I wasn't really thinking about much else; we were all laughing, talking, and enjoying the ride.

Afterward, over dinner, I expressed my trepidation over the next day's clinic, saying I hoped I could keep up, and despairing (as I always do) over my lack of formal training.

My friend looked across the table at me and remarked with a laugh, "You're kidding, right?"

I was puzzled. "About what?" This was no laughing matter to me.

"Oh my gosh! I can't believe how hard you are on yourself," she exclaimed. "I was watching you guys lope around, and I was pretty much green with envy, wondering if I'll *ever* be able to ride that way. You can't seriously think you're not as good a rider as the rest of the people here." She laughed again. "You're a MUCH better rider than you think you are."

Her shocked sincerity was hard to discount. I realize now, after digging around in all this affirmation stuff, that I have spent so much time focused on what's *wrong* with my riding—and with me—and the *holes* I can never seem to fill, no matter how much I learn and do, that I have never learned how to internalize any of what I'm doing *right*. Because I tend to focus so much on what I'm *not* doing right or *can't* do as well as I'd like, I automatically assume inferiority to anyone I talk to or ride with. This isn't humility. This is *genuine* perception.

Has this negative self-perception changed how I ride? Maybe. But more important to our purposes is that it changed *my experience of riding*. There's really is no way to count the cost of lost joy and missed opportunities.

Louise Hay says that once she began to realize that "all good begins with accepting that which is within one's self, and loving that self which is you," she began to develop over time a peaceful, loving, and appreciative relationship with herself. To get to this place, she says, she began by searching out little things that she thought were good qualities. As she began noticing these things, the good feelings about one part of her life began to spread into the rest.

This, Hay teaches, is exactly how affirmations take root and grow, transforming *words* into *perception* into *reality*. She predicts that in working with one or two affirmations to start, focusing in one area, other parts of our life will also improve. It really doesn't matter where we begin: with our horses, our riding, our diets, our fitness, or our mind-body connection. As we begin to affirm the little things that are already good in each area, these positives will ripple into other areas of our lives in which we'd like to find joy.

"I learned to love and approve of all of me," Hay writes, "even those qualities I thought were 'not good enough'....That was when I really began to make progress."

So what is *already* good about your body and your riding? Let's start some positive affirmation ripples for you:

- "My riding muscles are strong, flexible, and toned—I can ride all day!"

- "When I ride my hands stay light, in perfect communication with my horse."

- "I stay 'grounded and centered' in the saddle. My balance is unflappable!"

- "My mind is clear and focused; I am present in every moment of my ride."

Goals Count

With Coach Daniel Stewart's help, let's now figure out how to set some achievable goals in terms of fitness, nutrition, mindfulness, and mental training. Coach Stewart says that goal-setting, while nothing new, is still one of the most beneficial skills any of us can develop. A goal helps us use our time more efficiently, stay better focused on what's important, identify strategies that lead to success, seek feedback on our progress, keep going when faced with adversity, and develop a clear vision of what we want to accomplish. And yet, goal-setting remains a struggle for many of us. Here are a few things that may be getting in your way:

- **Fear of failure.** "What if I can't really achieve a goal I set?"

- **Fear of success.** "What if I do achieve it? Then what? And what if I can't keep it up?"

- **Others' impressions.** "What do my friends, family, and peers think about my goal?"

- **Past experience:** "I failed in the past and got discouraged; what could be different now?"

- **Willpower:** "Do I really have what it takes to see this through?"

- **Time:** "Will all the time and effort this takes today really benefit me tomorrow?"

Coach Stewart says that understanding *why* we don't set goals is only half the battle; the other half is learning *how* to set them. Regardless of whether we're training a young horse, learning to jump, developing a conditioning program, or just riding recreationally with friends, goal-setting is already an integral part of what we do with our horses. With a little deliberate thought and planning, we can build on this natural base to learn how to set more specific and intentional goals, along with plans for achieving them.

Exercise for Your Brain:
How Do Your Goals Measure Up?

As you start to set new goals, it's important to run a few traps to make sure each one is solid and indeed one you want to commit yourself to. Ask yourself if the goal you're setting is:

- **Right for you, right now?** Your short- and long-term goals must build upon your skills, experience, and capabilities rather than those you perceive others to have.

- **Worthwhile?** Reaching a goal requires hard work and dedication; be sure this goal will be well worth the effort.

- **Realistic?** A goal should be challenging but achievable. If it's too easy, your motivation will fizzle; if it's too far out-of-reach (for now!), you'll be setting yourself up for frustration and disappointment.

- **Self-determined?** A goal you set should be all about *you*—meaningful and fulfilling for you, first and foremost (that is, avoid at all costs setting goals just to please others).

- **Reasonably spaced?** Remembering that quality is better than quantity, goal-setting works best with only **one** long-term goal and no more than **three** short-term goals at a time; it's best to update your short-term goals every six months or so.

- **Measurable?** The best kind of goal lets you know if you've achieved it or not. To create real change, your goal must be specific enough to be measured.

- **Time-bound?** Establishing a target date for your goal will help you plan your action steps and track your progress. While timeframes need not always be set in stone, having a target date helps avoid the time snares of procrastination or complacency.

- **Believable?** A stretch can be healthy and good for sparking growth; however, if the gap between your current ability and your desired goal is too big, your mind can't accept its reality. Is there an intermediate step you can set as your first goal to narrow that believability gap?

- **Perpetual?** A single long-term goal that requires a lifetime commitment is fine, but success is more achievable—and trackable—when you can plan your work toward this goal one day at a time, setting smaller, periodic, complementary goals you can meet on your way to the top.

- **Ethical?** Every goal you set must align with your own moral compass, including all the steps you have to take to reach it. True success means following what is morally right and responsible (such as healthy weight maintenance over bingeing on diet pills) for the sake of your self-concept.

As you probably know by now, it's very easy to let a stated goal drift away in the busyness of your day-to-day life—and be snuffed by the "must tend" priorities that always have a way of popping up to challenge your commitment. Things happen, detours are inevitable, and setbacks occur, but once you commit to a goal, make up your mind to hold firm, claim space, and renew your commitment as many times as it takes until you reach the finish line.

In *It's Not Just About the Ribbons* (the follow-up book to the seminal *That Winning Feeling!*) reserve rider for the 1992 Olympic dressage team Jane Savoie says that another way to look at goal-setting is *defining your destination* with your end-result or long-term goal.

"In order to reach your personal best in any area of your life," writes Savoie, "you need to set definite, long-term goals so that you know exactly where you're

Jane Savoie's *It's Not Just About the Ribbons* and *That Winning Feeling!*, both from Trafalgar Square Books (www.horseandrider-books.com).

heading. Think of how futile it would be for you to get into your car to go to a horse show but not know where it is or how to get there! How can you arrive someplace if you don't know where you're going?"

Then, says Jane, the interesting stops and motivational "fuel stations" (otherwise known as your manageable, short-term goals) provide a "road map" telling you you're on the right route to that afore-mentioned destination.

Coming back to our own meandering trail ride, this metaphor seems almost too perfect!

RIDE FOR YOUR BRAND

In his 2010 *Harvard Business Review* article "What's your Social Media Strategy?" Soumitra Dutta explored the role of personal branding via social media in the business world as a means of helping executives "strengthen and leverage relationships, show commitment to a cause, profession, company, or product; and demonstrate a capacity for reflection instead of just action." Today, the rising phenomenon of companies using social media platforms to build a "personal brand" has settled deeply into the mainstream, and anyone who hasn't jumped on board this train is left far behind.

As a communications director by day (and sometimes night), I know all too well the difference strong branding makes in a company's overall image and perceived strength in its target market. Think about Starbucks, Google, Amazon, McDonald's...and the dozens of other companies whose brand is so strikingly clear you can't think of the company or its product without that carefully constructed brand image popping into your head. But this phenomenon is about far more than a snappy logo: A brand *packages* everything a company believes and represents into a single, striking image, sometimes paired with a catchy jingle or a memorable tagline. It's powerful. It's pervasive. And billions of dollars say it works. Companies use branding (and sometimes re-branding) to repair, establish, or strengthen their image and align everything they do behind it. And now, individuals do it, too: Think about the way authors, artists, and designers package themselves "for sales" on the Internet and via social media.

Going back to that *Harvard Business Review* article for a moment, Dutta wrote that branding is also about learning and seeking feedback to improve strategy, bring everyone on board, and smooth implementation. Branding in this light is something a company or individual does to: show commitment, enhance image, become known for ideas, and build peer recognition.

Among the first to take this powerful corporate and professional idea to horse-back, Coach Stewart says that as riders (at any level) establishing a personal brand applies this same kind of thinking to our goal-setting and the building of our *self-* *image*. By creating a mark and tagline for ourselves that says, "This is who I am, this is how I roll, and this is what makes me awesome," we set into motion for ourselves the same kind of momentum those out there crushing it on social media are gaining for business and professional success.

Exercise for Your Brain: Build Your (Riding) Brand

According to Coach Stewart, here's the secret to adding this amazing tool to your rider's toolbox:

1 **Identify a few physical and/or mental goals that are important to your enjoyment of riding and being with your horse.** To model this process for you, I'll go back to the life-changing toe epiphany Wendy Murdoch shared with us earlier in the book (p. 196) about remembering to spread our toes inside our boots while relaxing and rotating our "seat bones" downward to open up the lower back and deepening the seat (see p. 194). I now know that when I do these things, I am able to release my lower body tension, improve my stability in the saddle, and really feel the "dance" with my horse. Since this *was* such a game-changer for my riding, I want to brand it!

2 **Create an acronym.** To capture this short-term, continuous goal I want to make sure I commit to it in every ride, enhance my riding image, and become known for this quality (in my own mind, at least). Following Coach Stewart's advice, I've now chosen an acronym to describe this quality. (If the acronym doesn't work, just pick a representative word of five letters or less. Once you do this a time or two, you'll get the hang of it.) In my case, a bit of wordplay yielded my acronym: **STARS** (**S**pread **T**oes **A**nd **R**otate **S**eat-bones).

3 **Find your jingle jam.** Find a song that contains your acronym, either in the title or in the lyrics. (If something doesn't come immediately to mind, go to lyrics. net and use your acronym as a search term.) In my case, the 1980s Manhattans hit "Shining Star" came to mind. ("You are my shining star, don't you go away....") Coach Stewart advises us to then create a "brand playlist" to hold this song and other additions containing the acronym we may want to add later (the search can become addictive!). Listen to your "jingle jam" often, and as you do, visualize yourself doing whatever the acronym stands for *to the music* to create neural pathways that mentally and physically connect the music to the attribute or action your acronym describes.

4 **Create a logo to capture your brand.** In my example, I think it's fairly obvious. (I purchased myself a sheet of sparkly star stickers.) Place a graphic representation of your logo in places where you can see it all the time. Coach Stewart says that some riders sew their logos on their saddle pads, wear T-shirts with their logos on them, glue their logos on the butts of their crops, or wear temporary tattoos of their logos while working out or riding. Have fun with this and see how many ways you can keep that image in front of you, playing your mental visualization every time you do to keep that connection strong.

5 **Develop a tagline or a motivating statement for your brand.** Since no one has to know about this but you, let your imagination romp. Coach Stewart says that it needs to be memorable, and it can even be goofy if that will help stick it in your mind. Mine, for example, is "Dancing with STARS." (Don't judge. I didn't have to tell you.)

Georgia

"The picture of me on my horse represents pride, it represents happiness, it represents freedom and the beginning of a whole change of heart about how I felt about myself."

This branding process works for all kinds of reasons. "Riders who are able to build brands in this way often find that they're actually able to *become* their brands," says Coach Stewart. "Just seeing their logos (on their saddle pads, for example) reminds them of their acronyms, songs, and taglines. In this way, they're much more likely to remember to use positive reinforcement with themselves when they need it."

Find Your "Zone"

When we're trying to make an authentic connection with a horse—the kind where energies merge and we move as one in the dance we all aspire to—we must first be very well-connected to our *authentic self* (who you really are and what you value most at the core of your being...see our previous discussion on p. 32). While this is a subject addressed in all kinds of ways in countless books, articles, and by mainstream self-help thought leaders, Coach Daniel Stewart is once again at the forefront of applying a powerful mainstream concept to working with horses. "When you become disconnected from your authentic self," he says, "you have trouble in your relationship with your horse *and* within yourself. When you re-establish that connection, you get 'in the zone' where you and your horse are one."

If you're now waving your arms and shouting "sign me up!" (I know *I* am), we must first learn the answers to a few questions: What exactly *is* "the zone"? *Where* is it, and *how* do we get—and stay—there? Coach Stewart demystifies this mysterious process with some reassurance, saying:

- It gets easier with practice.

- It comes in small steps.

- It is a matter of retraining your mind to think differently.

- It brings together many little pieces of the larger puzzle we've already been exploring: health, fitness, and the mind-body connection that helps you find unity with your horse.

FIND THE FLOW

This mind-body connection that creates unity with your horse (as you may remember, this is what Susan Harris says will keep her riding until she's 95—see p. 159) requires a "state of flow" in which your ride feels effortless and automatic. I don't know about you, but it's easier for me to recall all the times when everything felt just the opposite, and no matter what I did to try to correct and rebalance, the whole ride just felt, well, clunky and clumsy and like a whole lot of effort—for me *and* for my horse.

What's the difference between these two rides? Coach Stewart says that in the first type (the effortless one), you're feeling "the flow." And in the second (clunky and clumsy), not so much. "When you develop the sensation of 'flow,'" he says, "you step into 'the zone.' No 'flow,' no 'zone'; it's as simple as that."

Not so fast, Coach Stewart. If "stepping into the zone" were *simple*, wouldn't we all be "stepping into it?" While lots of athletes may relate to this idea of "getting in the zone," as riders we face a challenge unique to our sport: There's another independent being beneath us. While *we* may find ourselves "feeling the flow," the unpredictable nature of horses, the cornucopia of things that can happen unexpectedly when riding, and the variables beyond our control mean our "flow" can be snatched from us in a moment and without warning. Horses can trip, refuse, spook, miss a change, or indulge themselves in a sideways hop or happy buck. As far as we know (and Coach Stewart attests), none of these things *ever* happen with a pair of skis or a golf club. (Although I did have a moody and vengeful tennis racket once.) The more often these unexpected events happen, the harder it gets to find (or regain) our sense of flow.

Nevertheless, since "flow" is the Holy Grail for all who ride horses, it stands to reason that we'd want to learn all we can about how to restore it any time it scoots out from under us. Here are a few quick fixes:

- **Cadence.** Recapture the sensation of flow by rhythmically whispering a cadence in time with your horse's movement like, "One, two, one, two…"

- **Rhythm.** Focus on an audible rhythm, like the squeak in your saddle, or the sound of your horse's breathing.

- **Trust.** Stop thinking so hard about riding and remind yourself that your practice and conditioning in and out of the saddle has prepared you well for the demands of your ride. *Trust* in your ability to find it in the quality of your riding.

- **Stop thinking. Just relax and soften.** In Sally Swift's second book, *Centered Riding 2: Further Exploration,* she explains this kind of softening as something that starts with relaxing the eyes (this is actually more of an awareness-expanding philosophy than merely a new way of using your actual eyes), and learning to use more of your peripheral vision to take in the largest possible area around the object in the center of your field of vision. See the exercise on p. 284 for more.

- **Stay present.** Since the state of "flow" can only occur in the present, this is where our work with meditation, mindfulness, and breathing will help us stay in the moment. According to Coach Stewart, we can easily succumb to anxiety and fear that takes us out of the present moment (and therefore out of the flow).

Whether we're talking about riding in the flow or meeting our body image struggles head-on, the lesson from this section of trail is the same: contrary to popular belief, our focus should never be on any specific outcome: "Successful outcome is our *reward* for achieving our short- and long-term goals—and not the goal itself." Instead, we should keep our focus on the positive processes we engage in to get to our end destination. The ability to Be Positive *invites* the flow we seek.

Exercise for the Body and Brain:
Sally Swift's "Soft Eyes"

The "soft eyes" technique from Sally Swift's *Centered Riding* and *Centered Riding 2* can literally expand your body awareness in connection with the movement of your horse. It's Swift's "Third Basic," and here is how to do it:

1 Sitting on your horse, choose an object in front of you and fix your eyes on it; then let your eyes relax.

2 Keeping the object at the center of your field of vision, use your peripheral vision to take in the largest area possible around the object.

3 As you allow your peripheral vision to dominate, notice your increased awareness of your surroundings, your body, and your horse's body.

Swift's books say that learning to soften your eyes helps you with *proprioception*, or the body's ability (originating in the nerve endings) to sense where all its parts are. "You will find it is much easier to feel how the horse moves your body when you are using soft eyes," she wrote.

Sit Back with Your Setbacks

It's going to happen. Whether we want to talk about it or not, there will be times during this shift to a new lifestyle that we're going to have a day—or maybe several—when we feel ourselves starting to spiral back down into that place we've all been before. This is the time to remember that we *always* have a choice. A slip or a spook (even a big one) doesn't have to be the end of the trail. The trick is to learn how to make sure a mistake (or a series of them) is just a brief hiccup, and not a deal-breaker. To help us learn how to shorten our time in the fear-and-panic realm to move past any lapse with ease, Coach Daniel Stewart offers us the "5 Rs"—words to memorize and call on as reminders when the going gets rocky.

- **Release.** Immediately after making a mistake, *let go* of frustration and disappointment to avoid dwelling on it. Example: "Well, that didn't go the way I hoped it would; next time, I'll do better."

- **Rethink.** Quickly replace any negative thoughts with positive ones like the motivating motto from the comedy *The Best Exotic Marigold Motel:* "Everything will be okay in the end, so if it's not okay, it's not the end."

- **Relax.** Let go of any tension by taking a slow, deep breath while repeating the word, "Relax," or a phrase like, "Let it go." (Sometimes I like to say "Let" on the in-breath, and "Go" on the out-breath.)

- **Refocus.** Benefit from a mistake or slip-up by telling yourself what you learned from it (find your own feedback).

- **Rehearse.** Practice using the "5 Rs" when you make mistakes in your day-to-day so that you'll be well prepared for them when they occur when it really matters— in high-pressure situations or when the going gets tough.

Coach Stewart says that when we learn to view *mistakes* and *setbacks* only as *learning opportunities*—another chance to practice and strengthen everything we now know how to do right—we not only shorten their duration, we also weaken their effect on us.

"SURF" YOUR STRESS WAVES

There's an ebb and flow that often accompanies the pursuit of health and fitness goals. One minute we're highly motivated to get healthier and feel better about our bodies, and then our best positivity is crushed by a wave of hopelessness and despair. Especially once we're starting to notice results (like that emerging ab muscle I saw in the yoga room), a setback or lapse that threatens our success is just about as depressing as it gets.

The good news is, there's a technique we can learn that will help us treat all such tumbles from progress as just momentary blips on our success radar. During those times when a stressful situation moves your lifestyle upgrade to the bottom of your priorities, Coach Stewart says the trick is to learn to "surf."

Huh?

"Becoming *more* confident, focused, and mentally tough (especially about keeping our health and fitness priorities high on our list) in the face of adversity," he writes in his monthly "Ride Right" newsletter, "keeps us moving forward *toward* our goals rather than allowing ourselves to be pulled helplessly out to a sea of anxiety." By amping up our focus, confidence, and tenacity during stressful times, we avoid getting knocked around by wave after wave, barely keeping our heads—and our good intentions and healthy practices—above the surface.

Coach Stewart says that by consistently practicing the healthy lifestyle improvement strategies and techniques we've discussed in previous pages *before* we need them, we'll have what we need to face down the "stress waves" with what some hot yoga practitioners call "Bengal tiger strength and bulldog determination." And, lucky for us, the significant "stress wave" challenges we quite naturally experience when riding horses, especially in competitive arenas, create the perfect practice field for "stress surfing" in other arenas of our lives. (Yep, it's all connected.)

Let Go of the Past

We've touched on this a bit already, but it's so important to our moving forward from here that we're going to double back for a moment to emphasize the importance of learning to let go of our painful past memories, whether we're talking about things that happened in our riding or in regard to our body image, or both. Keeping our negative past memories from interfering with our joy today—and especially our potential future happiness—is a line we must work hard to hold. And, borrowing from our reframing exercise, the trick here is going to be learning to tell ourselves these stories in ways that help us shape our "now" and our future in a positive ways.

Monica

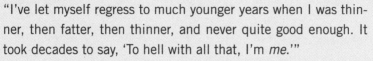

"I've let myself regress to much younger years when I was thinner, then fatter, then thinner, and never quite good enough. It took decades to say, 'To hell with all that, I'm *me*.'"

"It's up to each of us to decide how we're going to interpret these memories," Coach Stewart writes in his April 2013 "Ride Right" newsletter. "We can either see them as valuable lessons that promote learning, or we can see them as hurtful experiences that cause us to doubt our potential, lower our self-confidence, and perhaps even consider giving up (or avoiding future challenges) all together."

So, starting to pull together what we've learned so far about Being Honest, Being Fair, Being Proactive, Being Mindful, and now Being Positive, let's begin the transformation and reframing of the "bad from back then" into the unique potential for personal growth soon to be reflected in our riding and in our lives. Sit deep for one more climb and more than a little underbrush (but don't worry, we'll cut our way through it together)—I promise you the fresh view of your potential will be well worth it.

#Hoofpicks

In this chapter we explored how visualization, affirmations, and realistic goal-setting can be cultivated in our daily lives. This will help us in our work with horses by developing our mind muscles so we begin to intuitively work better under pressure and are better prepared to challenge ourselves. This will be a game-changer in the battle against negative body image because these practices, when used repeatedly, are proven to lift self-esteem.

Your Chapter 9 **#Hoofpicks** include:

1 **Check your focus.** When you catch yourself thinking about a ride, an event, or an entire day as an insurmountable hurdle on your happy trail, remember Coach Daniel Stewart's directive: "It doesn't matter who you are or what your challenges are, there is something special in you that can help you become great. Find it and make it your focus."

2 **Strategize!** The key to making the plethora of mental riding practices in this chapter work for you is identifying in advance which ones you will call into action when you need to. Spend some time trying each one and getting good enough at it that when you *do* reach for it, it will be there. Once you've made some these practices your own, think of situations when they would be helpful to you. Which ones will you call on first? What will remind you to try them? If the first one doesn't work as well as you'd like, what's next?

3 **Just say "WHOA!"** Habitual thoughts and thought patterns can be insidious—you're hock deep in them before you even realize it. Stay on the lookout for "stinkin' thinkin'" and stop those negative thought patterns in their tracks. The instant you recognize their chattering, sit deep and say, "WHOA!"

4 **Set your head for success.** When people consciously reshape their environment in a way that sets up success, the right behaviors begin to emerge almost on their own. As you take a look at your habits and behaviors, see if you can identify those thought trails that lead nowhere good. Nurture environment-builders with things like creating order in your tack locker, making sure to allow enough time after each ride or barn visit to just hang out with your horse. Simple mindfulness exercises, especially while grooming and during routine barn chores, continually work to "set your head" for success.

10 | Set Your New Course

Let's take a moment to remember Dr. Ira Progoff's imagery of the "weak stream" and the "boulder" back on p. 240. Another of my favorite visuals common in his meditations is that of a well and an underground stream. The picture he paints in his guided meditations offers an overarching view of our lives in which there is surface area—the parts of our lives that are visible to others—and far beneath that runs a current of inner wisdom that is always flowing within our reach. Whenever we find ourselves in need of simple mental refreshment *or* essential hydration, Dr. Progoff's meditations (and with practice you can do this on your own) can take you there, almost instantaneously. Sometimes, however, our well dries up. It may be a personal struggle, it may be horse trouble, or it may be just a bout of *ennui*; in these times we just have to go a little (or a lot) deeper to reconnect with our own personal aquifer.

To tap into this "underground stream" of inner wisdom that helps us be all we're meant to be—with our horses, family, friends, work—we must descend through all our past choices, emotional baggage, and belief systems (sometimes with a pick and shovel in tow) to clear away the debris that limits us. In a way similar to all we've explored in this book so far—diet, exercise, mindfulness, and biomechanics (and how our work with our horses crisscrosses *all* these paths)—we must *find our own way* to the joyful and productive existence we want and deserve.

The first section of this next stretch of our trail together is where we at last enter new terrain. Here's where we learn how to make lifestyle and behavioral changes stick. Whether your body image issues are based on real, serious, weight and shape challenges or are products of skewed perception and negative thought patterns, this is your path to freedom from inner *and* outer struggles.

Thought Patrol

It doesn't matter if you are brand new or a seasoned veteran in the "battle of the bulge," it's no secret that dealing with body image issues is stressful—whether it's real and impeding excess weight, or just unhappiness with the frame you're in. And whether you're trying to diet it off, work around it, defend it, or just simply live with the excess you feel, this stress can be omnipresent and debilitating to your self-image.

Citing the physiology of stress explored in too many well-known studies to count, Jill Valle says that our hard-wired, primitive, "fight-or-flight" hormonal response to stress (real *or* imagined) creates a powerful enemy in our war on negative body image. To address any resulting weight or body image issues, she adds, requires that we first calm the mind. As we learned in our Be Mindful section (see p. 209), by simply becoming aware of the actual thoughts (and associated feelings, but we'll cross that bridge next) driving our behavior and choices, we can begin to stem the stress reaction they create in our bodies.

AN ENDLESS LOOP

Valle explains that because our thoughts, feelings, and behavior are actually just points on a continuum (which in this case describes the "endless loop" of connection between related-but-slightly-different things in which any change to one affects the other two), when it comes to making important lifestyle changes, it really doesn't matter where we start. Instead of worrying too much about *which* change should come first, she advises us to just choose whatever is easiest and most doable, and trust that this ripple will occur.

• **For some, replacing a thought is the easiest place to begin.** Eventually new emotions begin ride along with the new thought, and the change in behavior that seemed unlikely (or impossible!) is suddenly within our reach. For example: My *thought* about kale was that it was disgusting, foul, strong tasting (remember that episode of *Cheers* where Woody was trying to convince everyone to try it?), and based on that thought pattern, there was simply no way I'd ever eat it on purpose. But then a dietician friend began extolling its many virtues, replacing my previous thoughts with some that were far more positive. She convinced me to try a kale salad she makes—and, incidentally, it wasn't terrible at all. After a few more successful kale adventures, I started *feeling* a little bit smug about my budding relationship with this unsuspecting vegetable, so you know what happened next, right? My *behavior* began reflecting this new attitude. I ordered the stuff off restaurant menus. And now I not only regularly add it to my shopping cart, I pick it up from the deli as a side dish whenever I need a quick, nutritious meal.

• **Other positive lifestyle changes start with the behavioral change, such as choosing a specific action to begin creating a new habit.** Then at some point, *feelings* begin to change about the behavior, and the next thing we know our *thinking* has changed, too. For example: It wasn't too long after I started taking Pure Barre classes (and I experienced the same phenomenon with hot yoga and Pilates years before) when I realized that when I ate proper quantities of light and nutritious food, I was able to finish strong and recover quickly from each class. The *behavior* change of regular conditioning made me *feel* better about my body and my riding. As a result, my thoughts about planning, shopping, and preparing light simple nutritious food (to sustain me through my classes) went from, "That's way too much trouble, and besides, I don't have time," to "I'm going to make time because it's worth it—and so am I!"

- **Still others find it easier to initiate change with their emotions and how they feel about something by focusing instead on how they want to feel.** Some call this "fake it till you make it," but with new information and ideas we'll explore in coming sections, learning to "pivot your feelings" (see p. 322) can be an amazing shortcut to the behavior change that suddenly seems as obvious as it is logical. For example (and I'll call out the points of our continuum as I circle the loop: I *felt* fear and dread as I began the riding portion of a clinic. *I'm an OK rider,* my thoughts reasoned, *but I'm not sure I can do this. I'm larger, older, and less experienced than any of the other riders here. And more afraid. Look at them, they're not bothered by this at all! What's wrong with me? Why am I even here?* The very thought of putting my silly little cutting-bred, highly competitive Rio on a loose rein and "cantering" all around a giant indoor arena with 20 other people doing the same had my guts in a knot, questioning my own sanity as well as the wisdom of this well-known exercise. I wasn't sure whether my fear had more to do with falling off, getting hurt, or making a complete fool of myself in front a large crowd of people. Still, I had committed to this, and my *feelings* drove me right up into the saddle as I switched my focus from fear to my deep desire to ride better and more freely. Because it was a prescribed exercise, I matched my *actions and behavior* as well as I could to the clinician's directives. It was every bit as insane as my emotions predicted: at one point we were going "upstream," cantering the opposite direction of all the other horses, then Rio was reaching out to bite anyone who got within reach, but before my thoughts could return to the negative place they started, I took a deep breath. Then another. I felt my body settle deeper into the saddle and connect with Rio's back. I felt his hind legs beneath me pushing off as he changed directions yet again, and I felt my body just fluidly follow. *Hmmm,* a new thought rolled quietly across my mind and came to a stop in the center of my awareness. *This is actually kind of fun.* I took another breath and thought about elongating my body and sitting back more. Something clicked. Suddenly Rio and I were literally floating around that arena together, my mind a blank canvas, my heart as filled with joy and gratitude as it had been with fear and dread. (And I didn't think once about the size of my thighs or try to suck in my belly as I crossed in front of the spectators and auditors.)

This kind of bouncing between thought, emotion, and behavior is not unusual, experts agree, and it may even change from situation to situation. Once you are aware of it and understand it, however, it becomes easier and easier to use this process to your advantage. The key, Valle says, is to look at whatever negative stress cycle is getting us down and choose and entry point. The entry point you choose may vary from situation to situation, and you may even change entry points several times before you find one you can nudge in a more positive direction.

"What most people don't realize," Valle assures us, "is that not only can you enter this continuum at any of these three points (thoughts, feelings, behaviors), but you may even bounce back and forth between *thoughts* and *feelings* for a while until you get the *behavioral* change you're looking for."

Building on what we've already learned about mindfulness, how thoughts work, and how to quiet, replace, or provoke different thinking, with the help of our experts and some real life applications, we're going to examine the powerful, lifestyle-influencing, workhorse nature of our thoughts (and patterns of thinking). This is most often the best place to begin reshaping the continuum to turn the corner to positive change.

BREAK IT DOWN

When you recognize a limiting or negative thought (and this gets easier and easier with practice), Valle says that there are three important questions to ask yourself:

1 Is this really true?

2 What is the evidence?

3 Even if it's true, how can I replace this thought with the positive version?

So if you catch yourself, for example, in the thought: "My thighs look as big as Dallas in these tan breeches," before you go digging through the hamper for a pair of black breeches (or decide to abandon your riding plan for an evening on the sofa) stop that thought and ask:

- **Is this really true?** Maybe, but probably not. (Have you *been* to Dallas?)

- **What is the evidence?** Who is looking at and thinking about the size of your thighs? (Other than you?)

- **Now replace body-bashing blather with something better:** "I have strong thighs to keep me stable in the saddle over all kinds of terrain."

Another important technique to learn as we start to build our awareness of the quality of our thoughts is something Valle calls "thought interruption," similar to the technique you learned from Coach Daniel Stewart called "thought-stopping." Valle drills deeper into this idea (beyond the "WHOA!") to equip us for deliberate interruption of those negative thoughts and thought sequences we've heard playing in our heads *many* times before. You know the ones...and regardless of where they originated, you've pretty much come to own them. You can likely recognize these "thinks" the minute something triggers them (more on that coming up—see p. 296) even if you have no idea what pressed the "play" button. Before you know it, you're caught in a painfully familiar whirlwind of negative thoughts that spiral into feelings that trigger behaviors—and with us, this twister likely has something to do with body image, self-worth or how we ride. The key is, catching hold of those thoughts before they spin out of control.

Exercise for the Brain: Catch That Thought!

Here's how to press "STOP" on a negative thought pattern once it starts playing in your head:

1 **Notice that it's a cycle.** "Wow, this gets played all the time."

2 **Pause and breathe.** Take a deep, belly breath (see p. 236). And another.

3 **Write it down.** Use your journal if you can (see p. 244) to ask and answer: What happened to bring up this stressful feeling? What thoughts ran through your mind from the minute you first felt that stressor? List the progression of thoughts that are part of this pattern.

4 **Beside each thought, label it "rational" or "irrational."** If you need to, use the first two of Valle's questions from p. 293 (Is it true? What is the evidence?) to help you assess whether the thought is rational or irrational.

5 **Reframe.** How else can I see this? Building on the exercise you learned on p. 267, Valle recommends *cognitive restructuring* as your go-to mental technique for finding positive ways to view or experience what could be considered negative events, ideas, concepts, and emotions.

Ever have something happen to you one day, and it's just a hiccup, and on another day, a major upset? Something that feels like an interesting challenge one day and a complete deal-breaker the next? Countless studies have proven that changing the way you look at something (*perception*) changes your experience of it (positive or negative or somewhere in between). What if we could learn to shift our perceptions *on purpose* to transform something that feels negative into something that feels better—or at least helps us view it as a learning experience? This is *cognitive restructuring*—a very useful mental tool for challenging (and defeating) your negative thought patterns. Arising from the cognitive therapy world, cognitive restructuring has quick and useful everyday applications that will give us immediate and true power over our stinkin' thinkin.' These patterns can be sneaky, though, especially when we're caught in the grips of body image issues; it may take a while at first to realize we're under their spell. With practice, however, we can learn which thoughts and patterns need to go, what triggers them, and how best to stop them in their tracks and send them packing. Here's the beginner's guide to do just this.

Exercise for the Brain: Cognitive Restructuring: Rebuild that Thought!

1 **Identify your thought patterns.** What are the thought sequences that tend to repeat themselves when you encounter something that stresses you out or makes you anxious or sad? When you're riding and things start to go south for you mentally, back up and see what happened to start this negative spiral. When you consider your body and you go from feeling okay to not so much, what was the last happy thought you remember...and then what?

2 **Notice your individual thoughts.** I know. This is hard to do at first. When you consider the sheer volume of thoughts, even though most of them are repeats, it still isn't always easy to pinpoint an exact thought. If you get stuck and frustrated and just can't seem to catch those slippery rascals, wind your way back to the mindfulness section (p. 211) to help quiet your brain so you can isolate individual thoughts. Then imagine that you are a (tiny) bystander, leaning against the inside wall of your skull, just impartially observing your own brain. Watch the thoughts as they arrive, as if you're watching a parade. Notice *how* and *when* negative thoughts tend to make an appearance—and whether they are part of a pattern you've identified or they tend to trigger your pattern. When you get good at simply observing your thoughts without judgment, it is much easier to begin to recognize their patterns and characteristics.

3 Challenge your thoughts. In order to get to the actual reframing part of this process, you have to be able to "catch yourself" in a negative thought, and then put a full stop on that outlaw (go ahead and use Coach Stewart's "WHOA!" here to distract that thought, if it works for you). Once you have the thought's attention (is this starting to remind you of training a three-year-old filly?) ask yourself Jill Valle's three questions (see p. 293).

4 Replace your thoughts with more positive alternatives. When you "catch" a thought that feels negative, change your self-talk to use more neutral emotions. It's important not to *deny* the negative situation; you're just looking for the "gift" (some would call this the "silver lining"). The trick here is to try to shift the way you see things (perception) in a way that is more optimistic and positive, yet still fits the reality (verifiable facts) of your situation.

"It's important to remember that our mind cannot think in opposites," Coach Stewart says, "so we cannot think the opposite of what we tell ourselves." Realizing this great truth, why not use it to our advantage? What if instead of always telling ourselves what we *can't, shouldn't,* or *won't* be able to do with our horses because of the way we look or how our body is shaped, we tell ourselves that we *can, should,* and *will* follow our joy by making small changes for our own health, the comfort of our horse, and the betterment of our overall lives?

What if?

Strengthen Your "Frame of Mind"

In earlier sections we covered most of what's required to improve the more technical points of creating a light-riding "framework." But as helpful as that may be to our riding, anyone struggling with body image issues understands that's only a fraction of the story. We know all too well how body anxiety can permeate every part of our lives. Regardless of our riding goals, discipline, or level, the real game-changer we're looking for is learning how to shore up our "frame of mind" in a way that will vanquish our *mental* riding problems as surely as the *physical*.

According to Coach Daniel Stewart not only *what* we think but also *how* we think has a profound impact on *our body's physical performance* when we ride. The first thing we need to know, he says, is that every rider generally has two main mindsets: 1) a *problem-focused mindset*, and 2) a *solution-focused mindset*. An example of a problem-focused mindset is: "I'm too big to ride well; my legs are too thick to give clear, subtle aids." A solution-focused mindset, on the other hand, would likely yield this statement: "I'm going to start a fitness program; I'm going to limit my portion sizes at meals."

"Humans are better at seeing problems than solutions," Coach Stewart says. "This is because problems hurt our feelings and create stronger emotions." This explains why even though most people actually receive a 3:1 ratio of positive to negative feedback each day, we still tend to dwell on the negative.

Exercise for the Brain:
Develop Your Solution-Focused Mindset

The first order of business in developing a stronger "frame of mind" is to train ourselves to find and reinforce our own personal *solution-focused* mindset. To do this, let's get out that journal, a clean sheet of paper, or cue up the computer so we can walk through this process together. (My own examples will hopefully help you feel better about yourself *and* inspire you to come up with a few mindsets of your own to switch.)

- **Problem-focused mindset.** Write a few sentences describing some of your perceived problems pertaining to your body and/or your horses. Here's mine: *I'm just too tired to go ride after work in the evenings, and on the weekends I have too much to do. I can't make progress in my riding because I never get to spend enough time with my horses. All I do is feed them, pat them, and make empty promises even I'm tired of hearing.*

- **Solutions-focused mindset.** Now write how all those issues could be resolved. For example: *First, I'm going to start going to bed a half-hour earlier. Second, I'm going to put some razor-wire boundaries on my work time to better protect my personal time. Third, I'm going to pack my riding gear, a healthy snack, and a bottle of water in the car each morning so I can go to the barn straight from work. I'll also schedule a one-hour "appointment" with my horses on Saturdays and honor that time like I'm seeing a doctor (because let's face it—I am!) so I can get my weekend chores and errands done but still spend consistent quality time with my horses.*

According to Coach Stewart, there are also two other, related mindsets to be aware of:

- The *scarcity mindset* (what I *don't* have).

- The *abundance mindset* (what I *do* have).

Applied to horses and riding, Coach Stewart says that these secondary mindsets often play a significant role in our "frame of mind." Things like leg length (not long enough), height (not tall enough), and weight (not the right shape or size) can invade our thinking to cast a negative light on everything we do. Similar to the problem- and solution-focused mindsets, the more we focus on what we *don't* have (*scarcity* mindset), the more we limit our ability to find what we *do* have (*abundance* mindset). "And no matter who you are," Coach Stewart reminds us, "you're always going to have some of both."

By putting deliberate focus on what you *do* have on your side rather than what you're battling (or think you are battling), you can train your mind to focus on the two key positives—solution *and* abundance. "It takes no talent to see a problem," Coach Stewart says. "Talent is being able to look *beyond* the problem."

So go ahead...try it!

✳ Exercise for the Brain:
Flip Your Focus

1 Choose something about yourself that you'd like to get beyond. For example: You're overweight, out of shape, and you feel out of balance when you ride.

2 Find your solution-focus. Change your behavior patterns to get fit and flexible.

3 Focus on the abundance mindset. You have *many* small opportunities in your day to make minor behavior modifications ("Small changes, done consistently, add up quickly," Coach Stewart insists):

• Make a point to take the stairs as many times each day as you can—wherever you are and whenever they are available.

• At each meal or snack, make the healthiest choice available to you.

• Cut the size of your current portions by at least a quarter.

Coach Stewart says that once your mind starts searching for *solution-focused*, *abundance-minded* opportunities every day, you will start to build upon your little successes to get where you need to go.

The Road to Self-Image Repair

Since Coach Stewart and others agree that the best antidote to negative thought habits is a strong self-image, it follows that for many of us who struggle with body issues, that sounds a little like the old quip, "If you don't have an oil well, get one!" The self-image we hold is complicated, and it is influenced by many different things, most of them beyond our control. But, as we're beginning to understand with the help of Jill Valle and Coach Stewart, we *can* learn to monitor and get some degree of control on our thoughts. (Think of that high energy,

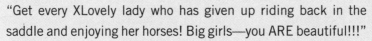

combustible horse that needs a calm, steady hand, knowledgeable and firm aids, good balance, and just the right amount of rein to do spectacular things. *Your thoughts are that horse.*)

Now that we have our "thought-stoppers," reframing techniques, and affirmations all installed, we can at last begin the process of repairing our self-image. Note the use of the word "process." In other words, this doesn't happen overnight. "If someone is in a deep self-image hole," Coach Stewart emphasizes, "climbing out is a matter of baby steps. You can't go from completely negative to completely positive in one step. Expect success, but realize that it takes a while."

SUCCESS BUILT IN LAYERS

If you're starting to sense some overlap here, this is probably a good place to explain that these are skills and strategies best built in layers. We started working through a few of these points earlier to lay your foundation; as we add new information and subtle shifts, we need to circle back to apply the same or similar mental techniques in a slightly different way, armed with our new understanding. That's how building mental muscles works and how we can make these new habits and behaviors really stick for good.

You're now familiar with identifying the factors you think are causing your negative thoughts. You know this may include things related to your age, weight, body image, riding ability, life circumstances, and occupation. Coach Stewart says that sometimes our negative thought habits are just about our riding issues, and sometimes (maybe even most of the time) our riding issues are likely also our life issues. "Who we are as riders mirrors who we are as people," he explains. And vice versa.

The key here is to pick the *one thing* that seems to be causing you the most trouble. Focus your attention on this *one thing* first. (The others will keep...and may even diminish or disappear once the "big one" leaves the building.) Coach Stewart describes this for us in simplified military terms: "If you want success, you have to send a strong army in one direction," he says. "Napoleon's army, the strongest, largest army the world had ever known at that point in history, lost the Battle of Waterloo because he split his army into too many small pieces and tried to fight on too many fronts at once."

Many if not most of us realize that our list of complaints and our continuous fight to "get things right" will scatter (and therefore weaken) our energy if we try to fix everything at once. This creates the same sort of downfall (on a much smaller scale, of course) Napoleon experienced, and for exactly the same reason.

"To win the self-image war," Coach Stewart says, "we have to focus all our strengths on one single point at a time."

BEYOND POSITIVE THINKING

While it may seem a little bit "wiggly" to try to pin down the exact emotions lurking beneath your thoughts, and harder still to figure out how your thoughts and feelings play together and off one another, therapist Jill Valle reiterates that getting good at *isolating* and then *examining* your thoughts individually is the key.

"Aligning your thoughts and feelings inspires different choices," she adds. "This is just something you have to experience one time to really understand the potential for change you have there." It's also important, Valle says, to recognize this progression as a completely normal growth process. "It's just what your mind will do if you let it; however, it's also very easy for old belief systems to get in the way and to dismiss all this as woo-woo poppycock," she cautions.

Esther and Jerry Hicks' *The Astonishing Power of Emotions* asserts that everything that exists in the world we live in began as a thought or idea. According to the oft-argued realm of quantum physics, our thoughts carry a vibrational frequency that attracts other thoughts (and ideas and people and things) humming on that same frequency. If you subscribe to this and related theories, thoughts are actually vibrational concepts that eventually mature into physical reality.

With this idea of thoughts becoming things in mind, lets begin to monitor our thoughts. Practice sorting thoughts about what you *do* want more of in your life and thoughts about things you are just *done with*. This is empowered thinking. By simply recognizing your actual thoughts, analyzing the emotions behind them in real time, and then sorting them according to "want" and "do not wants," you can put more deliberate attention on the ones you'd like to put to work attracting other thoughts, ideas, and people to you. "This goes far beyond just 'positive thinking,'" Valle says, "it's the manifestation of what you put your focus on."

According to *The Astonishing Power of Emotions*, the thoughts we have about what we want—our hopes and dreams, yes, but also our good intentions and ideas for improvement—are held within us in a sort of "vibrational escrow," just waiting for our withdrawal. The reason "thought work" such as what we've been discussing is so powerful in making our "thoughts become things," is that when we gather more and more similarly charged thoughts, our emotions come right along with them. And when our thoughts and emotions *align on the same frequency*, physical change is set into motion.

Exercise for the Brain: Turn the Key

Here's how to play with empowering your thoughts on your own:

1 Isolate a thought. This should be about something you really, really want to be true in your life. For example: "I want to feel skilled and confident on my horse every time I enter the show ring, knowing we look and perform great together."

2 Repeat this thought as an affirmation—as if it already is true. "I am skilled and confident on my horse, and we look and perform great together."

3 Visualize your success. Remembering to use all five senses, place yourself in the show ring on your horse and feeling the way you want to feel. Play the "video" of your perfect ride in your head, endless loop style, and remember to shift your perspectives (see p. 259) and let your skilled, confident, mental state infuse every cell in your physical body.

4 **Sit with this feeling for a moment, holding onto it for as long as you can.** Anything you think about over and over again *in this way* becomes a positive emotional investment without your having to do another thing. Your now pumped-up emotions, which carry the same vibrational charge as your original thought on the subject (see Step 1), add their energy to this collection.

5 **Pay attention and notice each time your physical world starts to respond.** The more you think and feel about this particular "want" of yours, the more people appear in your life with the same goal, opportunities for improvement "fall in your lap," even songs on the radio seem to be written just for you! Things all around you start to hum right along with this growing frequency. Whether it's something rather insignificant or a Very Big Deal, make a point of recognizing what happens in the physical world when your thoughts and feelings become aligned.

Eyes Forward!

If you haven't already noticed, this whole weight and body image struggle is a symptom of something much deeper going on inside each of us. The real answer is *not* in those size-6 riding breeches you may think are your end game. Nor is the prize we're seeking going to be hanging on any wall or adorning any trophy shelf. What we're really going for here is something you'll store inside you, and once you earn it, no matter where you go or what you do, on or off horses, you'll ride better, stronger, and lighter than ever before—it is yours to keep.

This goes furlongs beyond talk, miles past self-help, and over the horizon of how-to. This is about growth that will empower you to peel away layers that have accumulated over time so you can reconnect with your authentic self (who you

Myths of the Downward Spiral

BUSTED!

MYTH: "Once one thing goes wrong, it is always followed by another. It seems almost impossible to break the cycle of bad when the world seems to work against you."

TRUTH: It's easy, especially when we get overwhelmed by all the changes we are trying to make (or think we "should" make) in our lives, to give up on our goals. When our thoughts take a turn toward despair and feeling overwhelmed, all that "stinkin' thinkin'" we learned about (p. 264) can cue a downward emotional spiral in which each negative thought reminds you of another, and another... until you've revisited a kind of hopelessness that makes you want to give up riding altogether.

When we find our thoughts heading down this steep slope, all our expert sources agree that this is a good time for some "thought-stopping" or "thought interruption" (see p. 264). By simply recognizing and dealing straight-on with these moments of "funk," you can stop the spiral before it begins. In these instances, your job is *not* to work harder on whatever has you down—from extra weight to fitness procrastination to rampant disorganization eating up valuable "horse time." Just use what you've learned in this book to *replace negative thoughts* as soon as you catch them with thoughts and feelings that celebrate your worth and accomplishments *right now*.

"Counteract your inclination to go into negative thought spirals," Jill Valle advises. "We're so hard on ourselves. Try to have some compassion for yourself and your struggle."

Remind yourself that each new positive thought about yourself *right now* is a step in the right direction, no matter how small. "You're going for *just one step* at a time in the direction you want to go," Valle says. And, she reminds us, these steps by their very nature should be small in order to bring your emotions right along beside them. This takes time and patience and a willingness to allow the process to work.

"It's unrealistic to think you can go from total crap to completely elated in one step," she laughs. "Take as many baby steps as you need to until you reach higher ground."

truly are on the inside and all the wisdom she holds for you). You're in the process of opening up a new arena in your soul, where riding and being present in your body truly *is* the vehicle to spiritual growth you've probably known (or at least suspected) it could be all along.

So where to next? We've learned to isolate and examine our thoughts. We've learned to look for the emotion connected to our thoughts. Now we're going to take it a step further, drilling down to the beliefs that live *beneath* our surface. Once you begin this process, you may find some hidden beliefs that surprise you, or at the very least, have a bigger hold on you than you realize. This is not always the fun part, but the changes set into motion with the simple light of awareness could be profound.

DISTILL YOUR UNDERLYING BELIEFS

"Once we can recognize what our thoughts really are," therapist Jill Valle says, "we can then take each thought and run it through a simple process to distill its underlying belief."

First, we'll start on common ground:

- We all want to feel good about ourselves and our bodies.
- We're all searching for the same thing. (It's here—and it's been here all along. You just have to be willing to unpack and banish underlying beliefs that have been holding you back.)

Exercise for the Brain: Identify Your Beliefs

1 Get out that journal or fire up your computer! Spend three minutes writing as much as you can, as fast as you can, in answer to the following prompts:

- What do I believe to be true about myself and my riding?

- What do I believe would maximize my potential as a rider?

2 Now, choose *one* thought you've written in response to each question above. On two sheets of paper or two documents, isolate these thoughts—write each out, uncensored, in the greatest detail you can muster, at the top of each page. Now pick one and answer the following questions about it:

- What exactly is this thought, described more fully? Keep expanding upon what you have written, and then hone it down. Make sure your thought is stated as clearly and succinctly as possible.

- Where does it come from? Sift back through experiences, words of others, your own self-criticism arising from a past event or circumstance.

- What is the belief beneath it?

3 Next, ask the following in response to the third prompt above:

- How long have I believed this?

- What is the evidence of this belief in my life?

- Is it true?

Let me run through the exercise as an example:

- **What do I believe to be true about myself and my riding?** *I don't think I'm a very good rider and always feel "out of my league" regardless of the activity, event, or people I'm riding with.*

- **What do I believe would maximize my potential as a rider?** *Losing weight, getting in better shape, and working in a more focused way to fill in the gaps (real or perceived) in my riding education.*

- **What is this thought, fully expanded?** *I'm just so large and awkward; the minute we speed up I'm going to be flopping all over the place. How can I give my horse decent cues? I can't even control my own body, much less his! I'm not watching that video; I hate the way I look when I ride.*

- **Where does it come from?** *A random collection of memories and experiences: The reining clinic I attended when we were asked to cue with our outside leg at the canter and I couldn't imagine being able to do anything like that. My horse going faster and faster and trying to make him follow the same "cloverleaf" pattern as everyone else, but failing miserably. Trying but fearful and unable to use my legs effectively. Flopping around, almost falling off, sometimes actually falling off—and other early riding experiences just trying to stay on my first horse. Through the years, watching other riders sitting back, cantering easily, being able to use their hands and feet and legs to help their horses. Clinics and lessons where I was trying to keep up with people more advanced or less fearful than I was; trying to do things I wasn't yet ready to do.*

- **What is the belief beneath it?** *I'm too large, unbalanced, and uneducated as a rider to be able to do what I want to do and look and feel okay doing it.*

- **How long have I believed this?** *All of my riding life.*

- **What is the evidence of this belief in my life?** *Well, I did feel pretty out of control in those clinics—and I did nearly fall off that one time.*

- **Is it true?** *Well, yes and no. I am larger than I would like to be. But I'm very strong and usually stay in pretty good shape. Combining my lack of confidence with balance issues, I do feel less than beautiful and graceful in the saddle. Because I learned to ride sporadically and mostly on my own, I do run low on confidence, and as a result, I'm also reluctant to be firm enough with my horse when he starts falling apart to help him calm down and focus. But I have ridden quite a bit, in lots of different kinds of situations: Riding as a kid, all-day rides* in an open pasture full of "obstacles," a "racetrack" run at a full-out gallop, "jumps" (logs and stacks of branches), racing in the woods ("Duck!"); ranch riding on 500 acres in Hico, Texas, with my dad (no groundwork, round pens, or arenas there—horses stayed turned out and we showed up on weekends, threw on saddles, and took off in rough terrain without a second thought (or a cell phone!); trail rides with friends (on 35,000 acres in the LBJ Grasslands in Texas, camping overnight with horses on picket lines); ranch sorting (arriving with no idea what it even was but in one glorious run, sorting all the cows, in order!); surviving one-, three-, and five-day clinics (and riding through fatigue like I've never known despite Trace's bucking in front of a gasping crowd of women and Rio throwing a tantrum, running sideways through a group of people trying to listen to another instructor...good times, Rio). But I did survive all this unscathed (physically, at least!), and I'm still riding and learning and trying to do better.

"Once you expose the belief that lives on the third layer down," Valle says, "it then becomes a process of examining this underlying belief more closely for truth or value, and then laying down new beliefs that are more supportive of the change you are seeking."

Calling this something of a "fake-it-till-you-make-it" proposition, Valle says that the secret here is to ask yourself, "what would someone who rides well and is in the place I'd like to be in right now most likely believe?" The key to using this exercise to turn a new corner in your thinking is to always challenge yourself to go deeper. If you're tempted to say, "I don't know what to do," then imagine my riding friend Carole standing before you with her hands on her hips, asking *you*, as she always asks me: "What would you do if you *did* know?"

CUT A NEW TRAIL

In his fabulous book called *Leveraging the Universe,* author Mike Dooley tells us that when charting any new course we have three questions to answer:

1 What do I want?

2 Where am I today?

3 Which paths will I take to get where I want to go?

Dooley cautions us to beware of the "Should Trap" as we chart this course: "Our society is of the notion that if we don't figure out the 'shoulds' and 'hows' ahead of time," he writes, "we're being recklessly irresponsible." Instead, Dooley suggests that we allow ourselves to be led by what we want on the deepest level.

I've noticed that every time I replace "I should" with "I want," a fresh burst of clarity most often trots right along beside it. Sometimes the shortcut to what we think the "shoulds" will bring—comfort, safety, and even abundance—is just following our heart's desire. "The Universe and life's magic are best engaged when you're happy, doing what you want," Dooley says.

Dooley describes belief as the "fountainhead of our thoughts" and the expression "thoughts become things" as an immoveable Truth of Being: "Your thoughts will always, unfailingly, create your experience." By using the exercise we just learned, we can tunnel down from our thoughts to our underlying beliefs and excavate our own fountainhead—the source of our previous experiences. If we redirect that source into new ways of thinking (using the thought work and mindfulness exercises we've explored throughout this book), we *really can* change the content and quality of our future experiences.

How does all this pondering the "place" you're in—and how you got there—help you ride better or feel better about your body? I've already mentioned that our horses are our "mirrors":

Mike Dooley's *Leveraging the Universe: 7 Steps to Engaging Life's Magic* (Atria Books, 2011).

They reflect in their behavior, stance, and movement what's going on *inside of us*, whether we want to see, admit, or acknowledge it or not.

Picture Maureen (relax, Maureens—this is not a real person), a very self-conscious, anxious rider at a horse show. You've seen her. (Or maybe you've been her.) Rounded shoulders, eyes fixed (maybe darting a bit), hands in a death-grip on the reins. She's braced, tight, and stiff in all the key places. We can't see them, but her toes are probably clenched inside her boots, as if trying to grip the stirrup beneath her slightly turned-in toes. Everything about Maureen's body telegraphs self-consciousness and anxiety, both to her own brain and to her horse. To make matters worse, her pants are too tight and she's wearing the wrong bra. The main thing on her mind right now is her belly hanging over her rolled waistband, but her balance feels too precarious to try to adjust her belt.

How do you think Maureen's horse is going to move through the in-gate?

Now picture Janice, a calm, confident rider with steady control of her thoughts and movement. Janice is exactly the same size, shape and weight as Maureen, same level of experience, competing in the same class. Janice has taken a few moments to make sure she has wide-open shoulders, a flat lower back, and that her head, shoulders, hips, and heels are all aligned. She's relaxed, yet poised for performance. Her eyes are forward and calm (remember Sally Swift's "soft eyes" exercise on p. 284?), and Janice is ready to greet whatever this ride has to offer. She knows that whatever it is, it's going to be good. And, by the way, she's wearing comfortable, well-fitting pants—either because she bought the size that fit rather than the number she thought she needed to be or she jettisoned the extra weight. She's wearing the right bra, and she feels pretty good about her body because she's more tuned in to *what it can do* rather than *what it looks like*.

Imagine Janice and her horse move through that in-gate together, mirroring each other's confidence and ease.

Which rider do *you* want to be?

SEE EXCESS WEIGHT AS THE SYMPTOM, NOT THE CAUSE

Most of us think feeling good about our bodies is something that happens *after* we reach our goals, whether that includes losing weight or getting more fit, or both. Quite the contrary, as a whole lot of researchers are now pointing out. When you approach excess weight as *a symptom of an underlying cause, rather than the cause itself* by getting in touch and in tune with your body, recognizing your negative thought patterns and erroneous beliefs, and dealing with the layers of emotional issues getting in your way, you can then begin the work of *reclaiming* your body and mind so that *neither* wreak havoc on your horse time.

While there are a lot of schools of thought when it comes to weight loss/management (and not everything works for every body), reams of research shows that if you don't deal with underlying emotions, weight lost is going to come back—and bring friends. The challenge, then, is both healing our need to anesthetize emotions in unhealthy ways and making an ironclad commitment to our well-being and goals as a horseperson. Meeting this dual challenge is what will change your endgame for good.

As I've said a number of times (it bears repeating), it really doesn't matter where you start to untangle these issues, or in what order you address them, or how many times you bounce around between them while working through one particular challenge. What matters is that you *do* start, keep bouncing as needed. When I get stuck, discouraged, or just plain sick of one area that needs my attention (say, nutrition), I go back and take another look at something else (maybe the exercises that can bring my fitness up a grade level), concentrating my efforts there for a while. Not only do I make some new progress in that second area, but often when I go back to my first roadblock I find that it's resolved! Above all, *stay with your lifestyle changes* in each area we've covered until you get the results you're looking for across the board. If you, like me, have spent a lot of good time berating yourself for not having the body you desire, this three-point approach (*start, bounce if needed, stick with it*) is a tremendous load off a battered psyche: as long as we are working somewhere in this continuum, we're moving forward on the path to where we want to be. Who can ask for more than that?

"Emotions can be confusing for us," says Charles Gaby, MA, LPC. That emotions are part *biology* and part *biography* is a theory developed from the work of the late Silvan Tomkins, PhD, in the 1960s and explored in great depth by researchers worldwide and at the institute that now bears his name (www.tomkins.org). Tomkins, who found work during the Great Depression handicapping racehorses because of his ability to "read" their faces, first became fascinated with human personality while doing his postdoctoral work at Harvard Psychological Clinic. During his 18-year tenure in Princeton University's Department of Psychology, his interest in the study of human emotion and what he came to call *affect* became defining themes of his career. Researchers and scholars of the Sylvan S. Tomkins Institute developed his *affect theory* into *affect script psychology*. Tomkins believed that the blueprint for health lies in the way the body works best: Maximizing positive affect (opening up to greater experiences and expressions of excitement and joy) and minimizing negative affect (noticing our negative sensations and dealing with what is stimulating them).

So what the heck are affects? They look a whole lot like facial expressions but sometimes also include postures and vocalizations and reveal the underpinning of emotion. Tomkins identified nine archetypical facial affects as distinctive and recognizable by specific expressions and attributes of individual facial features, as well as an overall "look." Of the nine, only two are positive (Excitement/Joy and Interest/Excitement), one is neutral (Surprise/Startle), and six are negative (Anger/Rage, Disgust, Dissmell [looks like a reaction to a bad smell], Distress/Anguish, Fear/Terror, Shame/Humiliation).

It is the combination of an innate affect with the memory of our previous experiences of that same affect that creates what we know and recognize by its formal name: *emotion*. Or, as Donald L. Nathanson, an international leader in the study of human emotion and author of *Shame and Pride*, writes, "Affect is always biology, whereas emotion always represents biography."

So while each of us has the same nine innate affects, it is our *individual life experience* that makes the emotions we each attach to these affects a personal matter. We all develop general *scripts* (predispositions) for each emotion (as well as

RESOURCES Donald L. Nathanson's *Shame and Pride: Affect, Sex, and the Birth of the Self* (W.W. Norton & Company, 1994).

scripts that are dependent on particular kinds of scenes or in particular kinds of relationships that drive our thoughts and behavior).

Early Experiences Shape Scripts

Gaby, who is past president of the Tomkins Institute and now serves as a member of its board of directors, is uniquely qualified to help us understand where emotions come from, how our experiences and scripts influence our emotions, and how to deal effectively with what is stimulating negative emotions. He says that because so often it is our early experiences that shape the scripts we have for each emotion and all kinds of other things, what triggers a negative sensation (such as fear) in one person, can trigger excitement and joy in another.

For example, I can tell you that while the sight of a pony makes some of my friends wax nostalgic about their first pony ride, I look at a pony and get an ever-so slight, 46-year-old knot in my stomach as I remember *mine*. The pony in my early experience ran off with me, and because his cinch had worked its way loose (little jerk probably puffed himself up while being saddled), I ended up *under* this less-than-delightful steed as he galloped across a rocky pasture and away from anyone who could help me. (If I think about this long enough I can almost feel the physical sensation that accompanied the sickening thud when I finally gave up, let go, and hit the ground.) Let's just say my emotion around ponies is shaped by my early experience. So when someone in my family said, "Let's get the kids a pony!" I went straight to that *fear script* and said, with disproportionate vehemence, "Let's not!"

Yes, as Gaby admitted at the beginning of this section, emotions can be confusing, and sorting them out can be even trickier than isolating specific thoughts, particularly when our thoughts get entwined.

"What may be most confusing for people—as well as many psychologists—is that we tend to confuse the *experience* of emotion with the *thought* of emotion," Gaby explains. He likens this to the *thought* of having your toes in a cold stream as opposed to the actual bodily *sensation* from your toes in the icy water. "One is a sensation and the other is a mental image," he says. "Mental images play a big role in how scripts work."

Gaby says that training your mind to focus on the physical sensation an emotion creates in your body is key to allowing that emotion to dissipate, or pass through you, quickly. (Remember that body scan exercise on p. 233? Plug and play here!)

"If I feel anger and focus on the tension my anger creates *in my body*, the feeling of anger will pass quickly without an image to keep it going," Gaby elaborates. "If, however, I focus on the *mental images* of my anger (such as replaying past scenes and other associations), that anger—and its related tension—may last for days, and with enough feeding of scenes and associations, it may even amplify into rage!"

I don't know about you, but making this distinction between the physical sensations and mental images of emotions provided a 10,000-watt light bulb moment for me. Thinking about my horse who is a "recovering bucker," I can tell you that the emotion stirred when I feel that stiff-legged hop that always heralds an impending rodeo has both a physical component (holding my breath, tensing up my whole body, which as we all know does *not* help the situation) and a cornucopia of mental imagery from our past dalliances with bronc-dom. To test Gaby's point, the last time Trace stiffened into that first hop, I took a deep breath, centered and grounded, *released the tension in my body with my outbreath,* and kept riding. Within a few strides of my holding this course, he settled down and followed suit. He was still stiff and choppy and wringing his tail, but the response in my *behavior* as I rewrote that script allowed the *emotion* to dissipate and my *thoughts* to settle on the positive. (Yay! I did it!) Starting to see how the continuum can work in your favor now?

"Consciousness of our feeling body is one way to work with the emotional scripts that limit our freedom or keep us stuck in self-defeating patterns," Gaby says. He encourages us to practice *moving away from our mental images* and into sensation (you guessed it, there's an exercise for this—see p. 323) to get better and faster at calling up the ability to, as Gestalt Therapy Founder Dr. Fritz Perls put it, "Lose your mind and come to your senses."

Keep Your Scripts in Their Proper Places

Tomkins and others believed that human beings have affects and scripts to help them sort and process their experiences. "The world is full of stimulating things," Gaby elaborates. "Which ones are important and which ones aren't? Affect may have developed in humans as a primitive sort of triage system." Because affects are so basic to our consciousness, they literally drive our behavior: "When you are frightened, the fear affect makes you pay attention and it flavors that attention in a way that predisposes you to certain responses," Gaby says.

Likening this to the fight-or-flight instinct in horses, this amazing capacity to process our experiences can be very helpful to us. But like the horse that is ruled by his amped up fight-or-flight response based on a past experience of abuse, when our own life experiences shape our responses into scripts, we can get trapped in response patterns that do not serve us. "It can be a problem when life experiences shape our way of dealing with our affects in ways that rob us of freedom, flexibility, or hope," Gaby says.

Gaby tosses an example our way: Say a cowboy was scolded and shamed as a child with, "Big boys don't cry." A cowboy who can't feel his own distress may not be able to tune into the distress of his horse, his partner, or his children. Instead, when they seem distressed he is only conscious of feeling shame, disgust, or anger. Moving a little further into this idea as it relates to body image issues and riding, if we have once been hurt by others' comments about our size at a show, it can morph into a script *any time* we see others looking at us *at all,* triggering our shame affect and any and all mental images associated with that bad experience (they do tend to pile on). Pretty soon, just *thinking* of going to a show triggers emotions like shame and anger, and related scripted behavior (ice cream...Cheetos... wine...nachos) that takes us farther from—and not closer to—where we want to go.

"Shame is a feeling of loss and confusion that many of us avoid by doing something to trigger excitement or enjoyment," Gaby says. "If we sit with the sensation of shame/humiliation it will usually pass fairly quickly. But if we try to run away from it by distracting ourselves with food, alcohol. entertainment, or showing off, we often find ourselves running faster and faster and looking like addicts to those distractions. The more I eat or drink to escape my shame, the more shame I create, and therefore the more need to escape by eating or drinking."

Just like negative thought spirals (p. 265), emotional shame spirals, while they can be devastating, can also be broken.

So how do you change a script? If affects are fixed and unchangeable parts of who we are, as Tomkins asserts, and our experiences are often beyond our control, how can we keep our experiences from becoming harmful scripts—and how can we rewrite the scripts that are holding us back in our riding and in our life?

"To change a script we need *consciousness*, *creativity*, and *commitment*," Gaby says. "*Consciousness* to feel what we feel and question our images. *Creativity* to practice more emotional freedom as we allow the feeling to dissipate. *Commitment* to stay with new patterns until they become as automatic to us as the old ones."

The Direction of Emotion

Using Tomkins' work with affects as his springboard, human emotion expert Dr. Donald Nathanson devoted 20 years of research and clinical attention to something he calls the "Compass of Shame," which deals with the negative affect of shame/humiliation. Dr. Nathanson explains that when the shame affect is activated in us, for whatever reason, there are four possible patterns of reaction, which he identifies as four points of a compass.

Visualize with me here that on this compass *Withdrawal* is the North pole, *Avoidance* is the South, *Attack Self* is the East, and *Attack Other* is the West. It's possible when something causes us to feel shame/humiliation for our reactions to bounce back and forth and all around this compass—for example, from East/Attack Self ("How could I be so stupid?") to West/Attack Other ("How dare you!") to North/Withdrawal ("I'm going to go to bed for a few days with 'radio silence' and no texts, phone calls, emails, or knocks on the door will be answered") to South/Avoidance (overeating, substance abuse, distraction, busyness).

Remember that scripts are nothing more than emotional habits created when an experience triggers a specific affect, so perhaps a snarky insult about our weight triggers shame/humiliation, and we head South on the Compass of Shame where we avoid the resulting emotion with the anesthetic known as hot fudge. These are our emotional "autoresponders"; our job is to interrupt the process *before* it hijacks our emotions and form strategies for managing our responses. Understanding the Compass of Shame helps us classify our behavior (or desired behavior!) according to the emotion that likely triggered it, and then use what we learned about reframing (p. 267) and affirmations (p. 261) to *find a better feeling.* Unless our mood has moved into the clinical (and learning to use these tools can help us clue in when it has), *we can do something about our emotional state.* Charles Gaby said it takes *consciousness, creativity,* and *commitment* to change a script—we can use this new awareness of affects, emotions, and the Compass of Shame to practice recognizing our behavior (which pole am I on here?) and point our emotions toward a more balanced center.

Our Bodies—on the Compass of Shame
Depending on what we learned or experienced while growing up, we all have our own more-or-less typical ways of feeling and responding to the things that happen to us. Here we begin to see that, as a whole wave of current neuroscience now suggests, much if not most of our behavior is driven by emotions "scripted" from our own unique past experiences. These scripts run like a background program beneath our actions, impacting us in ways we rarely notice but are truly woven into all we do.

According to Gaby, there is more "Compass of Shame" around the female body than around just about anything else, activating in us any number of scripts we have likely developed over years upon years of battling body image issues. Shame scripts around body image issues, Gaby adds, generally hover around the "Attack Self" and "Avoidance" points on the Compass (see p. 317). An example he gives is likely familiar to those who grew up on a farm or ranch: As a young girl you grew up working hard all day, and after all the chores were done, what was your reward? A big, hearty home-cooked meal! (Likely with pie.) This, Gaby says, creates a powerful script rooted in all the things that have great meaning for us. And as time goes by, they may grow even more meaningful through the rose-colored lens of nostalgia.

So here you are, all grown up, working hard all day, and your inner script says, "Food is the reward you get when you work hard." Can you see what a fundamental problem it is, then, when you say in response, "I've worked hard. I deserve to eat something...low in dietary fat and sodium and high in nutritional value."

"WHAT?" argues your script. "Do you mean I can't have my reward? What about my pie?"

Learning to find alternative means of immediate gratification—not in a single grand way, but in daily ways, Gaby says—is the best way to deal with our old scripts related to food, exercise, and habitual responses to stress, frustration, anger, and disappointment. "The way we're scripted to feel is affecting us more than we think," he adds. And just *being aware* of what these scripts are, where they came from, and what habits they have formed is the first step toward breaking free of old behaviors that do not serve our healthy new lifestyle.

Digging in to our Avoidance Behaviors

Why *do* humans stuff themselves with food when they're feeling anxious, stressed, weary, frustrated, bored, or angry? Most of us, at one time or another (and some of us much more than that), have used food as an anesthetic: an immediate way to appease the desire to feel better. And while this may work for us short-term—that is, while we're digging into that hot fudge sundae or diving head first into that king-sized bag of Ruffles—the next thing we know we're traveling with the Compass of Shame as our guide. And when, after an extended bout of what I've referred to in this book as "stress eating," we can't zip our favorite riding jeans (or get our foot up and into the stirrup), the shame/humiliation escalates, and the next thing we know we're back in that fastfood drive-thru saying "yes" to the offer to "supersize it!" This cycle of shame-and-food-anesthesia can continue until you decide to do something differently.

So how do we break free of this shame chain? We know *what to eat*. We know *how to exercise*. We know *how to meditate* and *how to "thought stop"* and *how to visualize and affirm*. And yet, I admit it, it is distinctly possible some of us will still fall victim to the boilerplate scripted emotions that continually toss us back onto the Compass of Shame. First, Gaby advises, we need to raise our self-awareness around food.

"Every time you're about to eat, ask yourself, 'What emotion am I feeling right now? What else besides food might help me deal with this emotion? How else can I explore what's happening inside me besides stuffing myself with food in a false attempt to feel better?'" he says. "We have to learn how to *recognize* and *tolerate* the emotional distress we're feeling *without* eating." Just as we learned to "clear our skies of clouds" in our meditative practice (p. 220), we now have to learn to recognize a crummy feeling—and let it pass—as we identify things other than food that will now soothe us in healthier ways. Here are a few examples to show you how this can work:

- **Am I really just tired?** Have a large glass of water (sometimes when we think we're hungry we're really just mildly dehydrated) and take a power nap before you follow through on that snack. "I've read some studies that say that as many as 90 percent of us are walking around each day with some level of physical exhaustion—and more often than not, some degree of dehydration," Gaby says.

- **Am I feeling stressed and frustrated?** Do some deep breathing exercises or a five-minute meditation, followed by some journaling (see pp. 176, 219, and 244). In other words, how can you occupy your mind and address what's going on in a way that allows *energy* to pass through you instead of cheese-drenched tortilla chips? "When we use food to medicate a negative affect, we create more of the same," Gaby observes. "When we find something *besides* food that will medicate that affect, something that is actually good for us and even addresses the affect at its roots, then we're using the power of our responses for our own good."

Once when he was visiting a gambling addiction clinic, Gaby says he couldn't help but notice that *none* of the participants were overweight. "When people are caught up in sensory stimulation, they don't need food," he observes. "They 'medicate' their addiction in another way." Taking this observation to our lifestyle drawing board, it likely follows that we could use *any* addictive tendency we have to fuel positive behaviors and practices to substitute for our more negative, destructive ones. "People with weight and body image issues generally have some level of addiction to the immediate gratification of food," Gaby says.

So…instead of a cheeseburger…groom your horse. Instead of a donut, play in the round pen. Who needs wings at Happy Hour when you can be in the woods on your horse, watching the sky turn orange after that five o'clock whistle blows? Take a cue from these unsuspecting gambling addicts and feed your "avoidance urges" with horse time. After all, isn't that the win-win that gives you what you *really* want?

Anticipate Your Future Self

Applying these ideas from affect script psychology to our life with horses, it's no secret that our horses and our horsemanship are a part of our identity. There's a certain "image" we all want to project when we ride, both in representing ourselves and in providing leadership to our horses. Knowing exactly what this image is can be a huge motivational tool, Gaby says, when we realize that this image we hold of ourselves in the saddle is part of our *anticipated future.*

We all have an "anticipated future," Gaby says. Those of us who are fairly adept at introspection have a head start on those who aren't used to thinking in those terms. Nevertheless, your anticipated future is right there, lying dormant, waiting for you to drag it out and examine it! Typically built from your past experiences and current habits, your anticipated future is who you expect—and most often, hope—to be at some hazy point in the future. Spend some time with this future you! Fold in your goals and dreams and engineer for yourself an anticipated future based on things that will make you feel good instead of bad about your body. Much of the meaning we create in our lives is defined by what our anticipated future is, and how important creating that reality is to us. "Our anticipated future," Gaby reminds us, "not only impacts our image of self, but it also dictates our feelings now, moment-to-moment, as well as the meaning we make from what we're feeling."

If what we're trying to do is change our thoughts and perceptions about our bodies, it makes sense to align our current thoughts with our *new and improved* anticipated future. To that end, Esther and Jerry Hicks' *Ask and It Is Given* offers us a process called *pivoting* that is as simple as it is powerful: when you "catch yourself" in a thought or feeling you *don't* want to be having about something, stop, wait, and then allow that recognition to point you toward the feeling's opposite to reverse the direction of your energy to align with your positive imagined future.

"When you pick up a stick, you pick up both ends," the Hicks write. "This pivoting process will help you be more aware of which end of your stick you are currently activating: the end that is about *what you want*, or the end that is about the *absence of what you want*. Whenever you know *what you do not want*, you also know even more clearly *what you do want*."

With pivoting in our toolbox, we can begin to manage our emotions by being able to clearly define *exactly* what we desire. From there it is just a hop, skip, and a jump to shifting our "thought habits." Use pivoting whenever you detect or even suspect a negative emotion (they can be subtle and slippery) or when you are aware that a thought or statement is the opposite of what you want. Once you get good at "catching" the negative thoughts and emotions *before* they take hold, you can start using pivoting to override patterns of self-dislike or self-doubt. Even when things are feeling pretty good, but you know they could be better, call on pivoting to *redirect* even your "neutral" thoughts toward your ultimate goal. With this shift, it will get easier and easier to send your thoughts, emotions, awareness, and attention toward your positive anticipated future.

This process—like everything else we've discussed—does take some practice, and more than a little bit of determination. Most of us have no idea of the barrage of negative thoughts and feelings that pound us, 24/7, until we start trying to rope them, rebrand them, and herd them to higher ground.

Exercise for the Soul: Pivot Practice

1 Take out your journal or tablet and choose a thought or feeling that's floating around in your head right now (or one you've had recently) that is *not* what you want to think or feel. Write it down.
Caught thought: "I'm flopping all over this saddle."

2 Now write what the *opposite* of that thought or feeling is. Be clear and specific. Opposite thought: "I'm sitting deep, centered, and grounded. Nothing can separate me from the back of this horse."

3 Create a visualization (remember to use all five senses—see p. 259) of this "pivoted" thought or feeling that ties directly into your anticipated future. Sit with this visualization for at least 30 seconds.

Visualized anticipated future: "I enter the covered arena on a crisp, sunny autumn morning. There's a slight breeze ruffling the turning leaves; some of them flutter to the ground. I hear the mower in the adjacent pasture and smell the freshly cut grass as Trace and I circle the arena, walking slowly at first, and then picking up speed. I can feel his hind legs engage, one at a time, and I am aware of his footfalls. I feel grounded, my center is deep and low, my lower body relaxed, yet ready to respond. My legs stretch forward and down and my heels have settled into a natural down position, and my toes are spread but relaxed inside my boots. I cue Trace into a canter and he moves out willingly, picking up the correct lead and stretching his body forward as he moves easily into a nice, collected lope. I sit back and breathe deep, calm and confident, as we float effortlessly around and around the arena."

"SWITCH" YOUR GEARS

We've already been through *a lot* of information about how our thoughts, perceptions, and beliefs about ourselves, our bodies, and our abilities affect how we ride, how we feel about our bodies, and how we behave with our horses. All well and good. But how do we make these changes *real* and *integral* parts of our lives—and our very best anticipated future?

In the bestselling book *Switch,* authors and brothers Dan and Chip Heath explore the process of making serious changes stick—whether on the individual, group, or societal level—with an overarching analogy that hits home especially well for those of us who ride horses. The brothers Heath purport that the complex process of creating the brain-rewiring change in our lives that current neuroscience now deems possible is "like riding an elephant." Drawing upon the image of a "rider," an "elephant" (a few of our horses may well qualify!), and a "path," *Switch* teaches us that in each and every lifestyle change we make, we must "Direct the Rider," "Motivate the Elephant," and "Shape the Path."

RESOURCES

Esther and Jerry Hicks'
Ask and It Is Given
(Hay House, 2004).

Dan and Chip Heath's *Switch:
How to Change When Change Is
Hard* (Crown Business, 2010).

- **Educate your "change jockey."** The Heath brothers explain that the "rider" (remember, this is *their* analogy) is the brains of the operation. The Heaths use this term to describe the part in our world that holds the reins, gives the cues, and spurs the action (the *rational* side). This is the part that looks at ideas for change (such as those in this book), maps out a strategy, constructs a to-do list, and nags at us constantly when we deviate from any one of our plans to do better, be better, and (in our case) vanquish our body-image demons.

- **Adopt the "baby step."** *Switch* says we need to pick *just one thing at a time* to work on, and the smaller that thing is, especially at first, the better (remember our short-term goals from p. 278?). Overreaching (for example, a general and unspecific call to "get in shape") is precisely what shoots many of us in the booted foot. Even though taking small steps means it will take longer to change the big things (such as your overall fitness level) when you follow this progressive process, it is much more likely these changes will become permanent.

- **Embrace what's working.** "Follow the bright spots," say the Heaths, calling for a little introspection around what's going well for you *right now*—in your life, in your riding (because our horses are mirrors, you know!), and around your body image. What have you *already* done that's helping your ride better, feel better, and enjoy yourself more? The specifics here are individual and open-ended.

Exercise for the Brain: What Are *Your* Bright Spots?

1 **Open your journal or cue up a new document. Title your page with a quick summary of the Big Change you'd like to make, stated in present tense as if it has already happened.** (See how we've picked up some of the affirmation language here?) So, for example: *I'm fit, strong, and confident in the saddle because I reestablished my regular yoga practice.*

2 **Underneath that, add the subtitle, "My Bright Spots," and list the positives in your life right now related to your Big Change.**

- I'm healthy and able to take on this challenge (just had a physical that says so).

- I'm in decent shape for my age.

- I've done it before, so my body will respond quickly ("Whew!)

- This worked well for my body in the past; it significantly improved my overall fitness level.

- I already know the rules for proper nutrition and hydration for this practice.

- I'm highly motivated to change: every bag of feed I unload from the truck reminds me how great it will feel to "unload" 30 pounds of *me*.

3 Map Your Course

You wouldn't enter the show ring without knowing all the things you will be asked to do; in the arena of significant life change, the same rule applies. The Heaths call this serious planning "scripting the critical moves." For any change you're contemplating, from changing your thinking to changing your pants size, take a few moments to boil it down to specific behaviors that will mark this trail for you. These are *not* "big picture" items; these are the smallest working parts of the change you've chosen. Think of the road signs along the way once you've "defined your destination," as Jane Savoie recommends (see p. 277).

Look to Where You're Going (Ever Hear That Before?)

Even when we're not exactly sure where our "destination" is, the more specific we can be, the more likely we are to get there. "Change is easier," the *Switch* authors say, "when you know *where you're going and why it's worth it.*"

Saying, "I want to lose weight and get in shape so I can be a better horse-woman," is well and good. And there's a certain amount of freedom that comes with committing simply to eating well, exercising regularly, and letting your weight settle where it needs to be without being too specific. In fact, part of what can hamstring us in this quest is the goal of a specific number on a scale or a certain size of jeans or riding breeches. But, as we have already discussed (see p. 276), study after study shows that goals are attained when they are specific and measurable and have a time frame.

Exercise for the Brain: Pinpoint Your Destination

Rather than naming a number (whether related to the scale or clothing size), use this exercise to come up with a healthy "end goal"—where do you want this trail to lead? In your journal or wherever you're taking notes, list reasonable destinations you'd like to reach. For example:

• All the clothes I own fit "comfortably loosely" (to quote an image consultant I know).

• I feel better, lighter, and stronger, regardless of what the scale says.

• There is improvement in my labwork, blood pressure, and heart rate.

• I can mount my horse easily and quickly.

• I can ride all day, remaining flexible and strong.

• I've eliminated belly and upper arm fat so I feel better riding in public.

One thing I've noticed about motivation is that it tends to come and go in our lives, usually pretty much of its own accord. Depending on *what we want* and *why we want it*, motivation can be strong and surefooted beneath our choices, actions, and behavior—or it can be flighty, jigging and bolting in every direction. Realizing this, we need to know how to lure, catch, and cross-tie our motivation when it's eluded capture.

Comparing the emotional drive beneath our behavior to an elephant, the authors of *Switch* say that when we are able to "motivate the elephant," we put the strong, powerful force of emotion beneath us. The converse is also true. Who among us hasn't ridden a horse that refused to stop or go or turn or slow down or travel in the direction and speed you planned, no matter what we do? An unruly steed—whether real or metaphorical—is no fun, and it keeps us from getting where we want to go.

Myths of the Subconscious

BUSTED!

MYTH: "Enough with all this soul-searching and self-examination. I can lose weight and keep it off with sheer willpower."

TRUTH: In her book *It's Not Just About the Ribbons,* bestselling author and reserve rider for the 1992 US Olympic Dressage Team Jane Savoie says, "Ultimately, you will achieve whatever your subconscious mind believes...I learned that if I relied on conscious willpower to reach a goal, I might be able to make a short-term change, but it would only become a temporary change. If I directed my energy to my subconscious mind, I could make a permanent change.

"I realized that as long as I subconsciously thought of myself as being overweight, I would always regain the weight I had so 'consciously' taken off," she continues. "In order to keep the weight off permanently, I needed to change the 'programming' in my mind so that I saw and thought of myself differently when it came to food. I began to think of food as a way to nourish my body so it could function at peak efficiency rather than a source of comfort when I was emotionally stressed. I trained myself to enjoy feeling 'empty' before I went to bed instead of thinking I needed a full stomach to sleep well...I even substituted the word 'fat' for the word 'cream.' As a result, the thought of putting 'fat' in my coffee or of having a nice big bowl of mint chocolate chip ice 'fat' really turned me off!"

Engage Your Heart

Having and loving horses ignites a passion undeterred by discomfort or inconvenience. And, when you think about it, working with horses provides its own built-in set of motivations: Horses have to eat on a regular schedule; we make sure it happens. We slop through mud, slide along frozen ground to break ice from their water buckets, load and unload hay and feed in 100-degree summer sun, muck stalls, tote or spread manure, and any number of other unmentioned tasks as needed to keep them healthy, happy, and sound. Horses get shoes, shots, and pedicures whether we do or not; when they colic, cut themselves, or throw a shoe, we stop what we're doing, get the right person there, and pay whatever it costs to make them feel better.

When we learn to tap into this same feeling for our own self-care, sisters—and apply this same heart-driven determination to the other parts of our lives—we'll own the key to profound personal change.

The difference, however, between caring for our horses and caring for ourselves is that our needs are less concrete. According to *Switch* and a nationwide study explained in *The Heart of Change* by John Kotter and Dan Cohen, most people think change happens in the order of ANALYZE-THINK-CHANGE, but the sequence of change is actually SEE-FEEL-CHANGE. What this means is that change doesn't feel compelling to us when we can't *see* or *feel* any good reason to make it.

Bringing this a little closer to home for those of us who struggle with body image and weight issues, *analyzing what we need to do* and *thinking about doing it* rarely move the needle on the scale. The weight starts coming off once we *see* our situation in a different way, engage our emotions so that we *feel* differently about what we're doing—and once we start to notice that it's working. When that happens, there's usually very little that can stop our momentum.

John Kotter and Dan Cohen's *The Heart of Change: Real-Life Stories of How People Change Their Organizations* (Harvard Business Review Press, 2012).

RESOURCES

Break Down Your Desired Change

The idea here is to isolate and define the very *smallest possible* forward increment of the change you seek. "Break down the change," the *Switch* authors quip, "until it no longer spooks the Elephant." *Now* we're using language horse people can all relate to!

So how does it work?

Let's take the change, "I'm going to ride three days a week," as an example. For some, making the affirming statement, "I'm going to go ride my horse after work on Tuesdays and Thursdays, and in the morning on Saturdays," may be a small enough step toward seeing through the changes. Voicing an intention aloud or to another is enough to get them over the hump and into the tack. The behavior change I need to start with is packing my barn bag on Monday, Wednesday, and Friday nights, and putting it in my car. (We'll get more into how to create these kinds of tiny habits in the next section—see p. 335.)

Now, the first few Tuesdays, Thursdays, and Saturdays, I may not make it to the barn in time to ride, but the very act of packing that bag and putting it in my car will at some point start to feel ridiculous if I don't actually follow through on my intent to spend time with my horse. And, because the goal is breaking the bigger behavior change ("ride three days a week") into a series of small, doable parts, it's easy to see what the next "baby step" could be: "Leave work on time so you can get to the barn, no matter what.".

For this to work, the Heath brothers assert that there must be some reward for every slightest effort your "steed" makes in the direction you want him to go. (Reward the try, right?) And, like my über-sensitive horse, the Heaths say that "the Elephant in us is easily demoralized…it needs reassurance, even for the very first step of the journey." The old sports and business analogy "raise the bar" is completely useless here, the Heaths add. This is a time to *lower the bar* and keep on lowering it until your elephant can step over it as easily as your trail horse steps over ground poles.

I have a friend who is a runner. He says that five days a week he lays out his running clothes before he goes to bed; each morning he gets up, dresses in his running togs, laces up his shoes, and heads out the front door. Some days he goes for a full run; others he shortens his course. Still others he oversleeps and only has time to get to the end of the driveway, but *his* reward is successfully reinforcing that new morning run habit, no matter what.

With this level of commitment in mind, I will pack my bag and leave work in time to get to the barn, three times a week; the next step might be to groom and saddle my horse when I get there, regardless of whether I actually have time to ride or not. (Yes, your horse might think you're crazy after a couple of these visits.) The step after that could be adding five minutes of groundwork. Then it will make no sense not to hop on for a short ride, even if it is just one lap around the arena. As each step is rewarded by reinforcing a new habit (and maybe a pedicure), they all add up (eventually) to the change I want to make.

I know what you're thinking: "At this rate, the ultimate lifestyle changes I desire will take *forever*." You may be in for a surprise. Once you get the full power of your emotions engaged beneath your first tentative "baby steps," there's a magic that happens. Somehow "The FlyLady's" five minutes here and there *do* turn into a cleaner house; Dave Ramsey's "debt snowball" *does* get people out of seemingly hopeless financial holes; and Clinton Anderson's 15 minutes a day *does* make for better behaved horses. Clean houses, smart money, and respectful horses everywhere say "breaking it down" works—and next I'll show you how to pull together all your "baby steps" into one reliable guide.

Check Your Trail Map

As the Chinese philosopher Lao-tzu said in the sixth century BC, "A journey of a thousand miles begins with a single step." And as James, my farrier (although he's always quick to clarify that he's a "horseshoer"—we are in Texas, after all) said last Tuesday, talking about another client's horse's monumentally messed up feet, "You have to pick one thing and just work on that one thing at a time. And once you get a little growth on there, then you can start to shape it a little bit and go to work on the next thing." He thought he was telling me about horse feet; I recognized the great metaphor for healing a misshapen, overgrown, out of control, twisted, and potentially crippling lifestyle. While every great journey (or hoof) does begin with a single change, remember that we've learned it's integral to have some idea of where you want to end up—a destination (see p. 327)—and a map of the journey ahead is essential.

Call our friend Coach Daniel Stewart back to front and center for a few final thoughts on how to put all this knowledge to work, we reference the Behavior Inventory Checklist he included in his first book, *Ride Right with Daniel Stewart.* This simple but very powerful mapping tool can help us identify, prioritize, and track specific behavioral changes we want to make so that even though we're only going to be working on one small thing at a time (those "baby steps" we just learned about), we'll keep a solid idea in our heads of where we're going and how we'll get there.

While Coach Stewart originally crafted this chart to be very specific to *riding* behaviors, for our purposes (and with his blessing) we're going to broaden the scope a bit. (Actually we're going to crack it wide open to put *you* in charge of mapping your own journey, starting right here and now.) With this tool you'll be able to pinpoint *what* you want to start with, focus on *just that*, and then *track it* until the transformation you're going for is complete. The number of action items on your chart depends on your own goals. There may be just a handful of things you want to work on, or you may want to continue all the way through the red-bustier-and-golden-lasso stage.

With Jill Valle's thought-feeling-behavior continuum in mind (see p. 40), whether your first choice for change is a *thought pattern* you have recognized, an *emotional script* that tends to take over and derail your best intentions, or a *behavior* that is getting in your way, it's up to you to choose the *first issue* that presents itself to you and put the identified exercises to work. Try hard not to think right now about any of the *other* changes you are going to make. All in good time. Give yourself a break from the torrential downpour of "shoulds." Be gentle with yourself and choose: Just. One. Thing. And trust the process.

What you may discover, as Horseshoer James *also* said about that wayward hoof, sometimes one change brings others right along with it, more or less organically, so when you get ready to make the next one, you might just find it's already well underway. Taking this back to the body image arena, if we concentrate first on getting stronger, we just might find that we're eating better. If we're working on grounding and centering in the saddle to improve our balance, we just might find that our posture improves, our lower back is flattening and our heels are settling in to a relaxed and natural "heels down." And following these natural connections, once you see the first change approaching completion, the next thing to work on is likely to be as obvious as the smile on your face.

Note: You can download the following exercise from the RT[3] page at Trafalgar Square Books (www.HorseandRiderBooks.com) or on my website (www.melinda-folse.com).

Exercise for the Brain: Draw Your Own Map

Remember how I said this process develops in layers? The first few steps of this exercise will feel familiar to you—in fact, you have maybe now used them in some form a few times. But then we'll push a bit further, adding *new* layers:

1 Describe one thing you'd like to change. Remember, it can be a thought, a response to an emotion, or a behavior/habit. But just choose one.

2 State the change as if it has already happened and is your new state of being.

3 Visualize the change using as many sensory observations as you can naturally incorporate. (Now that this change is real, look, listen, smell, taste, and feel everything that is going on in this single moment inside your new reality.)

4 Check in with the stress management techniques you've learned about in this book. (Are you breathing all the way into your belly? Is that mindful stillness in your center readily available to you? Is there any tension in your body that needs your attention?)

5 Choose a "cue" to help you get back on track if you start to slip because life throws you a curve. (Did I say, "if"? Make that "when"—it's inevitable that things will happen to block your path.) Just like a gentle squeeze with your calf or light bump on that inside rein will get your horse's wandering attention back on you, plan ahead by choosing a word, phrase (this is a great way to use your personal branding, p. 278), or image to help you get your own drifting attention back on the task at hand.

6 Now is where you go back and reference some of that great journaling I know you *really* did! Starting with our section on affirmations (p. 261) grab that list you made of all that apply to you and write them in the imaginary center column of a new page (in your journal, perhaps?). To the left and right of that column, use the five adverbs provided to sort out where you are on that particular affirmation: on the left, write the two you're going for (**Always** and **Often**) and to the right, add the ones you're looking to change (**Occasionally**, **Rarely**, and **Never**). Because your list of affirmations are written as though they are statements of truth, choose a "response" from the adverbs and circle it. How true is this statement *right now*?

7 Here's where this practice starts to work its magic: Each and every week (I recommend you set a standing appointment with yourself, same time each week—see p. 145 for ideas for organizing your calendar), read through your list again and see if you are able to move any of your "Never" responses to "Rarely," your "Rarely" responses to "Occasionally," your "Occasionally" responses to "Often," or your "Often" responses to "Always." (Now I know we're taught to, "Never say never," and most of us have had "Always" bite us in the butt at least once in our life, but for the sake of putting edges on this exercise, let's suspend our dread of those two no-no words.) Suffice to say if we can move *most* of our affirmations into the "often" column and not let them slip further to the right than "occasionally," we're going to stay within a few minor life tweaks of our ideal state of being. Not a bad place to hover, wouldn't you agree?

Example 1:

Affirmation: I look good in my riding breeches/jeans.

Always   Often   Occasionally   Rarely   Never

8 After you complete your first round of this inventory, take a look at all the affirmations that made your "Never" column. Which one jumps out at you as the
most urgent to address? Write this down on a new page. Next to it, think back
to the first thing that came to mind when you read that affirmation—why did
you choose "Never"? What else was going on in the moments surrounding that
thought that could have triggered the "Never" response? Using the example
of a *thought pattern* below, create three columns on your new page. In the
first write the affirmation again. In the middle column, write what you usually
think instead. In the right-hand column, try to isolate what usually prompts
this "instead" thought. (Note: As we learned on p. 290, it doesn't really matter
whether you start by targeting a *thought*, a *feeling*, or a *behavior*—just that you
start. For the purposes of this exercise, we're starting with a *thought* but the
order is completely arbitrary.)

"Never" Response	What I Think Instead	What Prompted This Thought
I look good in my riding breeches/jeans.	My butt looks huge squeezed into these stretchy pants!	Watching my lesson video.

9 Now that we've isolated your typical thought pattern around this affirmation,
we're ready to go to work. With the goal being to change the thought pattern
to match the affirmation, and remembering our thought-emotion-behavior continuum, think of what you might be able to do to start changing that automatic
thought. In our pants example, since we're just trying to move the needle to
"Rarely" what this means is every once in a great while you catch sight of
yourself in a mirror or video and think, "Hey, I look okay today in these riding

breeches." (Remember the example I gave in the yoga classroom when I glanced in the mirror and thought my arms actually looked somewhat toned? That would be *my* "Rarely" day!) With this as the goal for this stretch of road, what tiny changes could you make to get that "Rarely?" Could it be some better fitting pants, maybe in a size larger and a darker color? Write that as a short-term goal and give yourself a deadline. Meanwhile, could you see about cleaning up your nutrition a little bit? Set this as a second short-term goal.

Thought-Pattern Change: How I Look in My Riding Clothes	
Goal	**Baby Step**
Short-Term Goal 1:	I'll order some riding breeches/jeans that look and feel more comfortable when I ride.
Short-Term Goal 2:	I'll make healthy eating and fitness choices.

10 Moving now toward feelings, repeat this process for an emotion you are able to isolate. Where does it come from? What triggers it? Is it part of a script? Is there a truth beneath it? Once again, remembering that you are just trying to move the needle one word in the right direction, see what the tiniest changes in the reality beneath the emotion might be, and set these as your baby-step, short-term goals.

Example 2:

Affirmation: I love the way I feel when I ride.

Always   Often   Occasionally   Rarely   Never

"Never" Response	What I Think Instead	What Prompted This Thought
I love the way I feel when I ride.	I feel like a big, clumsy out-of-balance mess when I ride at any gait other than a walk.	My horse started trotting, and I couldn't get my balance; I was aware of how everything on my body seemed to be flopping around.

Emotional-Pattern Change: How I Feel When I Ride	
Goal	**Baby Step**
Short-Term Goal 1:	I'll evaluate and improve my alignment and position with the help of a positive riding instructor (see pp. 165 and 169).
Short-Term Goal 2:	I'll add some core work to my daily routine, and start doing some stretching and stability warm-ups before I ride (see pp. 138 and 168).

11 Moving to the last stop on our continuum, repeat this process with *behavior patterns*, remembering to isolate the baby steps and create a specific plan for accomplishing each one until you can improve your rating by at least one word.

Example 3:

Affirmation: I do some form of exercise to improve my riding every single day.

Always   Often   Occasionally   Rarely   Never

"Never" Response	What I Think Instead	What Prompted This Thought
I do some form of exercise to improve my riding every single day.	I sat on my couch and read an article about exercising.	I was exhausted and achy after a short and not particularly good ride.

Behavior-Pattern Change: Adding Exercise to My Daily Activities	
Goal	**Baby Step**
Short-Term Goal 1:	I'll pick one new exercise and do it every day.
Short-Term Goal 2:	I'll create a program for myself (see p. 124) that addresses my fitness needs in a doable yet comprehensive way.

Behold, Your Own Great Truth

I know what you're thinking. Who has time for all this homework and personal digging? Trust me. *This* is your private path to making a true difference in how you feel *and* how you ride—from now on. Isn't that a respectable trade for a couple of sessions of soul-searching?

You see, when you really *use* this exercise and return to it regularly as you move through the areas of your life that need anything from minor tweaking to major overhaul (and sometimes you may not know for sure which is which until you're in the middle of your inventory), you'll find yourself connecting all the trails we've traveled together through these pages. Please note that you *don't* have to do this exercise all at once. In fact, percolation time between sessions is a good thing. Set aside one afternoon to create or print out the worksheets and fill them out, and then come back once a week to check in and work with different parts of the continuum as they seem important. It's very important to give yourself time, space, and patience to gain all you can from what should be a long-term commitment to yourself. Minutes spent regularly *now* will pay off in hours of pure joy with your horse in ways you might have missed completely without working steadily toward change.

This, like the RT³ Test at the beginning of this book, is not a quiz with right or wrong answers. It is a *process* for creating a space where you know how to find your own answers. You'll know them when you see them; they're the ones that meet you exactly where you are now—and take you where you want to go.

Set Yourself Up for Success

I suggest to you (and mostly to myself) that the best use of the information in this book is finding the courage to turn that pointing finger we tend to aim at others, inward. One person I interviewed early on who later declined to be named in this book told me, "It's a really sensitive issue. I don't know why I can't lose weight. I do really want to. I'm really good at lots of other things, but this is something I just can't do. I've tried lots of times and failed. I guess overeating and procrastinating is just the way I am. I've learned to accept that being big is just part of who I am."

I walked away from that conversation feeling sad and frustrated. If she had made peace with her size and was joyfully accepting and working around it as some of the other people we've visited with, well, that would have been another matter entirely—one theme of this book that I hope has come through loud and clear is that *if* you want to make a change in your body that will help you enjoy riding and being with your horse more, here's a healthy approach to finding your "new normal." But, some people are perfectly okay with whatever size they are; they just want to ride better with the body they have.

But the mournful, desperate unhappiness in this woman's eyes as she spoke made it very hard for me to keep quiet. I was still at the very beginning of the searching and reading and thinking that went into the development of this book, and I did not yet have any idea how to open her eyes to the possibility of change—or to help her set up her own success.

Study after study of human and organizational behavior reveal that when

BUSTED! Myths of Habit

MYTH: "I've been living and riding this way for most of my life. There's no way I can change a lifetime's worth of habits, even if they would make me happier and healthier."

TRUTH: In Gretchen Rubin's latest book, *Better Than Before*, she delves once again into the deepest research of something most of us think we already know all about. How we form habits, what makes habits stick, what kinds of habits work best for us, and how to change, shift or improve our habits, it turns out, are as individual as we are.

One overarching concept in Rubin's fascinating book is the division of people into four categories: *Upholders, Questioners, Obligers*, and *Rebels*. She does a great job of explaining how we

can know which one we are in general terms (and I do hope you'll check that out!); trotting this brilliant sorting work into our own arena, here are some clues to get you started:

• **Upholders are rule-followers.** Do you have a binder for each horse with his shot, deworming, farrier, and dental records carefully organized by date? Do you always clean your tack after a ride? Do you feed, water, hay, change bedding, and clean stalls on a specific schedule every day, every week, rain or shine? Do you ride and exercise your horses and yourself as recommended?

• **Questioners follow rules, but they want to know why.** Do you research dewormers and vaccines before making a decision on which to use? Do people consciously recreate their environment in a way that *sets up success*, the right behaviors begin to emerge almost on their own. "Many people have discovered that when it comes to changing their own behavior, environmental tweaks beat self-control every time," the Heaths write in *Switch*.

Just like our "baby steps" toward new habits, it's the tiny tweaks to our environment that set up true and lasting change. We've all heard about serving meals

you like to wait and see how you are feeling and when you will have time before settling on when you will ride and what you will do during a training session?

• **Obligers are held more accountable by the expectations of others over their own internal barometers.** Do you make sure to coordinate with your barn buddies on vet and farrier and dental visits? Do you prefer to work with a trainer and ride with a group? Do you bounce endlessly between the advice of others when you are trying to settle on a solution? Do you schedule shows based on what others are doing?

• **Rebels march to the beat of their own drums.** Do you decide which shots you will give, when, and if at all? Do you train, ride, and work your horse however you think best, regardless of what others say, advise, expect, or want you to do? Do you ride when you feel like it and only in events you want to?

Rubin says that while we all have some of all of these basic tendencies, recognizing which is most dominant in you will help you create *habit strategies* that will really stick for the long run. As we move forward on making the healthy changes we need to in our lives and our riding, a little bit of deliberate work on how we set up better habits could make the difference between *this time*...and every time before.

RESOURCES

Gretchen Rubin's *Better Than Before: Mastering the Habits of Our Everyday Lives* (Crown, 2015).

on smaller plates and laying out our morning workout clothes on the foot of the bed. I used to hang the dog leash on the front doorknob. (This led to a 60-pound dog standing on me and staring at me until I opened my eyes, then running to the door and joyfully shaking the leash until I came when I was called...tell me *you* could say no to that!)

Grooming your trail to success, or whatever you want to call it, is about making your old behavior a little more inconvenient (don't purchase junk food) and new behavior a slam dunk (keep fresh fruit and veggies washed, cut up, and parked in prime refrigerator real estate). These need not be big changes. You are not altering your core character, and you may not *ever* grow to like oatmeal. But if that bowl of oatmeal is what's ready to go every morning, you'll learn to get to the bottom of it. Over time you'll look back and wonder how you ever did things any other way.

#Hoofpicks

In this chapter we explored how our thoughts and the scripts our emotions and experiences have written for us have created some well-worn paths of behavior and resulting beliefs that may or may not be true. This will help in our work with horses by enabling us to understand our fears and how we allow them to keep us from challenging ourselves so we can begin to do the work that will improve our bodies and our riding. We will no longer avoid putting ourselves in learning opportunities out of fear or preconceived outcomes. This understanding is a new and different game-changer in the battle against negative body image because the self-fulfilling prophecy of failure is a mighty one. If we can master our thoughts and understand where our emotional scripts and resulting behavior are coming from, we can begin to re-write new behaviors, and create new experiences for ourselves and our horses.

Your Chapter 10 **#Hoofpicks** Include:

1 **It's always a mixed bag.** For each of us who struggles with body image issues, understanding the *thought-emotion-behavior continuum* means knowing that all of these things are interconnected—and always in play. You can begin with any of these three points—whatever makes the most sense to make the turn toward freedom. The even better news is that when one thing doesn't work, you have two other points of entry for addressing whatever physical, mental, emotional, behavioral, habitual, or any of those other "-als" that classify our struggles.

2 **Success comes in layers.** While that's not to negate, "Success comes in cans," one of the favorite sayings of my high school tennis coach Cal Hopkins (he loved to make us say this out loud), for our purposes it is the *layering* of information that will *open* that can. By combining the mindfulness techniques we learned in chapter 8 with the thought-control strategies from chapter 9, we now have our hands on tactics for amping up our self-compassion. This, friends, will help us put down our body image baggage for good.

3 **Find and nurture supportive relationships.** Whether next-door neighbors, barn buddies, or Facebook friends, having people in your life who recognize your unique beauty, honor your self-care strategies, and validate your commitment to breaking free from your body image struggles will fuel success as you've never experienced it.

4 **Easy, now.** Be gentle with yourself. Start small. Make tiny changes, wherever and whenever you see opportunities. As ready as you are to do better, feel better, and be better with your body and your riding, it's important to learn to be satisfied with the small victories—they will layer upon one another to build our ultimate success. So ease up on yourself. Things didn't get the way they are overnight, and finding your own healthy balance is a bit-by-bit journey (horse pun intended).

Be
Authentic

11 | The Road Divides Here

That's right. We're coming to that place on this long and winding trail where this all becomes either a pretty book full of "someday, maybe" ideas that will live on your shelf (or in some ubiquitous stack), or you decide to take some of these ideas to heart, grab the massive set of new tools we've just delivered, and set to work creating the lifestyle changes that will make a real difference in how you ride and how you feel. Some of you are going to put down this book and say, "I really should do some of that stuff." And then you may go right on living just the same way, weighed down (sometimes literally) by the same frustrations. That's one road ahead. And to be honest, it's the more well-worn path.

But others, including you and I, are going to choose that second road, the steeper one leading to the panorama, the one *by far* less traveled, to borrow an image from my favorite Robert Frost poem. *Our* "Road Not Taken"—the trail of permanent change—offers us a completely different experience of our life and our riding. Yes, there are rocks and ravines—and some stretches may be washed out completely. It's not particularly well marked, either, but our horses know the way. And, if we can get quiet enough, and stay present with them and with ourselves, we will, too.

But we're not quite to decision-time yet. There's one more stretch of this journey to cover together, and ideas ahead that are important for tending to what's likely missing for most of us in our quest to "lighten up." The real key to feeling better about our bodies, regardless of their actual size or shape, can go unnoticed—and if you're not looking for it, you might just miss it this time around, as you probably have for most of your life.

What I'm talking about here is *self-compassion*—extending love and under-standing to *ourselves* when we struggle, fail, or suffer, and then using that true esteem to leverage the power of all we are and all we know to become the very best version of ourselves we can be. It's about empowering our courage and commitment to making the changes that have been blocking us from finding joy in the things we love most. We love our horses, we love to ride, and for all the time and energy we have poured into getting things just right for them, we've cut ourselves off from the happiness due to us. Whether physical, mental, emotional, behavioral, habitual, or any of those other "-als" that classify our struggles, know this: We deserve to be free of perceived boundaries set by any issues that limit who we

Kaleigh (kaileighrussell.blogspot.com)

Remember: At the end of the day, it should be about you and your horse, *not* you and the peanut gallery.

"Fat Rider Survival Guide"

1 **Surround yourself with good horse people.** Don't feel like you need to suck up and be friends with people who don't feel you're worthy of them.

2 **Ignore the comments.** This one is hard, trust me. People will be quick to tell you you're too fat to ride, whether they're friends, coaches, or even tack store associates. These are not the people that spend hours with your horse, walk him when he colics, work him through his bad days. These people don't want to face the fact that they might be shown up by a fat rider not wearing field boots because they don't come in her size.

3 **Know your limits.** You won't be able to ride everything or jump everything. It's not insulting, it's not rude—it's the truth. Don't let people belittle you

think we are or can be. Our horses deserve our joy in their company. Let's take this road together, shall we?

Absolving All Past Failures

That's right. All of them. If you've tried and failed before to make healthy changes in body, brain, and soul, it's time to forgive yourself, let it go, and repeat after me: *I'm done with that!* It's also time to stop blaming programs or strategies you've tried, the support you've enlisted, or any of the books, DVDs, or workshops you've purchased thinking, "Maybe *this* is it." (Ask me about *my* diet-book-and-workout-DVD

---

and make that fact a condescending dig. *Every single rider* has limits, no matter her size.

4 Don't take people's crap. Whether you call them on their ignorance or just walk away, you don't have to put up with it. If you can get a 1000-plus-pound animal to stop being a turd then I completely believe you can tell someone to go the hell away.

5 You can do anything you want. If you put your mind (and ass) to it.

6 If it's not constructive, it's white noise. Someone telling you fat people are ruining the horse industry and someone telling you how to balance yourself in the saddle as a bigger rider are *not* both advice. Pick which one you'd rather hear.

7 People suck, horses don't. Your horse will not tell you that you look fat in those breeches. Your horse will not tell you that you're disgusting. And your horse will never tell you that you don't deserve to have him in your life.

---

collection!) According to Christopher Germer, author of *The Mindful Path to Self-Compassion: Freeing Yourself from Destructive Thoughts and Emotions,* no matter where you started or where you are today, it is time to stop counting false starts as failures and learn a new way.

"The problem lies in our motivation and in a misunderstanding of how the mind works," Germer writes.

As it turns out, a lot of what we tend to do to *not* feel bad is more than likely going to make us feel *worse.* Calling into play the familiar "don't think about pink elephants" illustration, Sigmund Freud himself wrote that there's "no negation in the unconscious mind" (see Coach Stewart's insight on this on p. 267). Germer maintains that whatever negatives we've thrown at our "issues" in the past to try to get rid of them has actually ingrained them more deeply in our subconscious.

On the other hand, Germer says that simple acceptance of whatever we're facing offers an ironic key to overcoming it. "The only answer to our problems," he writes, "is to first *have* our problems, fully and completely, whatever they may be." Circling back to Joy Nash's "Fat Rant" that we snickered over in the beginning of this book (p. 43), it's easy now to see the wisdom underpinning Nash's assertion that when we start making "fat" or "thick-waisted" or "short-legged" or "pear-shaped" or "big boned" or *anything* more of a descriptor and less of a judgment, we've taken the first step toward making the changes we *can* and living well with those we *can't.* Germer affirms that as counter-intuitive as this may sound, this is precisely the first step in the right direction.

RESOURCES

Christopher K. Germer's *The Mindful Path to Self-Compassion* (The Guilford Press, 2009).

Kristin Neff's *Self-Compassion: Stop Beating Yourself Up and Leave Insecurity Behind* (William Morrow, 2010).

Think back to Coach Daniel Stewart's method of comparing rider body types to horse breeds (see p. 96). There was no judgment there—just a set of facts upon which to build a strategy. By making the most of our positives and accepting the rest—not as negatives, but simply as things that *are*—we *turn toward our emotional pain and "own it"* rather than trying to run away or ignore it.

Although our bodies may not be quite what we'd like them to be, our pain over the gap between what we *wish* were true and our plus-sized, short-legged, or pear-shaped reality only becomes *suffering* when we *resist* this reality. So does that mean it's okay to be fat or big-bottomed when riding horses is all we really want to do? After all this talk about change, are we now going to just embrace our flaws and forget about changing them? Shouldn't we resist this reality we don't want with all our might until the gap disappears?

What Germer suggests is that resisting (that is, obsessing, blaming, and feeling defective) only aggravates the situation that causes us pain in the first place. Accepting and letting go of *suffering* frees up the mental energy we need to embrace our new Be Proactive and Be Positive strategies, while adding a dash of self-compassion to our mix.

Germer says that academic psychology is beginning to understand that combining mindfulness with self-compassion offers a new way out of the seemingly endless loop that holds so many of us captive. "Accepting our flaws doesn't mean that our behavior can't or shouldn't change for the better," he writes. "Acceptance is in the present moment. Each one of us has room to grow, and grow we must. We start by befriending who we are today, no matter how fumbling, incomplete, or clueless we are. Full acceptance of ourselves, moment to moment, makes it easier to adapt and change in the direction we'd like to go."

What Exactly *Is* Self-Compassion?

Self-compassion is one of those terms we may hear and nod about, but do we really have any clue what it means? Even the terms "self-love" and "self-care," while also a little squirmy, are more concrete. Self-compassion is a stretch of an idea for most of us because it means extending good will—*to ourselves*. It's about being soothing, like that friend who listens quietly to our troubles without offering advice. The one who lets us vent without judgment or comment, giving solid support while allowing us the space to sort things out. "We don't need to be particularly adept at regulating our attention to get benefit from self-compassion practice," Germer writes. "We just need to know we're hurting."

As developer of the scale used by most researchers in studies of self-compassion (access this scale for yourself at www.self-compassion.org), psychologist Kristin Neff, Associate Professor in Human Development and Culture, Educational Psychology Department at the University of Texas, Austin, identifies the six key elements of self-compassion:

1 **Self-kindness.** When you miss a lead change in your pattern or test or forget to schedule the farrier before your horse tosses a shoe, do you judge and berate yourself for your flaws and inadequacies? *Self-kindness* means extending to yourself the same warmth and understanding you would to a close friend who has suffered a setback. If your friend flubbed a lead change, you'd assure her she'd nail it the next time, and if she was forgetful, you'd say it happens to the best of us (because it does!).

2 **Common humanity.** When you suffer a misfortune or disappointment, such as losing a horse, a partner, or a job, do you feel isolated and ashamed, as if you're the only one in the world this has happened to? *Common humanity* means having a wider understanding of the flow and interconnectedness of human experiences that brings relief from feelings of isolation. As long as there have been people and horses, people have suffered the loss of a favorite friend or exciting prospect. We all lose love. We all lose jobs. And somehow we get through it.

3 **Mindful Awareness.** When you're feeling down, do you tend to fixate on all that's wrong? A conflict at work reminds you of a quarrel with your spouse, and then your mind hops to your neglected social life, abandoned goals, and the stacks of bills, laundry, and chores you can't ever seem to get ahead of...and suddenly *everything* makes you want to crawl back under the covers for good. Mindful awareness in the context of self-compassion means that while you are aware of disappointment when things are not as you'd like them to be, you approach

these feelings with curiosity and openness, rather than obsessing and becoming more frustrated, angry, or sad. So: the work conflict becomes "Tomorrow is another day!" the spousal spat, "We just need to take some time to relax and have fun together without a to-do list," and the to-dos that didn't get done: "I'm going to stop, prioritize, and make a plan."

4 Self-judgment. When you see aspects of yourself you don't like, do you get down on yourself? "My balance is terrible—I'm all over the place! I'll never be a relaxed, graceful rider." A self-compassionate person responds to difficulties and setbacks with tolerance that refuses to add insult to injury. "I'm struggling with balance, so I need to go back to my biomechanics and see what I need to do to find my 'sweet spot.'"

5 Isolation. Do you feel shame when something disappointing happens, as if you alone are responsible for it? "How could I have turned Sparky out in that paddock? If I hadn't turned him out, he wouldn't have gotten hurt." Self-compassion means having awareness that everything that happens comes from a universe of causes, and not just by the "mistake" or "shortcomings" of one person. Sure, maybe if you had chosen a different paddock, Sparky wouldn't have spooked at the shadow in the corner and clipped himself when he whirled and ran. However, there were a-thousand-and-one factors that caused the injury, not you.

6 Over-identification. When you're experiencing painful thoughts and feelings, do your emotions kick into overdrive? "I will never be able to ride at the level I want!" leads to rage or uncontrollable tears. Self-compassion helps us accept these things with emotional evenness, and balance: "While I dream of riding at the highest levels, I know I face a number of challenges; I have to be willing to work hard to pursue this dream."

Building Your Self-Compassion Muscle

I went to Neff's self-compassion website and took the test she provides there. No, I'm not going to tell you my score, but let's just say I'm about a quart low on self-compassion. The questions on this test surprised me, too. (Go take it and let's see where *you* are—www.self-compassion.org.)

Contrary to what you may be thinking (I know what *I* was thinking just after flunking Neff's test), developing healthy self-compassion is not a difficult thing to do. In fact, we're already pre-wired for it, Germer assures. "Although our personal experience may tell us otherwise, self-compassion is the most natural thing in the world," he writes. "Deep within all beings is the wish to be happy and free from suffering."

Relax, we're not adding anything else to our self-improvement agenda. Instead, we're just going to fan the flames a little bit under what we've already got cooking.

Exercise for the Soul: Turn Compassion Inward

1 Think about someone toward whom you feel a natural sense of compassion.

2 The next time you start beating up on yourself about something, use a "thought stopper" from p. 257 ("WHOA!").

3 Then, after quieting your mind with a few deep breaths, imagine that whatever you're berating yourself about just happened to this other person. What would you say to him or her?

4 Now offer these same comforts to yourself.

"Self-compassion can seem quite elusive at times, but since the wish to be happy and free from suffering is innate, it can't be ignored forever," Germer assures us. "Some measure of success is virtually guaranteed."

SELF-CARE VS. SELF-COMPASSION VS. SELF-PITY—WHAT'S THE DIF?

While these terms do all start with "self," they are not even close to the same thing. For example, if you frequently find yourself bouncing between life roles such as wife, mother, daughter, sister, friend, or caregiver (not to mention horse-keeper), with precious little time to do any of these roles much justice, you more than likely feel a little bit guilty when you pay any attention to your own needs over those of someone else. "We all require some maintenance," writes Germer in *The Mindful Path to Self-Compassion.* "A little time dedicated to self-care is not a moral lapse." While in the beginning self-compassion may indeed involve a little self-pity, Germer asserts that this also means opening yourself up to the universal nature of suffering—of *all* human beings—and then to acknowledge your own pain with a balanced mindfulness.

In her book Kristin Neff says that, more often than we realize, we don't even recognize our own suffering. And most of us, especially as horsewomen, have internalized the notion that we *shouldn't* whine in the midst of difficulty (we have *Cowgirls Don't Cry* as our ringtone, "Keep Calm and Carry On" on our t-shirts, and "No Whining" signs posted in our kitchens); it can be hard to even *notice* what a hard time we're having. "And when our pain comes from *self*-judgment," Neff adds, "it's even harder to see these as moments of suffering.....Self-compassion involves wanting health and well-being for oneself and leads to pro-active behavior to better one's situation, rather than passivity. Self-compassion doesn't mean that I think my problems are more important than yours; it just means I think that my problems are also important and worthy of being attended to."

Developing self-compassion enables us to let go of any unrealistic expectations that have been holding us and our riding hostage. The side effect you may notice immediately is the falling away of all the old obstacles that, up until now, have refused to budge in the slightest, no matter what you've done to try to "fix" this perceived flaw. For the familiar saying, "What you resist, persists," the opposite is also true: "What you *stop* resisting (and accept), fades away."

"By giving ourselves unconditional kindness and comfort while embracing the human experience, difficult as it is, we avoid destructive patterns of fear, negativity, and isolation," Neff writes. "The nurturing quality of self-compassion allows us to flourish, to appreciate the beauty and richness of life, even in hard times. When we soothe our agitated minds with self-compassion, we're better able to notice what's *right* as well as what's wrong, so that we can orient ourselves toward that which gives us joy."

Yes, ladies, we've come to the place where we can finally stop asking the haunting questions: Am I good enough? Am I smart enough? Am I attractive enough? Am I thin enough? Am I a "pretty" rider? "When we give ourselves compassion," says Neff, "the tight knot of negative self-judgment starts to dissolve, replaced by

BUSTED! Myths of Selfishness

MYTH: "All this focus on my body and my happiness and loving and caring for myself—it's just selfish."

TRUTH: In her profoundly thoughtful treatise on riding, dressage, and caring for the horse entitled *Dressage with Mind, Body & Soul: A 21st-Century Approach to the Science and Spirituality of Riding* and *Horse-and-Rider Well-Being,* renowned animal behaviorist and horse trainer Linda Tellington-Jones claims that *loving* yourself is the greatest way to *improve* yourself, and as you improve yourself, you improve the world around you.

Tellington-Jones uses the Hawaiian practice of *ho 'oponopono* to remind herself to embrace what's within. "I have incorporated a four-line mantra—it can serve as positive self-talk, or even prayer—in my life," she writes. "If I feel frustrated, or without hope, even for a moment, I simply repeat the following lines, aimed 'inward' toward my soul, over and over: *'I love you.' 'Please forgive me.' 'I'm sorry.' 'Thank you.'*

"Surprisingly, these can be very difficult things for people to say to themselves. 'I love you,' especially, is almost impossible for many a feeling of peaceful, connected acceptance—a sparkling diamond that emerges from the coal."

So how does all this emotional alchemy happen? Will the self-compassion prescription make you feel better about your body, your life, and your riding overnight? Of course not! Like everything else in this book (and a whole lot like training a horse), self-compassion is a process. Take it one day at a time. It took you a lifetime to build up your self-critical habits; consider allowing a little of your present and future to be spent replacing them. And don't forget to open your heart—to yourself.

women to aim inward," Tellington-Jones remarks. "But it is this simple chant, four lines only, that can in its simplicity remind you of the constant potential for change that exists in this world. When you are frustrated with your riding, your trainer, or your horse, it can be as easy as four short sentences to *change your mind* about the situation, and thus *change the reality*.

"If you love yourself even when you immediately recognize a mistake you have made, the mistake is easily made up for and avoided in the future. I stopped saying, 'Gosh Linda, that was really stupid,' when I started to think about the 52-million-plus cells that make up my body and are

on the receiving end of that sentiment. Today, sometimes it might rise to my lips, and even escape part way, but I always stop mid-sentence, and replace it with ho 'oponopono. My body, mind, and soul are much happier for it, and I feel the world reflected back to me is a better place, as well."

Linda Tellington-Jones' *Dressage with Mind, Body & Soul: A 21st-Century Approach to the Science and Spirituality of Riding and Horse-and-Rider Well-Being* (Trafalgar Square Books, 2013).

RESOURCES

Wake Up Your Potential

Way back on p. 42, we learned a little bit about what *Radical Acceptance* author Tara Brach calls the "trance of unworthiness"—the state many of us probably live in when it comes to our weight and body image. Now that we've ignited our self-compassion fire, what will we do with this information? How can we rouse ourselves from our "trance thinking?" Were we born with it, or was it learned?

First of all, even though we've explored some of the causes of negative body image in these pages, it really doesn't matter where it comes from or how we "got it." This is not about blaming our parents, pointing to circumstance, or otherwise discerning the source of our self-dislike. That's good news for those of us living in Brach's "trance of unworthiness," because chances are, we don't even realize there *is* any other way to think and feel about our bodies.

For whatever reason, the "trance" leads us to think that we have to be better or different to belong. In trying to evade or avoid the pain of our "unworthiness," we evolve strategies that (we think) keep us safe, hide our "flaws," and somehow compensate for all we believe is wrong with us. In *Radical Acceptance* Brach reveals some common examples of these "evasive strategies"; see how many of what follows seem familiar to you:

- **You embark on one self-improvement project after another.** Through better eating, a ramped up fitness regimen, more meditation, or volunteering your time—are you constantly trying to "better" yourself? While self-improvement is definitely not in and of itself something to avoid (heck, that's what a great deal of this book espouses!), it *is* important to pinpoint your motivation. Are you looking to be a new, healthier, or more altruistic *you* because it will bring more joy to your life—or because you're haunted by the fears that you aren't "good enough?"

- **You "hold back" and "play it safe" rather than risk failure.** Rather than riding in that clinic and struggling, do you avoid disappointment and responsibility, as

Amanda (afatgirlafathorse.blogspot.com)

During a visit to the *Chronicle of the Horse* forum, I ran across a post and a link to a blog called, "A Fat Girl and a Fat Horse—A Blog for Plus-Sized Riders," which I then began to follow and highly recommend for its wit, wisdom, and insight into struggles over weight issues and riding horses. Thank you, Amanda, for the wonderful light (and lightness!) you bring to this topic for so many readers. Here, friends, we hear from Amanda in her own words:

"And *why* did I lose weight? Simply put, it had absolutely nothing to do with *anything* that *anybody* said to me. I did it because I came to a place with myself where I said, 'You know, I love myself and myself deserves the good things in life.' And that was not just good, wholesome food, and exercise for my body (*not* weight loss, but good things—and frankly, if I bottom out at 200, or even if I stop here, I'll still be happy) but was also having the relationships and the job and the lifestyle that I deserve.

"I don't have the genes to be 'skinny'—it's just not in my cards. I am 6 feet tall with a family that runs on the large side of things. I have size 12 feet and hands that rival the size of my boyfriend's (he's the over-six-foot, Viking variety) and a 7¾ head. I am a *big* person, and I will always have that large, stocky frame. I don't *want* to be skinny, and I am glad that there are options for me.

"I pay a lot of attention to my horse. I *always* think about my weight before I get into the saddle on *any* horse. I consider the way that my body moves when my horse moves. I consider the horse that I am riding, his 'bone,' age, level of fitness. You know the best thing I did for my big mare? It wasn't lose weight, because she was just as happy carrying me at 309 as she is carrying me at 260...it was buying a saddle that fit her well!"

well as the harsh self-criticism and potential critique of others that goes along with failing to negotiate a learning curve? On horseback, do you hold yourself to an unfair standard rather than a bar equivalent to your age, experience, and amount of time in the saddle? Remember how we learned to check our thoughts (see p. 257)? Sometimes we have to check our starting points, as well. As much as we'd all like to, mastering all of our challenges *instantly,* is unrealistic.

- **You withdraw rather than experience the present moment.** Do you make up excuses not to participate in shows or trail rides or overnight camping trips with your horse by creating unnecessary drama around these opportunities and telling yourself stories about what's "really" going on? Do the stories you tell yourself about your body image challenges, your "barn friends," and your riding have recurrent themes, patterns, and projections? Do these stories that you think will protect you from disappointment instead provoke a state of constant, free-floating anxiety that cuts you off completely from the fun and camaraderie of these experiences? What do you imagine your barn acquaintances think about you and how you ride? How are they supportive? How are they letting you down? Are you living in an illusion of your own making?

- **You stay busy. Very, very busy.** Do you keep your body, schedule, mind, and life packed to overflowing? In this socially sanctioned hideout Brach calls "the universal coping method," this constant "busyness," Brach says, "helps us bury the feelings of vulnerability and deficiency lurking in our psyche." I often whine and complain that I'm too busy to ride—and I am—but who *made* all those commitments in the first place? Anyone else out there sacrificing the hallowed horse time (that we all know keeps us sane) in favor of "everything else" you have going on to the point of feeling a little bit...crazy? It's at this point in our journey together that it's time to ask ourselves if we are "on the run" from our feelings of inadequacy and whether we try to steer clear of confronting our anxieties by filling our time—and then overfilling it.

- **You are your own worst critic.** Is there something in you that believes that if you focus on all the ways you have or are screwing up, or by dwelling on your imperfections and deficiencies, you will somehow be a better person? Is there a running commentary in *your* mind that is always keeping track and letting you know (in less than flattering terms) how you're doing? I know, for example, that whether I'm at work, in the barn, in the saddle, or working out, it's hard to stop the inner critic's running commentary: *I don't look good in these jeans. I'm not sitting this canter like I need to. I don't deserve to even be in this show/event. Everyone is probably making fun of me behind my back. There's no way I can finish this circuit, this class, this bike ride...*

- **You focus on the faults of others.** Is blaming or criticizing others your escape hatch from the weight of your real or imagined "failures" and "inadequacies?" Sometimes the harder it is to admit our own faults, the better it feels to condemn others: "Jenny *always* cuts me off on the rail." "I could work out more if my family did *anything* to help around the house." "The barn staff closed up the indoor arena and turned off the lights before I could ride last night." If our first impulse when something goes wrong with our best intentions is to try to figure out whose fault it is, it's time to retrain our focus on how we can simply make whatever the situation is, *better*. (How can you, literally or figuratively, turn the lights back on?)

The most painful thing about the "evasive strategies" I've just described with Tara Brach's help (and YIKES—was I ever busted in several of these!) is how deeply they reinforce the insecurities that keep us trapped in our "trance of unworthiness." When we voluntarily (and after a while, habitually) keep ourselves limited by self-judgment, anxiety, dissatisfaction, and restlessness—in the saddle and out—we become debilitated by our certainty that "nothing is ever going to change."

A PRISON OF OUR OWN MAKING

It is within this "nothing is ever going to change" mindset that our thoughts and emotions can travel, in the blink of an eye, from a truly positive experience to stepping off into the bog of stinkin' thinkin' (see p. 264). Mired in the stories we tell ourselves, we then vacate the good-feeling, present moment before our best intentions realize what hit them. This pattern not only robs us of more joyful moments than we can count, it taints the ones we do manage to experience with worry: "This was a fluke"..."This won't last"...or, worse, appreciation snuffed by the desire for more: "This is all I want to do, every second of my life."

Instead of absorbing every beautiful moment of that perfect fall trail ride, your mind clouds *obliterate* the glorious day with negative thought patterns that then cycle into complete despair, turning a happy ride with your horse into a state of mourning that you don't get to do it more often. Before you know it your thoughts spiral into why that is, your shortcomings as a human being, and how nothing is ever going to change, except maybe for the worse (as you get older, let's say). In other manifestations of this self-imposed incarceration, a few sweet seconds of watching your horse play and romp with his friends in the pasture spirals into worry about something happening to him. The cheeseburger and beer with friends after a long day at a great show is overwritten with guilt that you shouldn't be eating like that. Any "silver lining" we experience sends us scurrying to examine the cloud—and within seconds we are back where we started.

THE ROUTE OUT

When we consider acceptance as a solution, this is far from that "que sera, sera, whatever will be, will be" brand of acceptance you may be more familiar with. What we're talking about here is embracing *everything that is* with mindful awareness. That's right. Every. Single. Thing. And we must do this without fear, judgment, or Pinterest makeovers. We've prepared well for this, ladies. With the toolkit assembled on our journey together, we are now ready to do it!

This trance-busting brand of acceptance Brach describes in *Radical Acceptance* comes in two parts:

1 **Learn to see things as they really are.** Calling upon strategies including mindfulness (p. 213), breathing techniques (p. 236), and using the thought-feeling-behavior continuum to our advantage (p. 290), we can begin to wash our experiences in the clear light of awareness to see every one of them exactly as it is. The fall trail ride is a multisensory delight (and fodder for future "happy place" visualizations): a glorious riot of color, the soft, rhythmic thud of hooves on damp leaves, the tangy aromatherapy of horse sweat, and the sun's warmth playing tag with a crisp breeze on our skin. When we can learn to immerse in our own experiences, we enjoy them as what our *senses* say they are, and not through a view obscured by our scripts, filters, and a busybody mind.

2 **See every moment with compassion and love.** Brach maintains that when we learn to relate to what we're *truly* seeing in all our experiences with the kindness of a mother holding her child, we honor each experience to become "intimate with the life of this moment as it is." Once you learn how to wrangle your mind into this new place, it takes very little effort to delight in every aspect of that perfect fall trail ride. Gaze at the color around you. Inhale the sweetness of this moment. Adore its perfection. Go ahead. Coo.

With self-compassion and acceptance of what is working together, there is balance and clarity that frees us to make whatever choices and changes we'd like to make in our lives. Whether we're rocking 50 extra pounds, short legs, an unbalanced frame, or physical challenges that are never going to change, when we engage full-throttle self-compassion and radical self-acceptance, we'll be able to access and engage the positive attributes we may have overlooked in our blind obsession with the ideal. As Coach Daniel Stewart likes to say, "Everyone has challenges. And strengths. From these we can develop a nice list of abundances we can draw from."

Susan Harris agrees: "We need to make friends with the body God gave us and learn to work with the size, shape, and body type we have," she says. "And ultimately, you can do a lot with horses, regardless of your shape or size, if you'll just be safe and sensible. There's a lot of opportunity with horses. Just start safely, take it a step at a time, and you have no idea how far you may be able to go."

The Secret to Sustainable Success

We've all been there. We start a new program, whether it's fitness, diet, or both, and experience some degree of success—sometimes we even reach big goals. Then at some point something happens to interrupt our rhythm; one missed workout turns into two, then three, then a week, then several weeks. One dietary slip turns into, "Oh well, I've blown it now, so I might as well," and "It's my (choose one) horse's birthday/parent's anniversary/first day of vacation; I'm going to enjoy myself now and get back on my program tomorrow. Or Monday. Or..." And then, the next thing you know, you're back in a place you don't want to be.

I don't know about you, but I'm just not interested in putting myself through that cycle again. I want change that sticks, at all three points of our continuum. I want my behavior to reflect a healthy lifestyle, my thoughts to be as "forward and quiet" as we ask of our horses, and I'd like for my emotions to follow suit. In other words, what I'm after—and what I think most people on this trail with us want—is a way to create sustainable change built on a healthy and positive body image.

Family therapist Jill Valle directed me to a variety of good resources and models for sustainable success strategies. I found what I was looking for in The Body Positive (www. thebodypositive.org), a multifaceted resource established in 1996 by Connie Sobczak and Elizabeth Scott to "transform people's beliefs about beauty, health, and identity, freeing them to live balanced, joyful, and purposeful lives." They assert that encouraging people to use their talents and passion to change their *world* instead of their *bodies* leads to enhanced self-love and self-care. In the way of overall guidance for making solid lifestyle changes stick, The Body Positive model offers four fundamental competencies we can learn to use to map our personal plan:

1 **Reclaim health and beauty.** At the opposite end of the spectrum from losing weight and getting a makeover, the Reclaim Health and Beauty competency is about learning the fundamentals of Health At Every Size (HAES), a practical and research-based health model that honors the genetic diversity of human size and shape (www.haescommunity.org). Like Daniel Stewart's body-type-horse-breed comparison (see p. 96) and unlike any traditional diet program you've ever heard of, HAES encourages people of all sizes to listen to their individual needs for physical activity and nourishment and to adopt healthy lifestyles. For those of us who ride and work with horses, our assessment really must honor our body type and follow Coach Stewart's advice for making the most of what we've got.

2 **Practice intuitive self-care.** From what, when, and how to eat, to when to hydrate, sleep, meditate, exercise, set better boundaries, squash negativity, ride harder, focus better, or just hang out with your horses—the exact prescription for what you need to do to care for yourself, mind, body, and spirit, is all there in your own internal personal playbook. As you learn to incorporate the various best practices outlined in this book and discern which are most helpful to you, start building some daily rituals around a few of them to help you check in, take action, and stay connected to this vital personal "help desk."

3 **Cultivate self-love.** We've already learned in the pages prior that being critical and unloving of our bodies *does not* motivate us to take better care of them. "Whipping ourselves into shape" is about the worst thing we can do. Instead, we need healthy and enjoyable self-care choices, based in the realm of the self-compassion we explored back on p. 351. Ironically, as we discovered in several different ways throughout this winding journey we've been on together, once we learn to love the skin we're in, it is actually easier to make some of the very same changes we had in mind back when we were beating ourselves up! Coming from a place of love, these changes are suddenly within reach and doable.

4 Build community based on shared positive body image. By creating communities where we support one another in choosing to love and honor our unique bodies, we expand our potential to create positive change in our own lives, in our riding and the time we spend with horses, and in the world. And, where can we find and build community? Ladies, kinship potentially exists all around us..

NOW LET'S APPLY SOME LEVERAGE

If you're a woman working with horses, you already understand that leverage can be your very best friend when you need to get a big job done with strength limited (despite our best fitness routines) by physics and reality. In Mike Dooley's *Leveraging the Universe,* we find a new take on this old friend in a way that fits our quest perfectly (thanks again to the recommendation of therapist Jill Valle). Dooley peppers his narrative with a series of clever "Notes from the Universe," in which he alerts us to important truths to keep filed away in the naysaying parts of our brains. (I keep these somewhere near the habit-forming part, just under that tangle of frayed behavioral wires.) Among my favorites of Dooley's "Notes from the Universe" is this one:

"Do you know what happens in time and space just before something really incredible happens? Something mind-blowing? Just before a really HUGE dream comes true? Do you? Absolutely nothing. At least not in the physical world. So if, perchance, it appears that absolutely nothing is happening in your life right now… consider it a sign."

"The first time I can remember actually leveraging life's magic, quite accidentally," Dooley goes on to say, "was as a nine-year-old boy, fresh from a horseback riding competition in which I placed sixth (out of six). Determined to do better, and following my mother's sage advice, I prayed to God each night to 'help me do my best' in the next

RESOURCES

Linda Bacon's: *Health at Every Size: The Surprising Truth About Your Weight* (BenBella Books, 2010).

Body Respect: What Conventional Health Books Leave Out, Misunderstand, or Just Plain Fail to Understand about Weight (BanBella Books, 2014).

Myths of Good Health

BUSTED!

MYTH: "Women who are large are unhealthy."

TRUTH: Acknowledging that good health can best be realized independently from size consideration, the Healthy At Every Size (HAES) movement "supports people of all sizes in addressing health directly by adopting healthy behaviors."

According to Linda Bacon, PhD, who wrote the book, *Health at Every Size: The Surprising Truth About Your Weight* that inspired the HAES movement and an extensive community and smattering of blogs, books, media, and resources (available at www.haescommunity.org), "We've lost the war on obesity. Fighting fat hasn't made the fat go away. And being thinner, even if we knew how to successfully accomplish it, will not necessarily make us healthier or happier. The war on obesity has taken its toll. Extensive 'collateral damage' has resulted: Food and body preoccupation, self-hatred, eating disorders, discrimination, poor

health....Few of us are at peace with our bodies, whether because we're fat or because we fear becoming fat."

Calling HAES "the new peace movement," Bacon (I am not making this up) curates and promotes for the broader community (nope, still not a pun) exactly the same ideals we're embracing as riders. Rather than promoting diet and exercise as our *only* solution, the HAES emphasis is on being at peace with our own bodies and finding self-compassionate ways to

- Respect body diversity.

- Take better care of ourselves.

- Honor and protect health over some externally opposed body ideals.

- Find joy in our physical activity.

- Challenge cultural and medical bias.

The HAES website and online community gives members the opportunity to connect with one another, offer support, and share advice and resources.

competition. Nightly I prayed, imagining myself as the next champion, and those thoughts rather promptly became a first-place trophy."

The experience became the cornerstone of Dooley's core premise that "thoughts become things." After personally experiencing the power of this concept many times firsthand (beyond the first-place trophy) and helping countless others do the same, Dooley created a scrapbook to help visualize his dreamed-of life. (Fun fact: Dooley's first scrapbook was inspiration for the "vision boards" advocated in Rhonda Byrne's *The Secret*, in which Dooley was featured many years later.) Dooley's favorite story arising from this enlightening discovery of how "thoughts become things" is the day he recognized himself sitting, in his real life, in one of the *exact places* shown in a magazine photo he had pasted in his scrapbook two years prior when he didn't even have the same job: "I looked up over my coffee and out the two-story plate-glass windows surrounding me to suddenly realize that I was sitting before the exact same view of Hong Kong Island that I had cut and pasted into my little scrapbook just twenty-four months earlier."

Looping in what we learned earlier in this book about how visualization, mindfulness, and self-acceptance can indeed open us up to new possibilities, there's no way of knowing what huge dream (or even tiny wish) could be just around *our* next corner!

Lay Claim to Your Happy Place (Right There with Your Horse)

We've talked a lot in this book about "finding joy," "returning to the joy we were meant to have in our riding," and even "being comfortable in the skin we're in" (or at least our riding clothes). What I really want to do now is help you, right here, right now, regardless of size, shape, or BMI, to claim the happiness that is already yours to enjoy—with your horses, as you ride, and throughout your life.

RESOURCES

Rhonda Byrne's *The Secret* (Atria Books/Beyond Words, 2006)

But how do we do that? Is happiness something that's "out there somewhere," waiting for some magic moment when we finally get everything right. Is it trapped somewhere inside us, trying to find a way to bubble forth like Aphrodite's fountain? Is being happy, as so many say, just a matter of making up your mind? And if it is that simple, doesn't that beg some questions, such as:

- Why don't we *know* we're happy?

- Why don't we *feel* happy?

- Why do we make ourselves *miserable* over the size of our thighs?

One of the great full circles of this book became apparent to me when, quite by accident (if you believe in such things), I happened to hear an on-air interview with Dan Harris, co-anchor of ABC's *Nightline,* on the weekend edition of *Good Morning America.* Harris was talking about his book: *10% Happier: How I Tamed the Voice in My Head, Reduced Stress Without Losing My Edge, and Found Self-Help That Actually Works—A True Story.* Granted, it's a mouthful of a title, but it got my attention as I walked through a hotel lobby on the way to my "egg-puck" repast in the self-serve breakfast bar.

To back up for a moment: I was just entering the, "So what?" phase of this book. How was I going to make all this information feel relevant, useful, and compelling enough to empower and equip readers to make whatever changes they need to (guess what) *be happy* with themselves and their riding? We've talked about all kinds of ways to make that perfect ride happen. We've gathered up tools and strategies and all kinds of ideas for equipping you, the reader, in this hot pursuit of a sometimes elusive joy that, as Susan Harris described on p. 159, will keep us riding longer, better, and stronger than we ever dreamed possible. But what would make all this information packed into these pages "click" for this emerging book's readers?

With Dan's interview echoing in my head, I took a deep breath, a quick download, and dived head first into the deep end of "happy."

WHO'S HAPPY—AND WHY?

Author Gretchen Rubin apparently had some of these same musings on the elusive state of happiness, and she embarked on her own quest—a year dedicated to the pursuit and underpinnings) of happiness—that became a *New York Times* Bestseller:

The Happiness Project: Or, Why I Spent a Year Trying to Sing in the Morning, Clean My Closets, Fight Right, Read Aristotle, and Generally Have More Fun. Synthesizing the wisdom of the ages with current scientific research, what Rubin created has now become a movement that I think fits well with what we're trying to do with our bodies and our horses.

In her book, Rubin embarked on the now familiar "annualism" approach (which the *New York Times* defines as "Engaging in, or desisting from, an activity for a year, usually with a book contract in mind") to combine raising her own awareness with sharing what she learned about happiness with others. Like so many of us, Rubin wanted to know *what* happiness is, *where* it comes from, and *how* to get more of it.

"Whether it's because we measure our lives according to the passing of birthdays or holidays, or because of the influence of the school schedule," she says, "a year feels like the right length of time for an 'experiment in living,' to borrow Thoreau's phrase. A year feels like enough time for real change to be possible—but manageable." In most things, learning by someone else's example is far easier than by studying principles in the abstract. Would learning to claim my happiness be the same? I couldn't help but wonder.

Rubin says that what prompted her to write *The Happiness Project* was her feeling that she was in danger of "wasting" her life. Suffering from what she called "an adult malaise" and "a recurrent sense of discontent," Rubin realized that what was missing for her was...*happiness.* Looking at my own life, and especially my life with horses, I felt the echo of Rubin's sentiment. There was much to be grateful for—so much, in fact, that I tend to feel a little bit guilty for not being *more* grateful. Layer on top of all this a sense of urgency to enjoy my horses while I have the health and ability to ride and work with them. Sprinkle with the barn buddies, trainers, mentors, and opportunities that we all know tend to come—and go—on their own time and in seasons we can't really predict. Now add the body and riding insecurities you've already heard way too much about, and you get something we'll call "*rider's* malaise."

So what did Rubin learn during her Happiness Project? "That the biggest obstacle to my happiness was…me," she writes. You can almost feel the sheepishness wrapped around this revelation, yet I suspect it's the same for all of us. Rubin says that as soon as she started thinking about how she could be *happier*, she realized how happy she *already was*: "My appreciation for life increased dramatically once I examined it."

So there's your leg up on *happy*.

Am I saying we should follow Rubin's tracks and do a "Horsey" Happiness Project of our own? Maybe. Even if nothing else in your life shifts at first (we've talked about how big change takes time), just the act of recognizing and appreciating what's good in your life *right now* will fuel everything else you do. As you begin to repair and replace worn out ideas, retool your habits, and make small changes in how you think, feel, and behave with regard to your body and your riding, you'll stake that claim to your "happy place" and settle in, once and for all!

Exercise for the Soul: How to Get Happy *Now*

Based on Gretchen Rubin's five tips from her book *The Happiness Project* (and check out her blog for more great stuff at www.gretchenrubin.com), implement the following tools in your "hunt for happy." You'll see how they all track back to things we've already discussed at various twists and turns of this book. In fact, your toolbox is chock *full* of "happiness implements." Let's put them to work!

1 Think about your body. Get enough sleep, get some exercise, and don't let yourself get too hungry. Revisit our "framework" discussion, beginning on p. 157.

2 Figure out ways to have fun. Learn how to do something new, make time for hobbies, preserve happy memories, get into the spirit of the season. That's why we do this horse thing anyway, right? Because it is FUN. Make time for it—and keep those appointments (see p. 149).

3 Act the way you wish you felt. If you're feeling annoyed, act loving. If you're feeling tired, act energetic. If you're feeling shy, act friendly. It really works. Hello, affirmations! Goodbye, Compass of Shame! (See pp. 261 and 317.)

4 Get rid of things that make you feel annoyed, angry, or guilty. Show clothes that don't fit, relationships that don't work, habits that don't help you, and activities that eat into your horse time—kick them to the curb! Make those doctors appointments, call your grandmother, replace a light bulb, clean a closet, answer a difficult email, stop nagging yourself and others.

5 Whenever possible, connect with other people. Show up. Make plans. Join a group. Go to a party. Reach out. Help someone. Philosophers and scientists agree: close relationships with other people are perhaps *the* key to a happy life. So here's where that community we spoke of a few pages back comes in (and see the sidebar on p. 378).

The Voice in Your Head

Now to return to Dan Harris (and the book he wanted to call "The Voice in My Head Is an Asshole")—one of the things he noted in his *Good Morning America* interview continued to haunt me. Saying that he found himself falling prey to an "eroding interior dialogue," Harris began to explain how he discovered that his negative self-talk was compromising his career as a leading anchorman.

"Most of us are so entranced by the nonstop conversation we're having with ourselves that we aren't even aware we *have* a voice in our head," Harris writes.

"I certainly wasn't—at least not before I embarked on the weird little odyssey described in this book."

Harris' exploration chronicled in his book, *10% Happier,* shows us, much as Gretchen Rubin did in *The Happiness Project,* simple ways to apply complex concepts and new findings in brain science to our everyday experience for a firsthand, user-friendly understanding of how these insights actually *can* change our lives for the better.

"To be clear," Harris writes, "I'm not talking about 'hearing voices,' I'm talking about the internal narrator, the most intimate part of our lives. The voice comes braying in as soon as we open our eyes in the morning, and then heckles us all day long with an air horn. It's a fever swamp of urges, desires, and judgments. It's fixated on the past and the future, to the detriment of the here and now. It's what has us reaching into the fridge when we're not hungry, losing our temper when we know it's not really in our best interest, and pruning our inboxes when we're ostensibly engaged in conversation with other human beings."

While Harris is quick to point out that our inner voice isn't *all* bad—and that there is enough goodness, humor, and truth in its observations to keep us listening—it can be, as he puts it, "a malevolent puppeteer." As riders with some degree of self-consciousness about our bodies, this is the voice that spews the kinds of statements we're all too familiar with:

"Your pants are too tight. Can't you feel the fat hanging over your waistband?"

"You're flopping all over the place. Why can't you get it together?"

"If your legs weren't so short maybe your horse could feel that cue."

"Those people over there watching you ride are talking about the massive size of your butt."

"The other people in this clinic probably think you shouldn't be here at all."

"You're never going to win any serious events until you lose weight."

"Judges ignore large riders. Don't even bother trying to show."

Calling upon the work of none other than Jon Kabat-Zinn (revisit our own Kabat-Zinn discoveries on pp. 216–222), Harris adds his voice to a growing determination to move mindfulness practices from Eastern religion and New Age-y circles into the mainstream, tapping into the science behind how and why they work *for everyone*.

A Little Bit O' Buddha

Going deep and wide in his research, Harris shares what he learned in multiple face-to-face conversations with Harvard-educated psychiatrist and practicing Buddhist Dr. Mark Epstein, as well as a whole host of what Harris refers to his "Jew-Bu" friends. For me, it helped cut to the "So what?" chase with efficiency usually reserved for Wikipedia.

"In many ways, it was my craziest act of gonzo journalism," Harris writes. "If it could help a monumental skeptic like me, I could only imagine what it could do for others."

Whether you have any affinity for Buddhism or not, one Buddhist teaching is that *in a world constantly changing, suffering comes from clinging to things that won't last*. Think about that for a moment. When we are able to step back a bit and take a look at our own life's dramas and desires through a wider lens, we can, as the Buddhists say, "let go" of our suffering. This is much easier said than done. As we already know, we cling tightly to those "personal truths" we talked about early on—*that we're too large to ride well; that we can't balance because of our big boobs; that we'll only be happy when we somehow look different than we do right now*. Will all those "truths" we've carried for a lifetime suddenly melt away just because we decide to "let go" and start meditating? Of course not.

But here's what *will* happen. As I've asserted earlier in this book and as Harris assures us: If you can do *some* of these mindful practices *just enough* to become a *little bit* more aware of your negative or destructive thoughts and feelings and where they come from, you'll become *slightly* less attached to them. (Remember the meditation technique of visualizing clouds passing through our clear blue sky and right out of sight? Take another look on p. 220.) Build on this progress, and bit by bit, chances are good that one of these days you're going to look around and notice that while you do still have these same thoughts and feelings, their power over your choices has begun to subside.

"It's not that I have different feelings," Harris explains, "but I don't identify and attach to them—or make them such a huge drama. Mindfulness allows your emotions to pass through with ease."

Happiness Is...Doing One Thing at a Time

If you ever feel like you suddenly have the attention span of a gnat, there's a reason. Another important source Harris presents to the rest of us in *10% Happier* is Janice Marturano ("a hard-charging, no-nonsense, sensible-haircut corporate attorney") who, after discovering meditation and realizing what a powerful game-changer it was, began to help spread the practice more or less virally through the ranks of attorneys and executives she knew. Noting the term scientists have now coined for the crack-like call of our electronics, "continuous partial attention," Marturano challenged Harris (and I now extend that challenge to you—and to myself) to *do only one thing at a time.*

This is much harder than you may think.

The sad truth here is that we are so accustomed to multitasking it's really hard to even notice when we're doing it. Intrinsically related to what we discovered about being present back on p. 214, I invite you to take this challenge to the barn: See if it's possible to leave your phone in the car. When you brush your horse, engage your senses (see p. 218) and don't do anything else but let the brush glide over his coat. Or gently detangle that knot in his mane. One step at a time. When you feed, pour the grain. Watch your horse chew. Listen to the steady rhythmic crunch and watch the circular motion of his jaw. And yes, when you muck his stall, keep your mind only on the poop you're scooping—all the rest of your crap can wait.

In what Harris calls the "blitzkrieg of information overload," remember this: The results are in. This is not just opinion any more. Neuroscience has deemed our capacity to "multitask" as virtually nonexistent. Multitasking is a made-up word created by those who don't even know what they're missing in their drive to know-all-do-all-be-all—all at once. Here's the deal: our brain is a *solo processor*. And, while we may *appear* to be able to do seven things at once, if you've ever started dinner, talked on the phone, fed the dog, watered the cat, unloaded the dishwasher, warmed up the clothes in the dryer, opened the mail, and took out the trash as you "relaxed" upon returning home after work, only to spend half the next day looking for your car keys (which you find in the freezer...at least they weren't in the trash), you'll realize, as I did, that those white-coated geeks are right.

What we think is more efficient (multitasking) is actually making us *less* efficient. And what we *think* is a waste of time (sitting still for at least five minutes a day—see p. 222 for how to fit this in) could well be the key to getting control of whatever is blocking us from the happiness we crave, on horseback and off.

Small Moves...Big Results

Once you actually try—and have some degree of success with—some of the mindfulness, meditation, and breathing exercises such as those in this book, you're likely going to want to tell people about it. Harris says this is how he discovered his *10% Happier* "schtick." Frustrated by the glazed response he was getting from his coworkers every time he started talking about mindfulness, he made a slight adjustment to his delivery of this game-changing information. (You know the expression I'm talking about...or if you don't, tell one of your friends you've started meditating. Feel the "whoosh" as their attention leaves the conversation.) When Harris told his producer, "I do it because it makes me 10% happier," he says that the look on her face instantly changed from boredom borderlining on scorn to genuine interest: "Really?" she said. "That sounds pretty good, actually."

"If you can get past the cultural baggage," Harris writes, "What you'll find is that meditation is simply exercise for your brain. It's a proven technique for preventing the voice in your head from leading you around by the nose. To be clear, it's not a miracle cure. It won't make you taller or better-looking, nor will it magically solve all of your problems. You should disregard the fancy books and the famous gurus promising immediate enlightenment. In my experience, meditation makes you 10% happier."

To be honest, I autoresponded to Harris' statement, "I'm not interested in being 10% happier. I wanted to be *100%* happier!" The surprise I didn't realize awaited me was how just 10% really can open the door to a different place. Just like we can recognize from the way we train our horses (one small thing at a time) and from the "baby steps" we're now using to nudge our own thoughts, emotions, and behavior into line (see p. 324), everything breaks down to a "start." Once

Myths of Isolation

MYTH: "I'm all alone. No one understands my struggles reconciling my body size and shape with my riding."

TRUTH: When I first began working on this book, I admit to some lurking. With more than a little bit of timidity about approaching people to request interviews and stories on this subject, I began my research by dipping a toe (or several) in the vast sea of information called the World Wide Web to help shape our exploration of this very specific and sensitive set of topics. Specifically, I set off in search of forums, blogs, websites, and vendors dedicated to body image issues and riding. In that, I discovered an amazing network of support and space for sharing and learning from each other.

What I discovered was that the Internet is traveled by an amazing number of compassionate caring and thoughtful people joining together over any topic or issue you can think of. It is also a place where people can be unspeakably cruel to one another, mostly under that same cloak of anonymity that makes bonding easier. So be careful in your online travels, friends, but do seek like-minded others when you're looking for a little help. Support is out there, just waiting for your keyword. And, as I'm sure you've noticed by now, I've shared many of my favorite finds throughout the pages of this book as "Voices of Our Sisters" in quotes, sidebars, boxes, and pages to give you a bit of a head start on finding some of these kindred spirits.

One place I trolled is the *Chronicle of the Horse* discussion forum (chronofhorse.com). I first searched for conversations related to my question: "Am I too heavy to ride?" It was interesting to find not only a thread that lasted for more than five years (2006 through 2011) and contained 693 different posts and comments, but great variety and thoughtfulness in these posts. What I found there was both astounding compassion and unflinching explorations of the real issues surrounding a diverse group of plus-sized riders. The *Chronicle of the Horse* forum is a place where lots of riders go to get information, find support, ask and answer questions, and enjoy the community of like minds—and issues. It's a busy place: At the time of my last visit, it had 49,098 active members, 237,443 different threads, and 4,636,111 posts.

As you might imagine, both Facebook and LinkedIn have numerous discussion groups formed around some of the same thoughts and issues we've all been trying to sort out on our own. Sometimes we may confide in a barn buddy, but most often, we do not. Feeling shame about our bodies is a solitary activity, and in this isolation it's easy to imagine that we're all alone. We are not.

Finding one—or several—safely "anonymous" support groups that discuss topics that resonate with you can be key to:

- Dealing with your feelings of shame over real or imagined imperfections.

- Navigating the difficulty of making lifestyle changes.

- Bringing back—and celebrating—the joy of riding and working with horses.

If you've ever been in a real face-to-face support group, you know what I mean when I say "safely anonymous." When we can connect with like-minded (and bodied) "others" from the privacy of our own homes and handheld devices, we feel far more free to air out our anxieties, fears, despair, determination, plans, dreams, hopes, goals, successes, failures, intentions, and missteps. Even in a "safe" face-to-face group setting, it isn't nearly as easy to "get real."

we get used to tackling the tiniest pieces of a new behavior, we can start to stack them up, and before too long the simple exercise that seemed too inconsequential to bother with has amalgamated into a flying lead change, a 20-minute run, a 50-pound weight loss, or a 30-minute sitting meditation with complete inner stillness. Likewise, intentional moments of happiness created here and there, over time, will eventually fuse, leaving you downright giddy. (You do the math!)

STEP UP TO YOUR HAPPY PLACE

I don't know about you, but I'm ready to do something different. I'm ready *to be happy*. I'm ready to do what I need to do to and learn what I need to learn. I want to wring every bit of joy I can out of every single moment with my horse from now on. I'm ready to let go of worrying about the muffin top hanging over my jeans. I'm ready to quit bargaining, scolding, and chastising myself for the size and shape of my body, the length of my legs, and the look of someone I'm not.

In other words, I'm ready to calm down and lose the lie.

The lie I refer to here is one Harris identifies in his book, and the one we all tell ourselves our whole lives: "As soon as we get the next meal, party, vacation, sexual encounter, as soon as we get married, get a promotion, get to the airport check-in, get through security and consume a bouquet of Auntie Anne's Cinnamon Sugar Stix, we'll feel really good."

Sound familiar? And how about this: It's the next horse, the next clinic, the next trainer, the next diet, the next program, the next supplement—the next double cheeseburger and fries—*that's* when we'll feel good...we'll feel *happy*. But that's the lie. Happiness, it turns out, is *not* just on the other side of "next" or "should." It's been right here in our lap (or out there in the paddock) all along, just waiting for us to notice it. Happiness is the face that greets and nuzzles you when you do your evening barn check. It's the moment when you get on the back of your horse, when you settle into the saddle and let out that telltale sigh. It's those moments (even if they are few and far between) when you *are* riding in perfect sync with the magnificent animal beneath you. It's the smell of horse sweat, leather, and freshly cut hay; the "good tired" at the end of a long day at the barn. It's the unique view of the world we are privileged to have from the back of a horse. And it's the friends we make along the way.

Whether we need to make changes or not, whether we are, in fact, too heavy to ride safely right now, or if we're just keeping ourselves in agony over the mismatch between our "double digit" jeans and the size-6 bottom pointed at us in the glossy equestrian magazine, it's time to *stop* making our pursuit of happiness the source of our *un*happiness.

Step up. Be Happy. Now.

JOY IN A (PEA) NUTSHELL

Here's how: Martha Beck would probably be among the first to say that the ideas in her book, *The Joy Diet: 10 Daily Practices for a Happier Life* are very basic. In fact, she compares her "Joy Diet rules" to "Pack a lunch," and "Wear sunscreen," and "Keep your matches dry," in terms of advice classification. One thing Beck has noticed throughout her many years of practice as a life coach is that people seem to miss the simplest ideas that can make all the difference between life that is a "joyful journey" and "hell on wheels." (Or in our case, on hooves.)

Exercise for the Soul: A Horsegirl's Happy Place

There is, of course, no substitute for devouring *The Joy Diet* in its entirety (it's a heaping helping of soul food, I promise!); it's one of my all-time favorite capsules of Beck's unique ability to make whatever seems broken in us feel completely fixable. However, and keeping the peculiarities of our horsegirl lives in mind, here are a few basics from the only true "D-word" I can wholeheartedly recommend for everyone.

Myths of Changing Your Mind

MYTH: "I've tried to change my life a million times, but I always fall back into the same patterns of self-loathing. My brain is just wired that way."

TRUTH: If you've been struggling with body image issues for as long as I have, you're probably pretty sure you've heard it all. I know I was. Until, that is, I started prowling around in a concept I've already mentioned but need to return to—what brain scientists refer to as *neuroplasticity,* or the idea that changes in behavior, environment, neural processes, thinking, and emotions can actually create changes in neural pathways and synapses. The brain, it turns out, is an "organ of experience," and we're all within just a few small tweaks of a giant opportunity for changes we may never have thought possible. Scientists used to say that our brains were pretty much unchangeable after a certain period in our early childhood. Recent neuroscience findings, however, reveal that

neuropathways (which is how information travels through the neurons that transmit nerve signals to and from the brain) within the brain can actually be removed, created, or re-created, largely dependent upon how we use them. "It's possible to sculpt your brain through meditation just as you build and tone your body through exercise," Dan Harris tells us in *10% Happier*, "to grow your gray matter the way doing curls grows your bicep."

Remembering that researchers, neuroscientists, and philosophers estimate that the average person has between 12,000 and 80,000 thoughts per day, many of them repetitive, what's important about this is how our repetitive thoughts *create* neuropathways. When we establish habits (either consciously or unconsciously) our subconscious mind uses the habit's neuropathway to make this behavior more or less automatic; it's the neuropathway that sustains the routine.

Now here's the mind-and-life-changing part: When we alter an existing routine *deliberately*—and repeat the new pattern just a few times—it interrupts the old patterns and pathways and establishes a new one (think road work...striped barrels and orange cones lining up in your brain). In the beginning, the original neuropathway just gains a "new lane" of additional information; however, when you keep repeating the new pattern, a wide, smooth new neuropathway is paved.

In *Train Your Mind, Change Your Brain*, science journalist Sharon Begley explores the demise of "orthodox neuroscience" that assumed only the brains of children are malleable and morphable (in other words, plastic) and that as adults this capability is gone. "It turns out this theory is not just wrong," Begley writes, "it is spectacularly wrong." What this means to those of us trying to adopt new habits to help build a new lifestyle is that, as Begley expresses the hope common to all of us: "our emotional lives and personalities, far from being carved in stone by our genes and early experiences, will prove as sculptable through mental training as our bodies are through physical training."

What's exciting about all this? As we ride into the valley of habit formation (dotted with tips and ideas for shaping new ones), it's important to understand that when we work on creating a new habit, we're not just training our behavior—we're blazing neuropathways that will eventually help make that habit *automatic*. And, even when there are contrary, but well-traveled previous neuropathways already in place, the more we repeat a new habit, the stronger it gets and the weaker the previous one becomes. It's still there (which is why it's so easy to revert back to our old ways), but with our new superpowers of thought control and conscious decision, we'll manage any wobbles quickly and stay on the right track.

RESOURCES

Sharon Begley's *Train Your Mind, Change Your Brain: How a New Science Reveals Our Extraordinary Potential to Transform Ourselves* (Ballantine Books, 2007).

- **Sit and watch your horse for at least 15 minutes a day. Watch him walk around his paddock. Watch him eat all of his hay. Don't think. Don't move. Just watch.** "To really do nothing, you must vacate your own life," Beck writes. "On the Joy Diet, you do this at least once a day." Beck's own stress-related illness kept sending her to the emergency room, where she'd always draw the "maddeningly flaky doctor who prescribed 'mindfulness' instead of "good old-fashioned morphine," but it led her to what she now calls "the essential practice of doing nothing"—and creating a habit of seeking stillness on a regular basis.

- **Once a day, just spend just a few minutes (set a timer if you need to) thinking about riding and horses and the simple truth of why you want them in your life. Revisit the feeling Susan Harris described on p. 159. Sit with it.** Making a point of remembering this simple truth every day taps back into our exploration beginning on p. 2 of this book. Beck typifies this conscious commitment as being present with "the simple truths of basic experience: This is what I love. This is what I need. This is what makes me angry. This is what's happening, right now."

- **Each day, identify and explore what you want, more than anything else, to change about how you are with horses. What is your truest riding desire?** Beck says she believes we come into this world with an innate yearning toward the fullest expression of who we are meant to be, and this code is constantly live-streaming from our heart to our brain in the "language of longing." And because, as Coach Daniel Stewart told us, "As we ride, so goes our life," getting clear on what we truly want from our horses and our riding is the most powerful predictor of getting there—and what measures we need to take to create our success.

- **Each day, write down one idea that will help you get what you really want.** To start with, write down one of the ideas you've read in this book that you'd like to work on in your horse life—one that you're going to start *today*. We've talked quite a lot about visualization and affirmation, and stating our hearts' desires as if they are already granted. This is where we get to put some legs under them (maybe four?). In *this* daily practice, we move closer and closer toward each of our desires every day (more "baby steps"...more 10%...starting to get the picture?). Push youself just a little here—right up to a place that feels slightly uncomfortable, right up to the edge of painful like we did in our stretching (see p. 136). "Once you know how it feels to go to the edge of your creative capacity," Beck assures us, "you'll begin to see that problems are solved by *leaning into* this sensation, not *retracting from* it."

- **Now write down one fear you want to overcome on your path to enjoying the time you spend with your horse.** Following the old adage to "do one thing every day that scares you to death," it's time to confront something you usually avoid out of fear. From what do you shrink? What fills you with terror? "Almost all my clients eventually reach a point where they know what they want from life and have several creative ideas about how to make it happen," Beck writes, completely unaware these words would one day appear in a horse book. "Some clients go right out and grab this scary proposition by the mane and tail. Others stall...and stall...and stall." (So are you going to grab your fear by the mane and tail—or stall, stall, stall?)

- **Pick three kinds of rewards for any step you take in tackling a specific horsemanship challenge.** Examine every ride and barn experience for even the smallest thought, emotion, or behavior changes—and give yourself a "treat" to recognize each. (Oh yes, we've already touched on this idea, too! Go back to p. 330 for a refresher.) Although human beings are usually pretty good at deferring gratification, even the most determined of us eventually get tired of doing things without any apparent reward. Bottom line? Bribe yourself. Remember, however, to choose "treats" that are as good for you as the new behaviors you are rewarding. (So, no, a hot fudge sundae probably isn't the answer.) Journaling every morning? *Treat.* Fitting in your 20-minute walking meditation? *Treat.* Attending to "Joy Diet" menu items? *Treat.* Come up with a solid selection of treats (not food!) for a daily ritual of reinforcement that will ultimately add up to the biggest treat of all: a confident, happy, healthy self, in and out of the saddle. Here's what works for me: Complete another 10-class pass in yoga, Pilates, or Pure Barre? *Massage.*

Morning Pages every day this week? *A full afternoon or evening Netflix binge.* Meditation twice a day for a month? *A mindful stroll through our local Botanic Garden.* Riding three times this week? *Riding three times this week. (Some things are rewards in and of themselves!)*

- **Remember play time.** Still thinking about why you ride, where you started, and how far you've come, take a few minutes to just play with your horse. For most of us, our daily dose of "play time" naturally corresponds with our barn time, and in embracing this distinctive "Joy Diet" imperative as non-negotiable, we can now officially justify extending our barntime every day to just...*play.* As busy, self-important adults, not to mention riders with way too many other things pulling us in different directions, it may be hard to enforce this priority—and even harder for others to understand it. Do it anyway. "A playful mind-set allows you to master whatever is in front of you, to form symbiotic alliances and partnerships, to adapt successfully to any challenging situation, and above all," Beck adds, putting a deft cherry on top, "to find a sense of fun that makes the whole shebang intrinsically satisfying." We may expend buckets of cash, gallons of sweat, and tubs of tears in our "playtime" with our horses, but this is the biggest kind of fun most of us know.

- **Look for opportunities to laugh.** Think of all the really funny things you've encountered while owning and riding horses, and laugh. As you watch your horse (and your barn friends) for cues, try to recall any reason to laugh again. Spend enough time with horses and horse people, and the laughter will always appear, surely as horse droppings. Someone told me once about a monk who taught his students to lie on their backs each day and simulate the belly shake of deep laughter, over and over again. (Of course I had to try it.) He said that contracting the abdominal "laugh muscles" almost always provokes natural laughter (probably because it feels a little bit ridiculous)—and even when it doesn't, endorphins are still released and you feel better afterward. According to Beck, a small child laughs about 400 times a day, and the average adult laughs just 15 times. So if we make a conscious effort to laugh even twice as much as we do now, we're well on our way to feeling better. Pandora has a comedy station. YouTube offers a whole subculture of comedians, and both Buzz Feed and Vine offer a steady stream of snickers and giggles (and occasional opportunities for beverages to spew from your nose). There are comedy networks, and a plethora of late-night hosts whose job in life is to make us laugh. (I still have Craig Ferguson's rabbit-puppet monologue saved on my DVR.) Not to mention the "goofy equine antics" included on Facebook and Twitter feeds (I do try to share any that come my way!) as well as many equestrian-specific websites. So go ahead and laugh. The opportunity is out there.

- **Connect with likeminded others.** Apply something you've learned so far to the people and horses in your life to help create more powerful, healing, and enlightening relationships. The challenge of this exercise is to reflect upon what you've absorbed from this book, as well as others I've recommended, and see how this information fits with your life's unique opportunities to connect with others. (Ah, the "community" key again!) Applying these small-sounding tweaks to your relationships (with humans *and* with horses!), Beck says, is transformative.

- **Immerse yourself in the daily sublime.** It may sound silly to say we should make a conscious effort each day to really enjoy the sublime aspects of mundane barn and horse chores. This sweet rule of the "Joy Diet" reminds us to elevate things that might otherwise slip right by us as ordinary experiences to being the "feasts" they can be for "the appetites, the senses, the mind, the heart." By calling attention to the more uplifting aspects of things that otherwise might seem ordinary, we activate and strengthen our attention and capacity for day-to-day joy. Things like brushing our horse, for example. Or hosing him off after a long sweaty ride. Scratching his itchy spot. Emptying a new bag of feed into the bin, cleaning your saddle, and dare I admit it, that heady first whiff of fly spray in the spring. These things, to those of us who are horse people, are feasts for the senses. But how many times have we forgotten to stop and savor them? From now on, turn your conscious attention to all the ways your favorite horse-related sights, smells, and sounds affect your spirit to create comfort, enjoyment, and a sense of abundance.

Here's Your Invitation to the Buffet

"Just because the Joy Diet is for the soul, rather than the body," Beck writes, "doesn't mean it lacks strict rules about eating. In fact, there are two: 1) You must only eat what you really enjoy; 2) you must really enjoy everything you eat."

I think these are good rules across the board, don't you? According to Beck, when our emotions are in balance and all other things are equal, we will naturally choose a balanced, healthy diet. *Unless* we are eating for reasons other than physical hunger. (For those of us who tend to relate food to our emotional state, we may not even be able to remember the last time we were really, truly hungry.) In answer, Beck wraps the whole issue of emotional eating in one smart, funny statement: "Please remember this," she implores. "If you are unable or unwilling to sit still, face difficult truths, specify your desires, run risks, play, laugh, cry, or connect, then giving yourself permission to consume whatever you want will probably make you eat like an industrial wood chipper."

Beck's Joy Diet can be implemented one step at a time, allowing your life and level of happiness to improve steadily over time, or you can undertake all at once in a "crash diet" if your situation is one of emergency. Regardless, Beck says (and I concur), "The Joy Diet is simply what you can do to feel better, especially when you don't *know* what to do to feel better."

Now here's the thing: By this point in *this* book, we *do* know what to do to feel better. We actually know *lots* of things to do to feel better.

Press the Pause Button

Spending deliberate time unplugged is easier for those of us who have horses. Our horses demand that of us. It doesn't seem to matter what kind of day I've had; pulling up to the barn hits the pause button for me as nothing else can. My friends and coworkers know it's a conversation stopper: "Gotta go, I'm at the barn." Texting and email cease. Work squabbles, home concerns, and the bottomless to-do list always running through my head fades to black. I'll keep the phone with me, of course, for emergencies and family. (Only they can reel me back in: "Where are you?" "We're hungry!" "Are you *ever* coming home?" "ETA???????")

And, for those times when I'm not lucky enough to score some barn time, I do try to make sure to build some "purposeful pauses" into my day. (Remember when my friend, Len, reminded me to watch the fountain outside my office window for a few minutes every hour or two—see p. 242)?) Whatever you need to do to hit the pause button in your own life, *do it*, on purpose, several times a day. This is your medicine; don't miss a dose. No tools, tricks, fancy equipment, clinics, or New Age tinkle music required. It really is as simple as setting a timer for five minutes and just sitting still, paying attention to your breathing, and learning to *be*.

In *The Compassionate Equestrian: 25 Principles to Live by When Caring for and Working with Horses,* Dr. Allen Schoen and Susan Gordon call this Quiet Focused Intention (QFI), and recommend we do it before entering our barn each day. This is deep, inner work on your very small, subtle "mental muscles" that, once strengthened, will completely rebuild your interior life. If you, as one of my all-time favorite Facebook posted memes put it, "live in an ADD world where reality is like a constant, gentle shower of post-it notes," take heart. During our five minutes of QFI before we interact with our horses—or even once we're on horseback—we only have to notice, acknowledge, and dismiss the barrage of input and simply return to our breath, as often as we need to. In. Out. In. Out.

Remember that you can press the pause button at *any time* (not just during your regular meditation time, in your favorite spot, or under the ideal circumstances)—on the fly, in the middle of a crowded noisy room (or frenetic pre-show warm-up arena), when someone is coming unglued, yelling and cursing at you, or when it's your horse whose getting fractious. *Everyone* has times when thoughts and emotions get the best of them. Now we have one more way to build and strengthen our ability to be aware of them, return physically to our breath, and as needed, break the patterns and cycles that are doing harm to our well-being (or as they say in yoga, "stealing our peace," which my daughters and I have now converted to "stealing our peas"…but that's another story for another time).

"Re-member" Why You Ride

Creating the kind of joy ride we're all looking for, it seems, is a matter of remembering and embracing all facets of who we are, and then bringing those parts together into a healthy, unified whole. "In our human experience," writes Sianna Sherman in "The Dismemberment and Remembering of Yoga" on RebelleSociety. com, "we are learning how to see our whole self, and call the fragmented and rejected parts of self home once again."

Couched by several authors as the opposite of "dis-membering" (as in chopping off parts), "re-membering" in this context is the act of *putting ourselves back together*. And, playing off the words of the poet mystic Rumi, when we do this, we're stronger in our broken places; the act of mending creates a bond within us that wasn't there before.

When we knit body image with riding, most of what we're dealing with has an emotional basis. Remembering, too, that emotions drive thoughts, as we discovered back on p. 290, and thoughts drive behavior. Behavior drives habits, and habits build neuropathways that make behavior more or less automatic. The bottom line for us as riders trying to break free of deeply ingrained body image issues is that if

RESOURCES Dr. Allen Schoen and Susan Gordon's *The Compassionate Equestrian* (Trafalgar Square Books, 2015).

we're not careful about which behaviors we allow to become habits, we find our-selves living out this struggle in a place far from the trailhead we seek.

We've learned that despite our 3:1 positive to negative input over the course of an average day, our minds naturally gravitate to the negative, which tend to have a "narrowing effect" on our thoughts and emotions. Positive emotions, on the other hand, are designed to "broaden and build" our repertoire of thoughts and actions. *Joy*, that branch of happiness we've been discussing in this chapter, is what expands this base of positive emotions. *Joy* makes us want to *play*. And as we can learn from Martha Beck's *Joy Diet*—and from the Heath brothers' *Switch*—play beckons *more* positive experiences. When we learn to play on a regular, daily basis, we become more and more open to exploring, creating, and inventing new pathways to the "positive side" of the barn aisle.

So what does this have to do with our riding? *Everything*.

"Our horses mean the world to us, so we need to make sure that the time we spend with them is as enjoyable and fulfilling as possible," remarks Coach Daniel Stewart. "Regardless of whether you're a competitive or recreational rider, this should be one of your most important goals because you can really only achieve true greatness doing things you love and enjoy. Sadly, if you're not enjoying your-self, you'll probably struggle with riding to your true potential."

By understanding the special role of joy in the complex equation of body image and riding, we begin to find our way back the way we felt the first time we threw our leg across the back of a horse.

Celebrating Equus

When author Linda Kohanov wrote *The Tao of Equus: A Woman's Journey of Healing and Transformation through the Way of the Horse* she was bordering on blasphemy. To suggest that there was more to connecting with horses than riding, training, showing, and competing was laughable, she admits. Nevertheless, she felt compelled to share with the world what she was experiencing in her own time and space with horses, and now the rest of the population is finally catching up. It is of particular importance to you now, especially if there are circumstances in your life that are preventing you from riding, but you still feel drawn to spending time with horses.

"My horses were awakening something in me, something profound and, at that time, indescribable," Kohanov writes. "How do horses inspire us, open our hearts, and enliven our souls?"

You can discover this awakening and answer this question for yourself, whether or not you ever set foot in a stirrup. As Kohanov, and now others, express, whether you own a horse, borrow one, go on equestrian retreats or workshops, or just hang out at the barn whenever the opportunity arises (no riding required!), horses offer humans, and women in particular, a powerful form of healing and soulful exploration.

Why do we think we have to *ride* horses to enjoy them and grow from their wisdom? More importantly, why do horses *let* us ride them in the first place? The arrogance of humankind suggests this is due to some lack of brainpower, but if you spend any quality time at all in the company of a horse of any size, shape, or color, I think you, too, will agree that no matter how you choose to interact with them, these are, as Kohanov sums up, "sensitive, highly evolved beings, protecting us, nurturing us, gently guiding us, waiting for us to wake up to the wisdom they so patiently hold while we work through our adolescent fantasies of power and conquest, often at their expense."

"Being a 'rider' means you ride horses," Susan Harris clarifies. "Being a 'horseman' (or 'horsewoman,' as it were) is the work of a lifetime—it means you care about the horse, learn all you can, and become a true student of the horse. Even if you're not riding, simply learning to groom, driving, sitting in a cart—just spending time with horses is all part of the process."

While many of us focus on riding as the primary connection we have with our horses, plenty of people have discovered that there are other great ways to connect in a unique partnership with our equine friends. One such example is shared by Eunice Rush (we first met her back on p. 66), who is quick to agree that having horses does not automatically mean we have to ride them. She has an 18-year old horse named Dakota that went lame as a five-year-old. After traveling to vets, chiropractors, and trying everything she knew of to find the answer, Eunice gave up the idea of ever riding Dakota again. Then someone said to her, "Well, if you're going to keep and feed that horse, you might as well teach him tricks."

After trying for about six months to teach Dakota to bow and making absolutely no progress, a strange and remarkable thing happened that changed both of their futures: As a woman of faith, Eunice says she often turns to her Bible for answers to perplexing problems she can't solve on her own. So after one particularly frustrating training session with Dakota, she says she took out her Bible and said, "Okay, I'm going to open this Bible and close my eyes and point to a verse. If the verse I land on has something about horses in it, I'll know God wants me to teach this horse to do tricks."

It did. (Eunice doesn't remember the exact verse—for the record, there are 57 of them!) So with a deep sigh and a load of doubt, she stepped back into the barn, saying, "Well, God, here I am, back here in the barn to teach this horse tricks. What are we going to teach him first?"

Immediately, she says, she knew she needed to start with teaching Dakota to "smile." Not really knowing how to go about it, she just followed her "horse logic," and within 20 minutes, Dakota was giving her an

Linda Kohanov's *The Tao of Equus: A Woman's Journey of Healing and Transformation through the Way of the Horse* (New World Library, 2007).

RESOURCES

expression that looked like a "smile" on cue. Eunice was dazzled, but still a bit skeptical.

"So now what?" She asked God. The idea came, just as suddenly as the first, to teach Dakota to "pray." Again, the horse learned a position that looked like "praying" within 20 minutes.

Over the next two months Dakota learned a full repertoire of tricks; Eunice associated each trick she taught Dakota with a Bible verse or life principle the trick could illustrate. Then, driving home from work one day, she heard a radio ad for a local kids' carnival taking place the very next week, and she knew she needed to call them to see if they had an opening for a trick horse. When the person on the other end of the line asked what her act was called, Eunice heard herself say, "Galloping for God." All their entertainment was already booked, the man told her, but he invited her to try again the next year.

Then the next day the man called and said the pony ride had cancelled—could she still come? "God has *such* a sense of humor," Eunice says. "Who was I to say no?"

Still, the lack of detail in their "act" was daunting. Not only had Dakota never been in public before, much less performed his tricks in front of more than a few random friends and family members, Eunice didn't have any of the normal props or equipment necessary to such a venture.

"You'll be in the parking lot, next to the dunking booth," the oblivious carnival director informed her. "And, oh yeah, we're gonna have the hay ride circling around you. You'll be on for three 45-minute acts, and while it'll be kind of dark, there are spotlights." (Really, horse people, can you think of any worse scenario?) If going to the barn to attempt to teach Dakota a trick was an act of faith, this carnival was nothing short of a leap.

And so they went. To Eunice's complete amazement, Dakota unloaded, performed, received his admirers, and loaded back up to go home without so much as a single misstep. He performed each trick perfectly, as if it was something he had done all his life. Since then Eunice and Dakota have traveled to perform for children's programs, parties, nursing homes, and other events far and wide. Although she has never marketed "Galloping for God," and she and Dakota are paid by donation only, they've averaged 8 to 10 shows a year for 13 years and counting.

Consider what Eunice might have missed in her own life if she had subscribed to the notion that you have to *ride* a horse to enjoy and find purpose in owning one. Eunice says that Dakota's story perfectly illustrates that whether you're riding, driving, doing tricks, or herding minis, *you just never know where a horse might take you.* And, if you really *are* too heavy to ride right now, there are plenty of great ways to enjoy spending time in the company of horses.

And if anyone ever says you shouldn't get a horse because you *can't* ride, or that you should get rid of a horse because you're *not* riding, just remember Dakota.

#Hoofpicks

In this chapter we explored all the ways we can take the tools, strategies, and insights offered up in this book and make them our own—part of who we are and how we ride. This is where this book becomes a living credo for each of us: a trail map that evolves with us to take us to places we didn't even know we wanted to go. This will help in our work with horses by enabling us to become gentler with ourselves and embrace who we are on the inside, becoming more attuned with our own authenticity. You'll find a deeper connection with your horse as he sees and mirrors back to you your own clearer vision of who you are. This understanding is a new and different game-changer in the battle against negative body image because as we layer the strategies and insights revealed one by one in the pages of this book upon the foundation of our deepest authenticity, we begin to build a new self-awareness that's lock-step with the lightness we've been yearning for.

Your Chapter 11 **#Hoofpicks** Include:

1 **Trust the process.** It's hard to imagine how "baby steps" will ever add up to where we want to be (especially when you're facing a steep climb), but

remember that *each small step* in the right direction is one step closer to where you want to be. This is a different trail than the ones you've been on before; there's value in taking this journey slowly. Stop and smell those tiny blossoms of understanding along the way as you move with deliberate intent *forward,* in the right direction.

2 Stop "shoulding" yourself. Chances are this book stirred things up for you and likely awakened some habitual thought patterns (like a shot of espresso, maybe?) that may be making you feel overwhelmed and headed toward the inertia that tends to prevent us from forward progress. Just know, as you do with a young horse in training, that *you'll get there.* The outlaw "I should" thinking—the inner or outer dialogue that begins with "I should..."—that's likely been tormenting you is no match for your new arsenal of tools and strategies.

3 Don't ask for what you don't want. For me it was absolutely amazing, once I started listening more carefully to my own words and monitoring my behavior and choices, how much more energy and attention I was habitually giving to the negatives in my life over the positives. Whenever you feel yourself bemoaning or criticizing anything about yourself, your body, or your riding, take a pause (and a deep breath), and then reframe it (out loud if it won't cause a scene) with a positive affirmation of the change you're making.

4 Choose joy. Especially when you're feeling stuck in a situation that has persisted for a while, make a deliberate choice to do something that feels good *in the midst of a moment of angst* (anything positive will work here—a fresh stick of gum might be all it takes) and choose a different trail. Seek the path to the joy you envisioned for yourself the first time you put your foot in a stirrup and hoisted yourself onto the back of a horse. *Whatever* your dream—ride toward it!

12 | All The Difference

"I took the one less traveled by, and that has made all the difference."
— Robert Frost, "The Road Not Taken"

If you've come this far, you'll agree I've shared quite a bit. Now this is the part where *you* take the reins.

Will this book help spark a new fire burning within you, a true desire to make whatever changes you need to start living a life filled to the brim with joy, horses, and riding? Author Louise Hay has an exercise I love in her book *You Can Heal Your Life* called "I Should…" I know, I know, we are trying to shake free of "shoulds"… but there's more to it—check out my take on this exercise, with our body image goals in mind:

Exercise for the Brain: I Should…

1 At the top of a sheet of paper or a page in your journal write the words, "I should…"

2 **Write five or six ways to finish a sentence that begins with "I should," specifically with your body and riding in mind.** Write fast and don't think about this much—just write whatever pops into your head first. Here's my list:

I should ride more regularly.
I should take better care of myself.
I should lose weight.
I should get more sleep.
I should write in my journal every day.

3 **Read the list out loud.** Pause after each "I should" and wait for a moment, and then ask aloud, "Why?" Then write as many reasons as you can think of *why* it is something you should do. As an example, let's consider the first item on my list: *I should ride more regularly.* Why? Because:

It makes me feel better in body, mind, and soul.
It's good for keeping me, and my horses, "tuned up."
A routine will help "protect" the time I set aside for my horses.

4 **Now, take each "I should" from your list in Step 2 and rewrite the sentence to say, "If I really wanted to, I could..."** Hay says she believes that the word "should" is one of the most damaging in the English language, because it makes us wrong—either in the past, right now, or in the future. Instead, she suggests we substitute the word "could." This, she says, changes *everything.*

If I really wanted to, I could ride more regularly.
If I really wanted to, I could take better care of myself.
If I really wanted to, I could lose weight.
If I really wanted to, I could get more sleep.
If I really wanted to, I could write in my journal every day.

5 **Read the "I could" statements aloud, followed by a pause, and then ask yourself, "Why haven't I?"** Hay writes that people may find they have been berating themselves for years for something they never wanted to do in the first place. It may not have been their idea to begin with, but was just something that *someone else* said they "should" do.

Give Up What-You-Don't-Want Grief

Ladies, it's time to give up this lament once and for all. Has whining about what you *don't* want ever brought what you *do* want? I hope, if you've absorbed nothing else from these pages, that this one point sticks: Fighting the negative is a plain, old-fashioned waste of time. (And with all the potential for self-improvement, who wants to lose any time at all?) According to nearly every expert and psychologist I talked to or referenced while working on this book, the more you dwell on what's wrong with your body and your life, the more *wrong* you will create.

Looking at our life and our riding, it's very easy to spot what we *don't* want. Chances are, it's a list that has been with you for a while—maybe for as long as you can remember. More than likely, this "don't want" list has insidiously poisoned countless moments in your life and in your time with your horse, whether you realize it or not. Even if you have never actually articulated these "don't wants" in so many words, trust me—they're there. They haunt you, taunt you, and when you're not looking, according to Louise Hay, they grow.

Taking a cue from another of Hay's exercises and looping back to Coach Daniel Stewart's tips on p. 296, lets practice isolating our "don't wants" and turning them into affirmations.

Exercise for the Brain: Ditch Your "Don't-Wants"

1 **Structure a page in your journal or in a document with two columns.** In the column on the left, list your "don't wants," such as the examples I've provided here. In the column on the right, turn these "don't-want" statements into positive, present-tense affirmations of the condition or situation at the "opposite end of the stick" (see p. 322). "Always make your statement in the *present* tense," Hay coaches. "Your subconscious mind is such an obedient servant that if you declare your want in the *future* tense, such as 'I want,' or 'I will have,' then that is where it will stay—in the future and just out of your reach!"

Here's my list to help you get started:

I don't want to be a "heavy" rider.	I am fit and strong; my body weight has settled where it needs to be and I am joyfully accepting of who I am.
I don't want to be a floppy, sloppy rider.	I am balanced and flexible in the saddle and I move in sync with my horse.
I don't want to be "that old lady" in my show classes.	I ride better now than I did when I was 20. I am ageless in the saddle.
I don't want to be out of balance with my horse when I ride.	I have worked hard to create a wonderful new strength and balance, and it shows in how I ride and in my improved relationship with my horse.
I don't want to be unhappy with my riding.	I look for and find the beauty in the most mundane moments of every single ride.
I don't want to be stuck in a body that's not the ideal for riding.	I celebrate the unique capabilities of my body, and what it can do on horseback.
I don't want these big boobs to flop around at the trot and canter and ruin my balance and my ride.	I stabilize my breasts when I ride so I can enjoy my riding more.
I don't want to be lonely.	I seek out like-minded horse people who are traveling the same trail for support, encouragement, and kinship.
I don't want to be an "ugly" rider.	I ride with grace and ease in perfect harmony with my horse.
I don't want these short stubby legs to make it so hard to communicate aids to my horse.	I enjoy the natural balance my low center of gravity offers; my legs are strong and effective!
I don't want my big-butt pear shape accentuated on horseback.	My broad base of support gives me natural balance and stability in the saddle.

2 Now we're going to put this practice in place in your life! Begin by catching any negative thought as early as you can (see p. 211 for help with this).

3 Use our thought-stopping technique (see p. 257) and yell, "WHOA!" (In your mind, please; I don't want to be responsible for scaring people—or your horse!)

4 Imagine your negative thoughts rocking back into a dramatic sliding stop.

5 Take a deep, belly breath (see p. 236).

6 Create a present-tense, positive form of your negative "think," and lope off again in your new frame of mind.

It's probably going to feel weird the first few times you do this exercise. Stay with it anyway. The process will get faster and faster until it becomes habit, and your correction (and the supporting mental imagery) will also become automatic. It's also important to understand that you won't stop *having* negative thoughts; you *will*, however, redirect them before they cause harm to what you want.

Here's another way to look at it: How do you anticipate your horse's inclination to spook at a garbage can? You see one ahead, you apply rein, leg, and seat, and then you just sit deep and keep your horse traveling straight. Your horse may *never* stop spooking at strange objects, but you can learn to catch and redirect his energy before he whirls for the barn.

Martha Beck wrote in her blog (find it on marthabeck.com) that we all have a choice when something we don't want is prevailing in our lives. Observing the community of critters surrounding her rural California home, Beck says she realized that within each of us lies the capacity to be both a small, vulnerable "critter" living at the whims of a capricious universe, or a vast and powerful "creator" taking charge of *making* what we want.

"When we stop feeling victimized or abandoned and resolve to design and build stuff, we align our identity with our creator-selves," Beck writes. "Instead of persecuted critters, we become heroes on a quest. A difficult quest, to be sure, but that's how it's supposed to be."

This assessment mirrors the experience I've had in writing this book. When the idea appeared to write *Riding Through Thick and Thin*, I wasn't sure I could do it. What could I say that hasn't already been said, plenty of times? How could I lend aid to this struggle, and yet dictate neither weight loss nor embracing your "fluffiness"? How in the world could I possibly straddle that line of demarcation between fight and flight? And when the first person I interviewed told me I was going to cause horses to be injured by encouraging large, unskilled riders to just jump on without regard for the animal's well-being, I nearly ran for the hills.

Then, that very same day, another person opened my eyes to the idea that I could *create* something *completely* different. Something that would pull together insights and ideas that had not been assembled this way before, and certainly not for this audience. Not only could I help provide what was in fact missing (a book on this topic for horse people), but I could empower readers to *create* whatever solution was missing in their own lives.

Whether or not I succeeded is for you, the reader, to judge, but I will tell you that when I made that mental shift and embraced the opportunity to create "what isn't yet," random, previously unconnected people, ideas, and sources began to show up to help, each in surprising and exciting ways. Slowly, the concepts and building blocks began to connect and take shape until they became the pages you have before you.

So, I join Beck's expressed sentiment: "The clear thought and hard work of aligning with your creator-self will empower you, fulfill you, and teach you who you truly are. And that, it turns out, was the real goal all along."

Which Trail Will You Take

Here's what this unique journey is asking of you, friends:

- **To be willing to begin by looking at ourselves deeply, honestly, and with compassion** without need for excuses, explanations, or justification. We are who we are. It's as simple as that—and we've gotten here as quickly as we can.

- **To be committed to peeling back the layers of understanding** about where we are and how we got here without condemnation or shame, but with compassion and acceptance.

- **To look unflinchingly at our horses and our saddles and the clear realities** of math and physics to see what adjustments we need to make, whether short-term or long-term.

- **To objectively assess how our lifestyles and habits** could be contributing to whatever situation we may want to change, and then to begin making these changes in small, real, and permanent steps rather than with another a quick-fix "diet" or "program."

- **To look at how we work in the saddle, what our bodies are and are not capable of,** and how we can improve our biomechanics to create unflappable stability and balance at any gait to achieve that ultimate "joy ride."

- **To understand what's really going on in our "frame of mind"**—to examine our thoughts, emotions, and patterns of behavior so we can "muck out" our minds along with our nutrition, fitness, and biomechanics.

- **To tap neuroscience for help in making permanent changes** to habits and behavior patterns that will fuel new mental strategies to change our experience...for good!

- **To pull all this together into a focused quest** for the same sense of utter happiness we felt the very *first* time we got onto the back of a horse and thought, *I'm home.*

Remember the 6 Keys to "Be": Be Honest. Be Fair. Be Proactive. Be Mindful. Be Positive. Be Authentic.

No, I'm not going to say the "less-traveled" terrain is easy. I've admitted a number of times that, in fact, it decidedly is *not.* Few worthwhile stretches are. But here there can be frequent stops in the clearings to enjoy the stillness of a quiet mind, to breathe in the sweetness of all you truly are and all you are meant to be, and to absorb all that is the horse beneath you. Here, there are no shortcuts (a dear old tennis coach once told me there's no such thing), but stick with it and you'll find yourself on a lifelong lope through a dazzling summer meadow, in complete harmony with the magnificence of the horse you are lucky enough to call your friend.

Afterword | RT³ Roundup

MINDFULNESS BY THE NUMBERS

Here's a sample calendar to help get you started— feel free to make your own combinations and shape your own plan from there!

1 Meditation	**4** Journaling	**7** Daily Affirmations
2 Mindful Walking	**5** Conscious Breathing	**8** Brand Self-Image
3 Body Scan	**6** Visualization	**9** Music Playlist

WEEK 1						
Sun 1&7	Mon 1&7	Tue 1&7	Wed 1&7	Thu 1&7	Fri 1&7	Sat 1&7

WEEK 2						
Sun 2&8	Mon 2&8	Tue 2&8	Wed 2&8	Thu 2&8	Fri 2&8	Sat 2&8

WEEK 3						
Sun 3&9	Mon 3&9	Tue 3&9	Wed 3&9	Thu 3&9	Fri 3&9	Sat 3&9

WEEK 4						
Sun 4&6	Mon 4&6	Tue 4&6	Wed 4&6	Thu 4&6	Fri 4&6	Sat 4&6

WEEK 5						
5 Pick one!	5 Pick one!	5 Pick one!	5 Pick one!	5 Pick one!	5 Pick one!	5 Pick one!

WEEK 6						
Pick two!	Pick two!	Pick two!	Pick two!	Pick two!	Pick two!	Pick two!

FITNESS BY THE NUMBERS

Similar to the "Pick Two Menu" I've just given you for incorporating **mindfulness** practices in your daily life, you can make a parallel commitment to taking care of your **body** with a solid and balanced approach to keeping yourself fit to ride. This flexible and fluid solution, designed to fit into even the busiest schedule, will keep you and your muscles aware of the job they have to do.

What this means is subscribing to a daily checklist that includes the three items from our Holy Trinity of fitness—strength, stamina, and flexibility. Here is a sample checklist to give you a jumpstart:

STRENGTH
• Weight Training (free weights or machines)
• Resistance exercises (with or without bands or tubing)
• Core work, such as Pilates

STAMINA
• Sustained cardio (walking, jogging, cycling, swimming)
• Logging 10,000 steps a day with a fitness-tracking device
• Circuit training (great way to check two boxes at once!)
• Interval training (for the time-crunched—gets more cardio in a shorter time-frame)

FLEXIBILITY
• Yoga sequence, class, or individual postures
• Resistance stretching

Make a daily commitment to do *something* in each of these three areas before you close your eyes on the day. I've given you tools in this book to help you make a schedule, but most important is the absolute commitment to do *something* in each area, even if your carefully planned calendar falls apart. Here's how that flux might look:

- Some days your **strength** work might only be a few pushups beside the bed before you crawl into it after a grueling yet sedentary day of meetings and commitments. Others it might be a full gym workout, Pilates class, core-strength DVD, or whatever free-weight routine you've established at home or the barn.

- Some days your **stamina** work might be taking the stairs or making a point to add steps wherever you can, all day long (FitBit, anyone?). Others it might be a walk/run with your dog or an hour on the elliptical with a good read.

- Some days your **flexibility** work might be a quick sun salutation or other favorite yoga sequence, a bout with flexibility bands or tubing at the barn before you ride, or a full-blown yoga class or DVD after work.

The point is, we're making a commitment to our bodies, and we're going about keeping that commitment systematically. Whether your fitness menu selections are small nibbles or full entrées, you're reminding yourself *and* your muscles that you are serious about keeping your body strong, fit, and flexible. You'll feel the difference fairly quickly, and the number on the scale will likely be sliding downward as you toggle between "At least I've done everything on the checklist," to "Pretty good," to "Great!" to "I am a FREAKIN' ROCK STAR!"

Bibliography

Arntz, William, Betsy Chasse, and Mark Vicente. *What the Bleep Do We Know?!: Discovering the Endless Possibilities for Altering Your Everyday Reality*. Deerfield Beach, FL: Health Communications, 2005, 2007, 2010 ebook.

"The Art of Riding with Karen Musson." Karen Musson. http://www.theartofriding.com.

Bacon, Linda, and Lucy Aphramor. *Body Respect: What Conventional Health Books Get Wrong, Leave Out, and Just Plain Fail to Understand about Weight*. Dallas, TX: BenBella Books, 2014.

Bacon, Linda. *Health at Every Size: The Surprising Truth about Your Weight*. Dallas, TX: BenBella Books, 2008, 2010.

Beck, Martha. *The Joy Diet: 10 Daily Practices for a Happier Life*. New York, NY: Harmony Books, 2003, 2008 ebook.

Benedik, Linda. *Longeing the Rider for a Perfect Seat: A How-To Guide for Riders, Instructors, and Longeurs*. North Pomfret, VT: Trafalgar Square Books, 2007.

Benedik, Linda. *Yoga and Riding: Techniques for Equestrians, Volumes 1 & 2*. North Pomfret, VT: Trafalgar Square Books, 2008, DVD.

Benedik, Linda, and Veronica Wirth. *Yoga for Equestrians: A New Path for Achieving Union with the Horse*. North Pomfret, VT: Trafalgar Square Books, 2000.

Blignault, Karen. *Stretch Exercises for Your Horse: The Path to Perfect Suppleness*. North Pomfret, VT: Trafalgar Square Books, 2003, 2013.

"The Body Positive." The Body Positive. http://www.thebodypositive.org.

Brach, Tara. *Radical Acceptance: Embracing Your Life with the Heart of a Buddha*. New York, NY: Bantam Books, 2003.

Byrne, Rhonda. *The Secret*. New York, NY: Atria Books/Beyond Words Publishing, 2006, 2007 ebook.

Cameron, Julia. *The Artist's Way: A Spiritual Path to Higher Creativity*. Los Angeles, CA: Jeremy P. Tarcher/Putnam, 1992, 2002.

Carroll, Robert. *The Skeptic's Dictionary: A Collection of Strange Beliefs, Amusing Deceptions, and Dangerous Delusions*. Hoboken, NJ: John Wiley & Sons, 2003.

Cash, Thomas F. *The Body Image Workbook: An 8-Step Program for Learning to Like Your Looks*. Oakland, CA: New Harbinger Publications, 1997, 2008.

"The Chronicle of the Horse." The Chronicle of the Horse. http://www.chronofhorse.com.

"The Complete Guide to the Alexander Technique." Robert Rickover. http://www.alexandertechnique.com.

"Cowgirls with Curves | A place for real sized cowgirls to be encouraged!" F.J. Thomas. http://www.cowgirlswithcurves.com.

Detrick, Janeen. "The Science Behind How the Law of Attraction Works: Quantum Physics, Quantum Mechanics, and String Theory." Good Vibrations Energy Clinic blog, June 18, 2011. http://www.goodvibesclinic.com/the-science-behind-the-law-of-attraction.

Dooley, Mike. *Leveraging the Universe: 7 Steps to Engaging Life's Magic*. New York, NY: Atria Books/Beyond Words Publishing, 2011, 2012.

Dossey, Larry, and Michael Toms. *The Power of Meditation and Prayer*. Carlsbad, CA: Hay House, 1997.

Duhigg, Charles. *The Power of Habit: Why We Do What We Do in Life and Business*. New York, NY: Random House, 2012, 2014 print and ebook.

Dutta, Soumitra. "What's Your Social Media Strategy?" *Harvard Business Review*, November 2010.

"Equifitt | Fitness & coaching for better riding." Equifitt.com. http://www.equifitt.com.

"An Eventful Life | Eventing News | Eventing Results | Eventing Photos | Eventing Videos." Eventing Life Pty Ltd. http://www.an-eventful-life.com.au.

"EZUP Stirrup Extender." E-Z UP Stirrup Extender & Stirrup Swivel. http://www.ezupstirrup.com.

"A Fat Girl & A Fat Horse." Amanda Neal. http://afatgirlafathorse.blogspot.com.

Folse, Melinda. *The Smart Woman's Guide to Midlife Horses: Find Meaning, Magic, and Mastery in the Second Half of Life*. North Pomfret, VT: Trafalgar Square Books, 2011 print and ebook.

Germer, Christopher K. *The Mindful Path to Self-compassion: Freeing Yourself from Destructive Thoughts and Emotions*. New York, NY: Guilford Press, 2009.

Goodwin, Shelley. "Too Fat to Ride?" *Horse Canada* vol 7, issue 5 (Sept/Oct 2008).

Harman, Joyce. *The Horse's Pain-Free Back and Saddle-Fit Book: Ensure Soundness and Comfort with Back Analysis and Correct Use of Saddles and Pads*. North Pomfret, VT: Trafalgar Square Books, 2004.

Harman, Joyce. *The Western Horse's Pain-Free Back and Saddle-Fit Book: Soundness and Comfort with Back Analysis and Correct Use of Saddles and Pads*. North Pomfret, VT: Trafalgar Square Books, 2008, 2015 ebook.

Harris, Dan. *10% Happier: How I Tamed the Voice in My Head, Reduced Stress Without Losing My Edge, and Found Self-help That Actually Works—A True Story*. New York, NY: Dey Street Books, 2014.

Hay, Louise L. *21 Days to Master Affirmations*. Carlsbad, CA: Hay House, 2011.

Hay, Louise L. *You Can Heal Your Life*. Carlsbad, CA: Hay House, 1984, 1994.

Heath, Chip, and Dan Heath. *Switch: How to Change Things When Change Is Hard*. New York, NY: Crown Business Publishing, 2010.

Hendricks, Dell. "Mapping Your Reining Win." *Horse & Rider*, September 2002.

Hicks, Jerry, and Esther Hicks. *Ask and It Is Given: Learning to Manifest Your Desires*. Carlsbad, CA: Hay House, 2004.

Hicks, Jerry, and Esther Hicks. *The Astonishing Power of Emotions: Let Your Feelings Be Your Guide*. Carlsbad, CA: Hay House, 2008.

Hicks, Jerry, and Esther Hicks. *The Law of Attraction: The Basics of the Teachings of Abraham*. Carlsbad, CA: Hay House, 2006.

Hicks, Jerry, and Esther Hicks. *The Law of Attraction Essential Collection*. Carlsbad, CA: Hay House, 2013.

Hicks, Jerry, and Esther Hicks. *Manifest Your Desires: 365 Ways to Make Your Dreams a Reality*. Carlsbad, CA: Hay House, 2008.

Hicks, Jerry, and Esther Hicks. *Money, and the Law of Attraction: Learning to Attract Wealth, Health and Happiness.* Carlsbad, CA: Hay House, 2008.

Hicks, Jerry, and Esther Hicks. *A New Beginning II: A Personal Handbook to Enhance Your Life, Liberty and Pursuit of Happiness.* Carlsbad, CA: Hay House, 1991.

Hicks, Jerry, and Esther Hicks. *Sara Learns the Secret about the Law of Attraction.* Carlsbad, CA: Hay House, 2007.

Hicks, Jerry, and Esther Hicks. *The Vortex: Where the Law of Attraction Assembles All Cooperative Relationships.* Carlsbad, CA: Hay House, 2009.

Kabat-Zinn, Jon. *Arriving at Your Own Door: 108 Lessons in Mindfulness.* New York, NY: Hachette Books, 2007, 2013 ebook.

Kabat-Zinn, Jon. *Coming to Our Senses: Healing Ourselves and the World through Mindfulness.* New York, NY: Hyperion Books, 2005; Hachette Books, 2005, 2006.

Kabat-Zinn, Jon, and Myla Kabat-Zinn. *Everyday Blessings: The Inner Work of Mindful Parenting.* New York, NY: Hyperion Books, 1997; Hachette Books, 1998, 2010.

Kabat-Zinn, Jon. *Full Catastrophe Living: Using the Wisdom of Your Body and Mind to Face Stress, Pain, and Illness.* New York, NY: Delta Trade Paperbacks, 1990, 2009 ebook; Penguin Random House, 2013.

Kabat-Zinn, Jon. *Letting Everything Become Your Teacher: 100 Lessons in Mindfulness.* New York, NY: Delta Trade Paperbacks, 2009, 2010 ebook.

Kabat-Zinn, Jon, and Richard J. Davidson, ed. *The Mind's Own Physician: A Scientific Dialogue with the Dalai Lama on the Healing Power of Meditation.* Oakland, CA: New Harbinger Publications, 2012, 2013.

Kabat-Zinn, Jon. *Wherever You Go, There You Are: Mindfulness Meditation in Everyday Life.* New York, NY: Hyperion Books, 1994; Hachette Books, 2005, 2010 ebook.

"Ki-Hara Resistance Stretching – Innovative Body Solutions." Innovative Body Solutions, Inc. http://www.ki-hara.com.

Kohanov, Linda. *The Tao of Equus: A Woman's Journey of Healing & Transformation through the Way of the Horse.* Novato, CA: New World Library, 2001, 2007, 2010 ebook.

Kotter, John P., and Dan S. Cohen. *The Heart of Change: Real-life Stories of How People Change Their Organizations.* Boston, MA: Harvard Business Review Press, 2012.

LeVan, Angie. "Seeing is Believing." *Flourish!,* December 2009.

"Linda Bacon, PhD | professor, researcher, author, consultant." Linda Bacon. http://www.lindabacon.org.

Lipton, Bruce. *The Biology of Belief: Unleashing the Power of Consciousness, Matter & Miracles.* Carlsbad, CA: Hay House, 2005, 2008, 2015.

"Martha Beck—Creating Your Right Life—inspiration & tools for empowered living." Martha Beck, Inc. http://www.marthabeck.com.

Murdoch, Wendy. *50 5-Minute Fixes to Improve Your Riding: Simple Solutions for Better Position and Performance in No Time.* North Pomfret, VT: Trafalgar Square Books, 2010 print and ebook.

Murdoch, Wendy. *Simplify Your Ride: Ride Like a Natural, Parts 1, 2, and 3*. North Pomfret, VT: Trafalgar Square Books, 2006, DVD.

Nash, Joy. "A Fat Rant." YouTube video, 7:45. Posted March 2007. http://www.youtube.com/watch?v=yUTJQIBI1oA.

Nathanson, Donald L. *Shame and Pride: Affect, Sex, and the Birth of the Self*. New York, NY: W.W. Norton & Co., 1992, 1994, 2015 ebook.

Neff, Kristin. *Self-Compassion: Stop Beating Yourself Up and Leave Insecurity Behind*. New York, NY: William Morrow and Co., 2011, 2015.

Peacock, Susan Hoffman. "Less Bounce to the Ounce." *USDF Connection*, October 2011.

Peeke, Pamela. *Fit to Live: The 5-Point Plan to Become Lean, Strong & Fearless for Life*. Emmaus, PA: Rodale, 2007 print and ebook.

Pickert, Kate. "The Mindful Revolution." *Time* magazine, 2014.

Pomroy, Haylie. *The Fast Metabolism Diet: Eat More Food and Lose More Weight*. New York, NY: Harmony Books, 2013 print and ebook.

"The Progoff Intensive Journal Program." Dialogue House Associates and Jon Progoff. http://www.intensivejournal.org.

Rashid, Mark. *Nature in Horsemanship: Discovering Harmony through Principles of Aikido*. New York, NY: Skyhorse Publishing, 2011 print and ebook, 2015.

"Real Beauty Sketches," video campaign by Dove brand of Unilever N.V., 20:36. Posted April 2013. http://realbeautysketches.dove.us.

Reno, Tosca. *The Eat-Clean Diet: Fast Fat Loss that Lasts Forever*. Missisauga, Ontario CA: Robert Kennedy Publishing, 2007.

"Ride with Your Mind – Rider Biomechanics." Mary Wanless. http://www.marywanless.com.

Rubin, Gretchen. *The Happiness Project: Or, Why I Spent a Year Trying to Sing in the Morning, Clean My Closets, Fight Right, Read Aristotle, and Generally Have More Fun*. New York, NY: Harper Publications, 2009, 2011.

Savoie, Jane. *It's Not Just About the Ribbons: It's About Enriching Riding (and Life) with a Winning Attitude*. North Pomfret, VT: Trafalgar Square Books, 2003, 2008 print and ebook.

Savoie, Jane. *That Winning Feeling!: Program Your Mind for Peak Performance*. North Pomfret, VT: Trafalgar Square Books, 1997, 2012 print and ebook.

Schleese, Jochen. *Suffering in Silence: The Saddle-Fit Link to Physical and Psychological Trauma in Horses*. North Pomfret, VT: Trafalgar Square Books, 2013, 2014 print and ebook.

Schoen, Allen, and Susan Gordon. *The Compassionate Equestrian: 25 Principles to Live by When Caring for and Working with Horses*. North Pomfret, VT: Trafalgar Square Books, 2015 print and ebook.

"Scientific American Blog Network." Scientific American and Nature America, Inc. http://blogs.scientificamerican.com.

"selfcompassion.org." Self-Compassion and Kristin Neff. http://www.selfcompassion.org.

Shaw, James. *Ride from Within: Use Tai Chi Principles to Awaken Your Natural Balance and Rhythm*. North Pomfret, VT: Trafalgar square Books, 2005.

"Step-Up Stirrup." Step-Up Stirrup LLC. http://www.stepupstirrup.com.

Stevic-Rust, Lori. "Color-Coding Your Life: A Surprising Look at Balance." The Huffington Post, January 24, 2015. http://www.huffingtonpost.com/lori-stevicrust-phd-abpp/balance_b_4628239.html.

Stewart, Daniel. *E-90-EQ—Equestrian Fitness Exercises, Bootcamps, Circuits and Cardio Classes*. StewartClinics.com, 2015, DVD.

Stewart, Daniel. *Pressure Proof Your Riding: Mental Training Techniques—Gain Confidence and Get Motivated So You (and Your Horse) Achieve Peak Performance*. North Pomfret, VT: Trafalgar Square Books, 2013 print and ebook.

Stewart, Daniel. *Ride Right with Daniel Stewart: Balance Your Frame and Frame of Mind with an Unmounted Workout and Sport Psychology System*. North Pomfret, VT: Trafalgar Square Books, 2004, 2015 ebook.

Strozzi-Heckler, Richard, ed. *Aikido and the New Warrior*. Berkeley, CA: North Atlantic Books, 1993.

Stubbs, Narelle C., and Hilary M. Clayton. *Activate Your Horse's Core: Unmounted Exercises for Dynamic Mobility, Strength, & Balance*. Mason, MI: Sport Horse Publications, 2008.

Swift, Sally. *Centered Riding*. North Pomfret, VT: Trafalgar Square Books, 1985.

Swift, Sally. *Centered Riding 2: Further Exploration*. North Pomfret, VT: Trafalgar Square Books, 2002, 2014 print and ebook.

"Team Beachbody." Beachbody LLC. http://www.teambeachbody.com.

"Tellington TTouch Training." Linda Tellington-Jones. http://www.tellingtonttouch.com.

Tellington-Jones, Linda, and Rebecca Didier. *Dressage with Mind, Body & Soul: A 21st-Century Approach to the Science and Spirituality of Riding and Horse-and-Rider Well-Being*. North Pomfret, VT: Trafalgar Square Books, 2013 print and ebook.

"Tomkins Institute." The Tomkins Institute. http://www.tomkins.org.

Torres, Dara, and Elizabeth Weil. *Age Is Just a Number: Achieve Your Dreams at Any Stage in Your Life*. New York, NY: Three Rivers Press, 2009, 2010 print and ebook.

Torres, Dara, and Billie Fitzpatrick. *Gold Medal Fitness: A Revolutionary 5-Week Program*. New York, NY: Harmony Books, 2010 print and ebook.

Torres, Dara. *Resistance Stretching with Dara Torres: 17 Easy Exercises to Stretch and Strengthen Your Body*. Miami, FL: Innovative Body Solutions, 2008, DVD.

"Trim Down Club." B2C Media Solutions Ltd. http://www.trimdownclub.com.

Wanless, Mary. *Ride with Your Mind Essentials: Innovative Learning Strategies for Basic Riding Skills*. North Pomfret, VT: Trafalgar Square Publishing, 2002.

Wanless, Mary. *For the Good of the Rider*. North Pomfret, VT: Trafalgar Square Publishing, 1999.

Williams, J. Mark G., John D. Teasdale, Zindel V. Segal, and Jon Kabat-Zinn. *The Mindful Way through Depression: Freeing Yourself from Chronic Unhappiness*. New York, NY: Guilford Press, 2007, 2010 ebook.

"Why Home Workouts Rock." American Specialty Health Incorporated. http://www.healthyroads.com.

Index